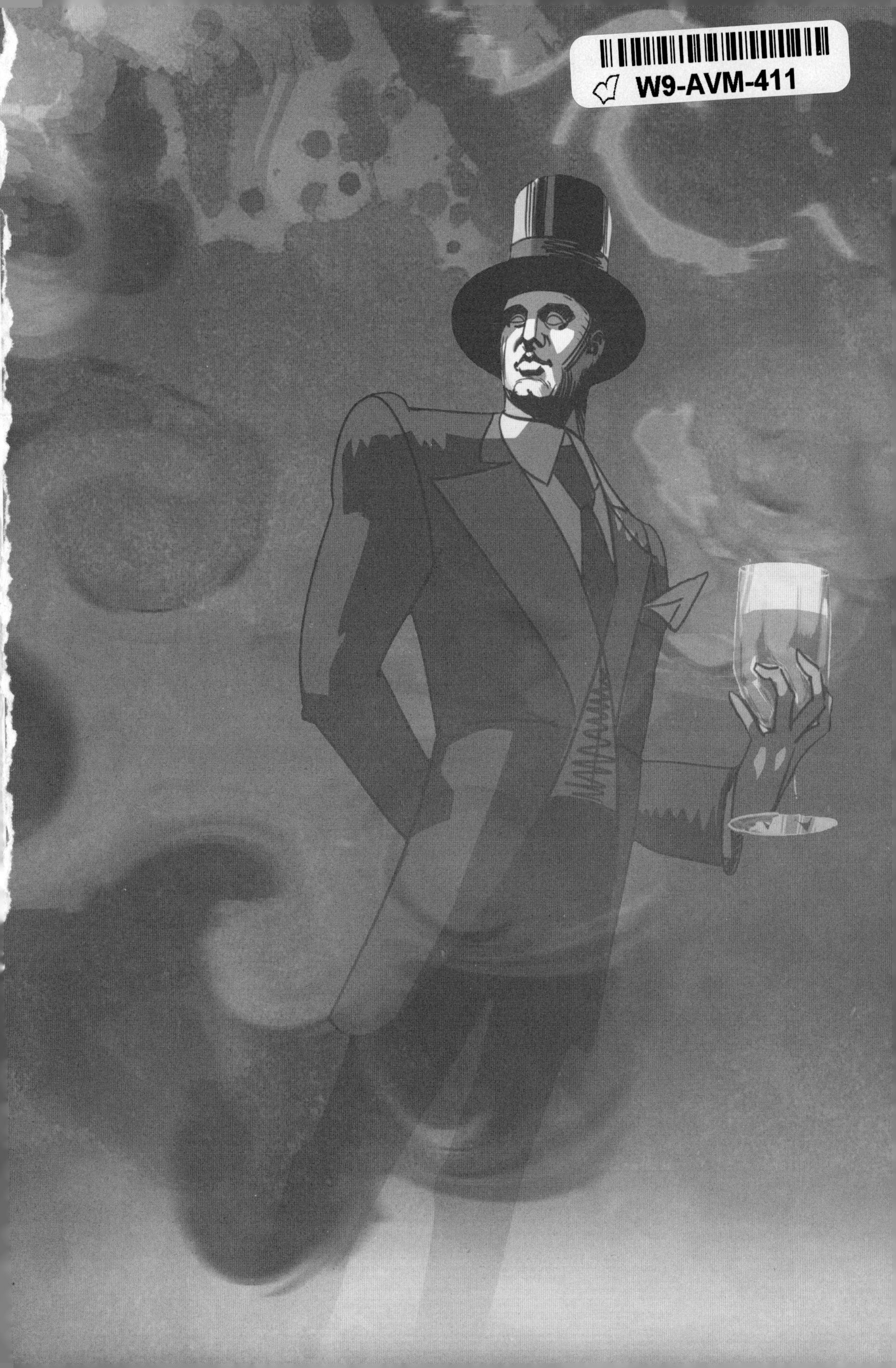

HARDEARS

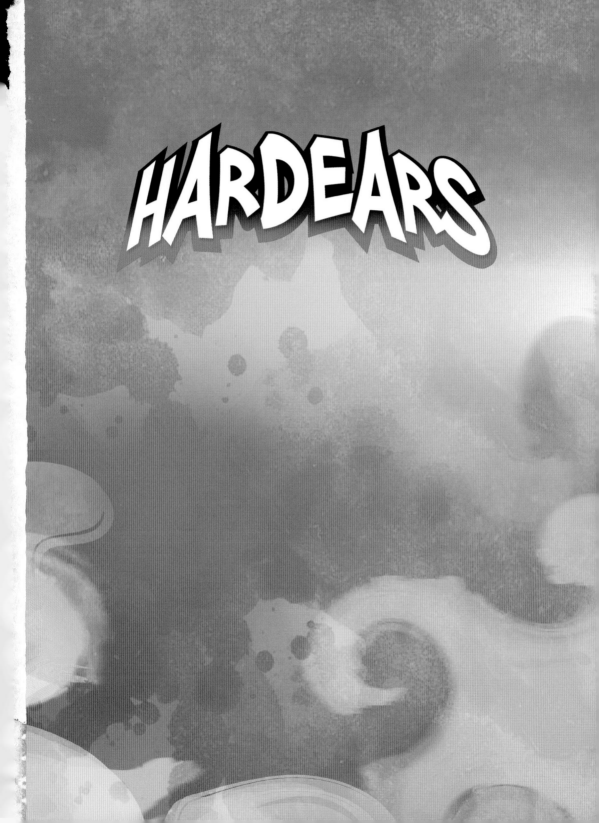

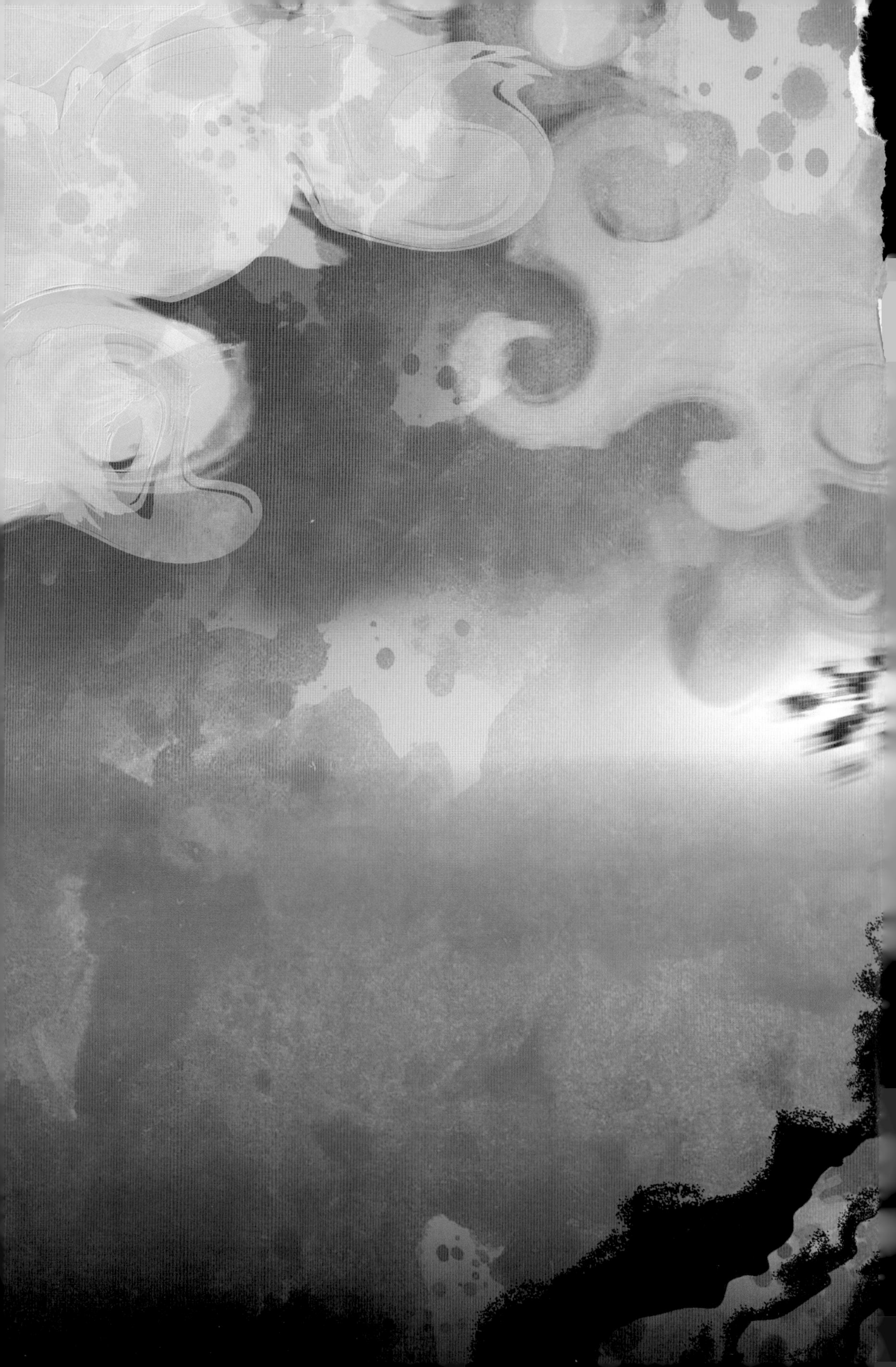

HARDEARS

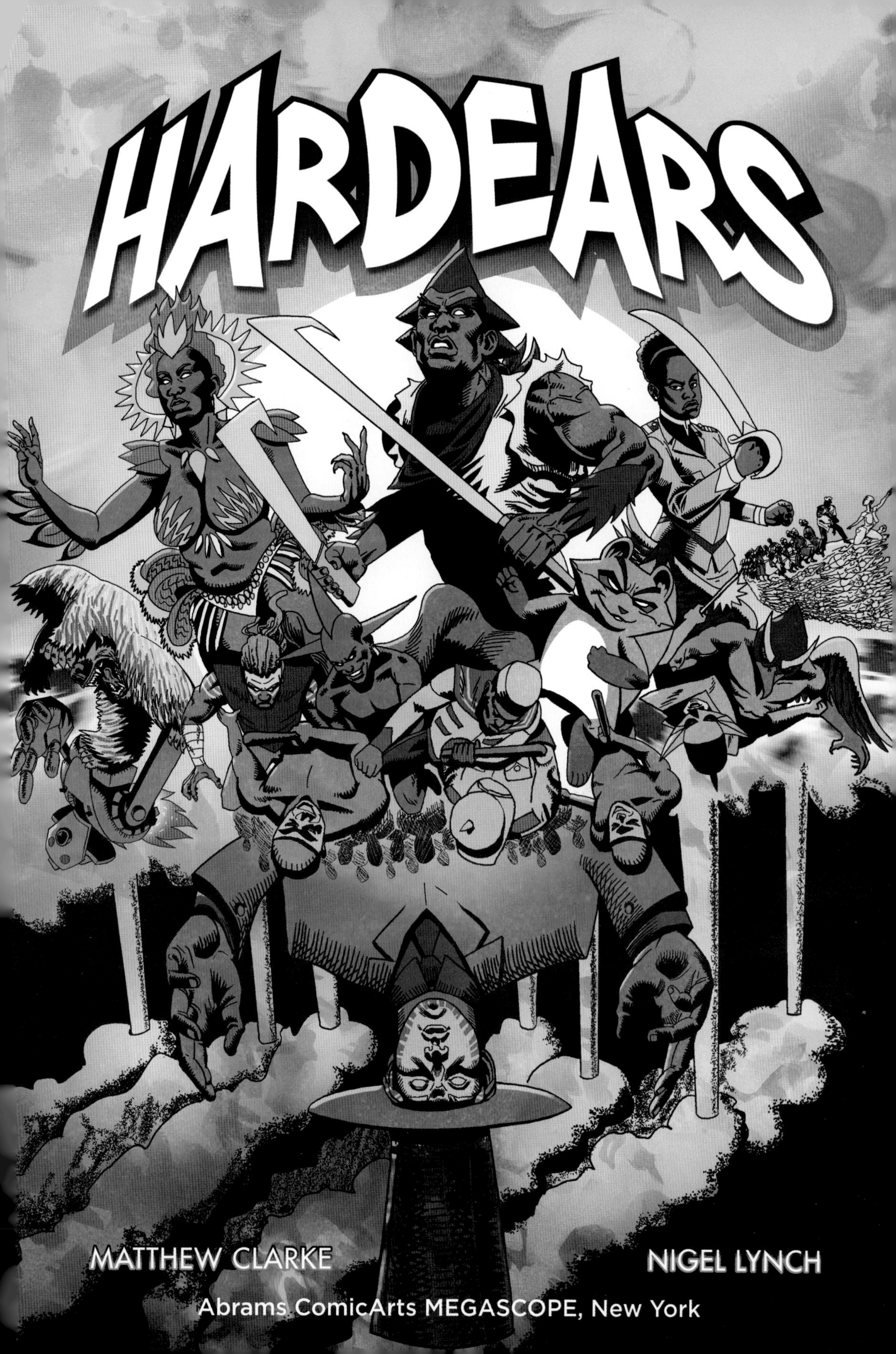

MATTHEW CLARKE

NIGEL LYNCH

Abrams ComicArts MEGASCOPE, New York

MEGASCOPE Curator: John Jennings
Editor: Charlotte Greenbaum
Designer: Kay Petronio
Managing Editor: Mary O'Mara
Production Manager: Alison Gervais

Cataloging-in-Publication Data has been applied for and may be obtained from the Library of Congress.

ISBN 978-1-4197-5192-9
eISBN 978-1-64700-191-9

Printed and bound in China
10 9 8 7 6 5 4 3 2 1

Abrams ComicArts books are available at special discounts when purchased in quantity for premiums and promotions as well as fundraising or educational use. Special editions can also be created to specification. For details, contact specialsales@abramsbooks.com or the address below.

Abrams ComicArts® is a registered trademark of Harry N. Abrams, Inc. MEGASCOPE™ is a trademark of John Jennings and Harry N. Abrams, Inc.

ABRAMS The Art of Books
195 Broadway, New York, NY 10007
abramsbooks.com

ABRAMS COMIC ARTS
MEGASCOPE

MEGASCOPE is dedicated to showcasing speculative and non-fiction works by and about people of color, with a focus on science fiction, fantasy, horror, history, and stories of magical realism. The megascope is a fictional device imagined by W. E. B. Du Bois that can peer through time and space into other realities. This magical invention represents the idea that so much of our collective past has not seen the light of day, and that there is so much history that we have yet to discover. MEGASCOPE will serve as a lens through which we can broaden our view of history, the present, and the future, and as a method by which previously unheard voices can find their way to an ever-growing diverse audience.

MEGASCOPE ADVISORY BOARD

THIS BOOK IS
DEDICATED TO
ANYONE WILLING TO
PURSUE A DREAM

THE WORLD OF HARDE

BACCOOCATCHER

FEW MEN ARE ABLE TO OCCUPY THIS JOB DESCRIPTION, HOWEVER THE ONES WHO DO TRAVERSE THE ISLES FOR HIRE, BRINGING RELIEF TO THOSE UNDER THE TORMENT OF A BACOO INFESTATION. CATCHERS OFTEN USE SPECIAL BOTTLES AND INTELLECT TO TRAP THESE PESTS.

JUMBEES

IS A GENERIC TERM GIVEN TO THE VARIOUS RACES OF SUPERNATURAL, MYSTICAL, PARANORMAL CREATURES OF THE HARDEARS ISLANDS.

THE BARBADOS RACCOON
(Procyon lotor gloveralleni)

Is an extinct subspecies of the common raccoon (Procyon lotor), that was endemic on Barbados in the Lesser Antilles until 1964.

DUPPY

A CHARACTER FOUND IN THE JOURNALS OF HARDEARS' GREATEST HEROES. HE IS THE LAST OF HIS KIND (BARBADOS RACCOON), SEEN ONLY BY A SELECT FEW OR THOSE WITH THE ABILITY TO DO SO.

BACCOO

THE BACCOO IS A DWARFLIKE TRICKSTER JUMBEE WITH THE ABILITY TO REWARD ITS "OWNER" WITH WEALTH UNTOLD OR GRANT WISHES ONCE FED WITH A STEADY AND CONSTANT SUPPLY OF MILK AND BANANAS. THEY HAVE POLTERGEIST TENDENCIES AND ENJOY CAUSING TROUBLE, TORMENTING THOSE AROUND THEM, MOVING ITEMS, STONING HOMES AND CAUSING GENERAL MAYHEM.

APART FROM THEIR MISCHIEVOUS TRAITS THEY ARE ALSO DEVIOUSLY INTELLIGENT AND SOME HAVE THE ABILITY TO SHAPE SHIFT AND BECOME INVISIBLE. THEY ARE MAINLY ACTIVE NOCTURNALLY. THEY ARE PRODUCERS OF NEGATIVE VIBES.

VIBES

Is produced by every living entity and some non-living objects. It is essential to existence itself, and as result, is a highly valuable commodity.

Vibes comes in many forms: solid, liquid, gaseous. Its appearance cannot be accurately described but generally a surreal, rainbow-coloured, neon glow is noted. Vibes has two stages, Basic Vibes and Complex Vibes. Complex Vibes only occurs when Basic Vibes is converted by a living creature. Usually Basic Vibes is extracted from plant sources such as sweet cane grass. All forms of Vibes sit on a spectrum of Positive and Negative Vibes, with the latter being the least desirable due to its adverse effects.

The Supernatural Guild has declared that humans produce the most potent form of Complex Vibes. However, this claim has been dismissed by the Scientific Guild.

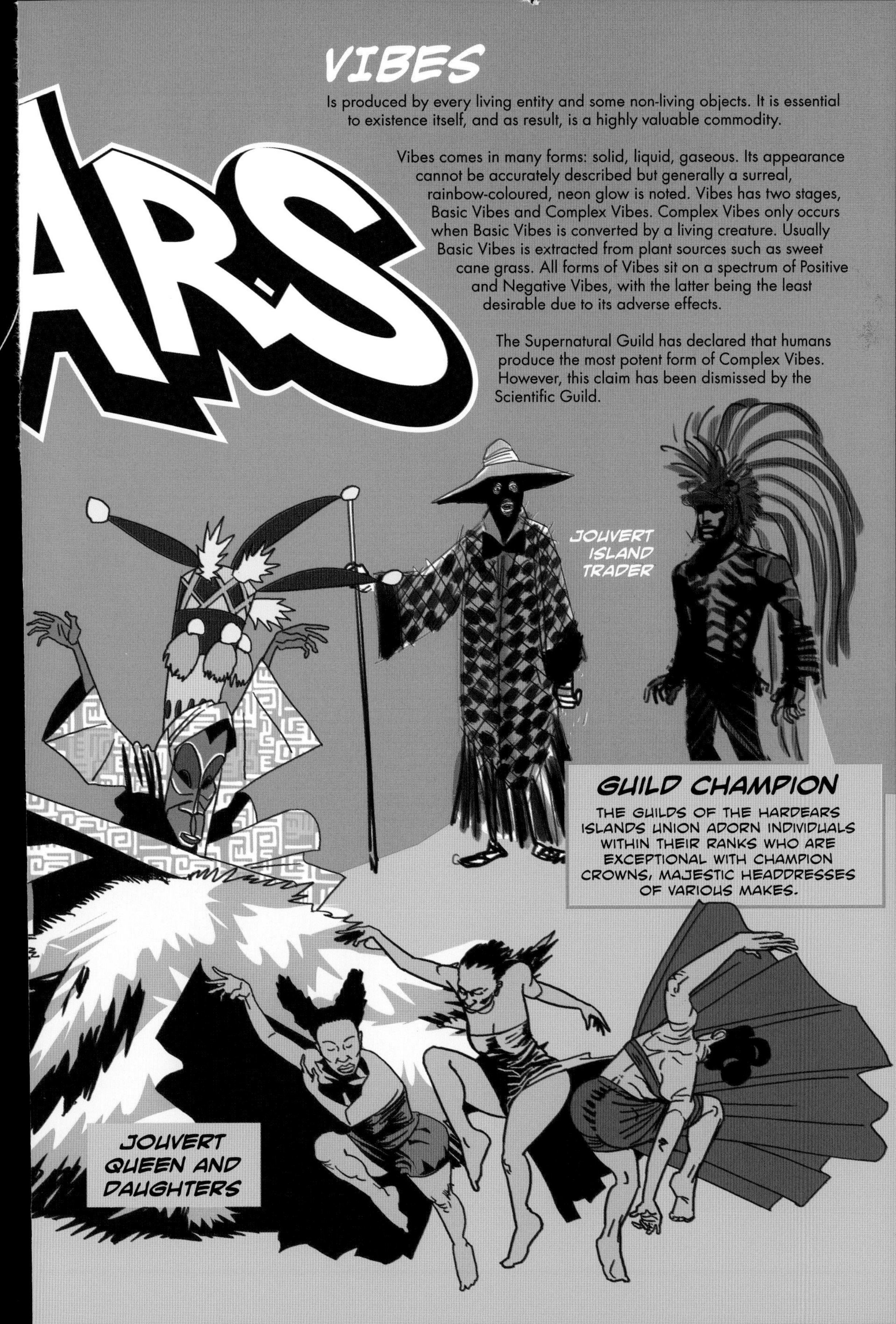

JOUVERT ISLAND TRADER
GUILD CHAMPION
THE GUILDS OF THE HARDEARS ISLANDS UNION ADORN INDIVIDUALS WITHIN THEIR RANKS WHO ARE EXCEPTIONAL WITH CHAMPION CROWNS, MAJESTIC HEADDRESSES OF VARIOUS MAKES.
JOUVERT QUEEN AND DAUGHTERS

LANDSHIP

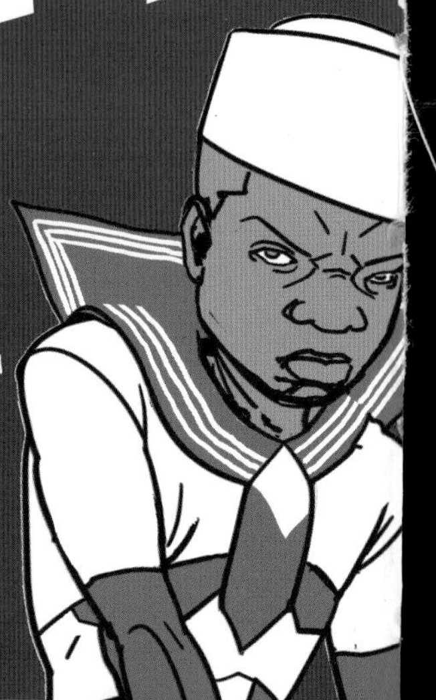

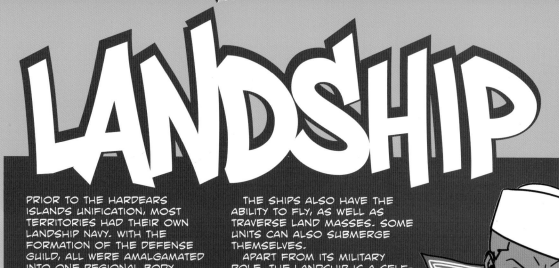

PRIOR TO THE HARDEARS ISLANDS UNIFICATION, MOST TERRITORIES HAD THEIR OWN LANDSHIP NAVY. WITH THE FORMATION OF THE DEFENSE GUILD, ALL WERE AMALGAMATED INTO ONE REGIONAL BODY.

THE LANDSHIP SERVES AS THE ISLANDS' MOST POWERFUL MEANS OF INTERNAL AND EXTERNAL DEFENSE, ABLE TO PERFORM PEACEKEEPING DUTIES TO VANQUISHING ATTACKS BY HURRICANES.

THE VESSELS OF THE LANDSHIP ARE NOT REAL SHIPS, BUT INSTEAD ARE ANCESTRAL SPIRITS JOINED BY THE RHYTHM OF EACH SHIP'S TUK BAND*, AND GUIDED BY ITS CREW.

THE SHIPS ALSO HAVE THE ABILITY TO FLY, AS WELL AS TRAVERSE LAND MASSES. SOME UNITS CAN ALSO SUBMERGE THEMSELVES.

APART FROM ITS MILITARY ROLE, THE LANDSHIP IS A SELF-CONTAINED INSTITUTION WHICH STRIVES TO BE RELEVANT TO THE VERY EXISTENCE OF ITS MEMBERS, PROVIDING THEM WITH CREDIT UNION, BANK, COUNSEL, ENTERTAINMENT ON SPECIAL OCCASIONS, COORDINATING TRAINING AND APPRENTICESHIP, AND IN GENERAL, A FRIEND AND FAMILY WHEN ONE IS NEEDED.

* A MUSICAL ENSEMBLE, WHICH PLAYS TUK OR RUKATUK MUSIC.

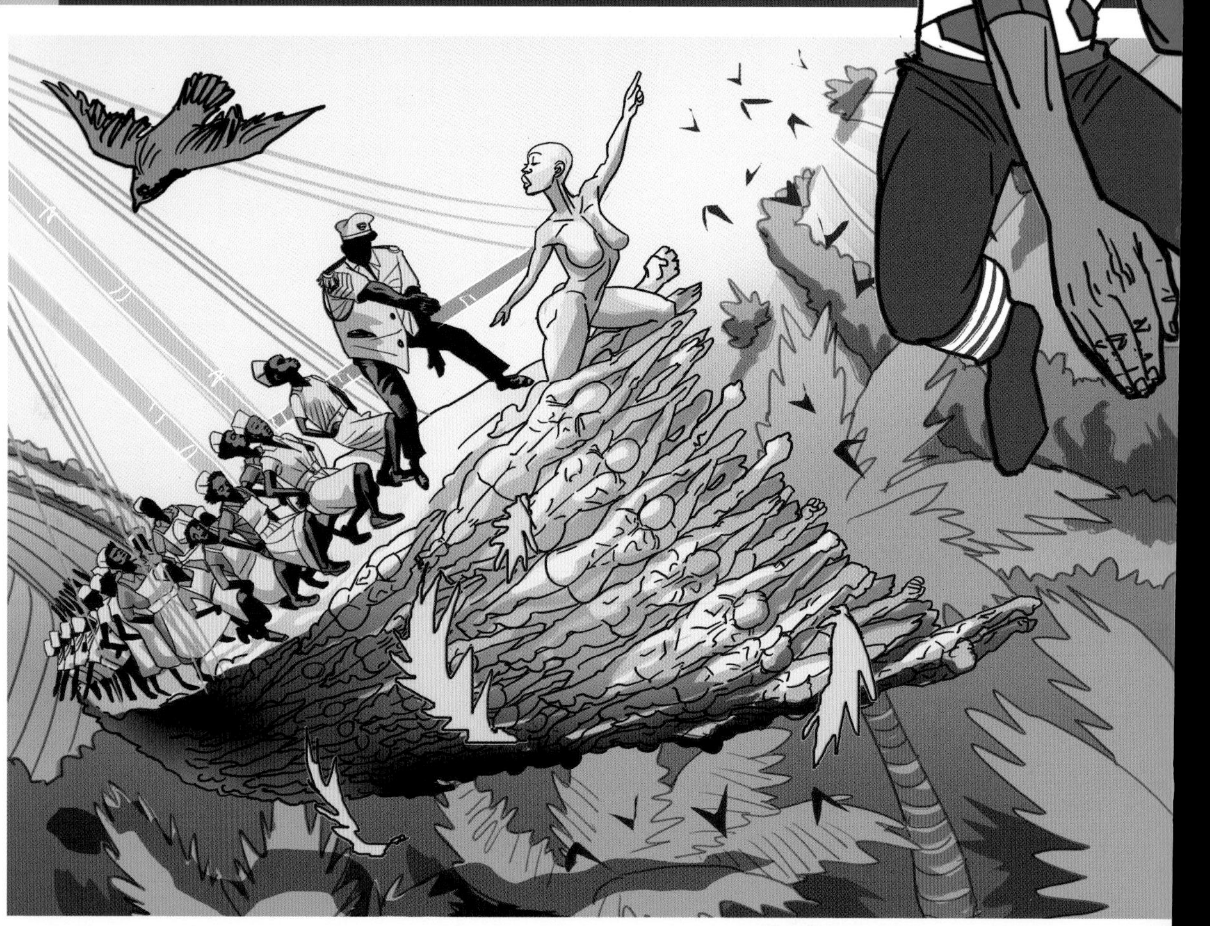

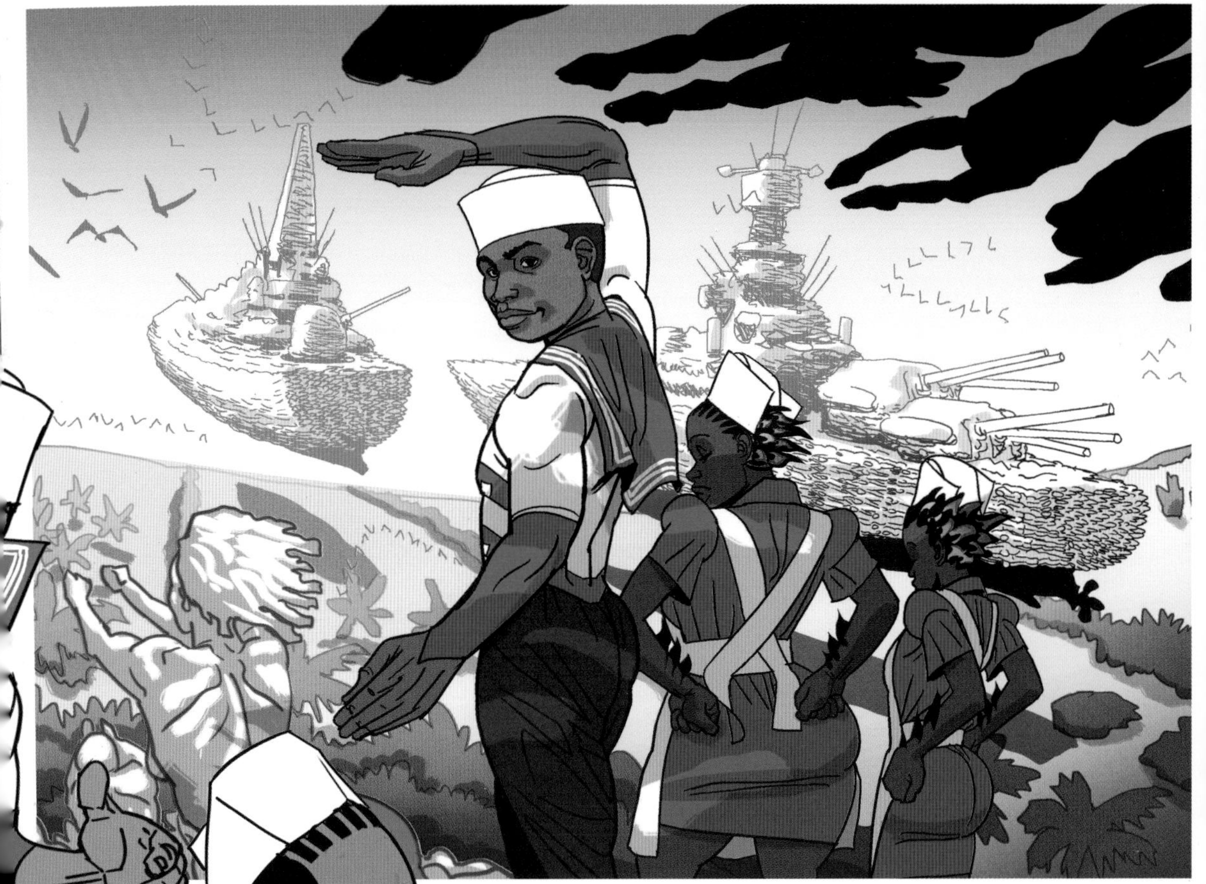

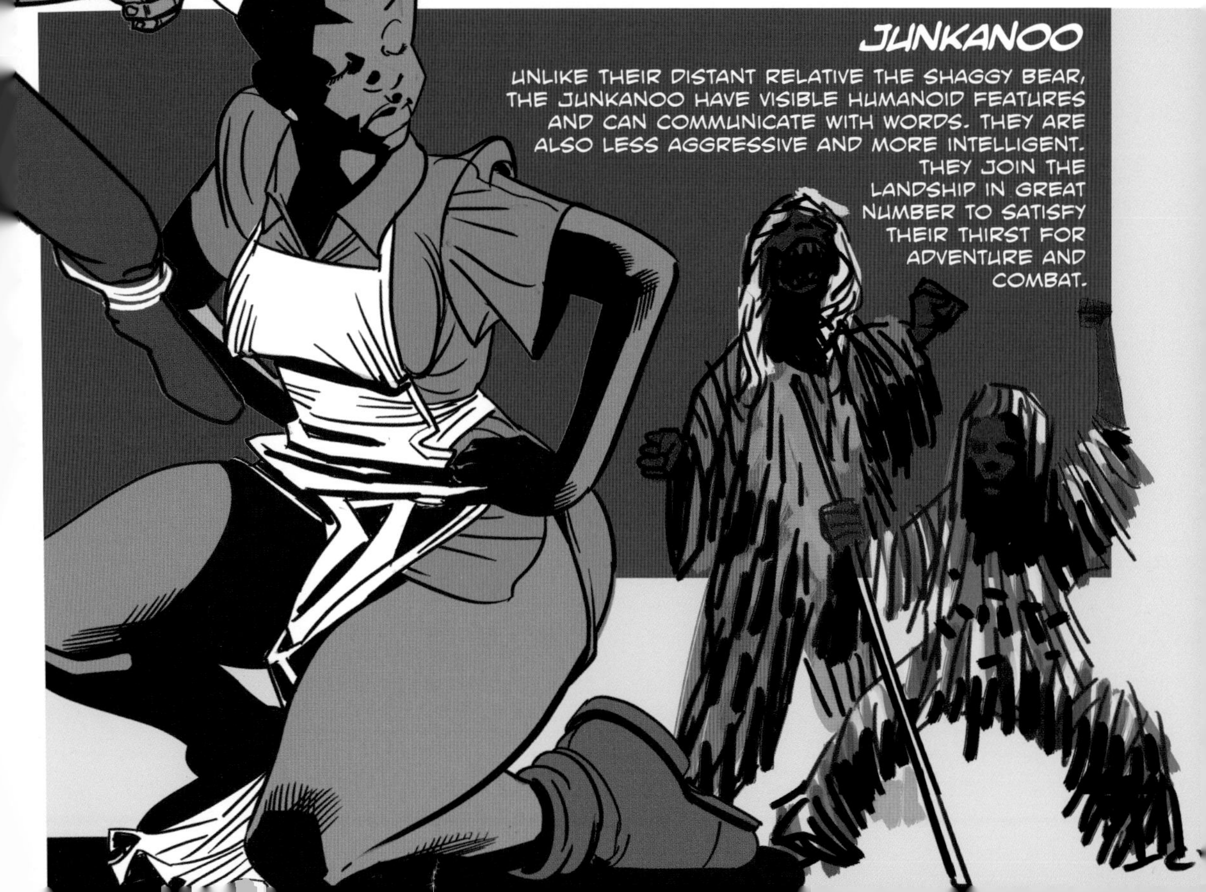
JUNKANOO
UNLIKE THEIR DISTANT RELATIVE THE SHAGGY BEAR, THE JUNKANOO HAVE VISIBLE HUMANOID FEATURES AND CAN COMMUNICATE WITH WORDS. THEY ARE ALSO LESS AGGRESSIVE AND MORE INTELLIGENT. THEY JOIN THE LANDSHIP IN GREAT NUMBER TO SATISFY THEIR THIRST FOR ADVENTURE AND COMBAT.

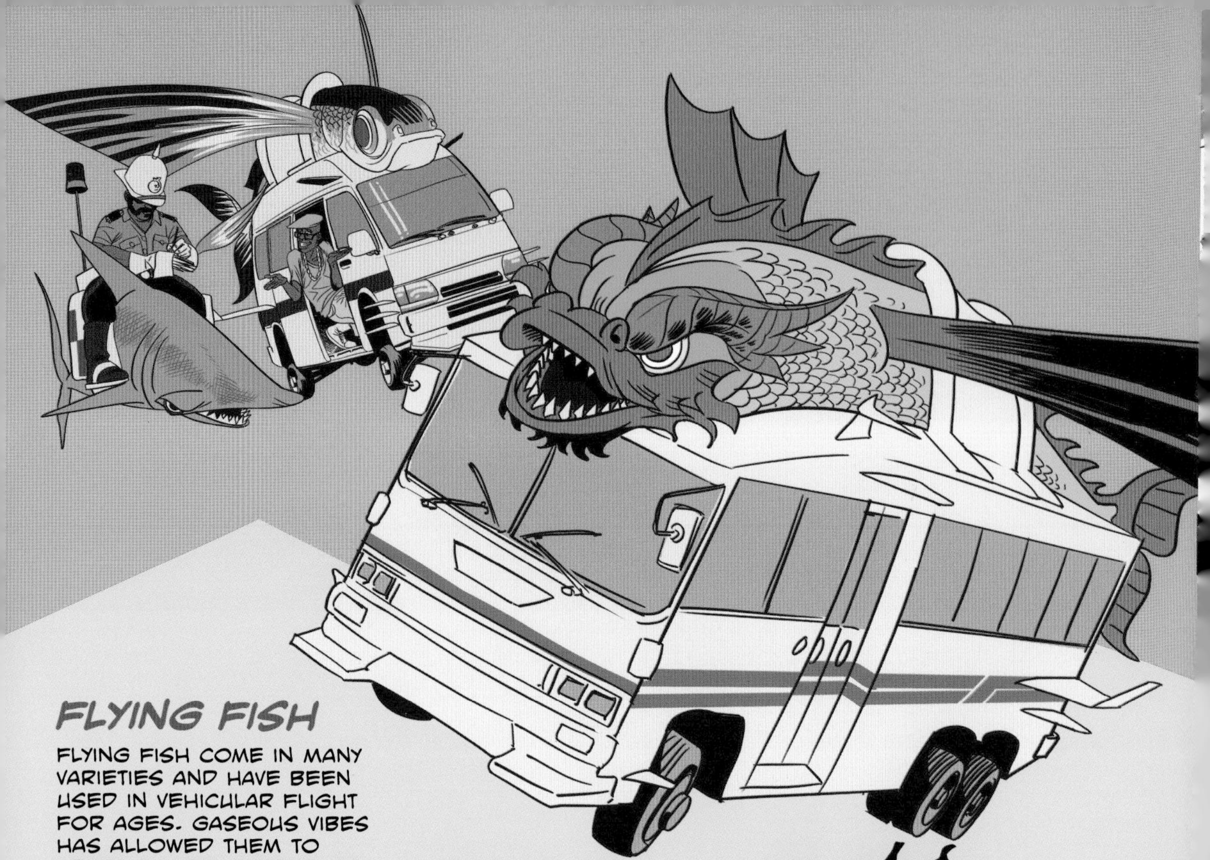

FLYING FISH

FLYING FISH COME IN MANY VARIETIES AND HAVE BEEN USED IN VEHICULAR FLIGHT FOR AGES. GASEOUS VIBES HAS ALLOWED THEM TO ADAPT TO LIFE OUTSIDE OF WATER.

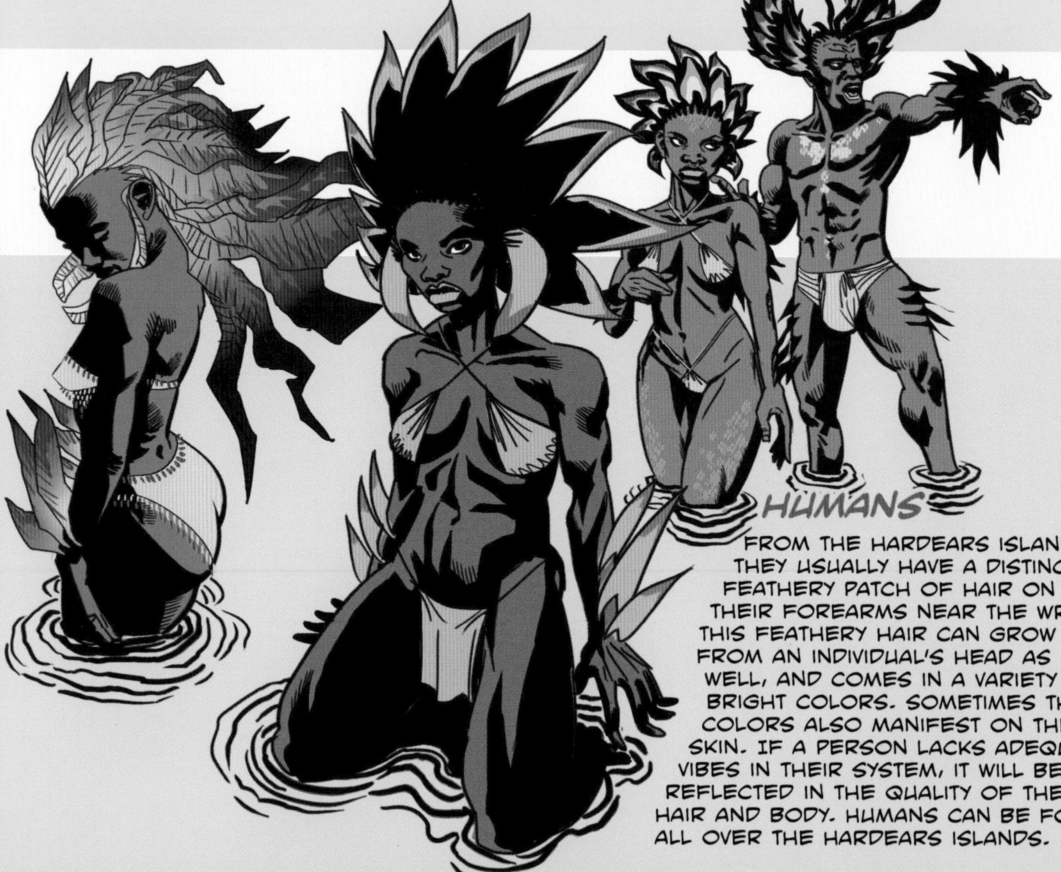

HUMANS

FROM THE HARDEARS ISLANDS, THEY USUALLY HAVE A DISTINCT FEATHERY PATCH OF HAIR ON THEIR FOREARMS NEAR THE WRIST. THIS FEATHERY HAIR CAN GROW FROM AN INDIVIDUAL'S HEAD AS WELL, AND COMES IN A VARIETY OF BRIGHT COLORS. SOMETIMES THESE COLORS ALSO MANIFEST ON THE SKIN. IF A PERSON LACKS ADEQUATE VIBES IN THEIR SYSTEM, IT WILL BE REFLECTED IN THE QUALITY OF THEIR HAIR AND BODY. HUMANS CAN BE FOUND ALL OVER THE HARDEARS ISLANDS.

AVIANS

WINGED HUMANOIDS OF VARIOUS SIZES, COLOUR, AND SHAPE CAN BE FOUND ALL OVER THE HARDEARS ISLANDS. THE CANOPY ISLANDS, HOWEVER, ARE CONSIDERED THEIR HOMELAND. THEY HAVE BEEN TRYING TO GAIN OFFICIAL RECOGNITION OF THE AERIAL LESSER GUILD HOWEVER, THIS HAS CONSTANTLY BEEN BLOCKED BY THE AGRICULTURAL GUILD. TENSIONS HAVE EXISTED FOR YEARS BETWEEN THE TWO, WITH THE AGRI GUILD ACCUSING AVIANS OF CROP THEFT AND AVIANS PROTESTING AGRICULTURAL EXPANSION, WHICH HAS ENCROACHED ON AND DESTROYED THEIR FOREST HABITATS.

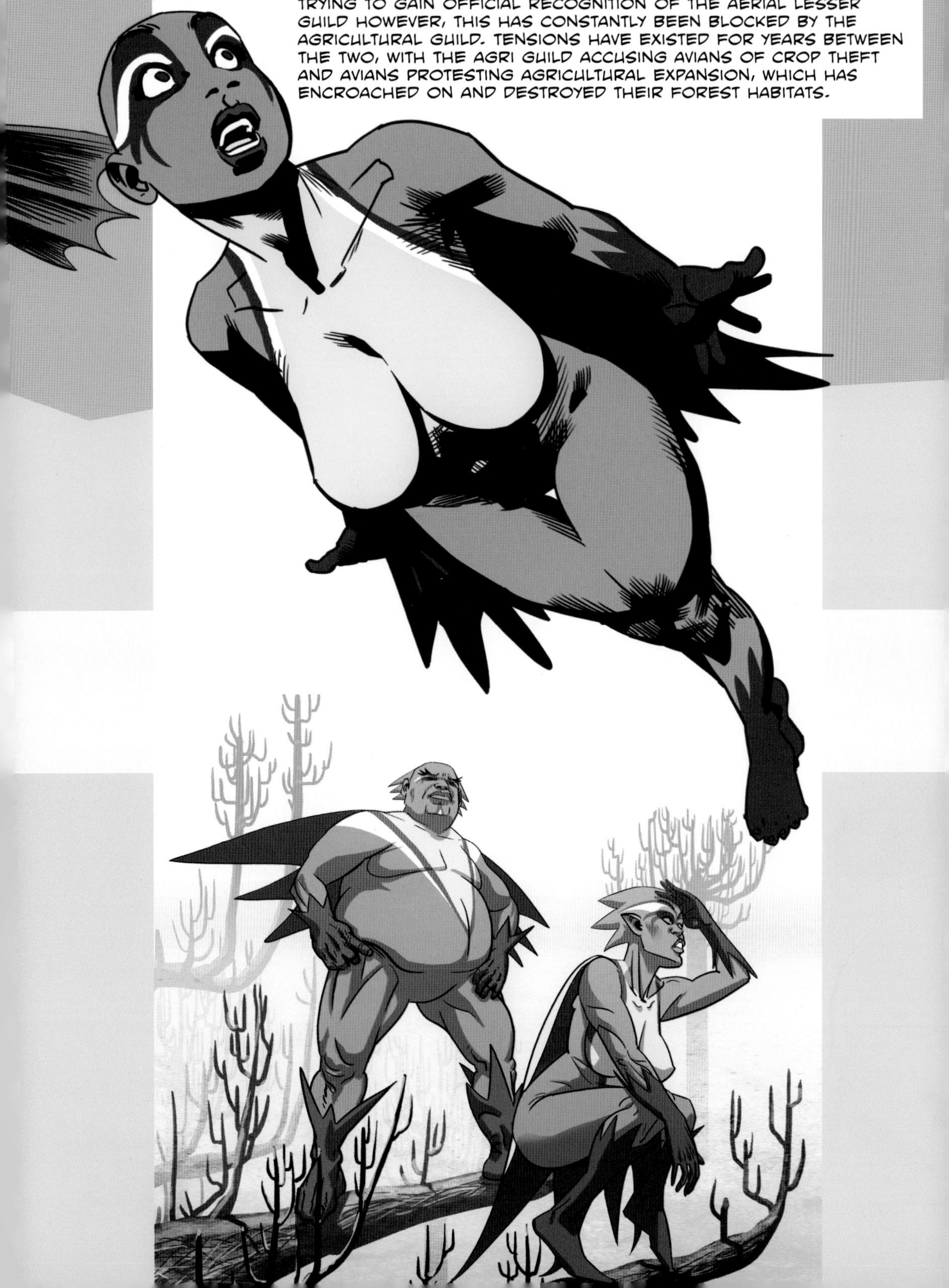

JUMBEES

IS A GENERIC TERM GIVEN TO ALL MYSTICAL BEINGS IN THE HARDEARS ISLANDS THOUGH OFTEN TIMES INCORRECTLY SO. TRUE JUMBEE OFTEN TIMES CANNOT PRODUCE THEIR OWN VIBES AND FEED ON THE VIBES PRODUCED BY OTHER BEINGS OR OTHER SOURCES. BECAUSE OF THIS THEY ARE VIEWED OFTEN TIMES AS MALEVOLENT ENTITIES.

MOONGAZER

THESE TOWERING GIANTS ORIGINALLY ROAMED THE SHORELINES OF SOME HARDEARS ISLANDS, BUT OVER TIME, WERE DRIVEN INLAND AS THEY CAME INTO CONFLICT WITH EVER-EXPANDING CIVILISATION.

MOONGAZERS, AS THE NAME SUGGESTS, SPEND MOST OF THEIR LIFE STARING AT THE MOON, ESPECIALLY A FULL MOON. OTHER LIGHT SOURCES, SUCH AS BONFIRES AND RESIDENTIAL LIGHTING MAY ATTRACT A YOUNG MOONGAZER AS WELL. THE REASON FOR THIS IS NOT FULLY KNOWN BUT RESEARCH CONDUCTED BY THE SCIENCE GUILD SUGGESTS THAT A MOONGAZER USES THE MOON'S LIGHT TO PRODUCE ITS OWN VIBES. THUS, THE MOON STARE MAY BE AN ACT OF FEEDING AS THIS CREATURE HAS NO VISABLE MOUTH. THEY WILL OFTEN TIMES STRADDLE ROADS AND PATHS AND CRUSH AN UNFORTUNATE PASSER-BY WITH THEIR LONG LEGS.

LEGEND HAS IT THAT PASSAGE THROUGH THE LEGS OF THIS JUMBEE CAN TAKE SOME, WITH THE KNOW HOW, TO ALTERNATE REALITIES.

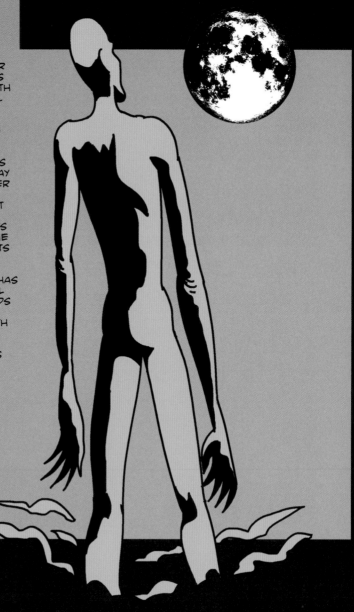

SOUCOUYANT

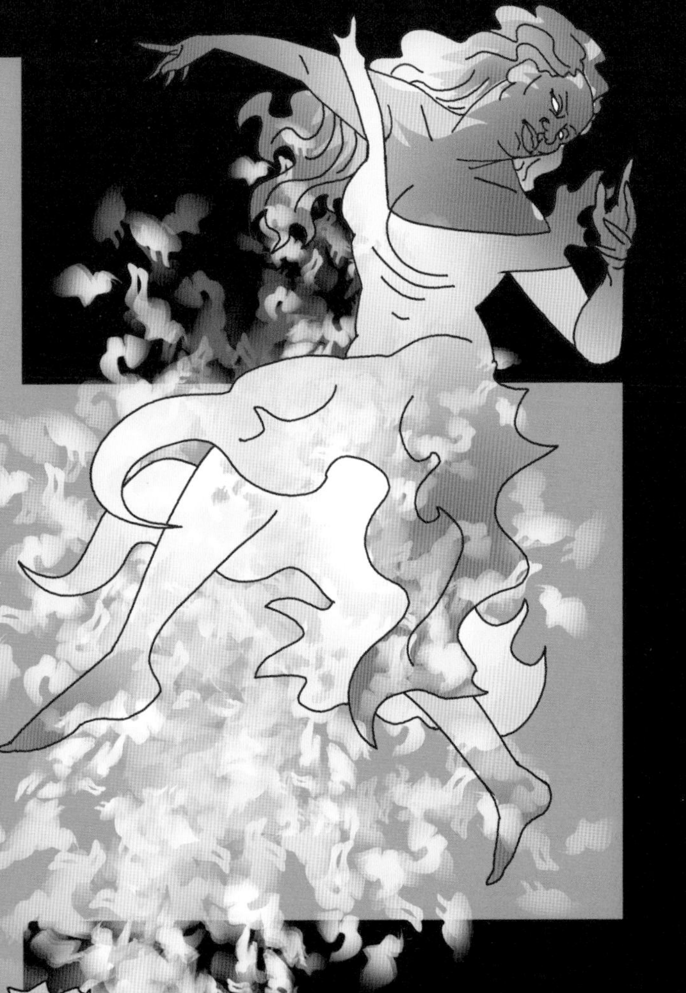

ALSO KNOWN AS FIRE RASS, ANGELI, LOOGAROO, HAG OR HAIG, THESE SHAPE SHIFTING JUMBEE ARE THOUGHT TO BE NEARLY EXTINCT. THEY CANNOT PRODUCE THEIR OWN VIBES AND MUST FEED OFF THE VIBES OF OTHER LIVING CREATURES. THEY CAN LIVE FOR HUNDREDS OF YEARS ONCE THEY KEEP FEEDING. DURING THE DAY THEY APPEAR EITHER AS A YOUNG WOMAN OR AN ELDERLY WOMAN BUT AT NIGHT WILL SHED THEIR SKIN AND TAKE THE FORM OF A FIREBALL AS THEY TRAVEL TO THEIR PREY. SOUCOUYANTS ARE KNOWN TO SEDUCE MEN AND THOUGH THEY CAN TOTALLY DRAIN AN INDIVIDUAL OF VIBES IN ONE GO, THEY PREFER TO BUILD A RELATIONSHIP WITH THEIR PREY AND DRAIN THEM OVER TIME. SOUCOUYANTS IN THE FORM OF AN ELDERLY WOMAN ARE ESPECIALLY LOATHED AS THEY TEND TO FEED ON CHILDREN OFTEN TIMES USING TREATS AS A LURE.

SOUCOUYANTS OFTEN HIDE THEIR SKIN WHEN TRAVELING IN FIRE FORM BECAUSE, IF FOUND, AND DESTROYED, WILL CAUSE THIS JUMBEE TO PERISH.

THESE ENTITIES HAVE A PECULIAR COMPULSION TO COUNT GRAINS OF RICE, A FACT OFTEN EXPLOITED BY PERSONS HUNTING THEM.

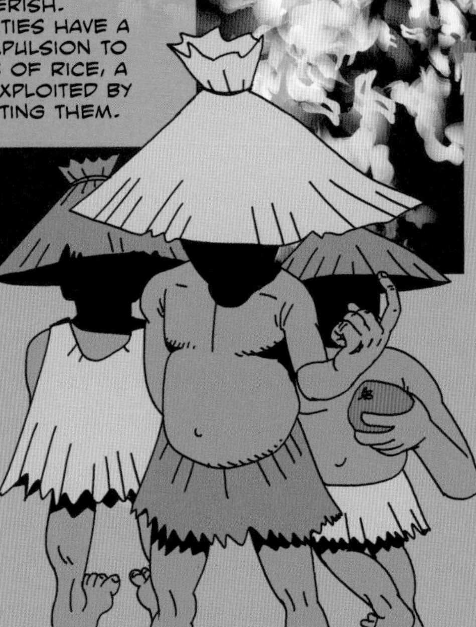

DOUEN

THESE JUMBEE ARE THOUGHT TO BE EXTINCT AFTER THE DESTRUCTION OF JOUVERT ISLAND'S MANGROVES TO MAKE WAY FOR CONSTRUCTION AND FARMING.

DOUEN ARE CHILD LIKE IN APPEARANCE AND OFTEN WEAR A STRAW HAT, BUT ONE NOTABLE FEATURE THEY POSSESS IS THAT OF HAVING BACKWARD FEET FROM THE KNEE DOWN. THEY ARE MISCHIEVOUS IN NATURE AND, ONCE THEY LEARN OF YOUR NAME, WILL CALL IT IN A VOICE FAMILIAR TO YOU AND ATTEMPT TO LEAD YOU INTO THE MANGROVE OR FOREST THEY RESIDE IN. DOUEN ARE KNOWN TO LEAD PERSONS TO GET LOST IN REMOTE AREAS. THIS ASPECT OF THEIR BEHAVIOR HAS LARGELY BEEN MISUNDERSTOOD AND SEEN AS AN ATTEMPT TO PREY ON THEIR VICTIMS WHEN IN FACT THEY ONLY FEED ON VEGETABLE VIBES.

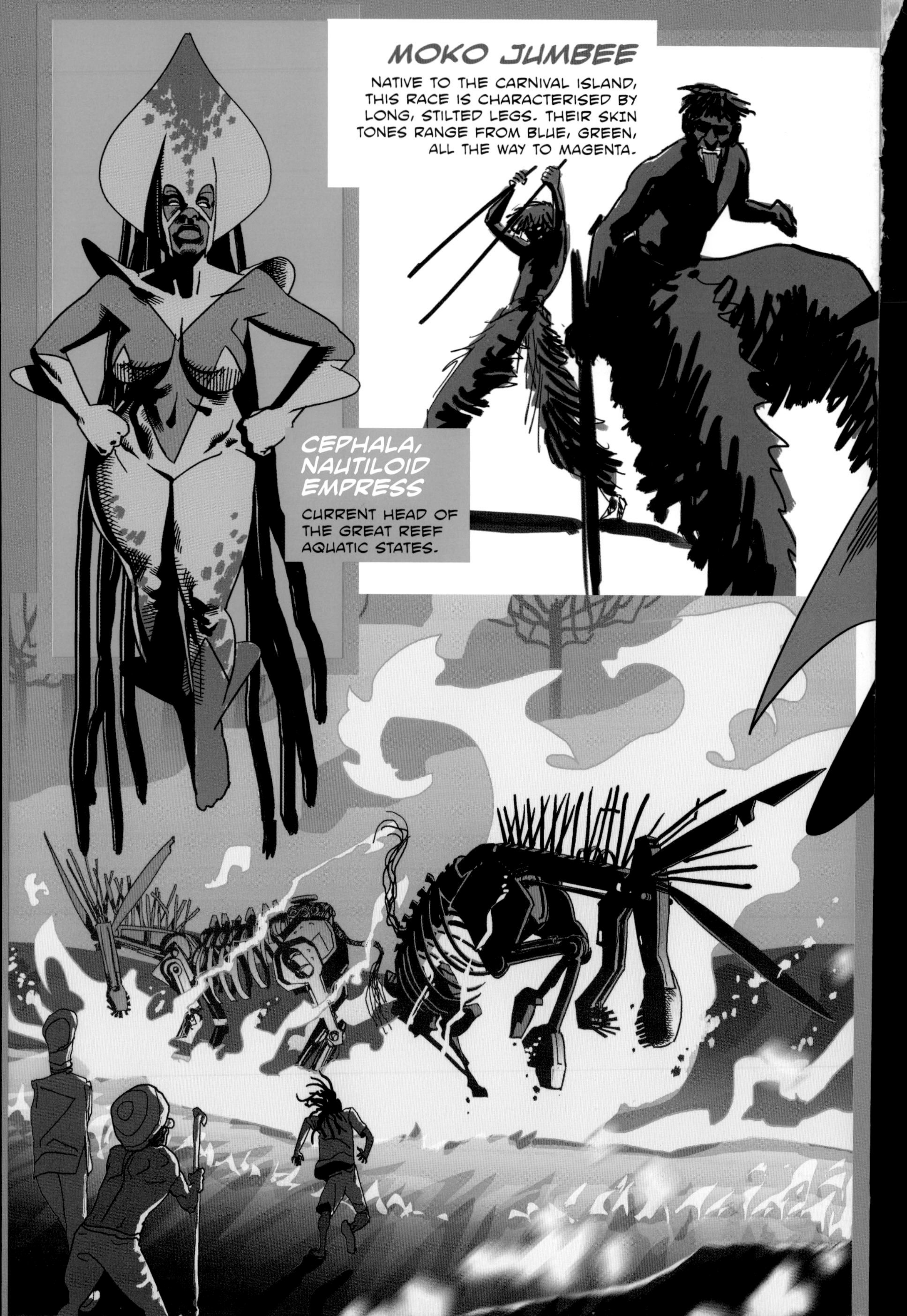
MOKO JUMBEE
NATIVE TO THE CARNIVAL ISLAND, THIS RACE IS CHARACTERISED BY LONG, STILTED LEGS. THEIR SKIN TONES RANGE FROM BLUE, GREEN, ALL THE WAY TO MAGENTA.
CEPHALA, NAUTILOID EMPRESS
CURRENT HEAD OF THE GREAT REEF AQUATIC STATES.

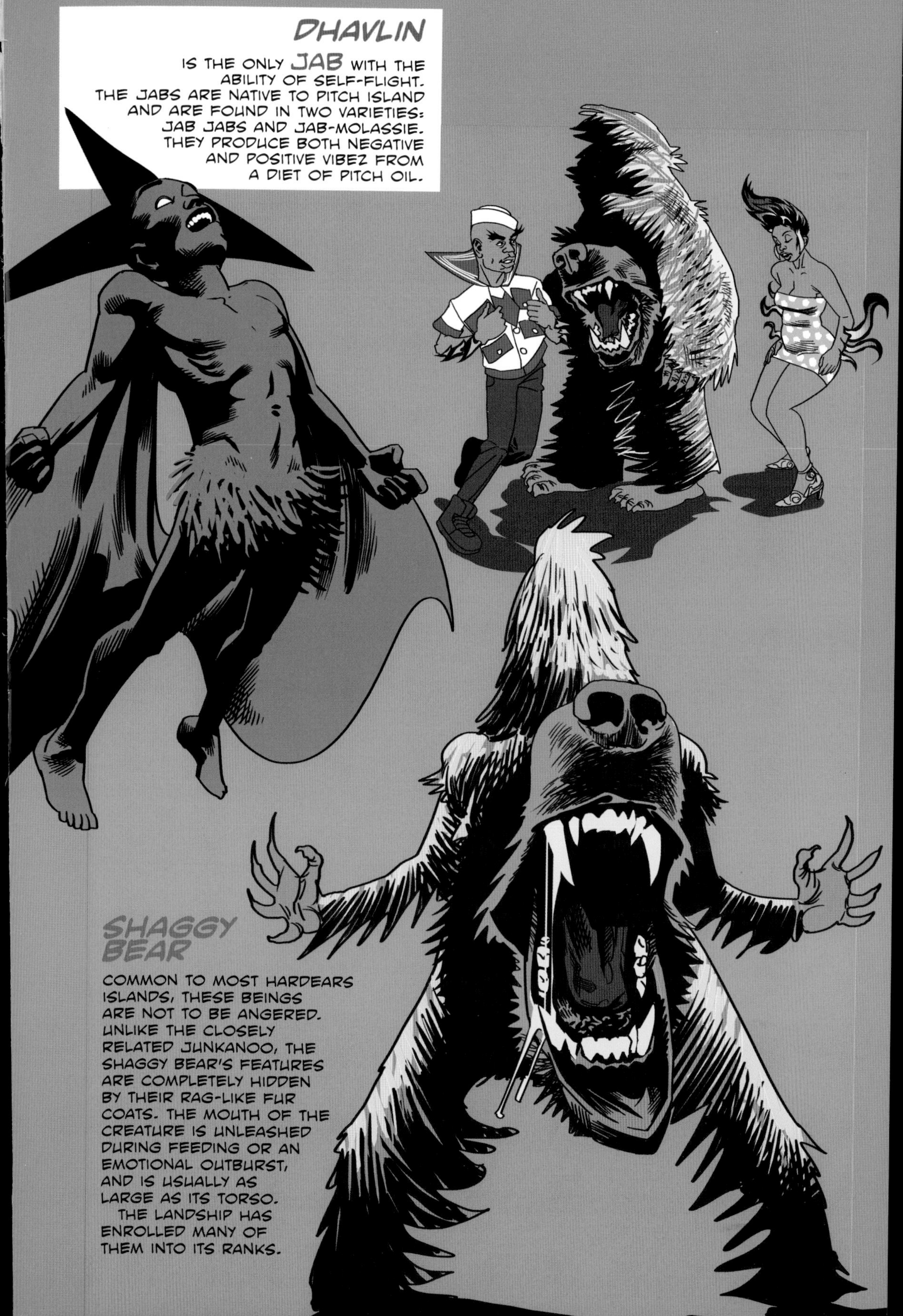
DHAVLIN
IS THE ONLY JAB WITH THE ABILITY OF SELF-FLIGHT. THE JABS ARE NATIVE TO PITCH ISLAND AND ARE FOUND IN TWO VARIETIES: JAB JABS AND JAB-MOLASSIE. THEY PRODUCE BOTH NEGATIVE AND POSITIVE VIBEZ FROM A DIET OF PITCH OIL.
SHAGGY BEAR
COMMON TO MOST HARDEARS ISLANDS, THESE BEINGS ARE NOT TO BE ANGERED. UNLIKE THE CLOSELY RELATED JUNKANOO, THE SHAGGY BEAR'S FEATURES ARE COMPLETELY HIDDEN BY THEIR RAG-LIKE FUR COATS. THE MOUTH OF THE CREATURE IS UNLEASHED DURING FEEDING OR AN EMOTIONAL OUTBURST, AND IS USUALLY AS LARGE AS ITS TORSO.
THE LANDSHIP HAS ENROLLED MANY OF THEM INTO ITS RANKS.

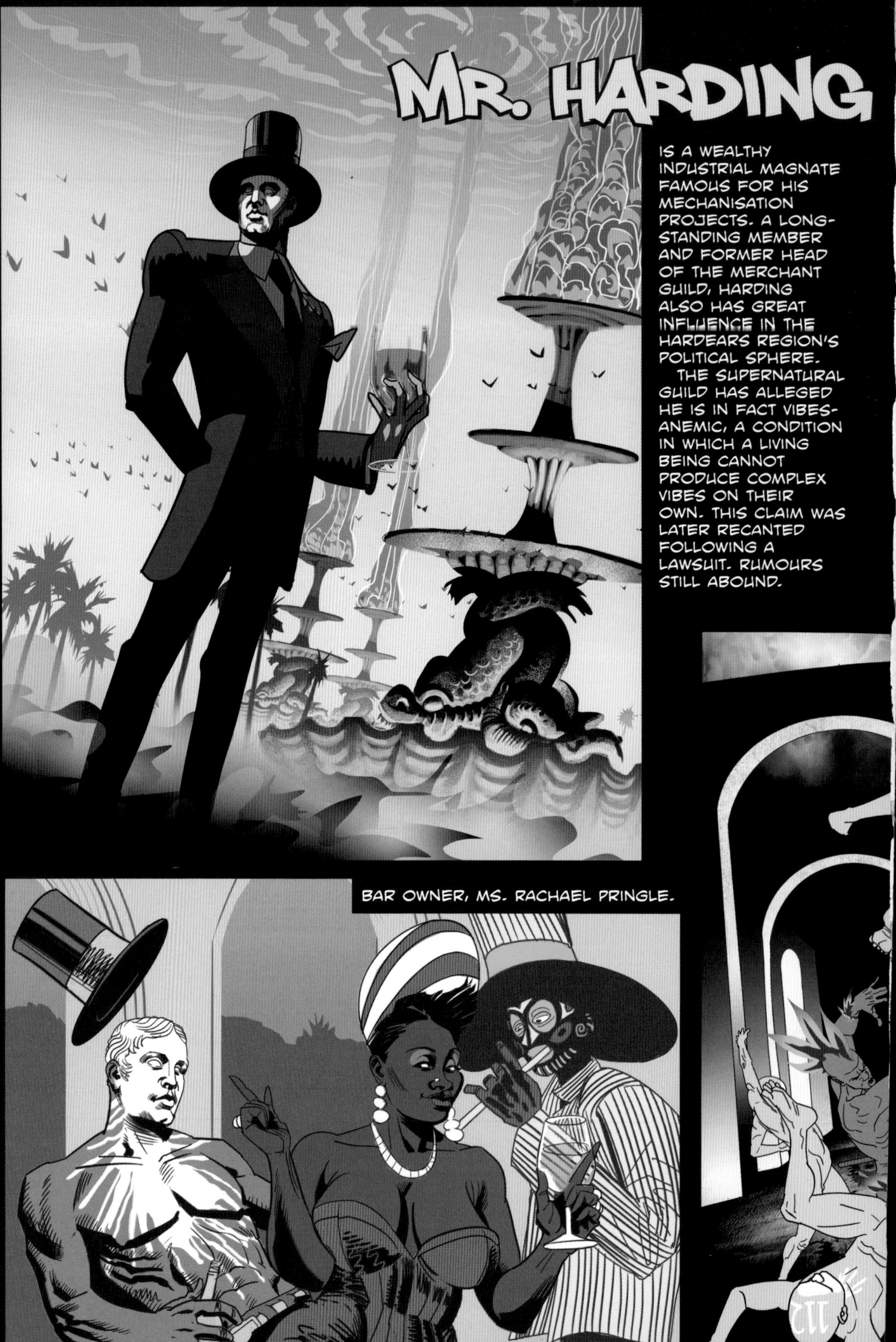
MR. HARDING
IS A WEALTHY INDUSTRIAL MAGNATE FAMOUS FOR HIS MECHANISATION PROJECTS. A LONG-STANDING MEMBER AND FORMER HEAD OF THE MERCHANT GUILD, HARDING ALSO HAS GREAT INFLUENCE IN THE HARDEARS REGION'S POLITICAL SPHERE.
THE SUPERNATURAL GUILD HAS ALLEGED HE IS IN FACT VIBES-ANEMIC, A CONDITION IN WHICH A LIVING BEING CANNOT PRODUCE COMPLEX VIBES ON THEIR OWN. THIS CLAIM WAS LATER RECANTED FOLLOWING A LAWSUIT. RUMOURS STILL ABOUND.
BAR OWNER, MS. RACHAEL PRINGLE.

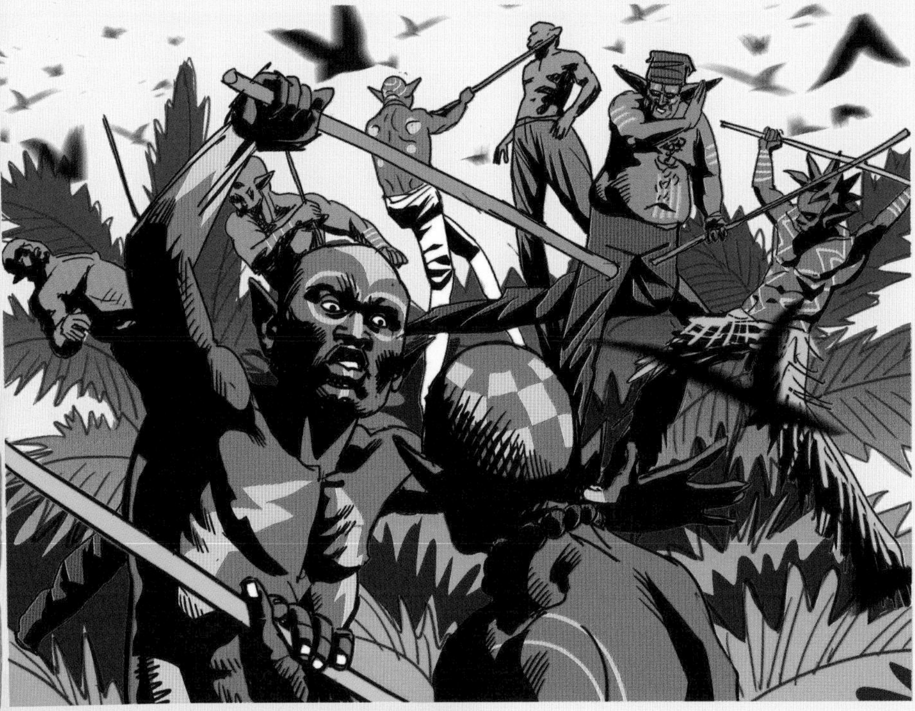

STICK COMBAT

(KNOWN AS STICK-LICKING OR STICK SCIENCE) IS A SYSTEM OF WEAPONS FIGHTING THAT FEATURES THE USE OF FIRE-HARDENED STICKS OF VARYING LENGTHS.

THIS MARTIAL ART HAS BEEN AN INTEGRAL PART OF HARDEARS ISLANDS SOCIETY AND IS SEEN AS A TEST OF MANHOOD, A SPORT, A MEANS OF SELF-DEFENSE, AND A METHOD OF SETTLING DISPUTES.

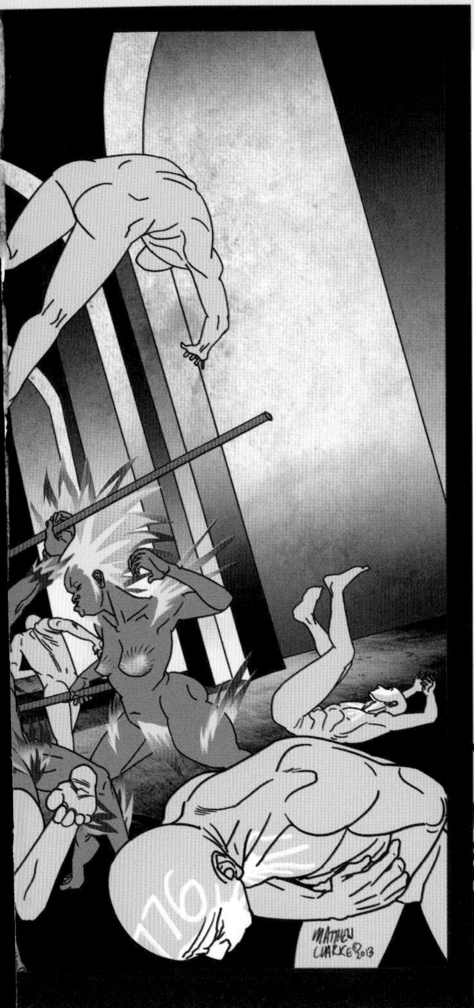
MATTHEW CLARKE ©2013

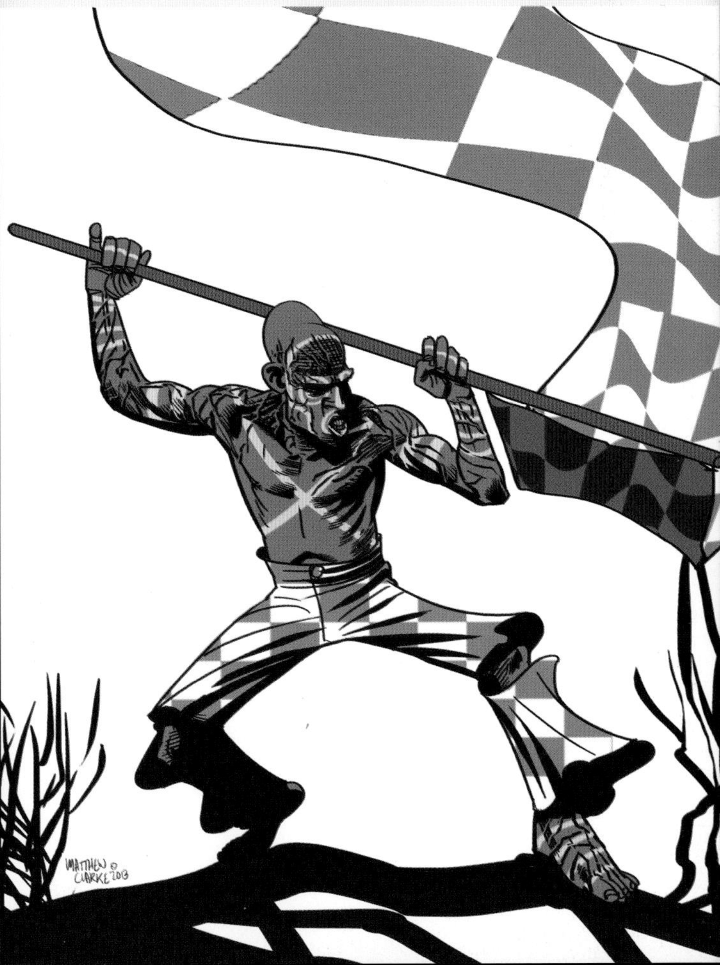
MATTHEW CLARKE ©2013

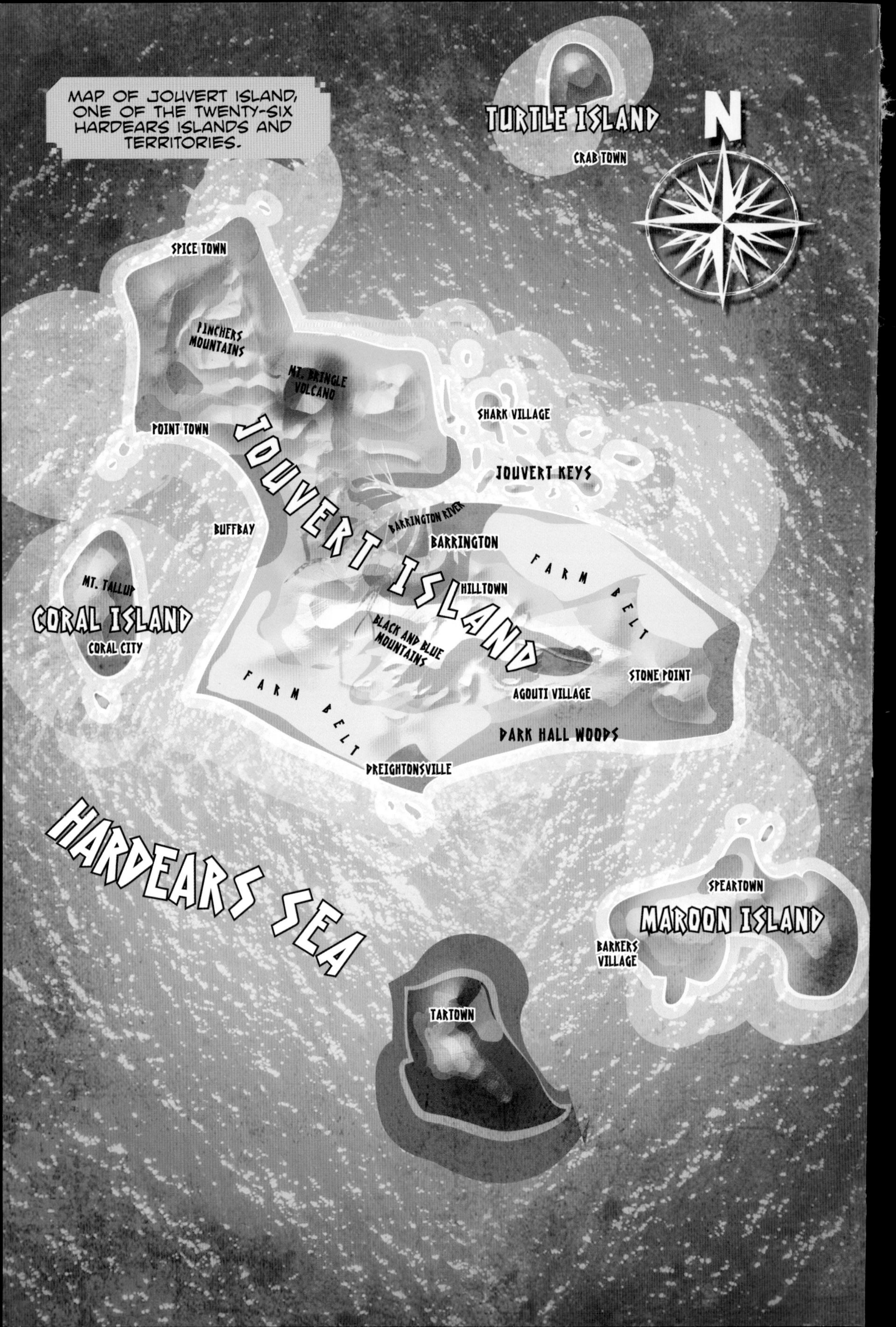
MAP OF JOUVERT ISLAND, ONE OF THE TWENTY-SIX HARDEARS ISLANDS AND TERRITORIES.
TURTLE ISLAND
N
CRAB TOWN
SPICE TOWN
PINCHERS MOUNTAINS
MT. BRINGLE VOLCANO
SHARK VILLAGE
POINT TOWN
JOUVERT ISLAND
JOUVERT KEYS
BUFFBAY
BARRINGTON RIVER
BARRINGTON
FARM BELT
MT. TALLUP
HILLTOWN
CORAL ISLAND
CORAL CITY
BLACK AND BLUE MOUNTAINS
STONE POINT
FARM BELT
AGOUTI VILLAGE
DARK HALL WOODS
DREIGHTONSVILLE
HARDEARS SEA
SPEARTOWN
MAROON ISLAND
BARKERS VILLAGE
TARTOWN

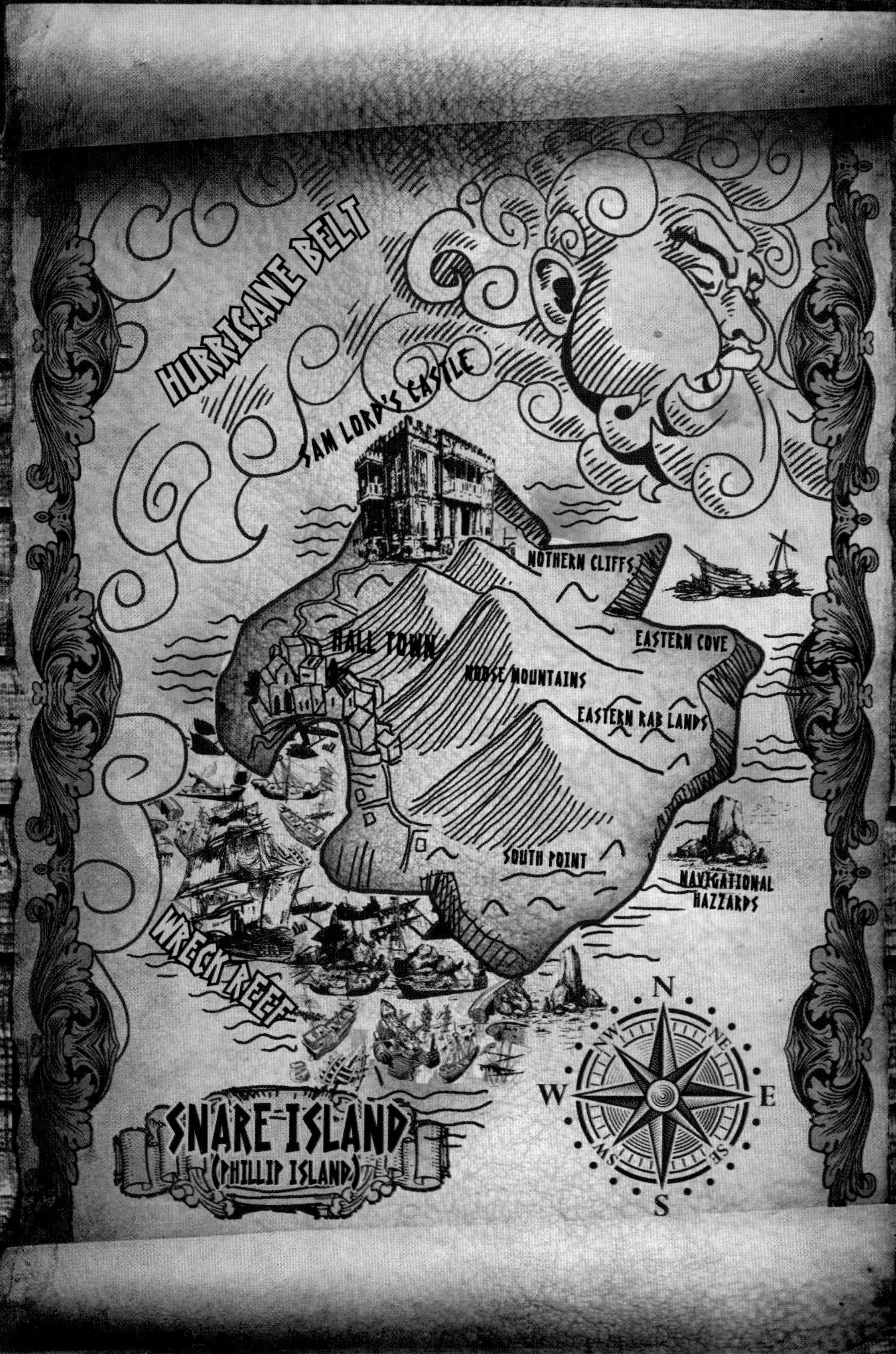
HURRICANE BELT
SAM LORD'S CASTLE
NOTHERN CLIFFS
HALL TOWN
EASTERN COVE
NOOSE MOUNTAINS
EASTERN RAB LANDS
SOUTH POINT
NAVIGATIONAL
HAZZARDS
WRECK REEF
N
NW
NE
W
E
SW
SE
S
SNARE ISLAND
(PHILLIP ISLAND)

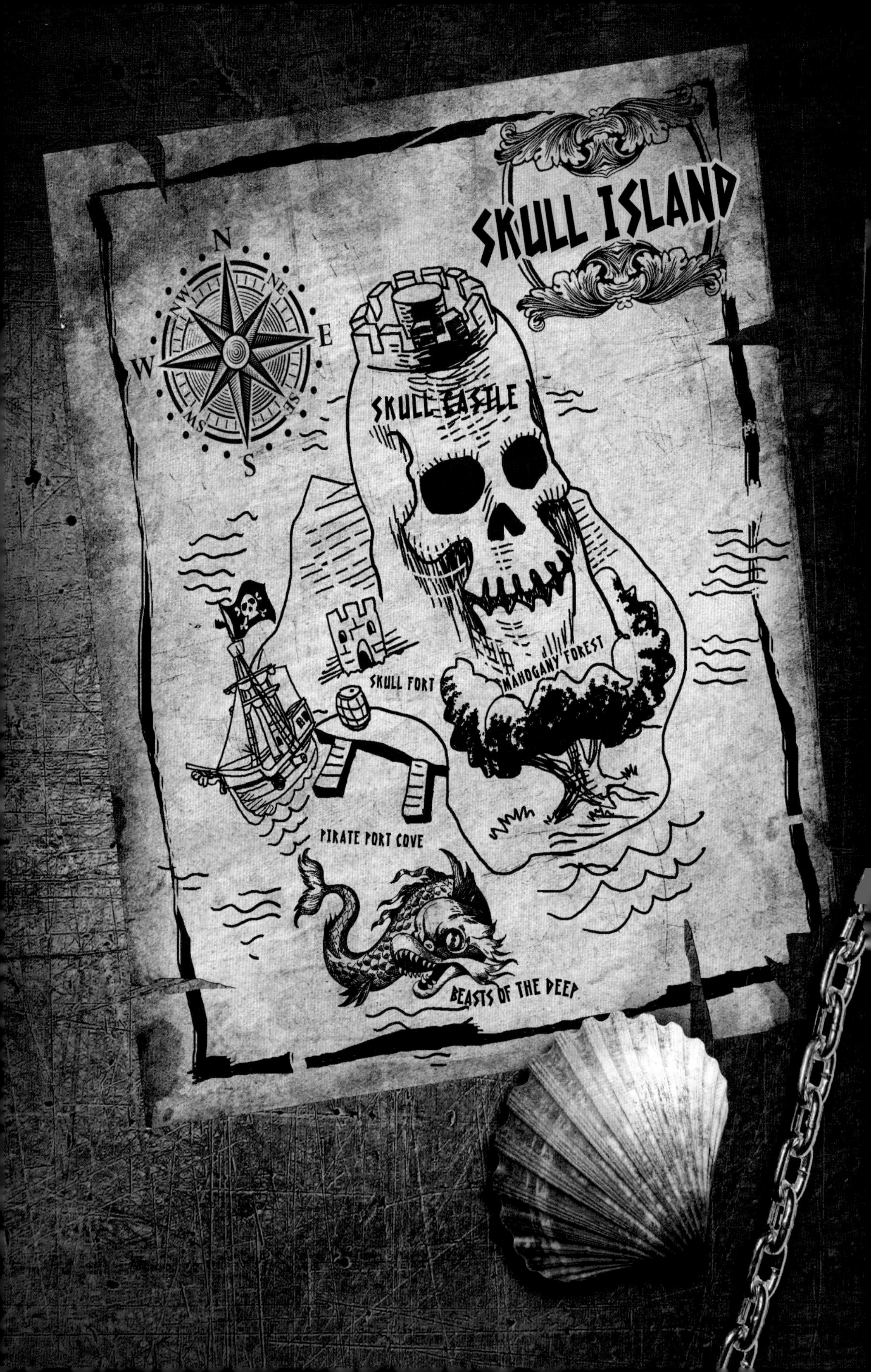
SKULL ISLAND
N
NE
E
SE
S
SW
W
NW
SKULL CASTLE
SKULL FORT
MAHOGANY FOREST
PIRATE PORT COVE
BEASTS OF THE DEEP

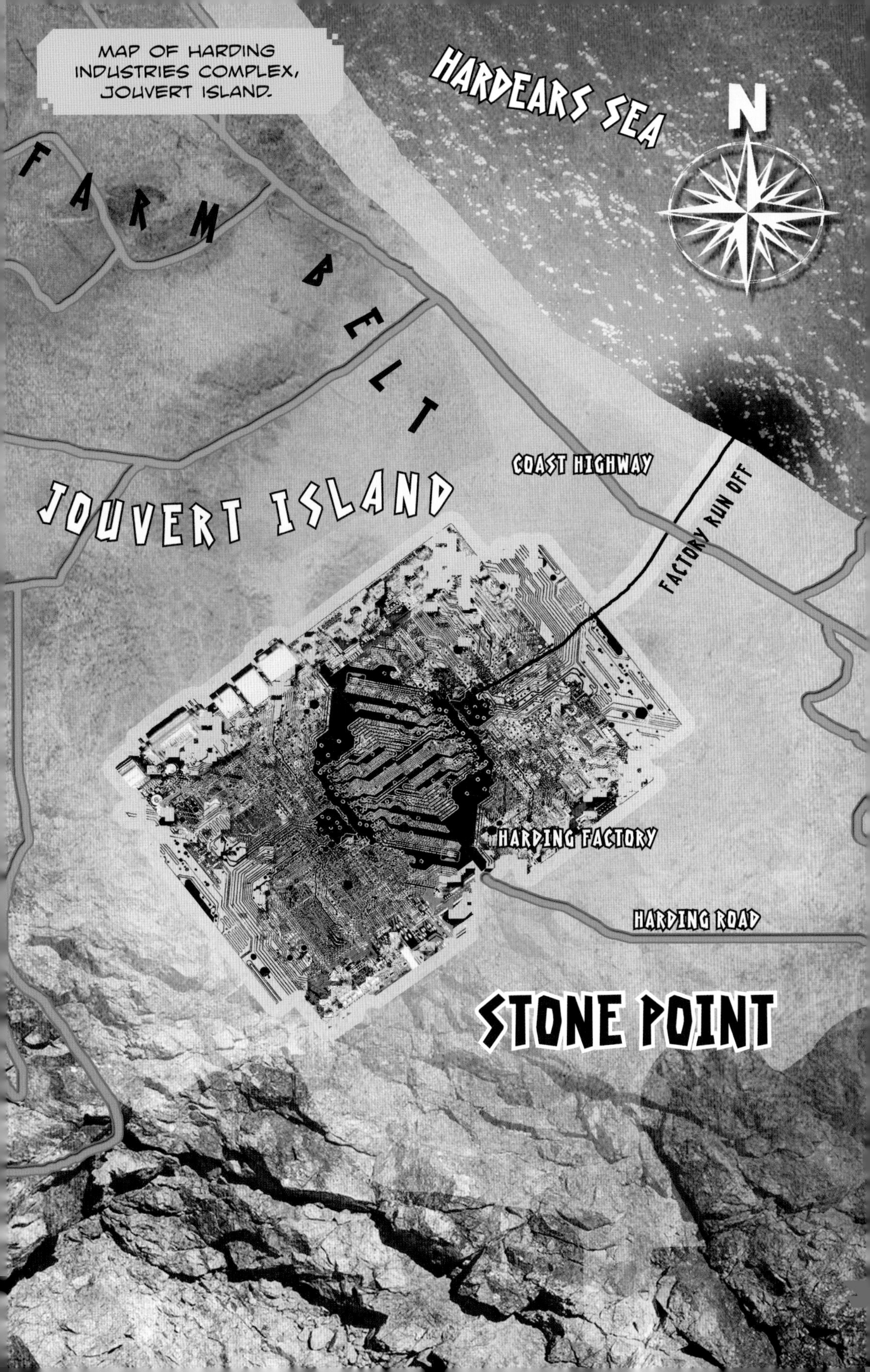
MAP OF HARDING INDUSTRIES COMPLEX, JOUVERT ISLAND.
HARDEARS SEA
N
FARM BELT
COAST HIGHWAY
JOUVERT ISLAND
FACTORY RUN OFF
HARDING FACTORY
HARDING ROAD
STONE POINT

GUILDS

OF THE HARDEARS ISLANDS UNION

The Federation of Guilds was established shortly after the Hardears Islands unification and functions as the Union's legislative and bicameral parliamentary body. The Union Parliament is comprised of the House of Elected Representatives and the House of Guilds.

CURRENTLY THEY ARE SEVEN MAIN GUILDS, other officially unrecognised Guilds exist, referred to as lesser Guilds. Their status the result of various political and social situations.

AGRICULTURAL

The largest and oldest guild, it pre-dates unification. Membership is mainly comprised of farmers, food producers, and retailers. In many remote areas, members of the Agri Guild also serve in defense militia. The expanding Defense Guild is attempting to phase this out, but has been met with great opposition from outlying areas many times, requiring delicate mediation.

SEA

Officially the guild of fishermen, aquatic dwellers, and traders, it is also no secret that pirates, smugglers, and the occasional sea monster fill its ranks, too. Many of its aquatic-dwelling membership cannot attend the land-based Union Parliament and have demanded the establishment of a Hall of the Sea.

DEFENSE

The Defense Guild was created as a unified army for the Hardears Islands. The various policing and security forces, including the Landship, combine to form this guild. Its authority, however, is unable to fully reach all areas of the Hardears region, most notably the aquatic realms.

TRANSPORT

The Transport Guild was formed as a means of getting the notoriously unruly transport and shiping sectors of the Hardears Region in order. Residents of the union are yet to fully feel any positive change from this ongoing process.

MERCHANT

From the big movers and shakers to the humble vendor, this guild forms the economic body of the union. Its biggest challenge when not dealing with an Agri Guild strike is maintaining an image of social responsibility. This often translates as distancing itself as much as possible from its black market.

SUPERNATURAL

The oldest existing guild and most talked about behind closed doors, the Supernatural Guild deals with all that exists above and beyond nature. Ironically, in a world that is paranormal, this guild is often times viewed with suspicion, yet all aspects of society secretly seek its services.

SCIENCE

Researching, discovering, and organising knowledge for the benefit and advancement of all is the driving force behind this well-respected body, which was formed from the much older Supernatural Guild. These two guilds have a love/hate relationship.

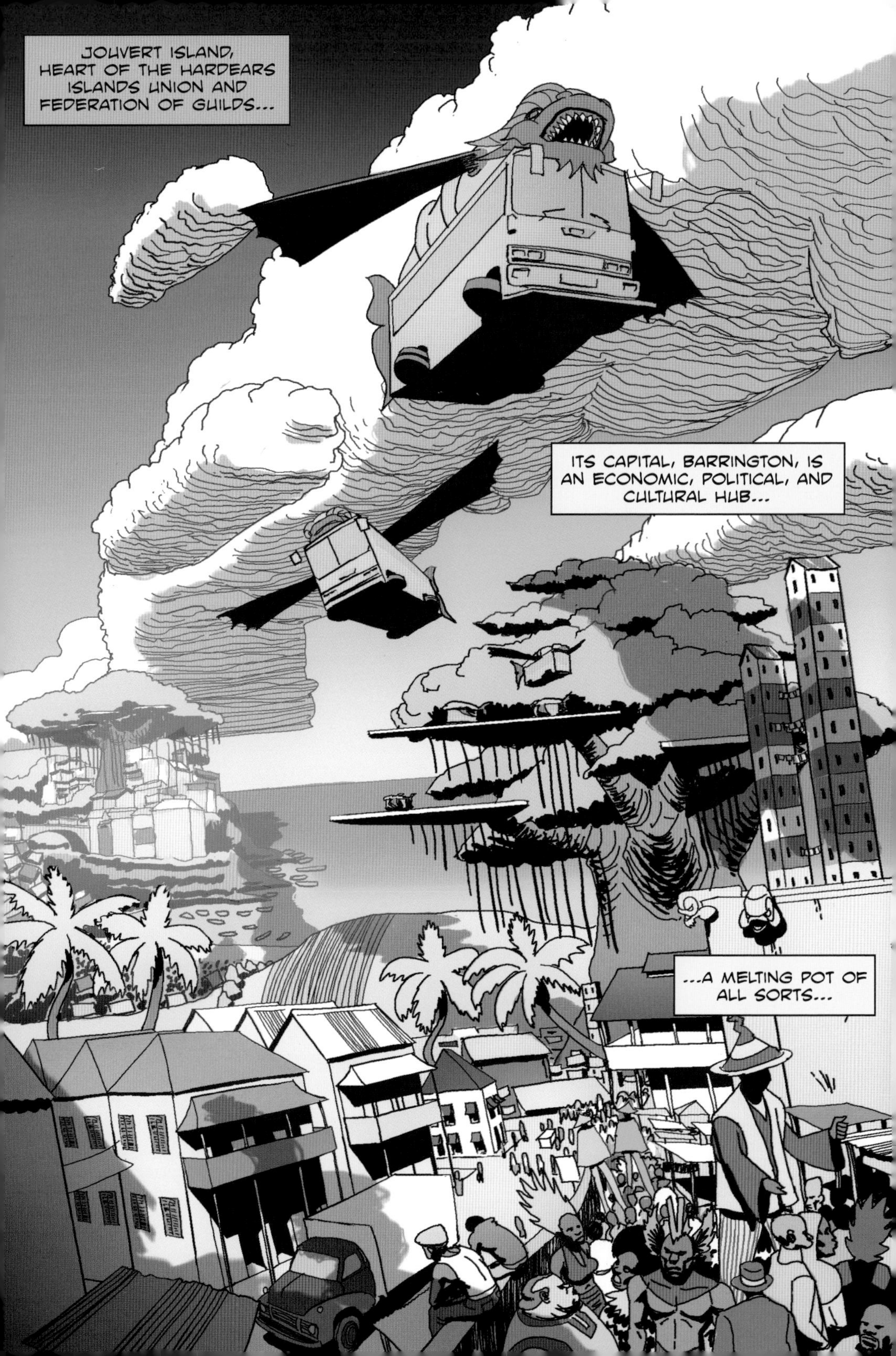
JOUVERT ISLAND, HEART OF THE HARDEARS ISLANDS UNION AND FEDERATION OF GUILDS...
ITS CAPITAL, BARRINGTON, IS AN ECONOMIC, POLITICAL, AND CULTURAL HUB...
...A MELTING POT OF ALL SORTS...

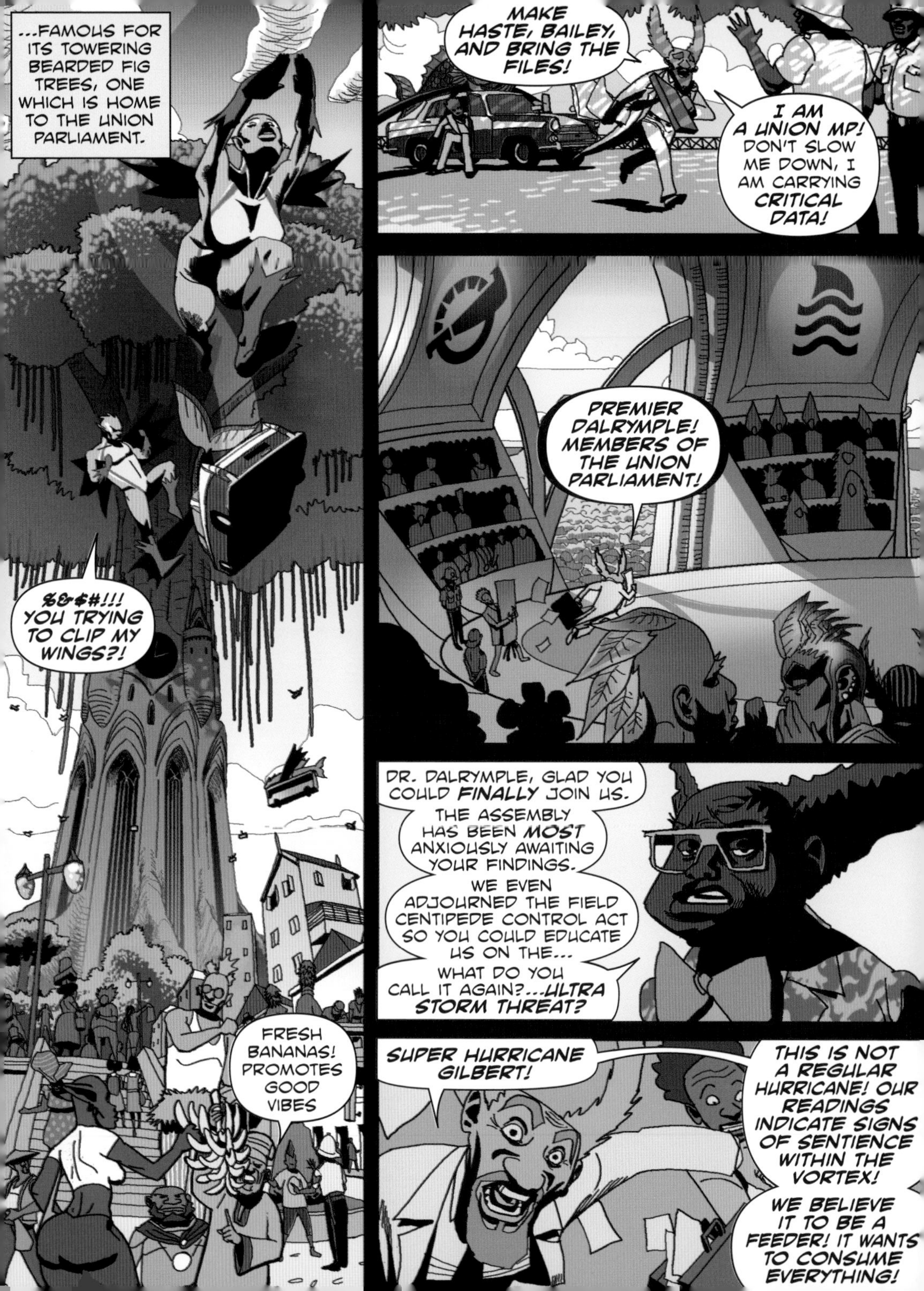
...FAMOUS FOR ITS TOWERING BEARDED FIG TREES, ONE WHICH IS HOME TO THE UNION PARLIAMENT.
%&$#!!! YOU TRYING TO CLIP MY WINGS?!
FRESH BANANAS! PROMOTES GOOD VIBES
MAKE HASTE, BAILEY, AND BRING THE FILES!
I AM A UNION MP! DON'T SLOW ME DOWN, I AM CARRYING CRITICAL DATA!
PREMIER DALRYMPLE! MEMBERS OF THE UNION PARLIAMENT!
DR. DALRYMPLE, GLAD YOU COULD FINALLY JOIN US.
THE ASSEMBLY HAS BEEN MOST ANXIOUSLY AWAITING YOUR FINDINGS.
WE EVEN ADJOURNED THE FIELD CENTIPEDE CONTROL ACT SO YOU COULD EDUCATE US ON THE...
WHAT DO YOU CALL IT AGAIN?...ULTRA STORM THREAT?
SUPER HURRICANE GILBERT!
THIS IS NOT A REGULAR HURRICANE! OUR READINGS INDICATE SIGNS OF SENTIENCE WITHIN THE VORTEX!
WE BELIEVE IT TO BE A FEEDER! IT WANTS TO CONSUME EVERYTHING!

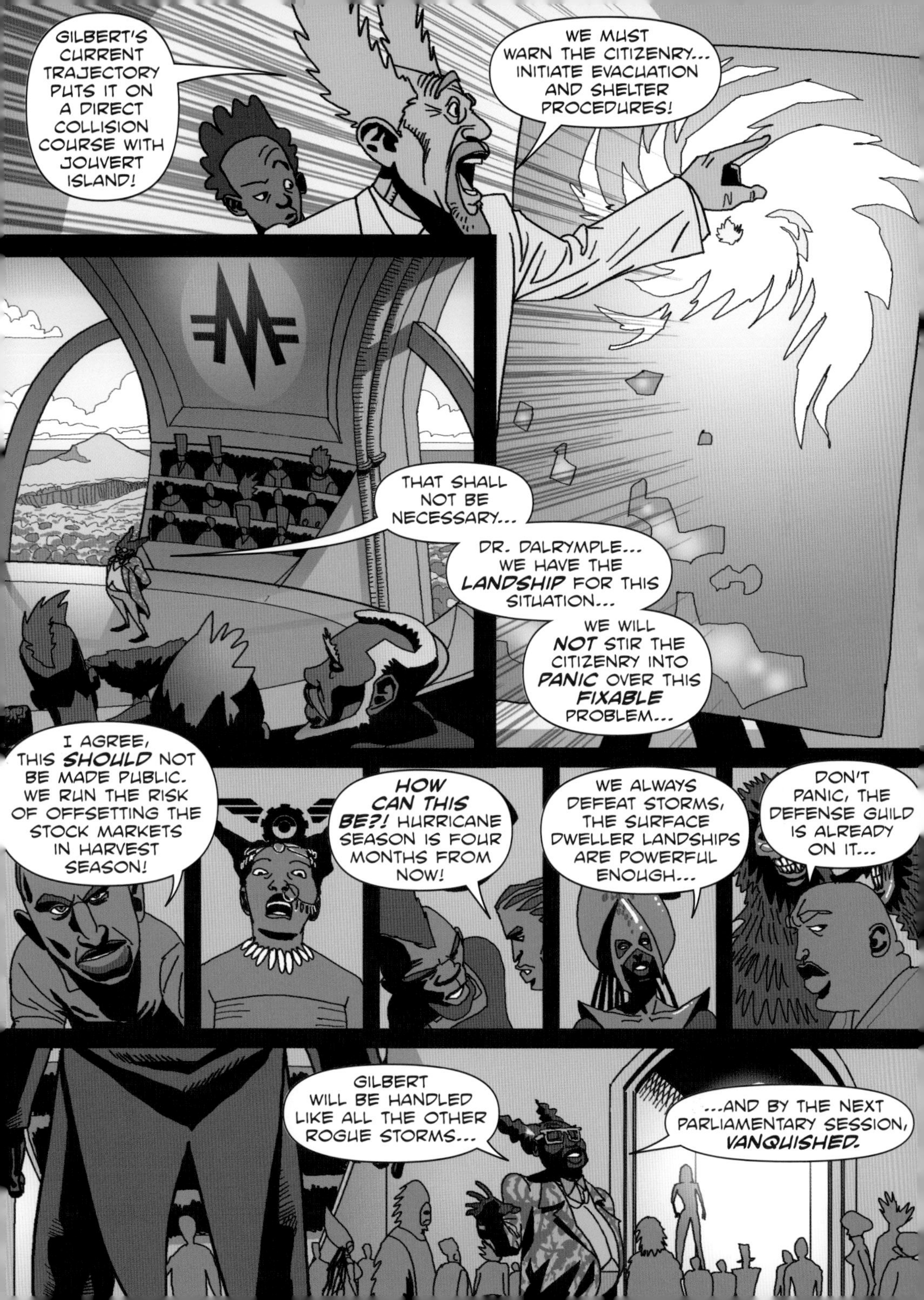
GILBERT'S CURRENT TRAJECTORY PUTS IT ON A DIRECT COLLISION COURSE WITH JOUVERT ISLAND!
WE MUST WARN THE CITIZENRY... INITIATE EVACUATION AND SHELTER PROCEDURES!
THAT SHALL NOT BE NECESSARY...
DR. DALRYMPLE... WE HAVE THE LANDSHIP FOR THIS SITUATION...
WE WILL NOT STIR THE CITIZENRY INTO PANIC OVER THIS FIXABLE PROBLEM...
I AGREE, THIS SHOULD NOT BE MADE PUBLIC. WE RUN THE RISK OF OFFSETTING THE STOCK MARKETS IN HARVEST SEASON!
HOW CAN THIS BE?! HURRICANE SEASON IS FOUR MONTHS FROM NOW!
WE ALWAYS DEFEAT STORMS, THE SURFACE DWELLER LANDSHIPS ARE POWERFUL ENOUGH...
DON'T PANIC, THE DEFENSE GUILD IS ALREADY ON IT...
GILBERT WILL BE HANDLED LIKE ALL THE OTHER ROGUE STORMS...
...AND BY THE NEXT PARLIAMENTARY SESSION, VANQUISHED.

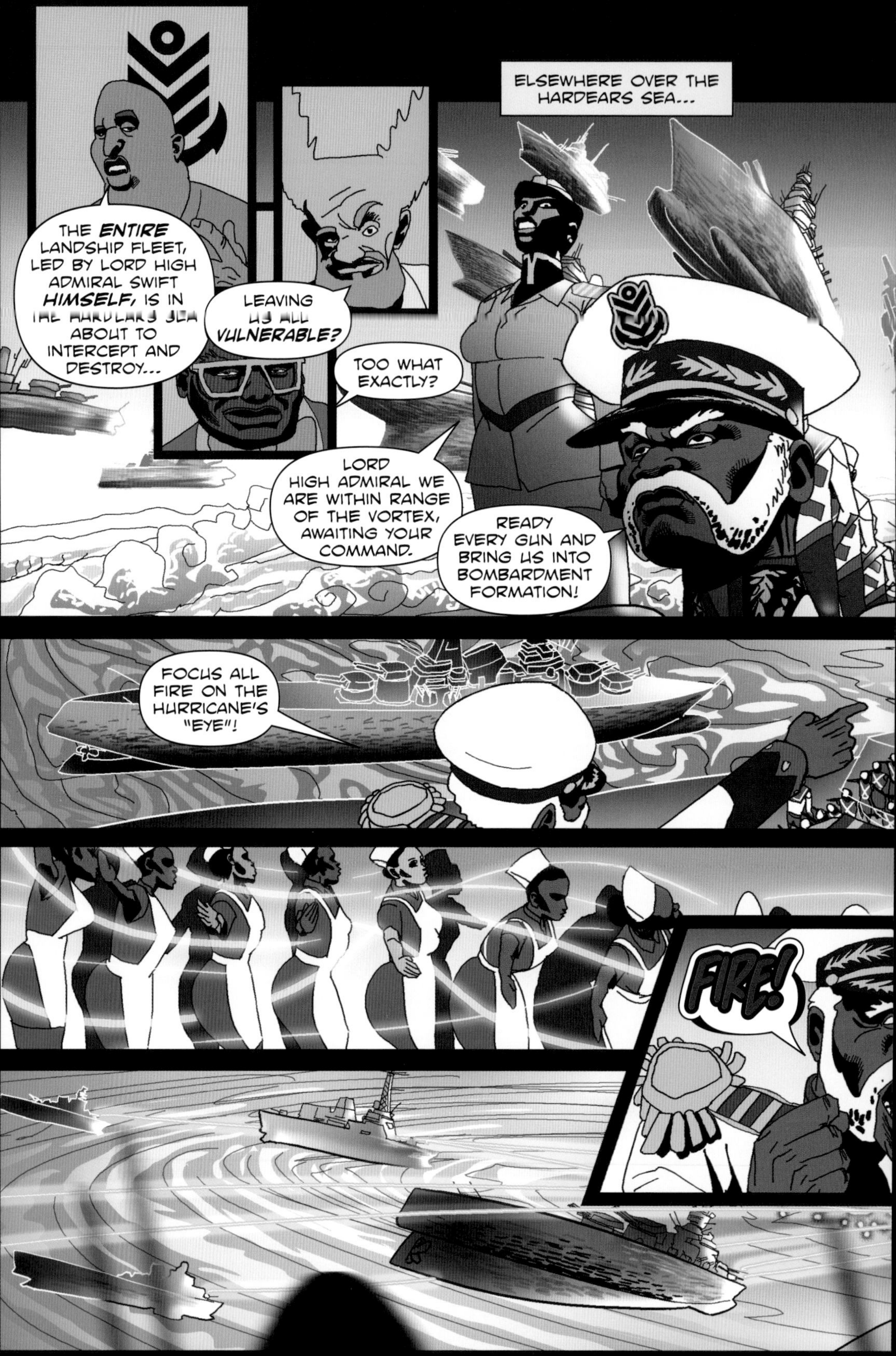
THE ENTIRE LANDSHIP FLEET, LED BY LORD HIGH ADMIRAL SWIFT HIMSELF, IS IN THE HARDEARS SEA ABOUT TO INTERCEPT AND DESTROY...
LEAVING US ALL VULNERABLE?
TOO WHAT EXACTLY?
ELSEWHERE OVER THE HARDEARS SEA...
LORD HIGH ADMIRAL WE ARE WITHIN RANGE OF THE VORTEX, AWAITING YOUR COMMAND.
READY EVERY GUN AND BRING US INTO BOMBARDMENT FORMATION!
FOCUS ALL FIRE ON THE HURRICANE'S "EYE"!
FIRE!

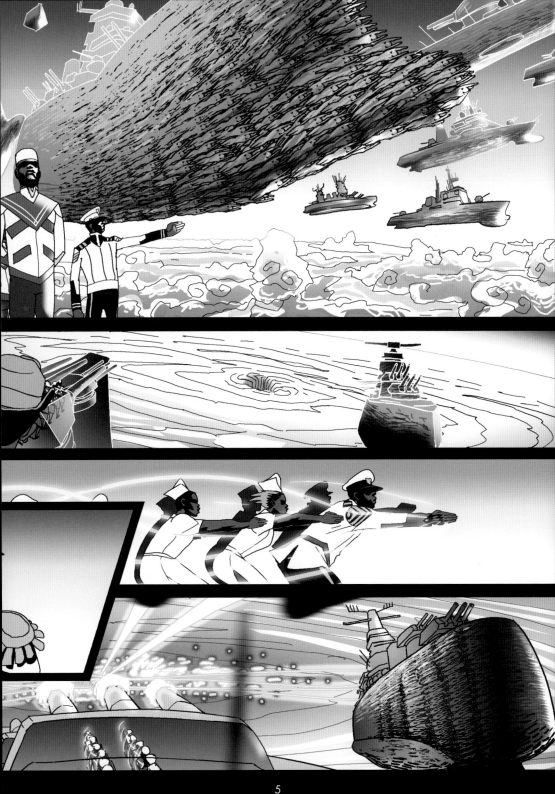

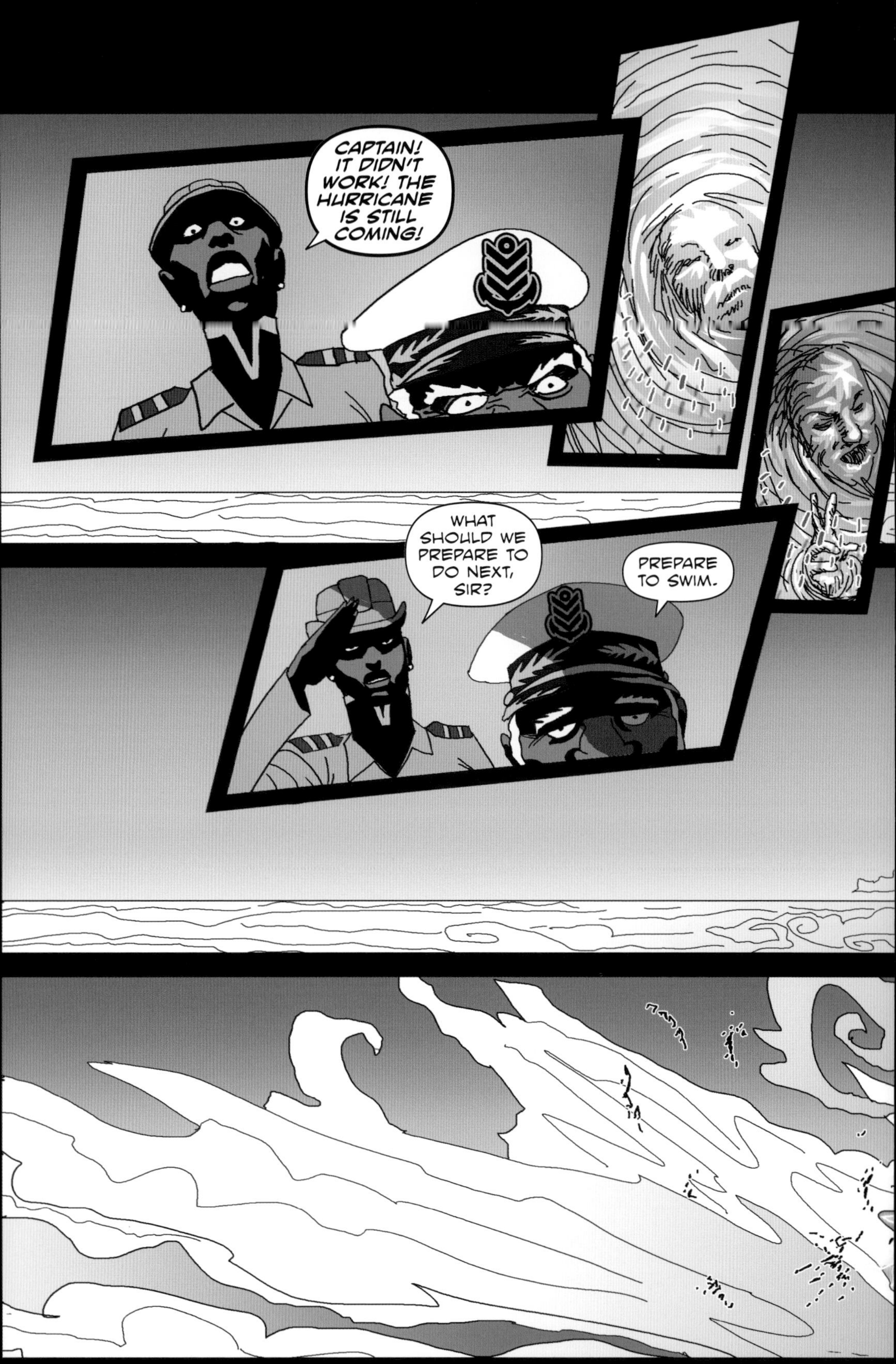
CAPTAIN! IT DIDN'T WORK! THE HURRICANE IS STILL COMING!
WHAT SHOULD WE PREPARE TO DO NEXT, SIR?
PREPARE TO SWIM.

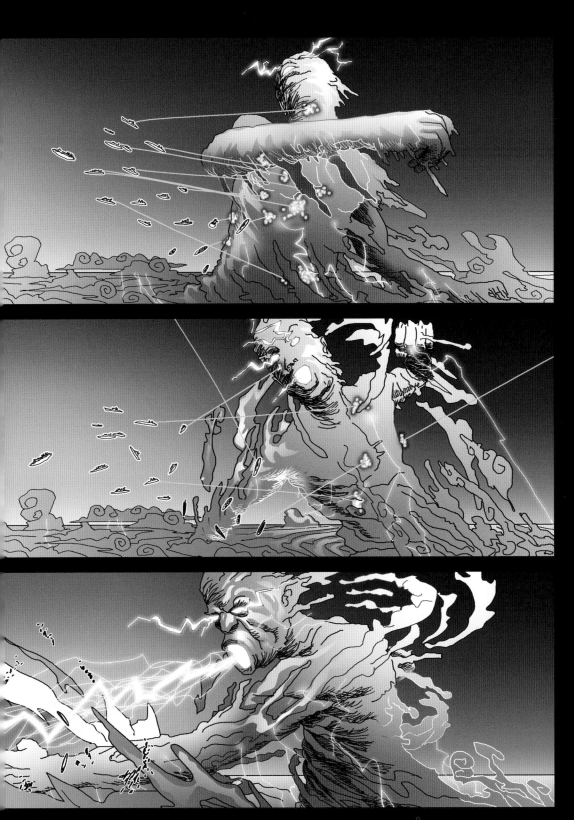

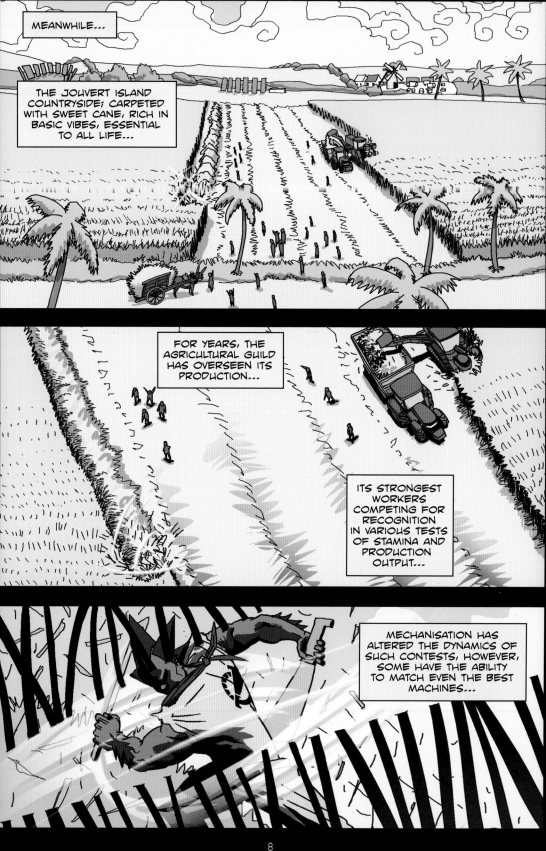

MEANWHILE...

THE JOUVERT ISLAND COUNTRYSIDE; CARPETED WITH SWEET CANE, RICH IN BASIC VIBES, ESSENTIAL TO ALL LIFE...

FOR YEARS, THE AGRICULTURAL GUILD HAS OVERSEEN ITS PRODUCTION...

ITS STRONGEST WORKERS COMPETING FOR RECOGNITION IN VARIOUS TESTS OF STAMINA AND PRODUCTION OUTPUT...

MECHANISATION HAS ALTERED THE DYNAMICS OF SUCH CONTESTS, HOWEVER, SOME HAVE THE ABILITY TO MATCH EVEN THE BEST MACHINES...

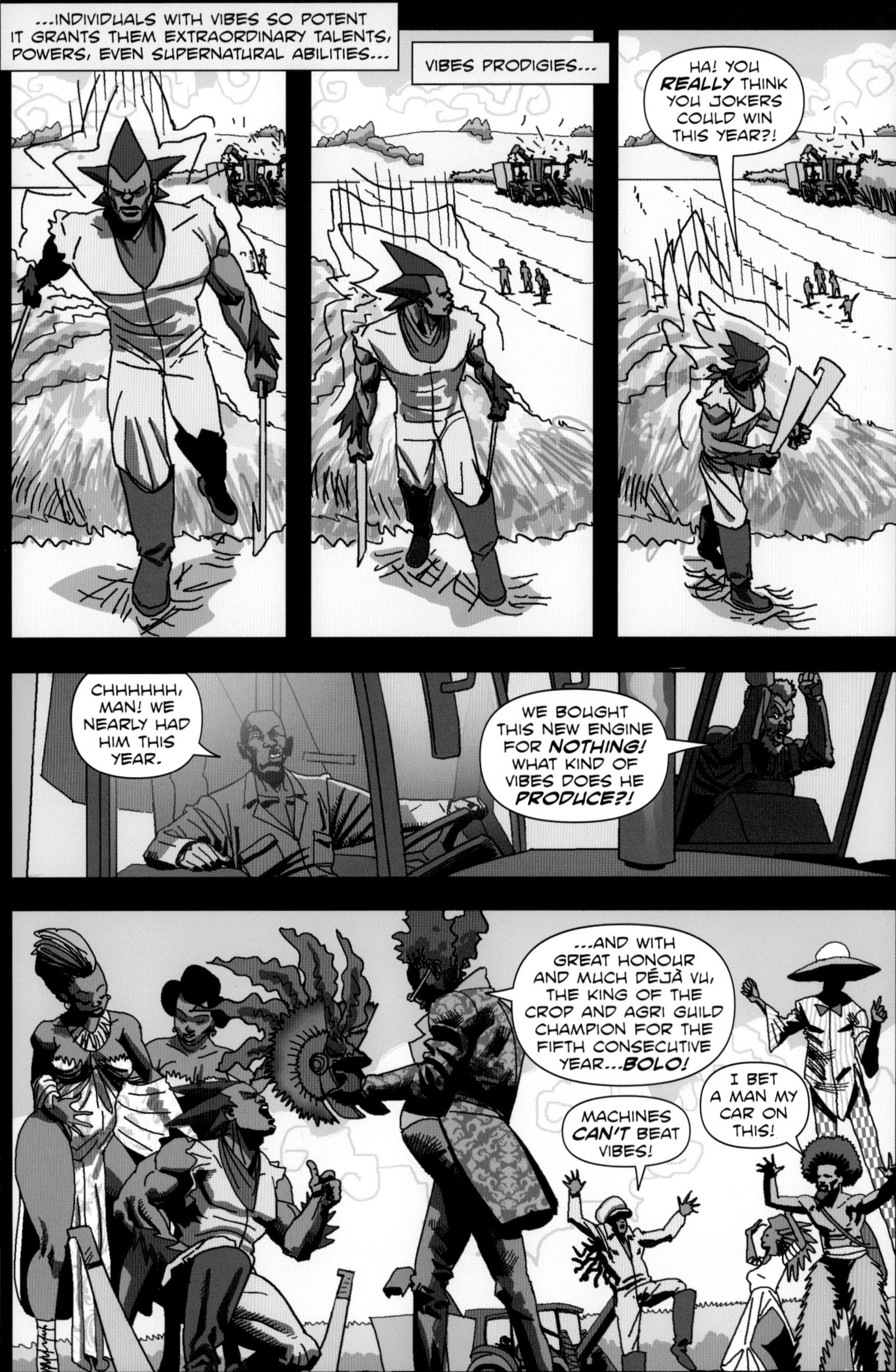
...INDIVIDUALS WITH VIBES SO POTENT IT GRANTS THEM EXTRAORDINARY TALENTS, POWERS, EVEN SUPERNATURAL ABILITIES...
VIBES PRODIGIES...
HA! YOU **REALLY** THINK YOU JOKERS COULD WIN THIS YEAR?!
CHHHHHH, MAN! WE NEARLY HAD HIM THIS YEAR.
WE BOUGHT THIS NEW ENGINE FOR **NOTHING!** WHAT KIND OF VIBES DOES HE **PRODUCE?!**
...AND WITH GREAT HONOUR AND MUCH DÉJÀ VU, THE KING OF THE CROP AND AGRI GUILD CHAMPION FOR THE FIFTH CONSECUTIVE YEAR...**BOLO!**
I BET A MAN MY CAR ON THIS!
MACHINES **CAN'T** BEAT VIBES!

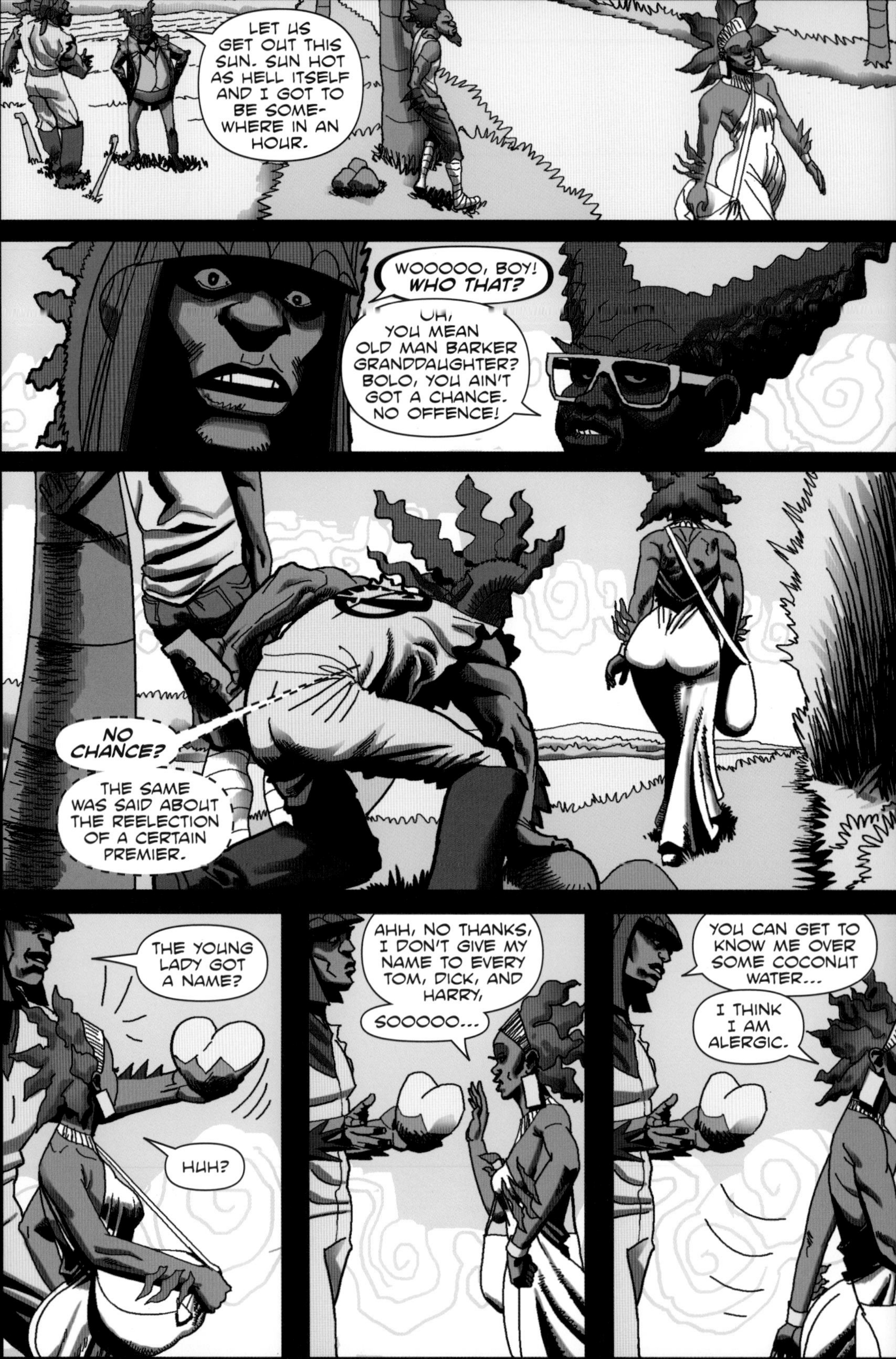
LET US GET OUT THIS SUN. SUN HOT AS HELL ITSELF AND I GOT TO BE SOME-WHERE IN AN HOUR.
WOOOOO, BOY! WHO THAT?
UH, YOU MEAN OLD MAN BARKER GRANDDAUGHTER? BOLO, YOU AIN'T GOT A CHANCE. NO OFFENCE!
NO CHANCE?
THE SAME WAS SAID ABOUT THE REELECTION OF A CERTAIN PREMIER.
THE YOUNG LADY GOT A NAME?
HUH?
AHH, NO THANKS, I DON'T GIVE MY NAME TO EVERY TOM, DICK, AND HARRY,
SOOOOO...
YOU CAN GET TO KNOW ME OVER SOME COCONUT WATER...
I THINK I AM ALERGIC.

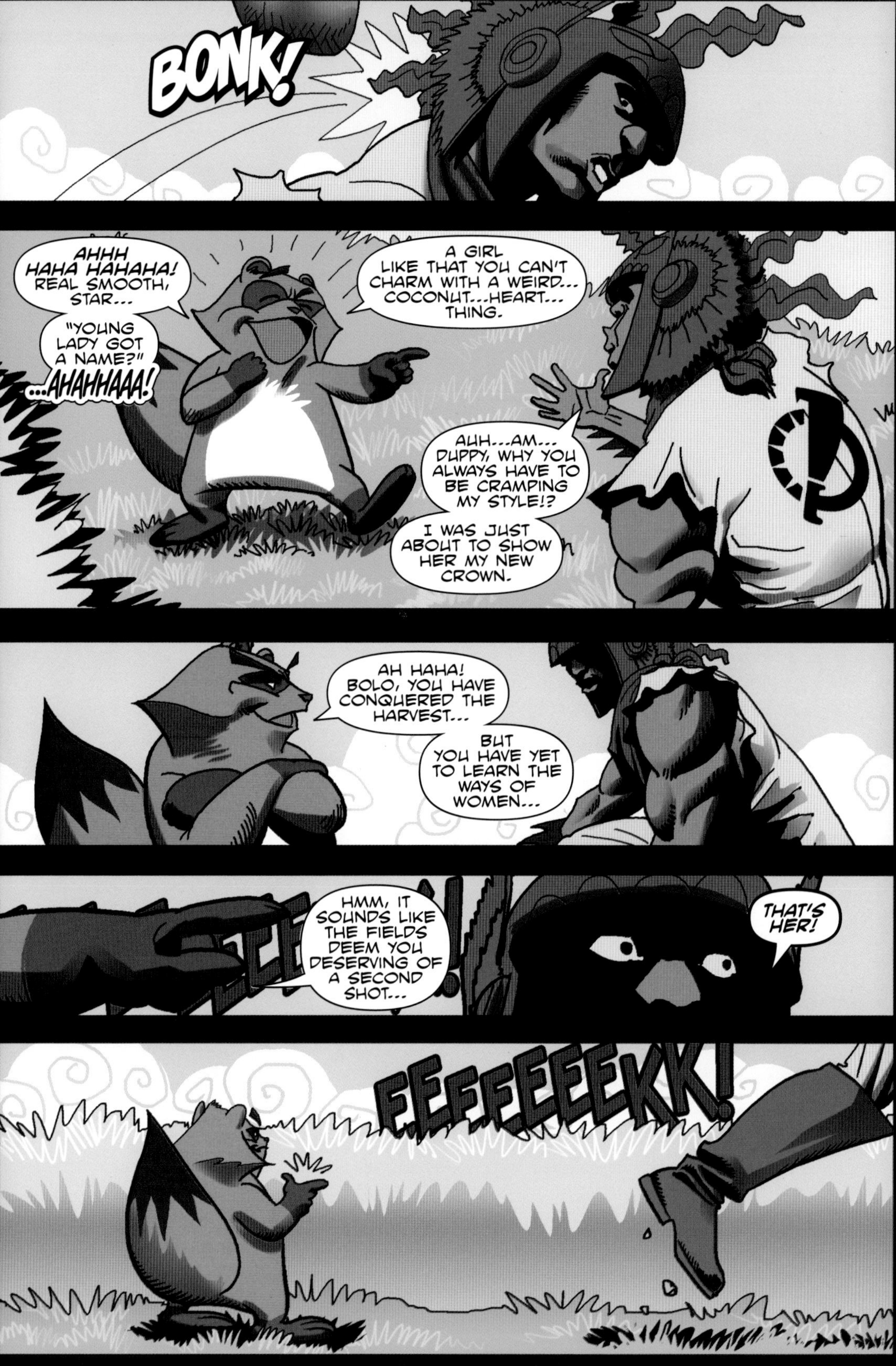
BONK!
AHHH HAHA HAHAHA! REAL SMOOTH, STAR...
"YOUNG LADY GOT A NAME?"
...AHAHHAAA!
A GIRL LIKE THAT YOU CAN'T CHARM WITH A WEIRD... COCONUT...HEART... THING.
AUH...AM... DUPPY, WHY YOU ALWAYS HAVE TO BE CRAMPING MY STYLE!?
I WAS JUST ABOUT TO SHOW HER MY NEW CROWN.
AH HAHA! BOLO, YOU HAVE CONQUERED THE HARVEST...
BUT YOU HAVE YET TO LEARN THE WAYS OF WOMEN...
HMM, IT SOUNDS LIKE THE FIELDS DEEM YOU DESERVING OF A SECOND SHOT...
THAT'S HER!
EEEEEEEKK!

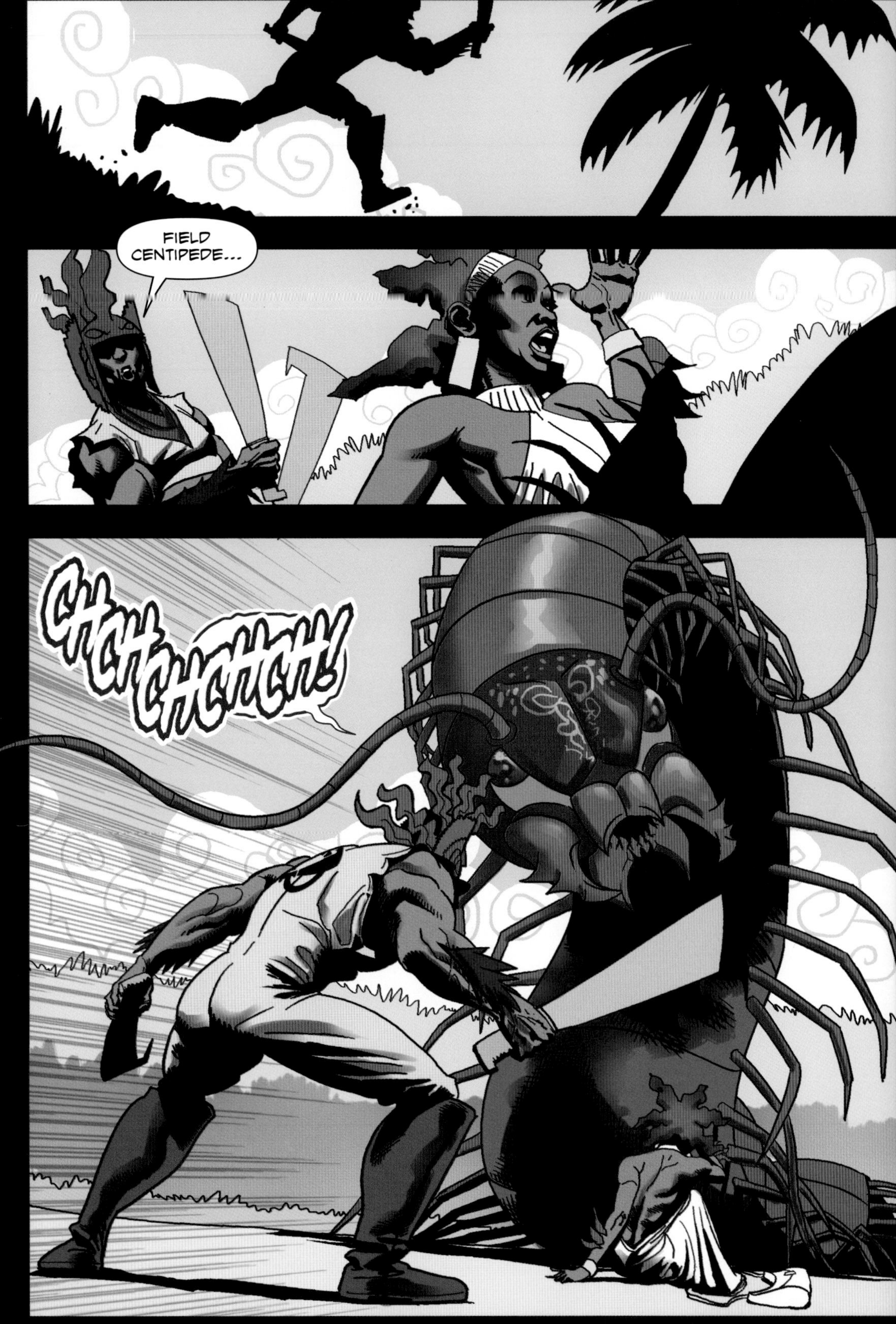
FIELD CENTIPEDE...
CHTCHTCHTCH!

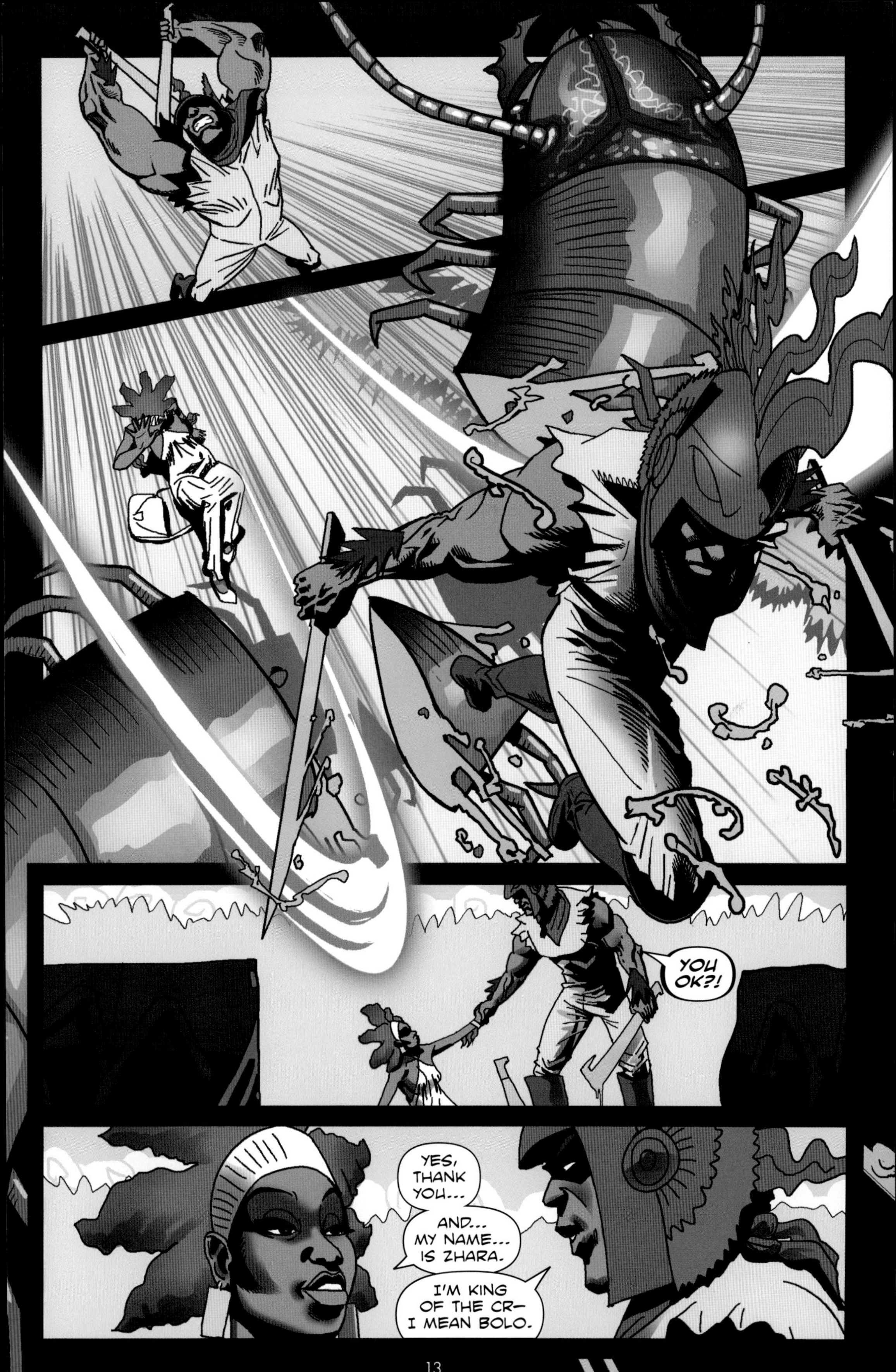
YOU OK?!
YES, THANK YOU...
AND... MY NAME... IS ZHARA.
I'M KING OF THE CR— I MEAN BOLO.

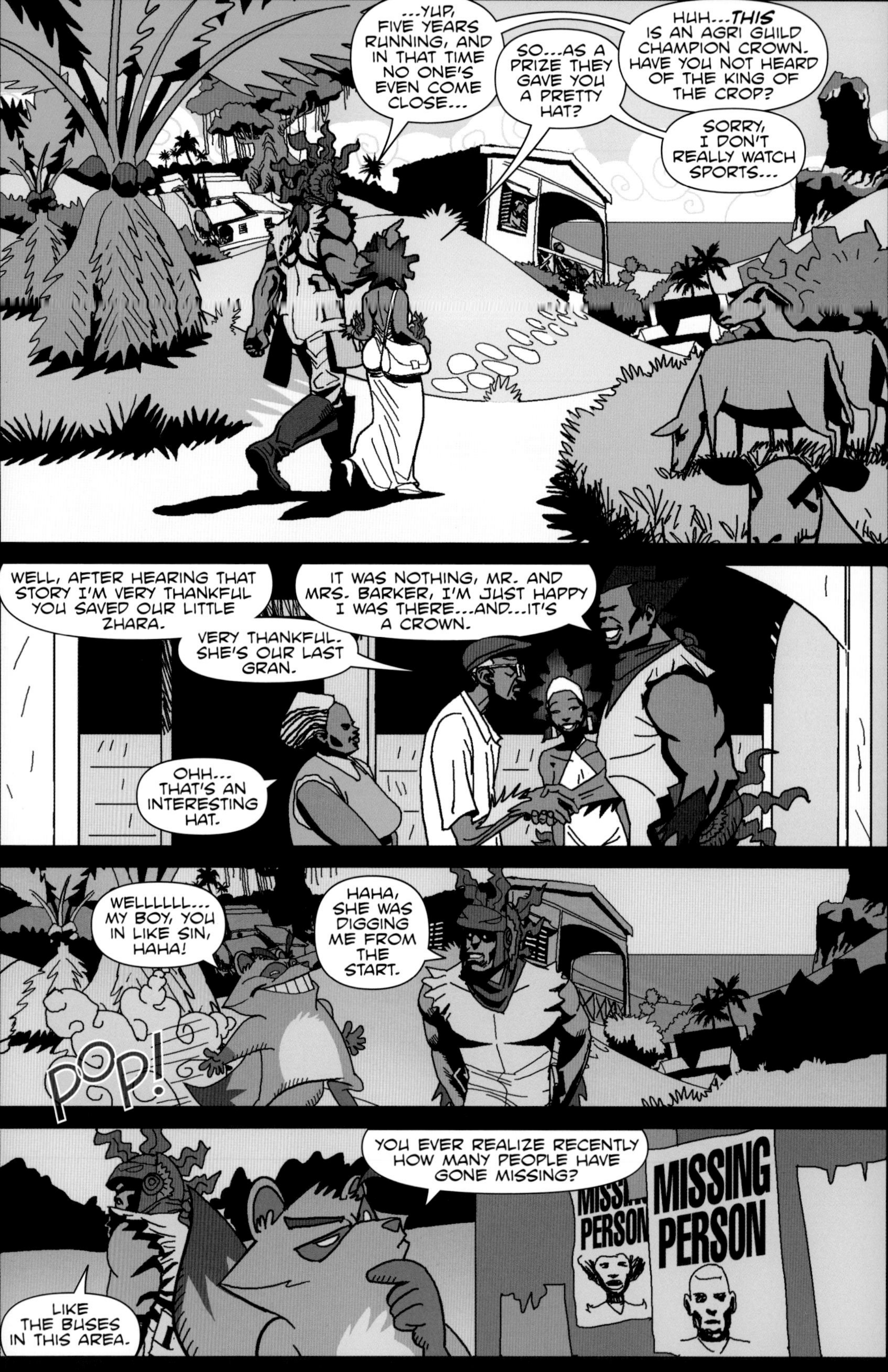

...YUP, FIVE YEARS RUNNING, AND IN THAT TIME NO ONE'S EVEN COME CLOSE...
SO...AS A PRIZE THEY GAVE YOU A PRETTY HAT?
HUH...*THIS* IS AN AGRI GUILD CHAMPION CROWN. HAVE YOU NOT HEARD OF THE KING OF THE CROP?
SORRY, I DON'T REALLY WATCH SPORTS...
WELL, AFTER HEARING THAT STORY I'M VERY THANKFUL YOU SAVED OUR LITTLE ZHARA.
VERY THANKFUL. SHE'S OUR LAST GRAN.
IT WAS NOTHING, MR. AND MRS. BARKER, I'M JUST HAPPY I WAS THERE...AND...IT'S A CROWN.
OHH... THAT'S AN INTERESTING HAT.
POP!
WELLLLLL... MY BOY, YOU IN LIKE SIN, HAHA!
HAHA, SHE WAS DIGGING ME FROM THE START.
YOU EVER REALIZE RECENTLY HOW MANY PEOPLE HAVE GONE MISSING?
MISSING PERSON
MISSING PERSON
LIKE THE BUSES IN THIS AREA.

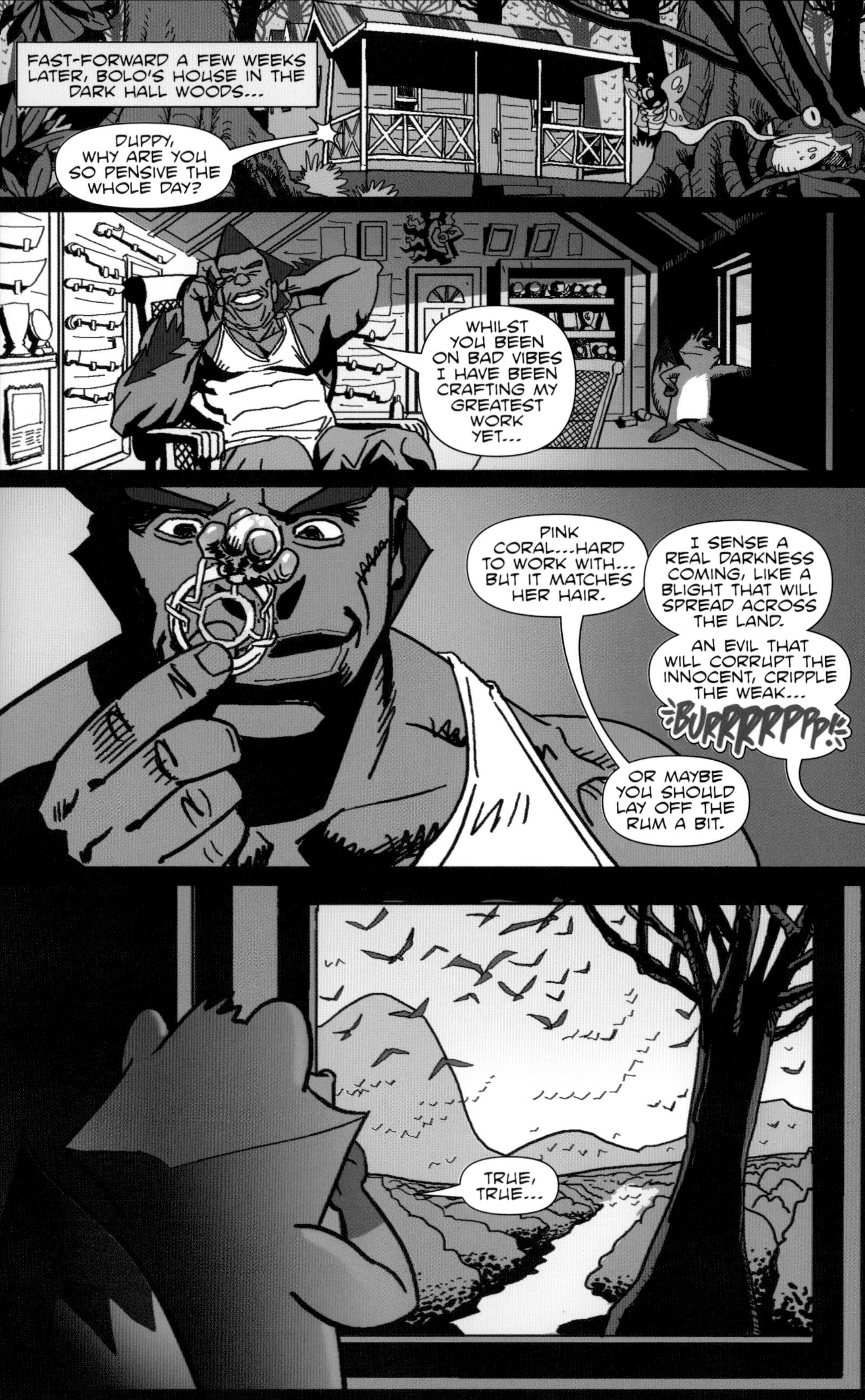
FAST-FORWARD A FEW WEEKS LATER, BOLO'S HOUSE IN THE DARK HALL WOODS...
DUPPY, WHY ARE YOU SO PENSIVE THE WHOLE DAY?
WHILST YOU BEEN ON BAD VIBES I HAVE BEEN CRAFTING MY GREATEST WORK YET...
PINK CORAL...HARD TO WORK WITH... BUT IT MATCHES HER HAIR.
I SENSE A REAL DARKNESS COMING, LIKE A BLIGHT THAT WILL SPREAD ACROSS THE LAND.
AN EVIL THAT WILL CORRUPT THE INNOCENT, CRIPPLE THE WEAK...
BURRRRPPP!
OR MAYBE YOU SHOULD LAY OFF THE RUM A BIT.
TRUE, TRUE...

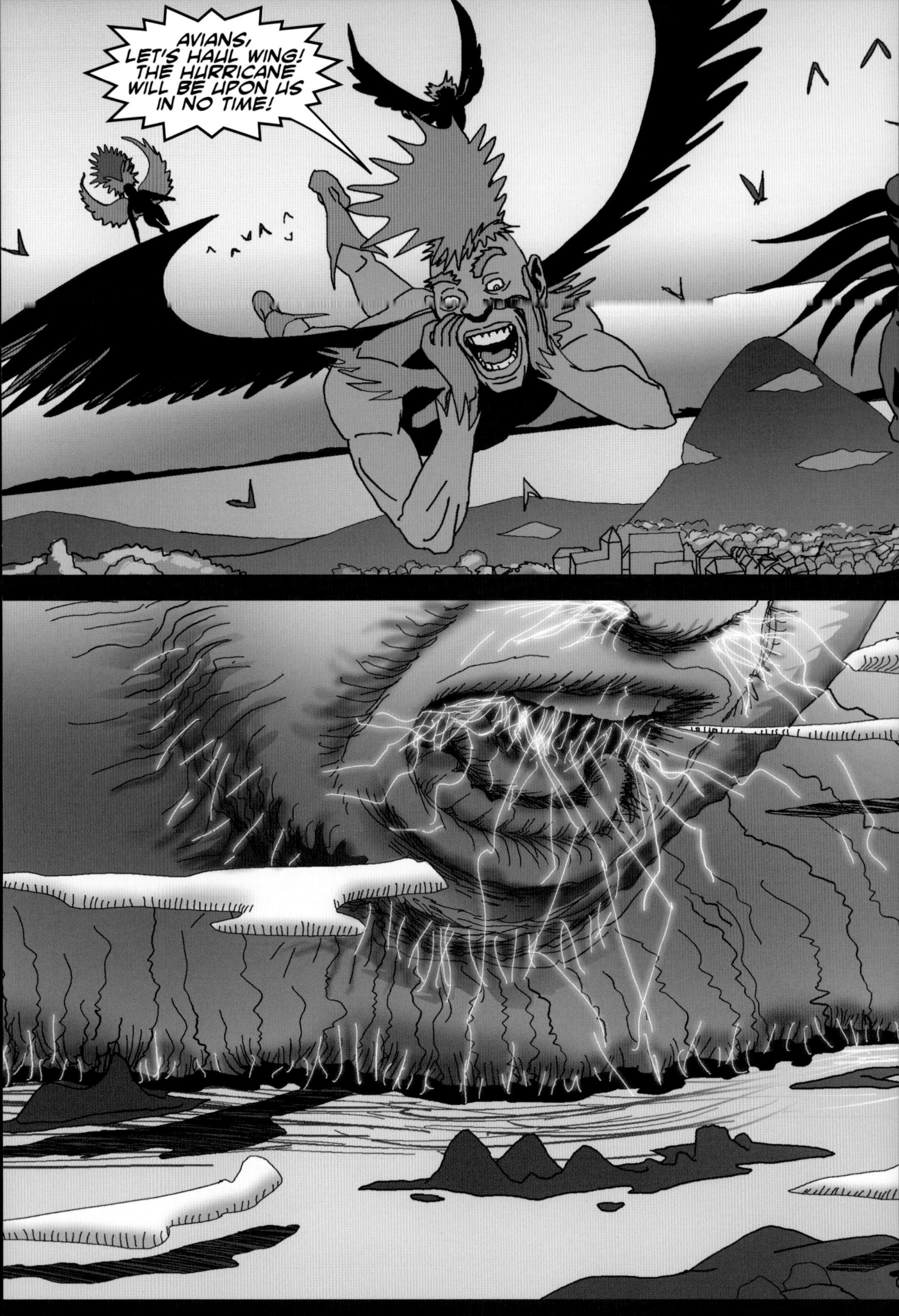
AVIANS, LET'S HAUL WING! THE HURRICANE WILL BE UPON US IN NO TIME!

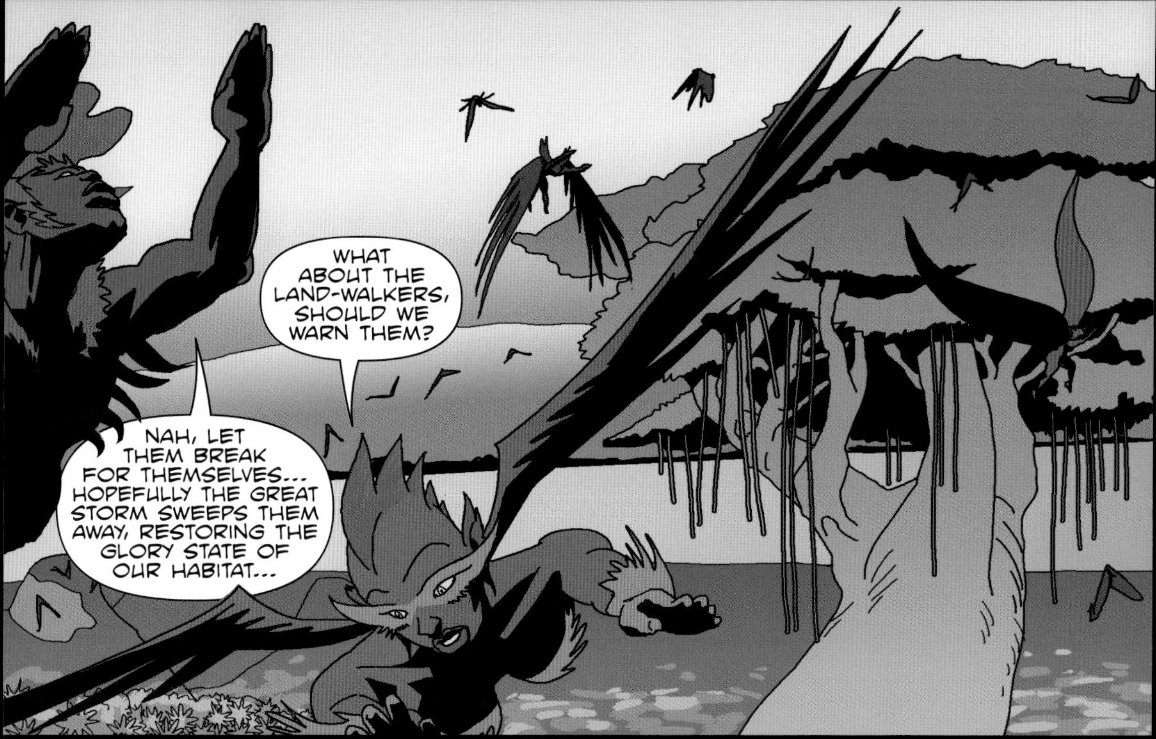
WHAT ABOUT THE LAND-WALKERS, SHOULD WE WARN THEM?
NAH, LET THEM BREAK FOR THEMSELVES... HOPEFULLY THE GREAT STORM SWEEPS THEM AWAY, RESTORING THE GLORY STATE OF OUR HABITAT...

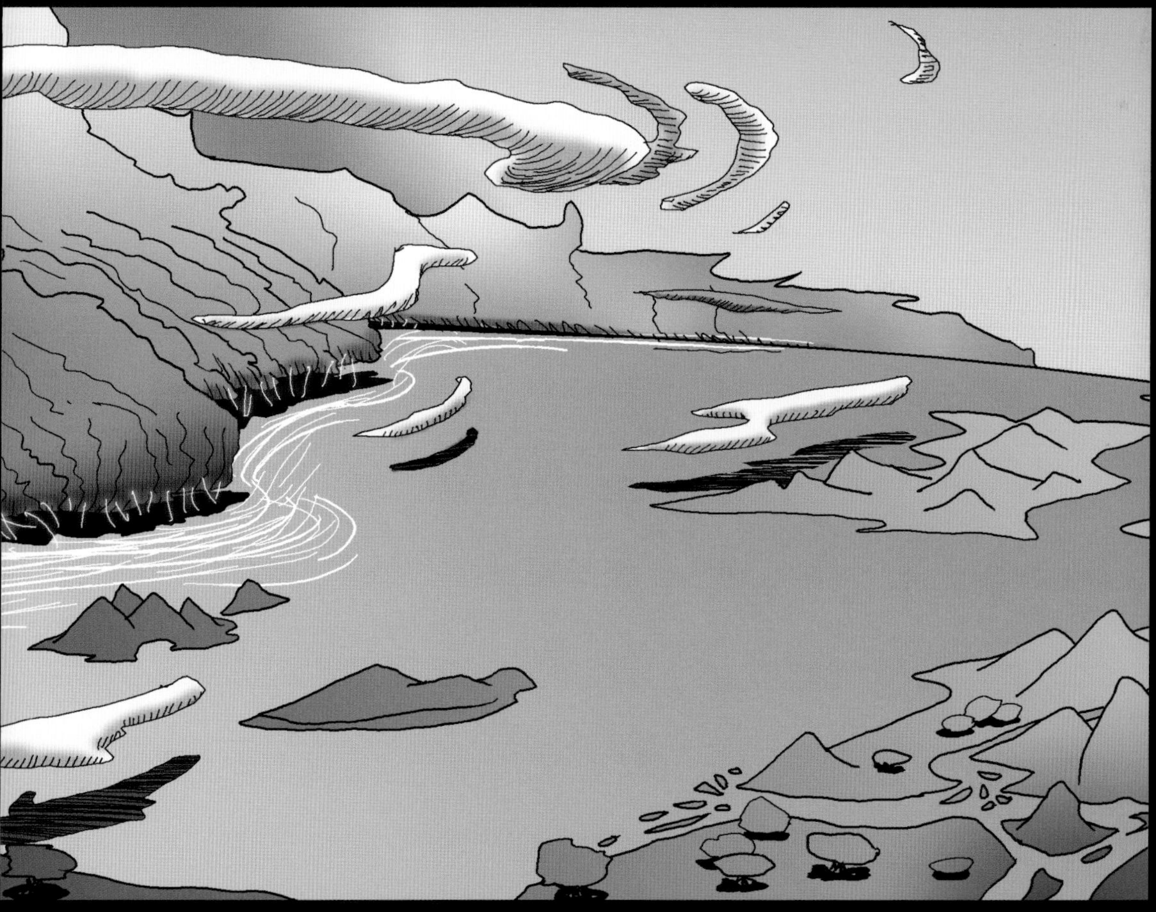

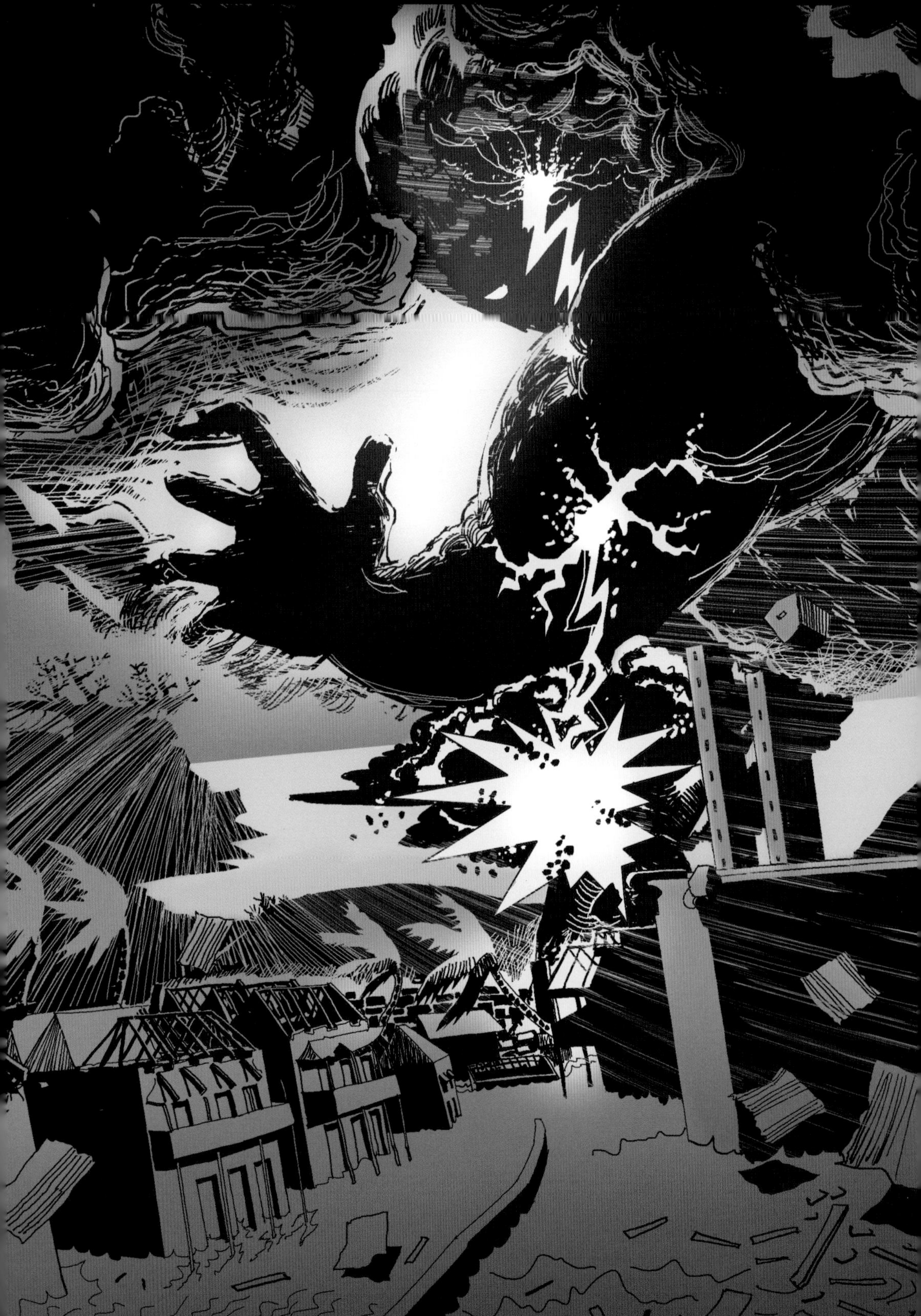

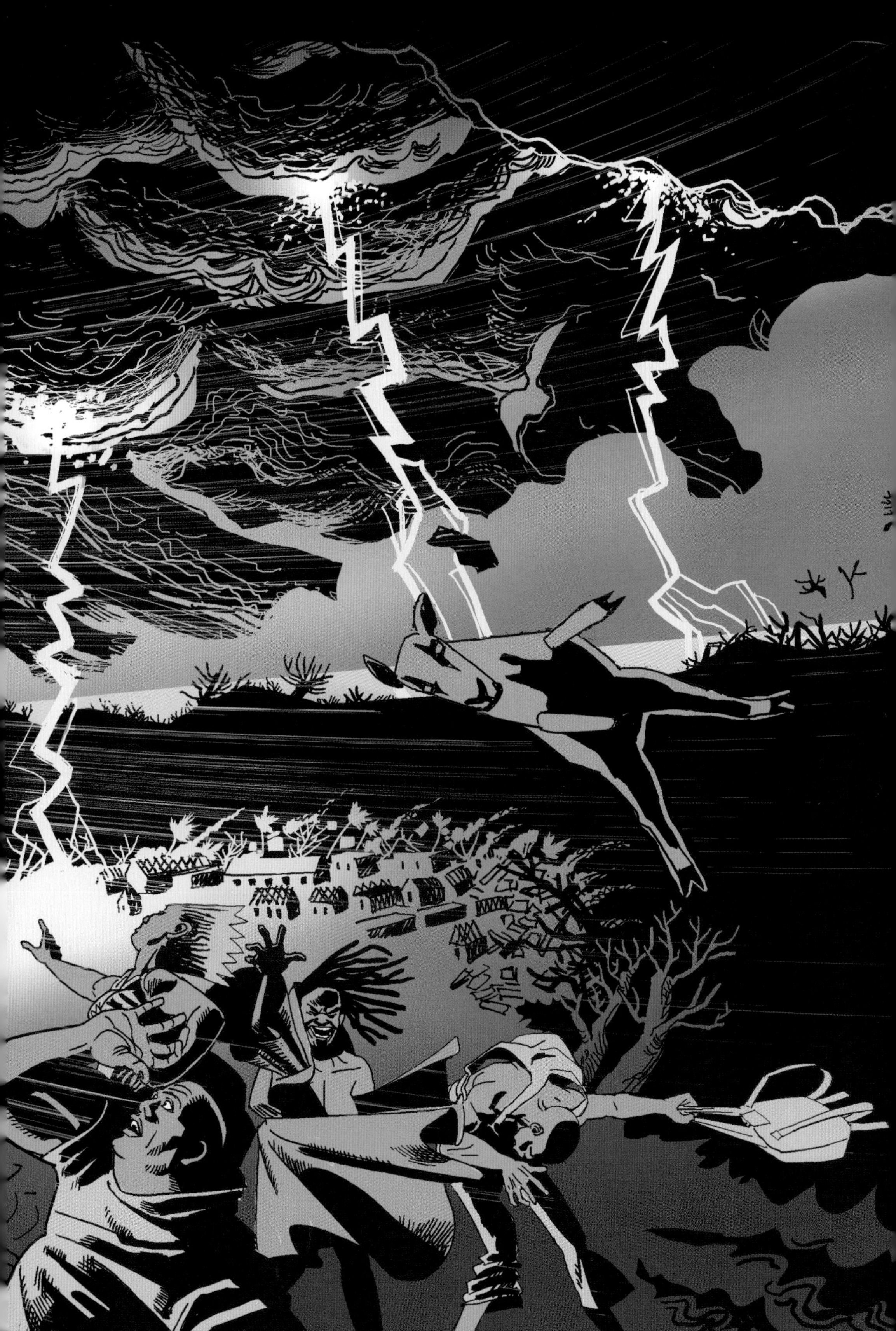

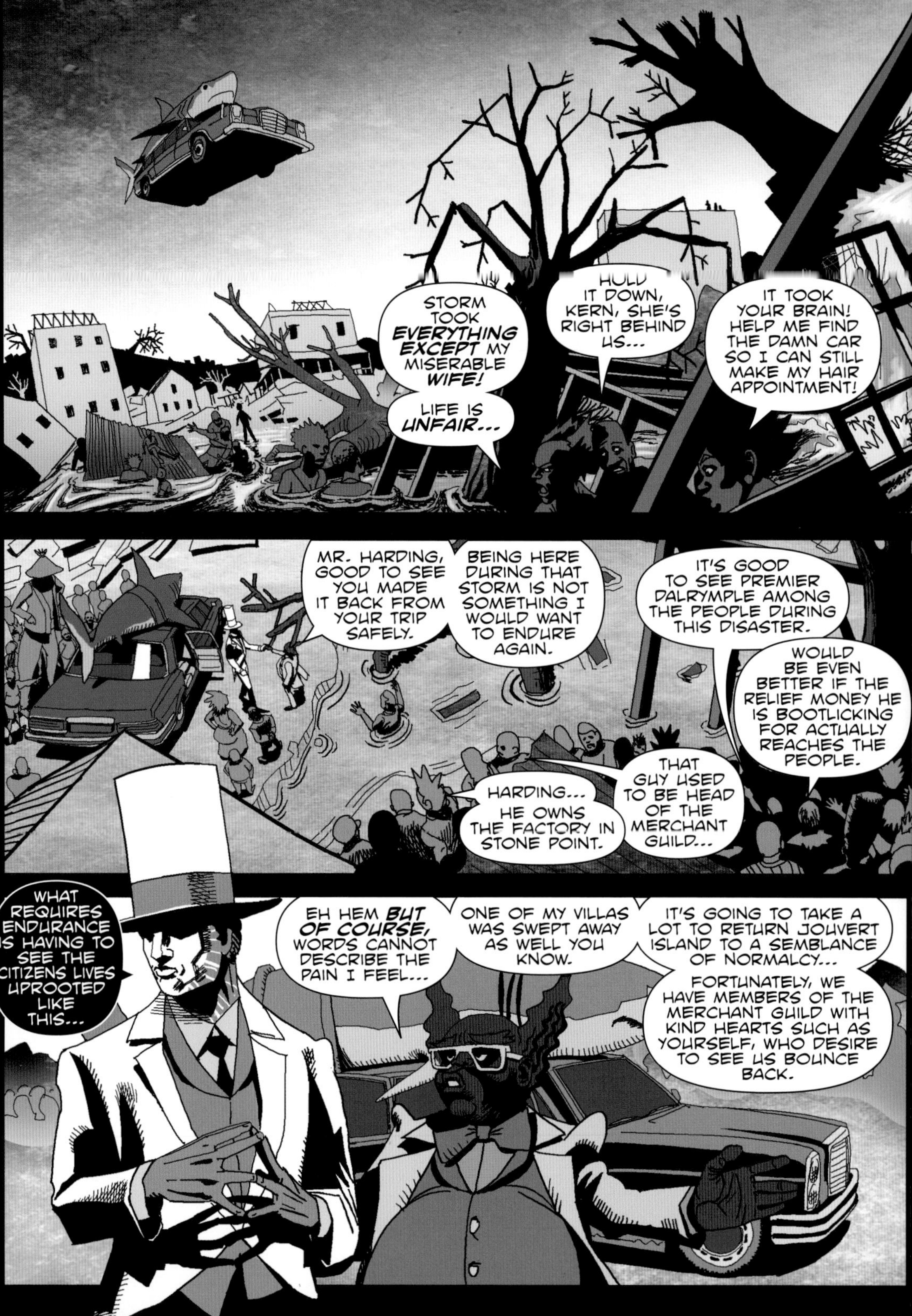
STORM TOOK EVERYTHING EXCEPT MY MISERABLE WIFE!
LIFE IS UNFAIR...
HOLD IT DOWN, KERN, SHE'S RIGHT BEHIND US...
IT TOOK YOUR BRAIN! HELP ME FIND THE DAMN CAR SO I CAN STILL MAKE MY HAIR APPOINTMENT!
MR. HARDING, GOOD TO SEE YOU MADE IT BACK FROM YOUR TRIP SAFELY.
BEING HERE DURING THAT STORM IS NOT SOMETHING I WOULD WANT TO ENDURE AGAIN.
IT'S GOOD TO SEE PREMIER DALRYMPLE AMONG THE PEOPLE DURING THIS DISASTER.
WOULD BE EVEN BETTER IF THE RELIEF MONEY HE IS BOOTLICKING FOR ACTUALLY REACHES THE PEOPLE.
HARDING...
HE OWNS THE FACTORY IN STONE POINT.
THAT GUY USED TO BE HEAD OF THE MERCHANT GUILD...
WHAT REQUIRES ENDURANCE IS HAVING TO SEE THE CITIZENS LIVES UPROOTED LIKE THIS...
EH HEM BUT OF COURSE, WORDS CANNOT DESCRIBE THE PAIN I FEEL...
ONE OF MY VILLAS WAS SWEPT AWAY AS WELL YOU KNOW.
IT'S GOING TO TAKE A LOT TO RETURN JOUVERT ISLAND TO A SEMBLANCE OF NORMALCY...
FORTUNATELY, WE HAVE MEMBERS OF THE MERCHANT GUILD WITH KIND HEARTS SUCH AS YOURSELF, WHO DESIRE TO SEE US BOUNCE BACK.

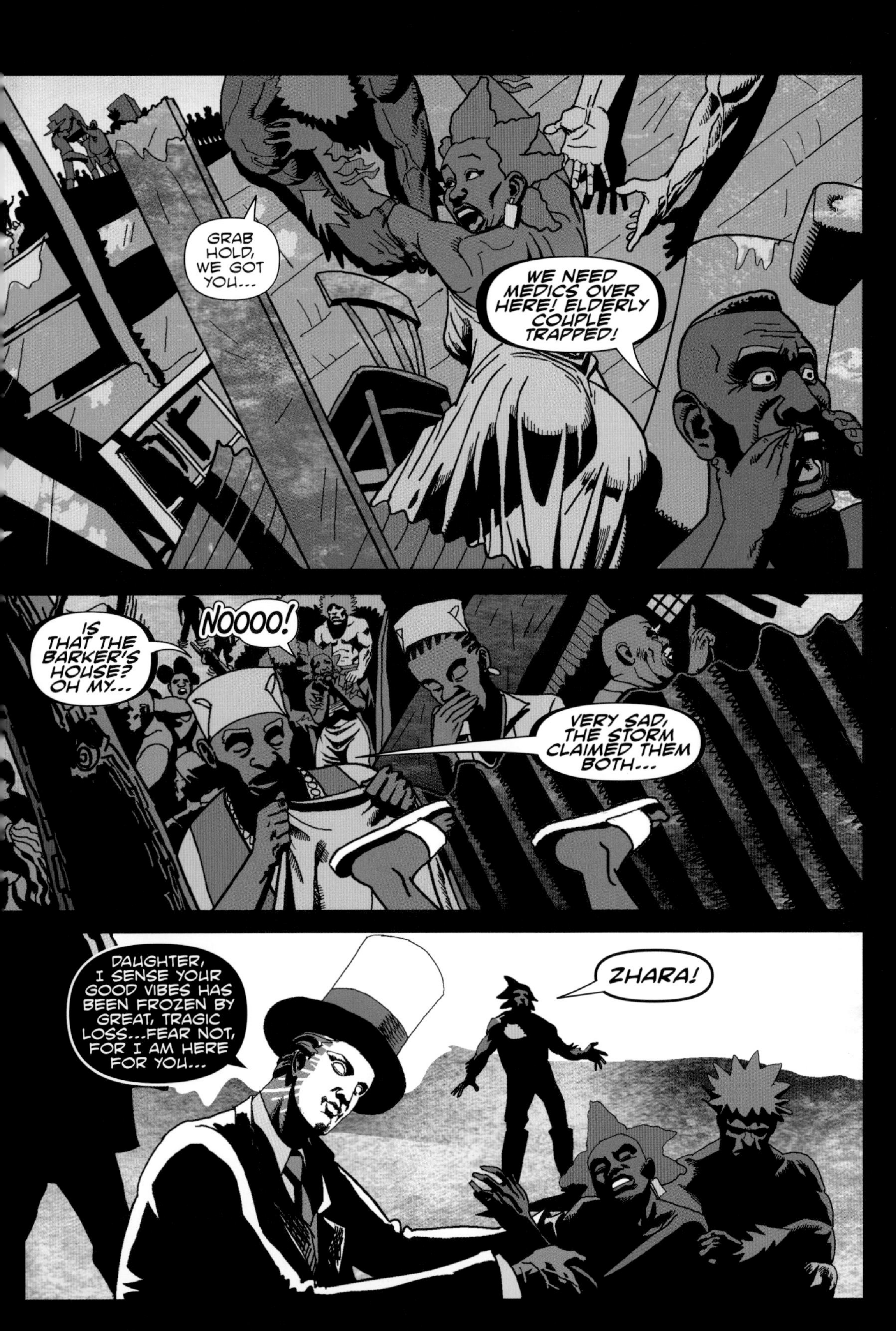
GRAB HOLD, WE GOT YOU...
WE NEED MEDICS OVER HERE! ELDERLY COUPLE TRAPPED!
IS THAT THE BARKER'S HOUSE? OH MY...
NOOOO!
VERY SAD, THE STORM CLAIMED THEM BOTH...
DAUGHTER, I SENSE YOUR GOOD VIBES HAS BEEN FROZEN BY GREAT, TRAGIC LOSS...FEAR NOT, FOR I AM HERE FOR YOU...
ZHARA!

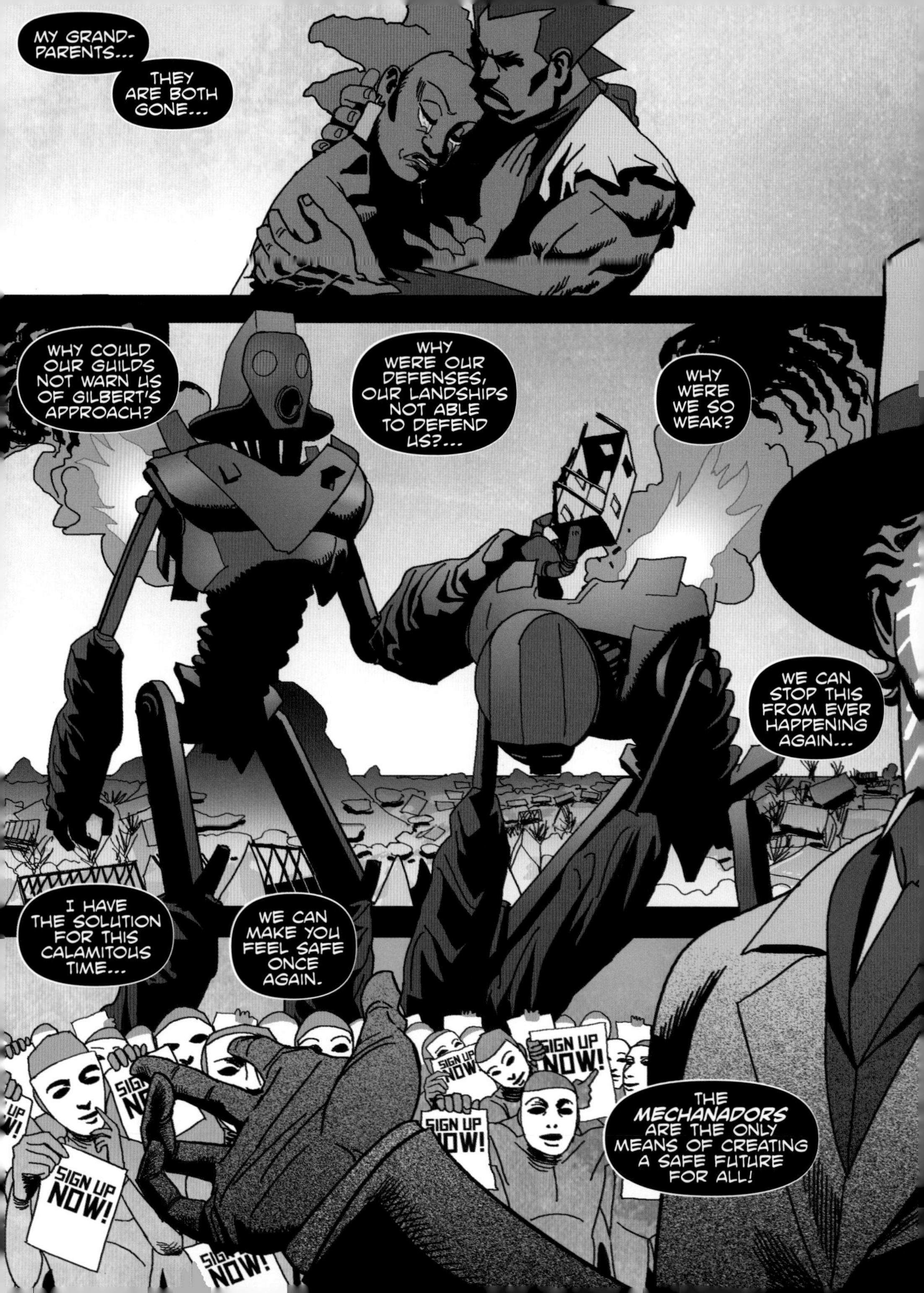
MY GRAND-PARENTS...
THEY ARE BOTH GONE...
WHY COULD OUR GUILDS NOT WARN US OF GILBERT'S APPROACH?
WHY WERE OUR DEFENSES, OUR LANDSHIPS NOT ABLE TO DEFEND US?...
WHY WERE WE SO WEAK?
WE CAN STOP THIS FROM EVER HAPPENING AGAIN...
I HAVE THE SOLUTION FOR THIS CALAMITOUS TIME...
WE CAN MAKE YOU FEEL SAFE ONCE AGAIN.
SIGN UP NOW!
SIGN UP NOW!
SIGN UP NOW!
SIGN UP NOW!
THE MECHANADORS ARE THE ONLY MEANS OF CREATING A SAFE FUTURE FOR ALL!

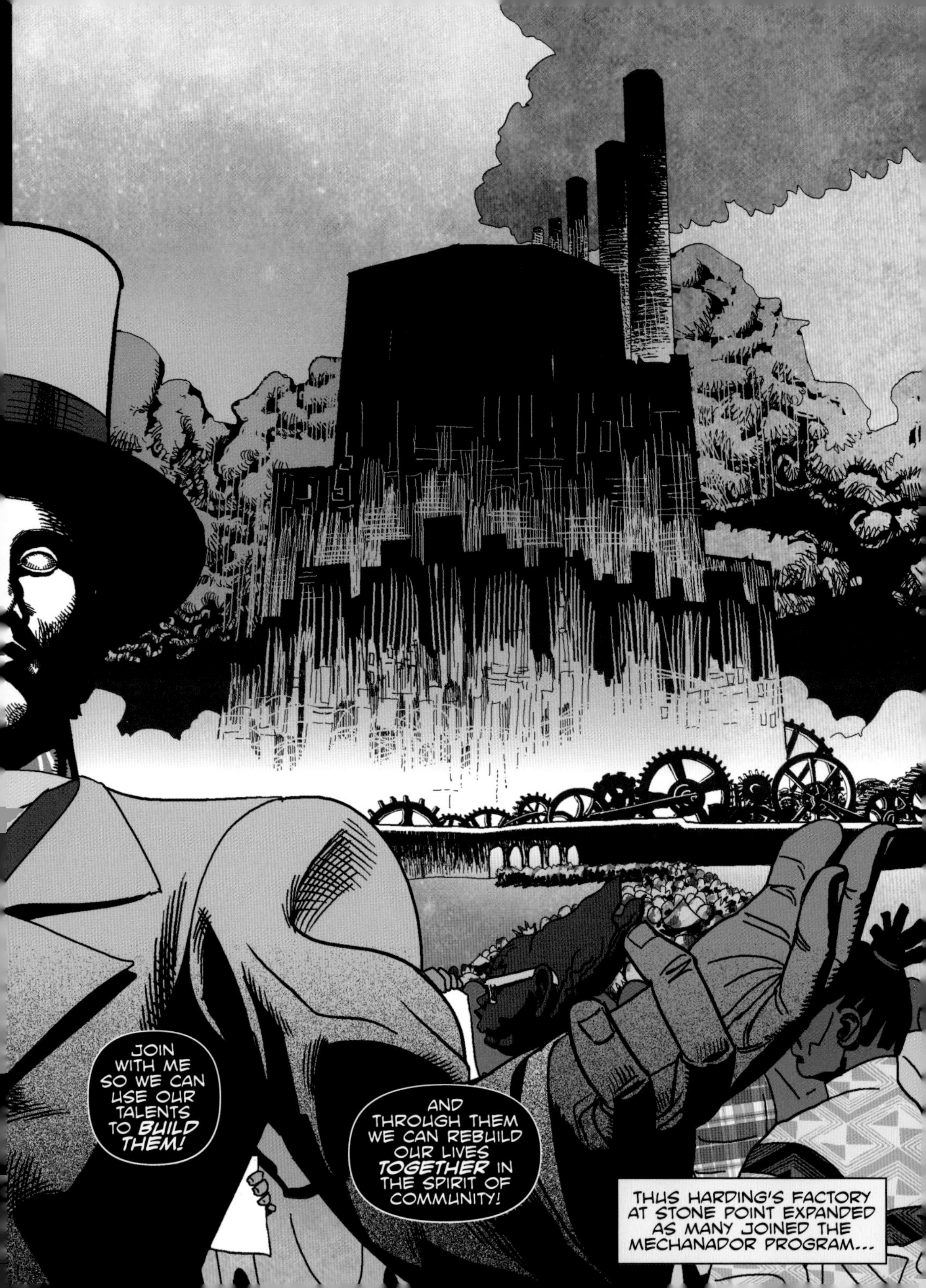
JOIN WITH ME SO WE CAN USE OUR TALENTS TO *BUILD THEM!*
AND THROUGH THEM WE CAN REBUILD OUR LIVES *TOGETHER* IN THE SPIRIT OF COMMUNITY!
THUS HARDING'S FACTORY AT STONE POINT EXPANDED AS MANY JOINED THE MECHANADOR PROGRAM...

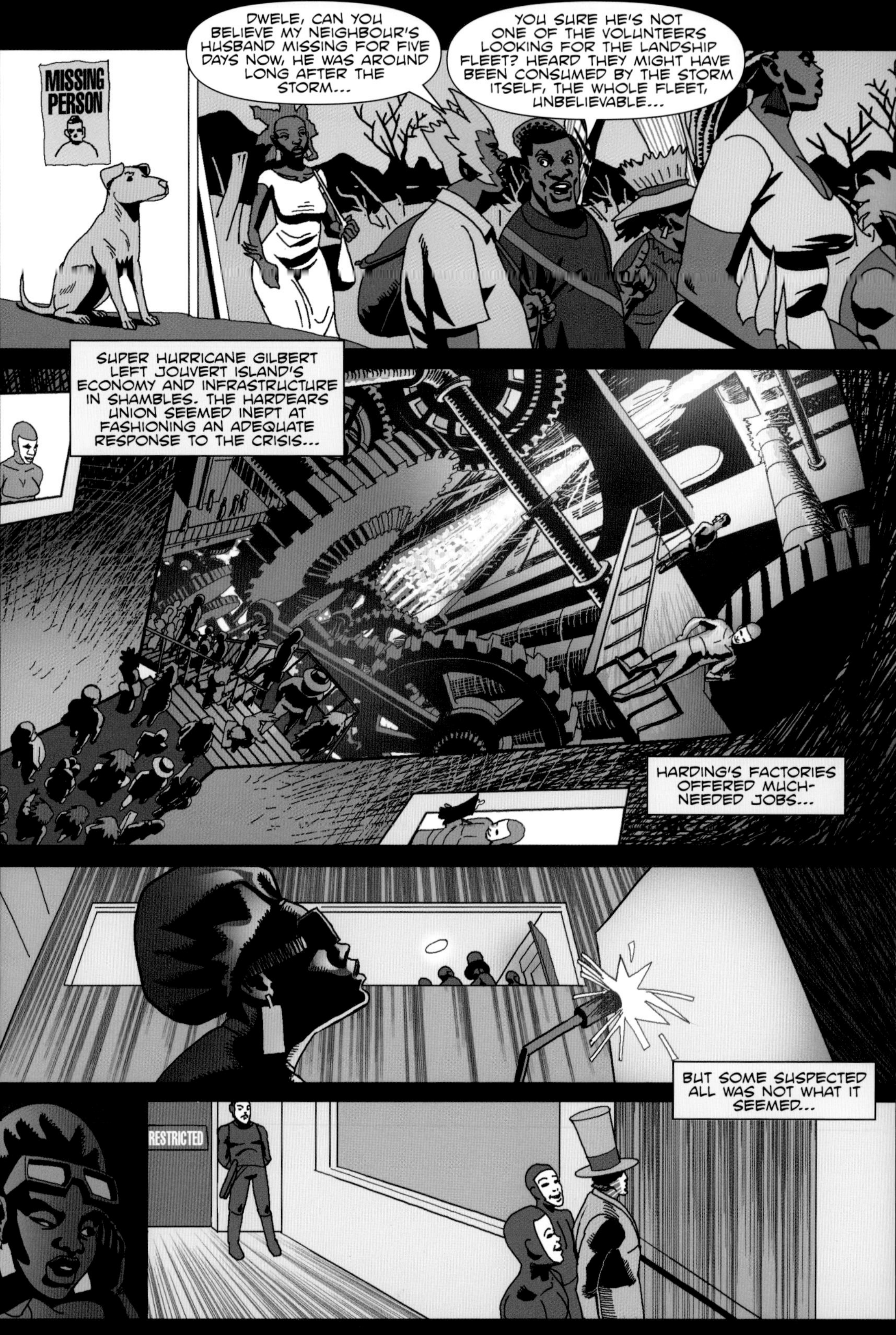
MISSING PERSON
DWELE, CAN YOU BELIEVE MY NEIGHBOUR'S HUSBAND MISSING FOR FIVE DAYS NOW, HE WAS AROUND LONG AFTER THE STORM...
YOU SURE HE'S NOT ONE OF THE VOLUNTEERS LOOKING FOR THE LANDSHIP FLEET? HEARD THEY MIGHT HAVE BEEN CONSUMED BY THE STORM ITSELF, THE WHOLE FLEET, UNBELIEVABLE...
SUPER HURRICANE GILBERT LEFT JOUVERT ISLAND'S ECONOMY AND INFRASTRUCTURE IN SHAMBLES. THE HARDEARS UNION SEEMED INEPT AT FASHIONING AN ADEQUATE RESPONSE TO THE CRISIS...
HARDING'S FACTORIES OFFERED MUCH-NEEDED JOBS...
BUT SOME SUSPECTED ALL WAS NOT WHAT IT SEEMED...
RESTRICTED

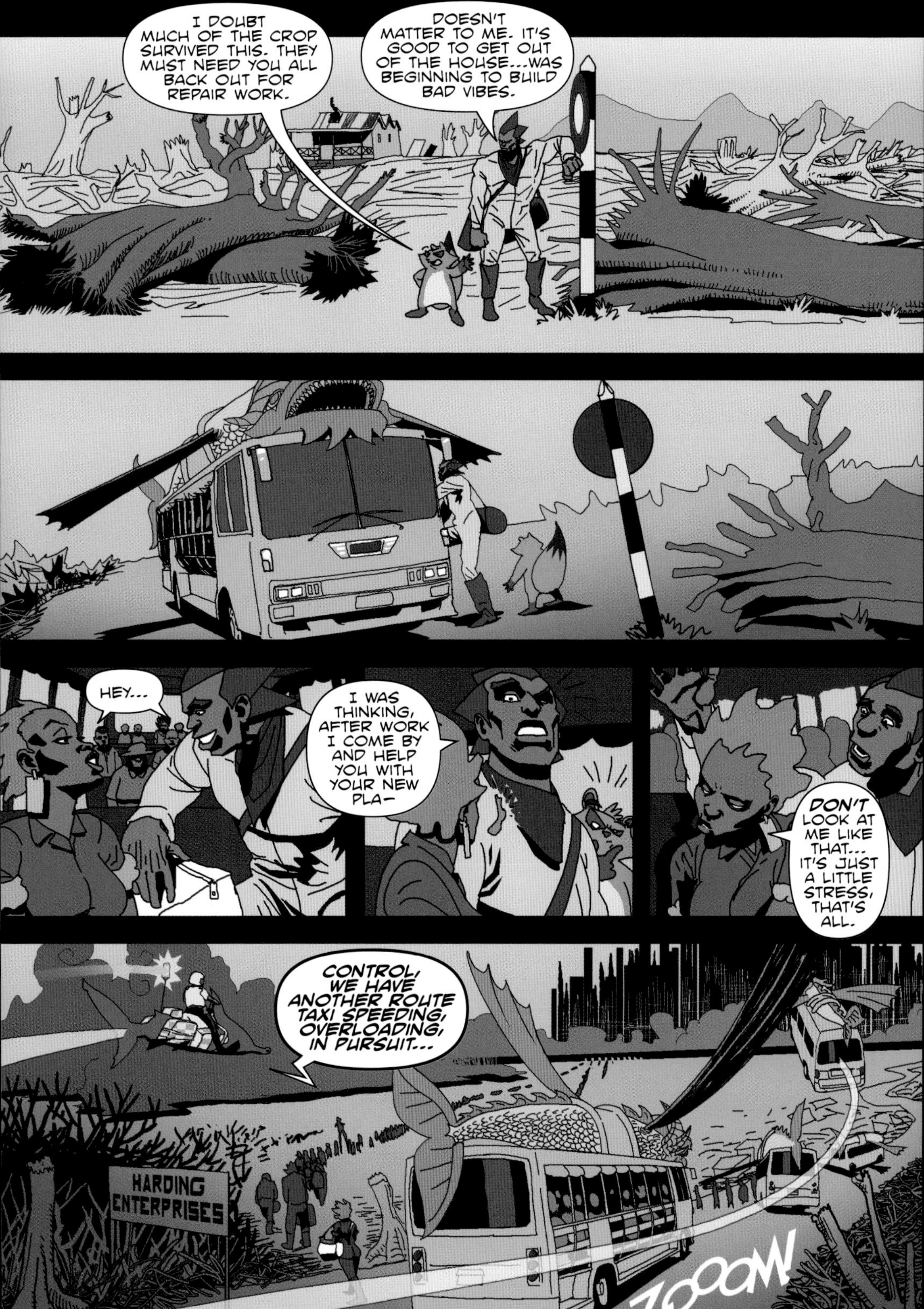
I DOUBT MUCH OF THE CROP SURVIVED THIS. THEY MUST NEED YOU ALL BACK OUT FOR REPAIR WORK.
DOESN'T MATTER TO ME. IT'S GOOD TO GET OUT OF THE HOUSE...WAS BEGINNING TO BUILD BAD VIBES.
HEY...
I WAS THINKING, AFTER WORK I COME BY AND HELP YOU WITH YOUR NEW PLA—
DON'T LOOK AT ME LIKE THAT... IT'S JUST A LITTLE STRESS, THAT'S ALL.
CONTROL, WE HAVE ANOTHER ROUTE TAXI SPEEDING, OVERLOADING, IN PURSUIT...
HARDING ENTERPRISES
ZOOOM!

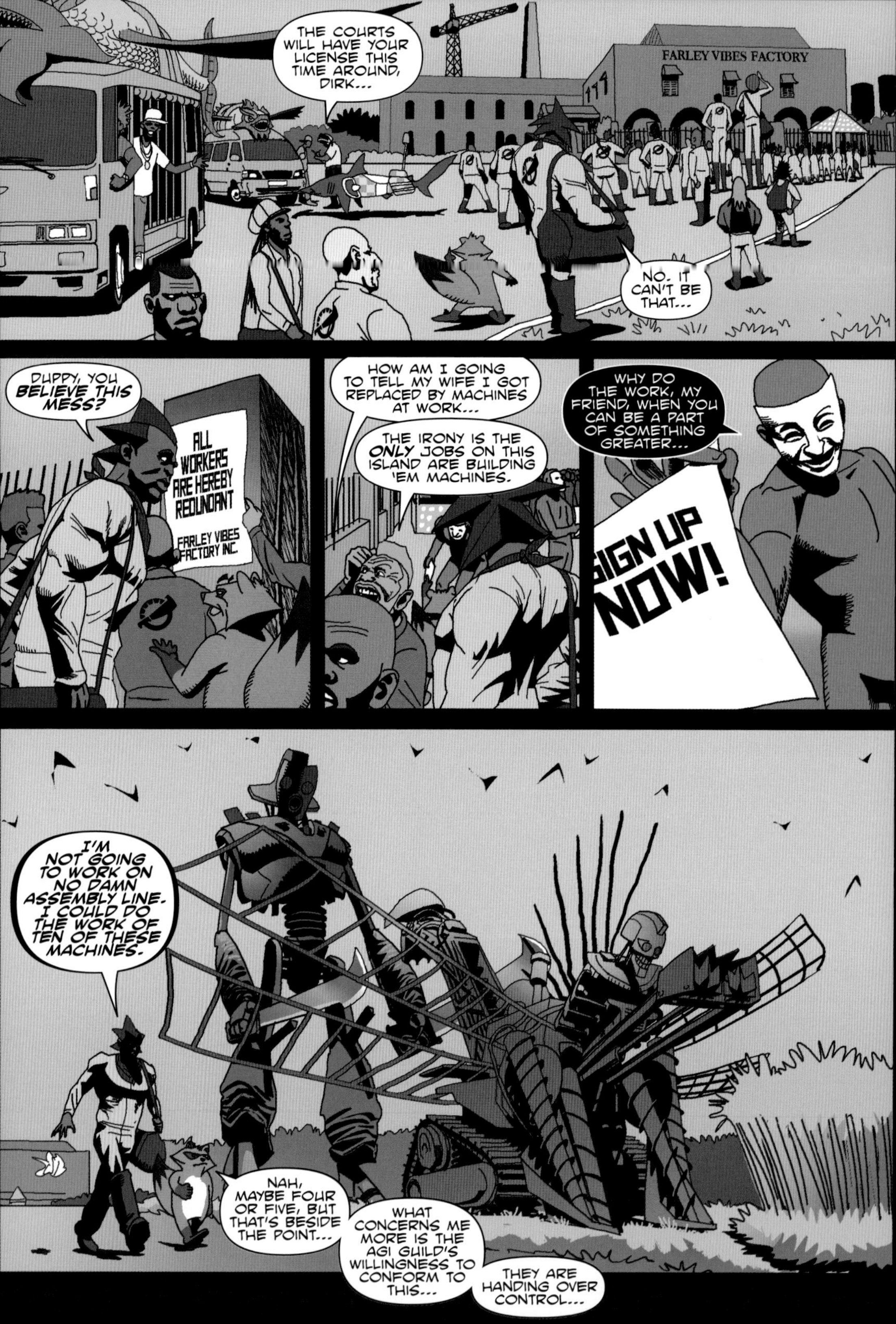
THE COURTS WILL HAVE YOUR LICENSE THIS TIME AROUND, DIRK...
FARLEY VIBES FACTORY
NO. IT CAN'T BE THAT...
DUPPY, YOU BELIEVE THIS MESS?
ALL WORKERS ARE HEREBY REDUNDANT
FARLEY VIBES FACTORY INC.
HOW AM I GOING TO TELL MY WIFE I GOT REPLACED BY MACHINES AT WORK...
THE IRONY IS THE ONLY JOBS ON THIS ISLAND ARE BUILDING 'EM MACHINES.
WHY DO THE WORK, MY FRIEND, WHEN YOU CAN BE A PART OF SOMETHING GREATER...
SIGN UP NOW!
I'M NOT GOING TO WORK ON NO DAMN ASSEMBLY LINE. I COULD DO THE WORK OF TEN OF THESE MACHINES.
NAH, MAYBE FOUR OR FIVE, BUT THAT'S BESIDE THE POINT...
WHAT CONCERNS ME MORE IS THE AGI GUILD'S WILLINGNESS TO CONFORM TO THIS...
THEY ARE HANDING OVER CONTROL...

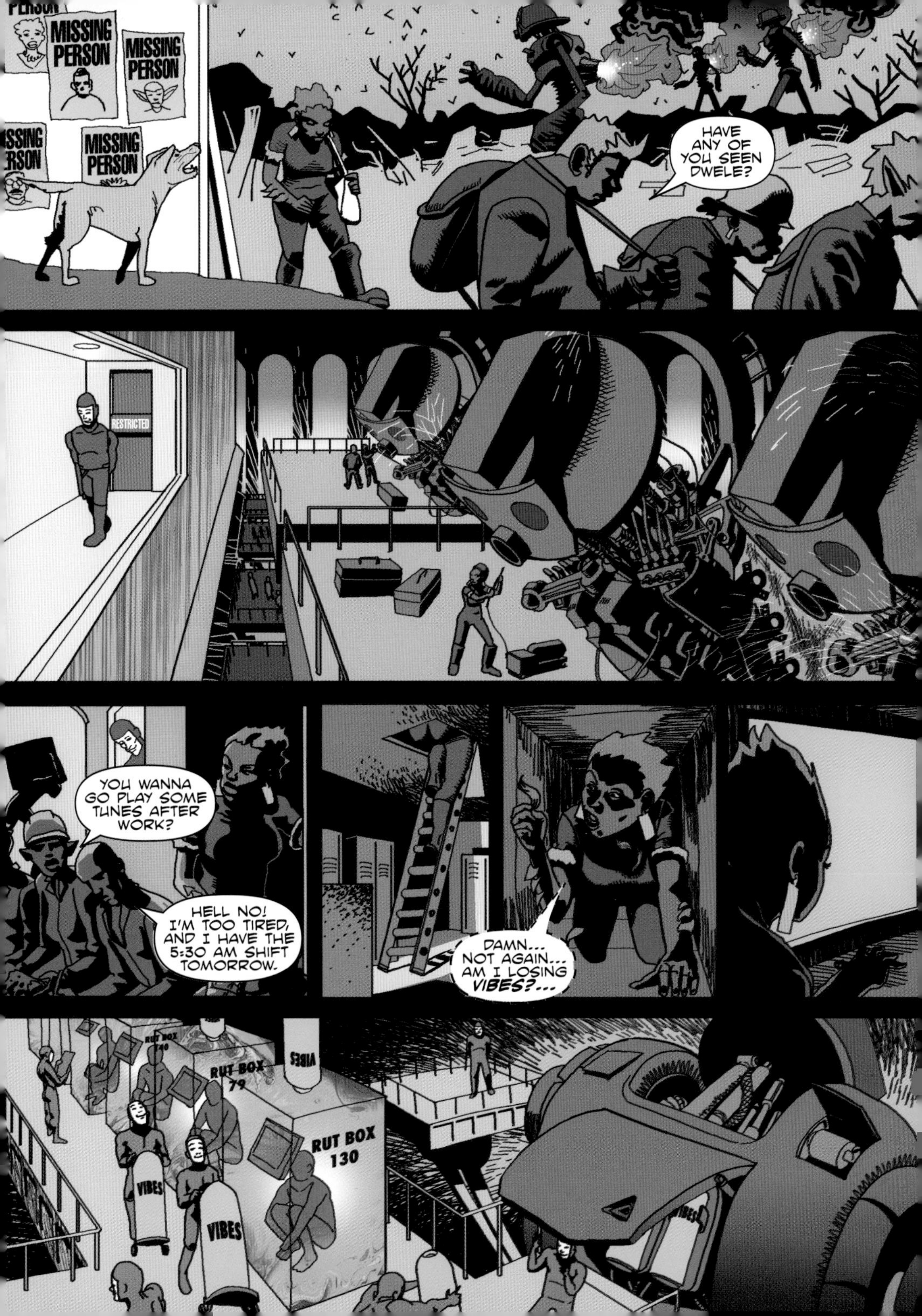
MISSING PERSON
MISSING PERSON
MISSING PERSON
MISSING PERSON
HAVE ANY OF YOU SEEN DWELE?
RESTRICTED
YOU WANNA GO PLAY SOME TUNES AFTER WORK?
HELL NO! I'M TOO TIRED, AND I HAVE THE 5:30 AM SHIFT TOMORROW.
DAMN... NOT AGAIN... AM I LOSING VIBES?...
RUT BOX 79
RUT BOX 130
VIBES
VIBES
VIBES
VIBES

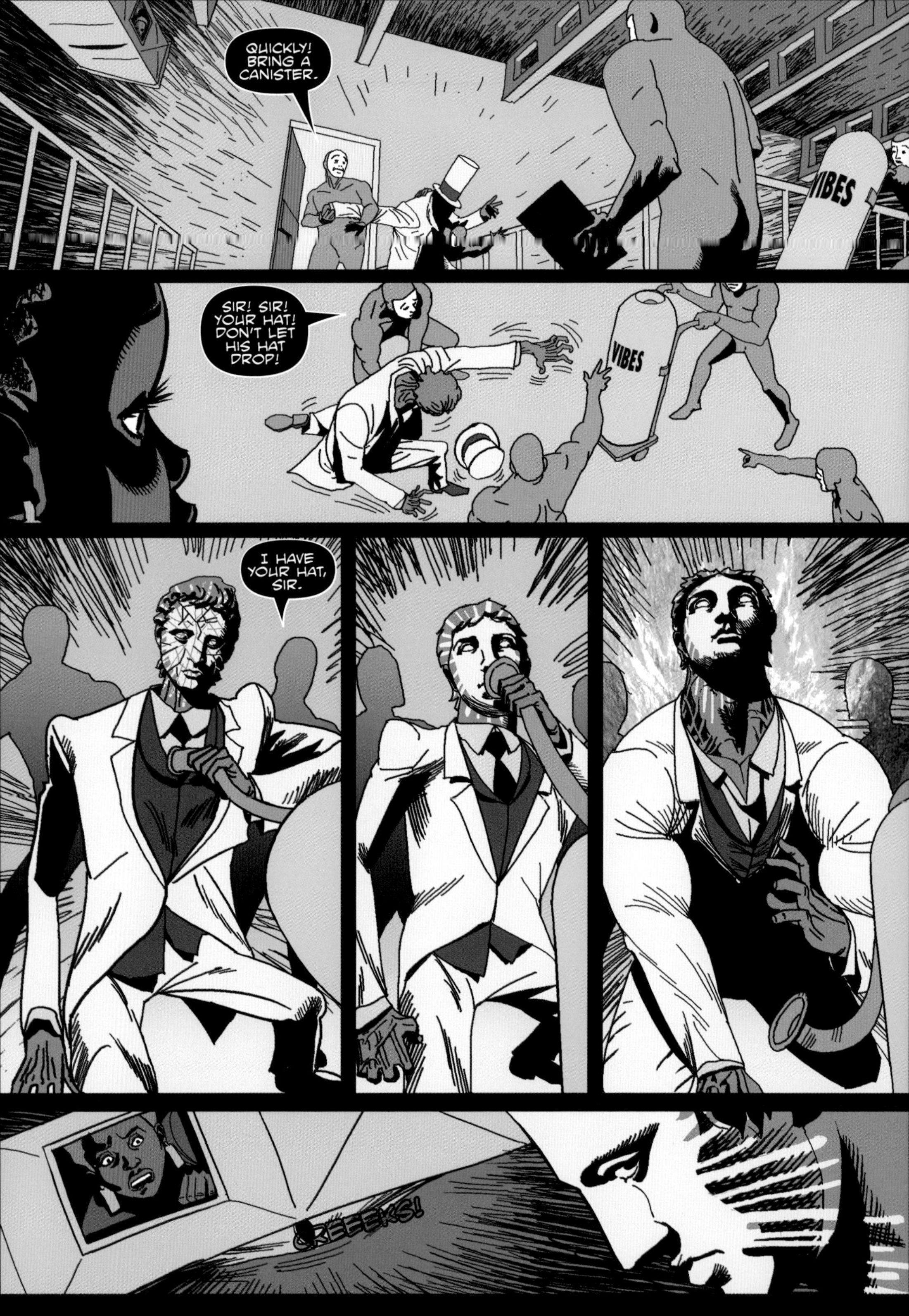
QUICKLY! BRING A CANISTER.
VIBES
SIR! SIR! YOUR HAT! DON'T LET HIS HAT DROP!
VIBES
I HAVE YOUR HAT, SIR.
CREEEKS!

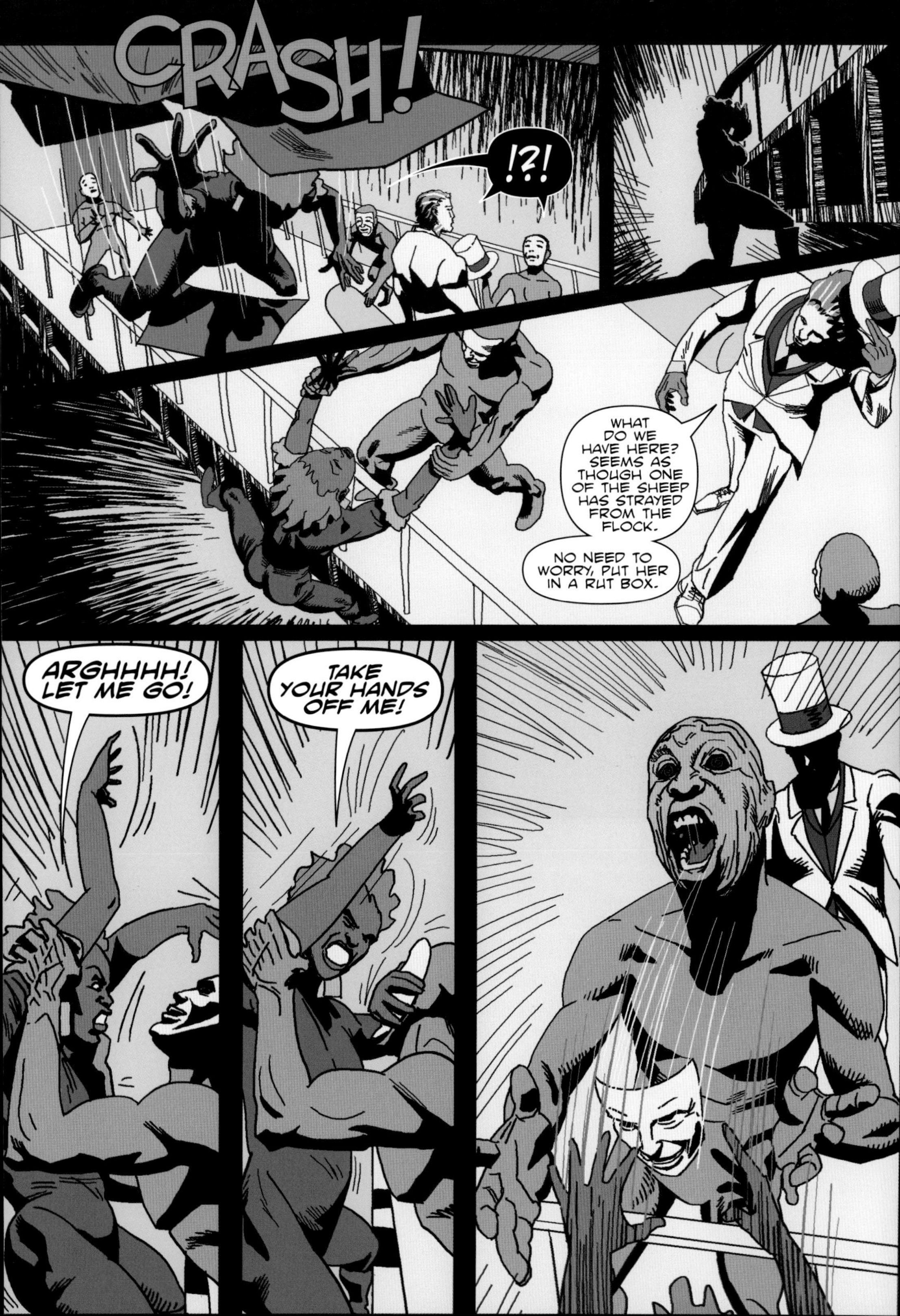
CRASH!
!?!
WHAT DO WE HAVE HERE? SEEMS AS THOUGH ONE OF THE SHEEP HAS STRAYED FROM THE FLOCK.
NO NEED TO WORRY, PUT HER IN A RUT BOX.
ARGHHHH! LET ME GO!
TAKE YOUR HANDS OFF ME!

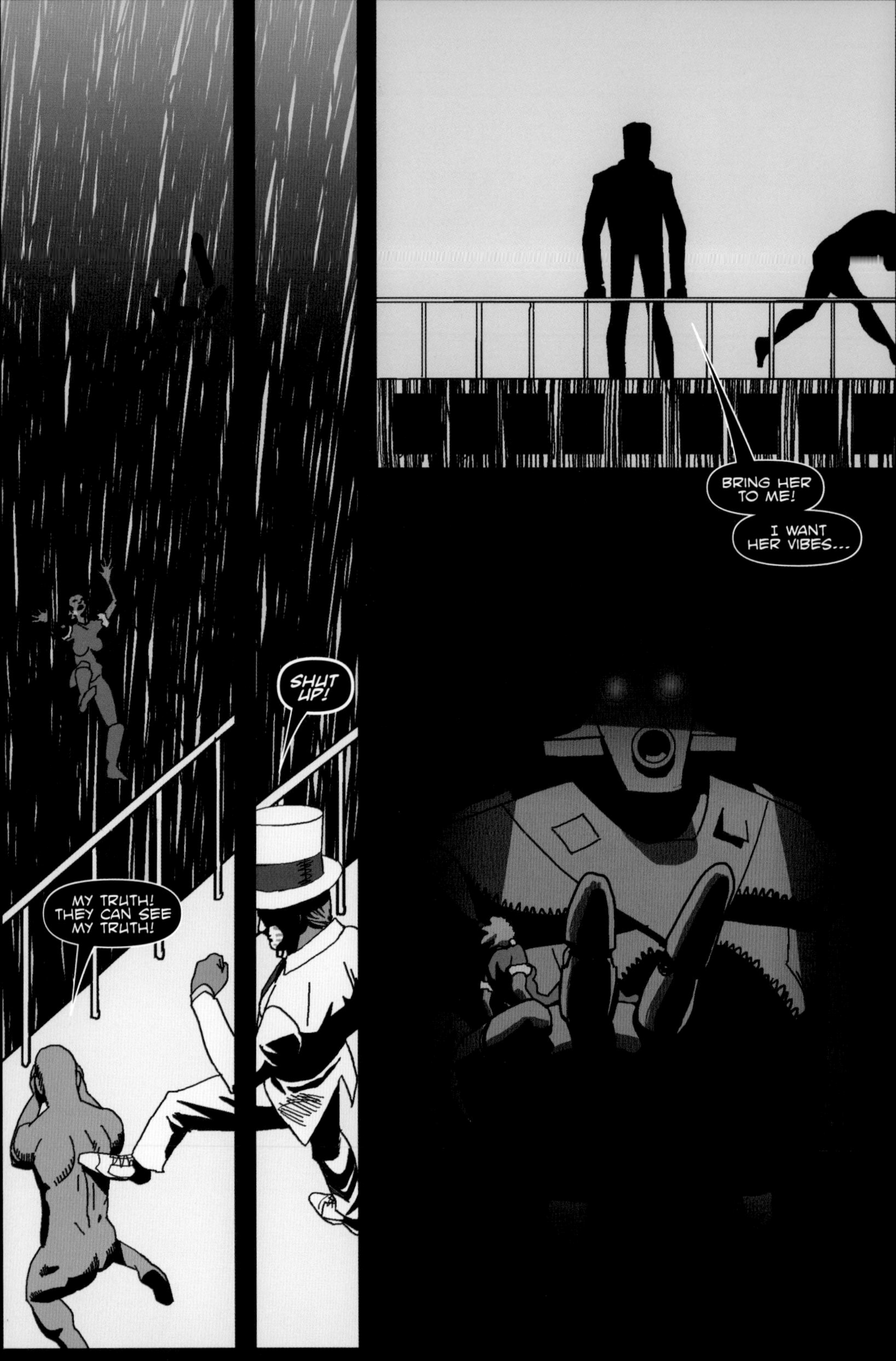
BRING HER TO ME!
I WANT HER VIBES...
SHUT UP!
MY TRUTH! THEY CAN SEE MY TRUTH!

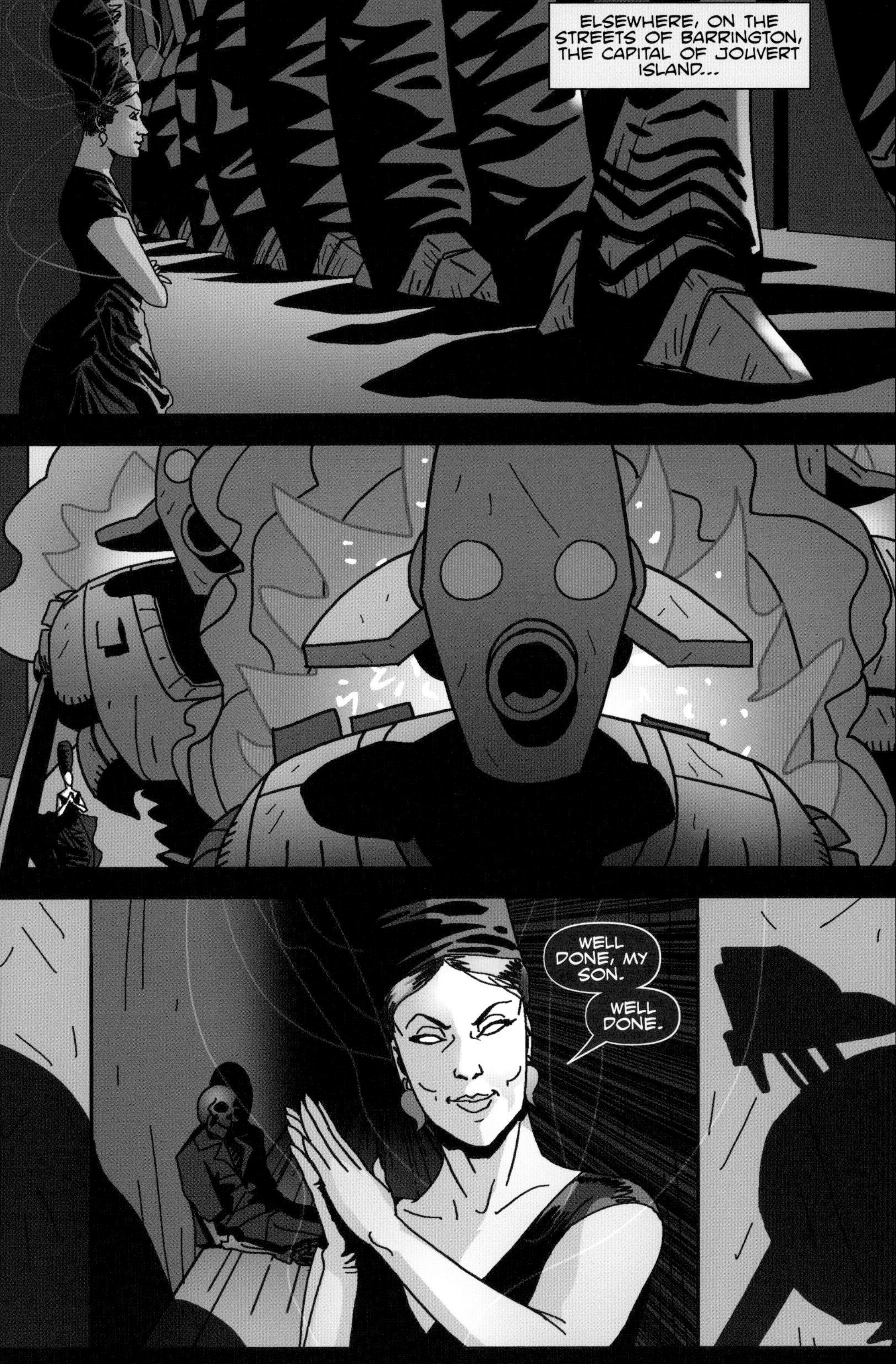
ELSEWHERE, ON THE STREETS OF BARRINGTON, THE CAPITAL OF JOUVERT ISLAND...
WELL DONE, MY SON.
WELL DONE.

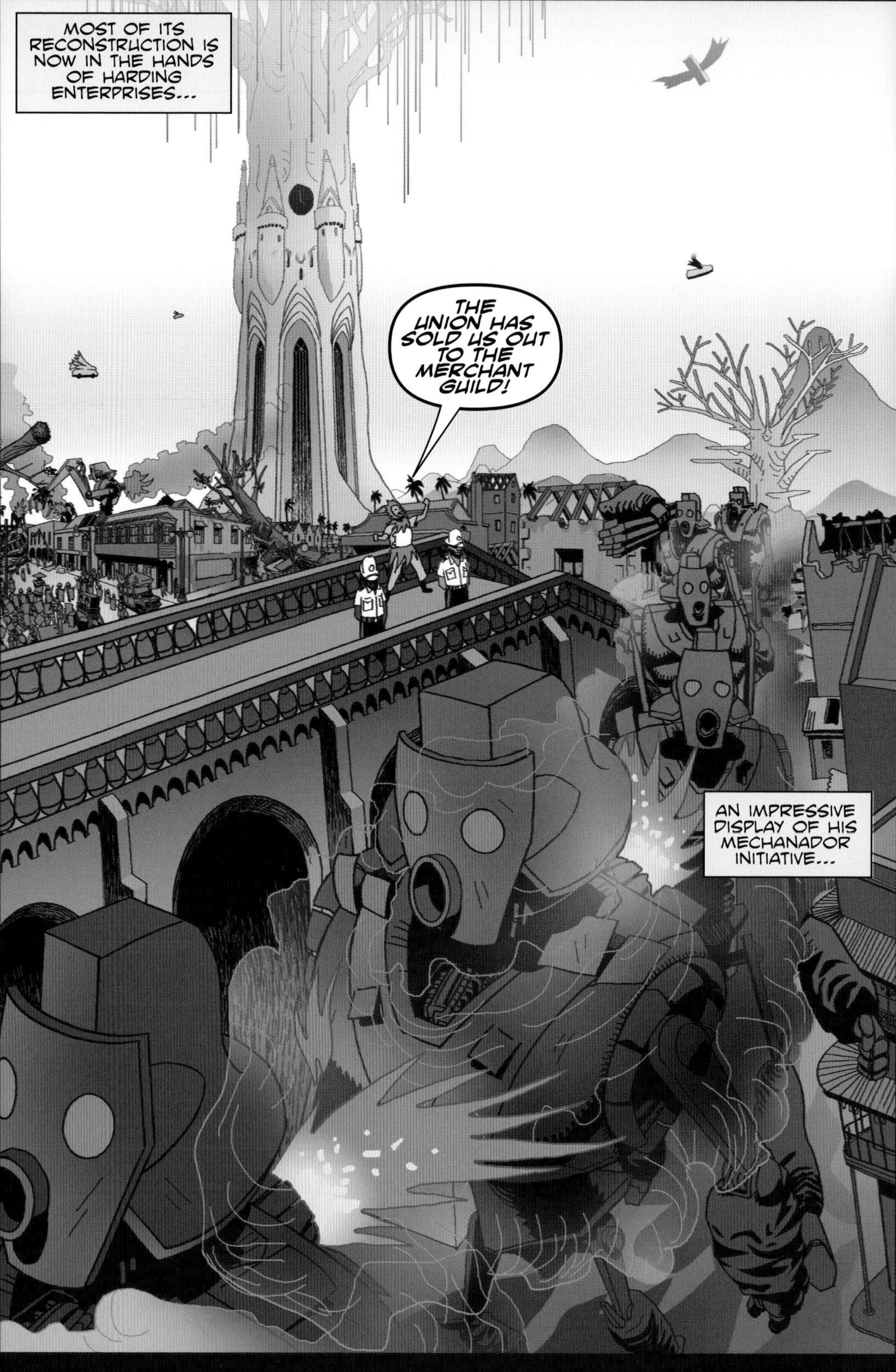
MOST OF ITS RECONSTRUCTION IS NOW IN THE HANDS OF HARDING ENTERPRISES...
THE UNION HAS SOLD US OUT TO THE MERCHANT GUILD!
AN IMPRESSIVE DISPLAY OF HIS MECHANADOR INITIATIVE...

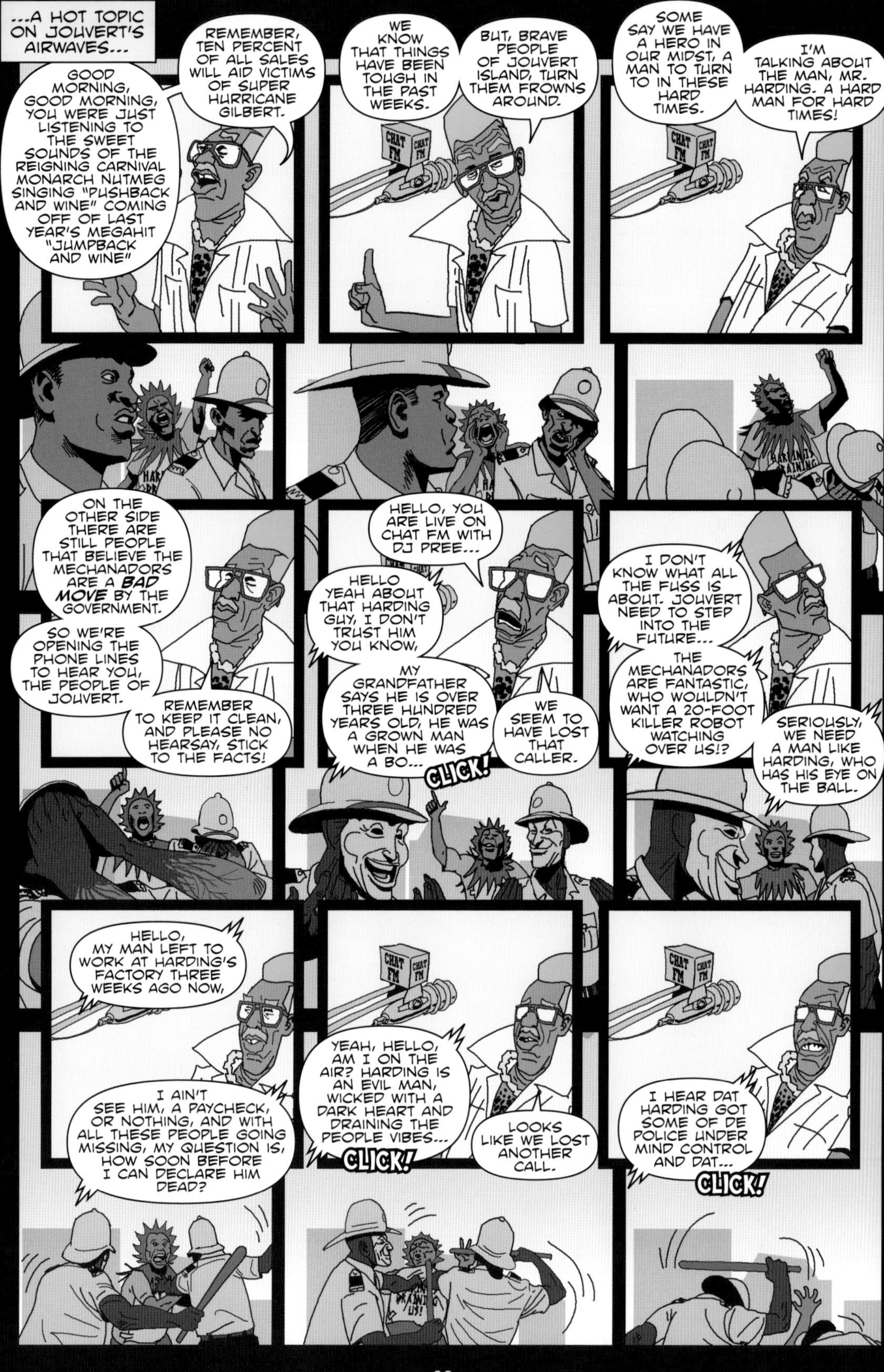
...A HOT TOPIC ON JOUVERT'S AIRWAVES...
GOOD MORNING, GOOD MORNING, YOU WERE JUST LISTENING TO THE SWEET SOUNDS OF THE REIGNING CARNIVAL MONARCH NUTMEG SINGING "PUSHBACK AND WINE" COMING OFF OF LAST YEAR'S MEGAHIT "JUMPBACK AND WINE"
REMEMBER, TEN PERCENT OF ALL SALES WILL AID VICTIMS OF SUPER HURRICANE GILBERT.
WE KNOW THAT THINGS HAVE BEEN TOUGH IN THE PAST WEEKS.
BUT, BRAVE PEOPLE OF JOUVERT ISLAND, TURN THEM FROWNS AROUND.
CHAT FM
SOME SAY WE HAVE A HERO IN OUR MIDST, A MAN TO TURN TO IN THESE HARD TIMES.
I'M TALKING ABOUT THE MAN, MR. HARDING. A HARD MAN FOR HARD TIMES!
ON THE OTHER SIDE THERE ARE STILL PEOPLE THAT BELIEVE THE MECHANADORS ARE A BAD MOVE BY THE GOVERNMENT.
SO WE'RE OPENING THE PHONE LINES TO HEAR YOU, THE PEOPLE OF JOUVERT.
REMEMBER TO KEEP IT CLEAN, AND PLEASE NO HEARSAY, STICK TO THE FACTS!
HELLO, YOU ARE LIVE ON CHAT FM WITH DJ PREE...
HELLO YEAH ABOUT THAT HARDING GUY, I DON'T TRUST HIM YOU KNOW,
MY GRANDFATHER SAYS HE IS OVER THREE HUNDRED YEARS OLD, HE WAS A GROWN MAN WHEN HE WAS A BO...
CLICK!
WE SEEM TO HAVE LOST THAT CALLER.
I DON'T KNOW WHAT ALL THE FUSS IS ABOUT. JOUVERT NEED TO STEP INTO THE FUTURE...
THE MECHANADORS ARE FANTASTIC, WHO WOULDN'T WANT A 20-FOOT KILLER ROBOT WATCHING OVER US!?
SERIOUSLY, WE NEED A MAN LIKE HARDING, WHO HAS HIS EYE ON THE BALL.
HELLO, MY MAN LEFT TO WORK AT HARDING'S FACTORY THREE WEEKS AGO NOW,
I AIN'T SEE HIM, A PAYCHECK, OR NOTHING, AND WITH ALL THESE PEOPLE GOING MISSING, MY QUESTION IS, HOW SOON BEFORE I CAN DECLARE HIM DEAD?
CHAT FM
YEAH, HELLO, AM I ON THE AIR? HARDING IS AN EVIL MAN, WICKED WITH A DARK HEART AND DRAINING THE PEOPLE VIBES...
CLICK!
LOOKS LIKE WE LOST ANOTHER CALL.
CHAT FM
I HEAR DAT HARDING GOT SOME OF DE POLICE UNDER MIND CONTROL AND DAT...
CLICK!

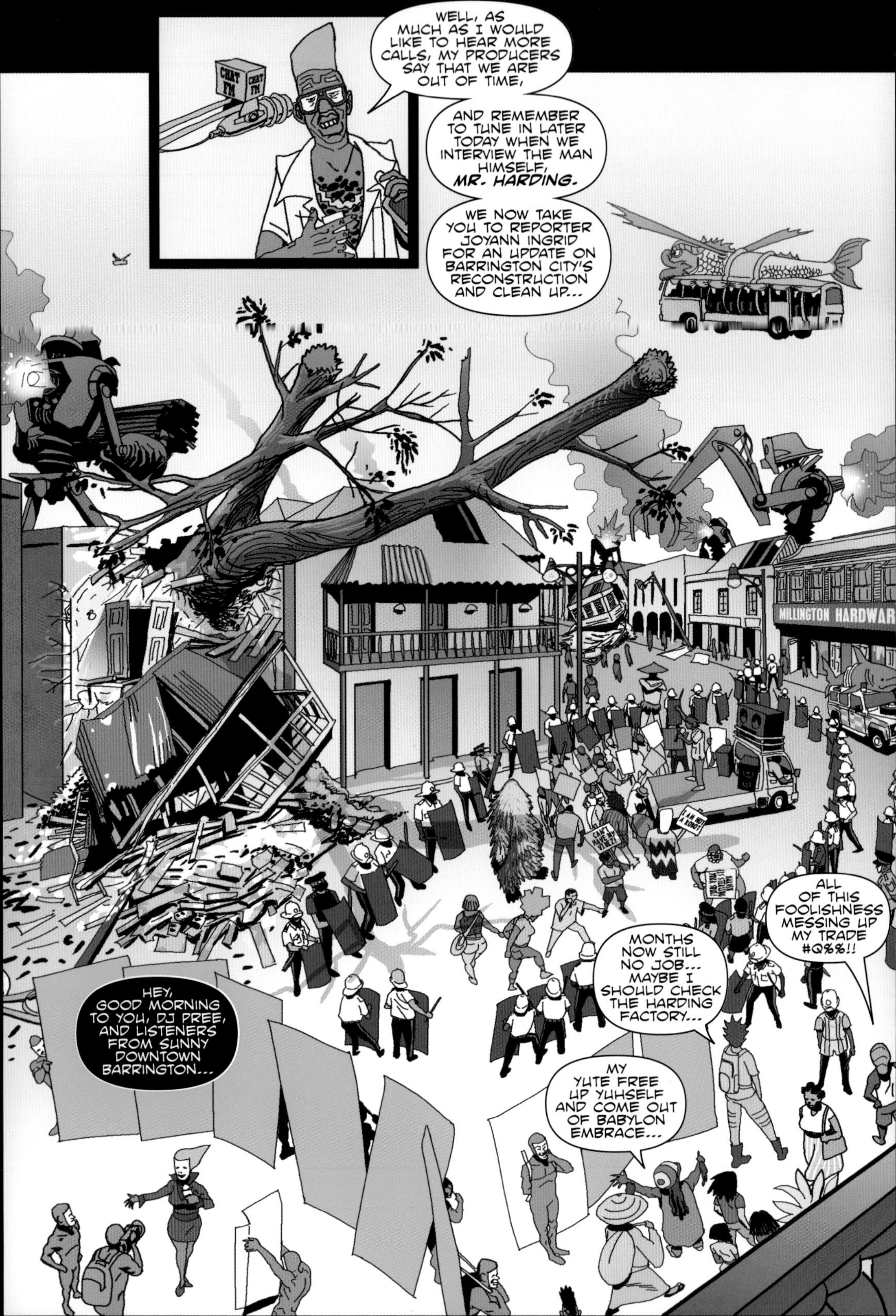
CHAT FM
WELL, AS MUCH AS I WOULD LIKE TO HEAR MORE CALLS, MY PRODUCERS SAY THAT WE ARE OUT OF TIME,
AND REMEMBER TO TUNE IN LATER TODAY WHEN WE INTERVIEW THE MAN HIMSELF, MR. HARDING.
WE NOW TAKE YOU TO REPORTER JOYANN INGRID FOR AN UPDATE ON BARRINGTON CITY'S RECONSTRUCTION AND CLEAN UP...
MILLINGTON HARDWAR
I AM NOT A ROBOT
CAN'T HAVE MY VIBEZ!
ALL OF THIS FOOLISHNESS MESSING UP MY TRADE #Q%%!!
MONTHS NOW STILL NO JOB... MAYBE I SHOULD CHECK THE HARDING FACTORY...
HEY, GOOD MORNING TO YOU, DJ PREE, AND LISTENERS FROM SUNNY DOWNTOWN BARRINGTON...
MY YUTE FREE UP YUHSELF AND COME OUT OF BABYLON EMBRACE...

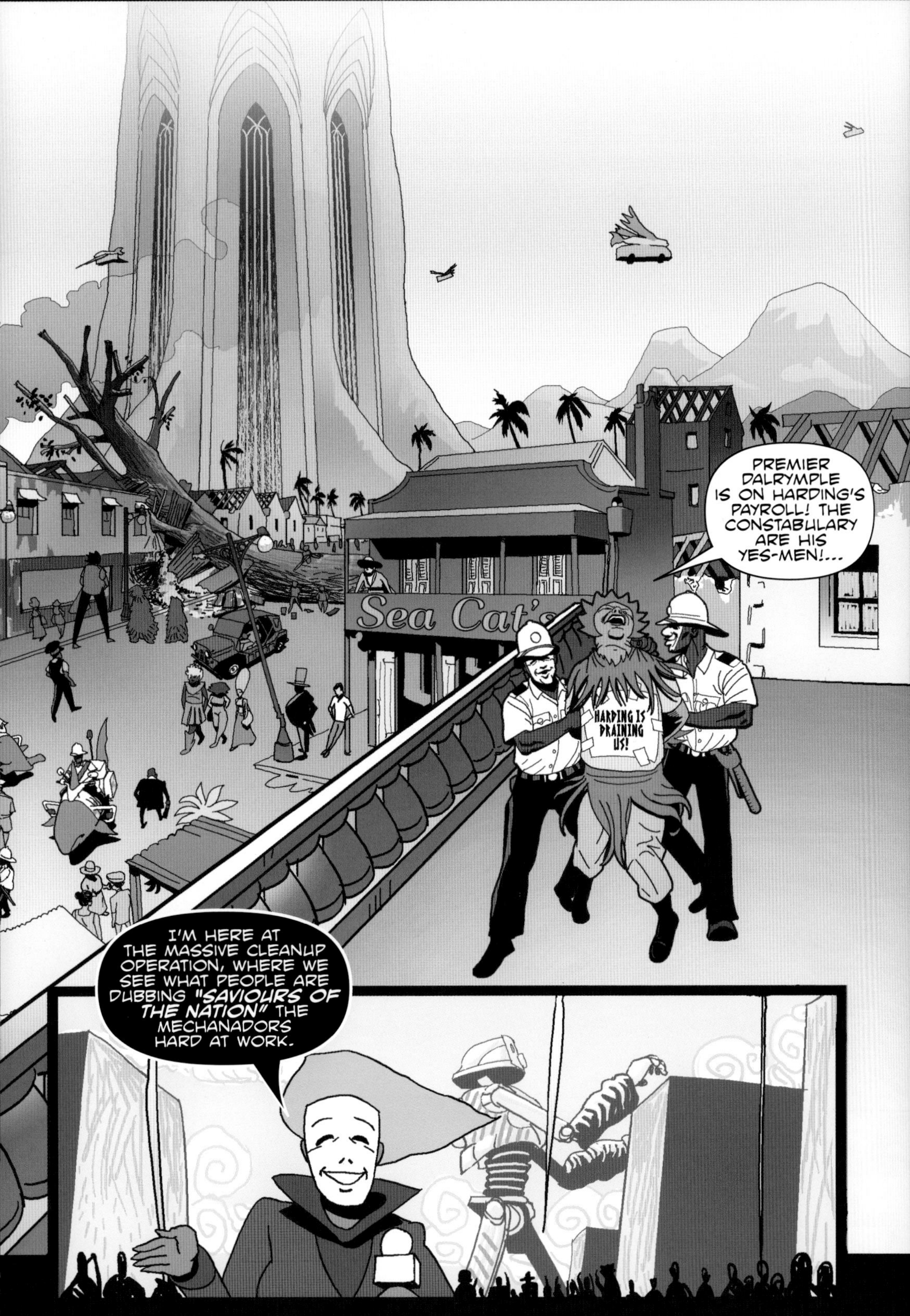
PREMIER DALRYMPLE IS ON HARDING'S PAYROLL! THE CONSTABULARY ARE HIS YES-MEN!...
Sea Cat's
HARDING IS DRAINING US!
I'M HERE AT THE MASSIVE CLEANUP OPERATION, WHERE WE SEE WHAT PEOPLE ARE DUBBING "SAVIOURS OF THE NATION" THE MECHANADORS HARD AT WORK.

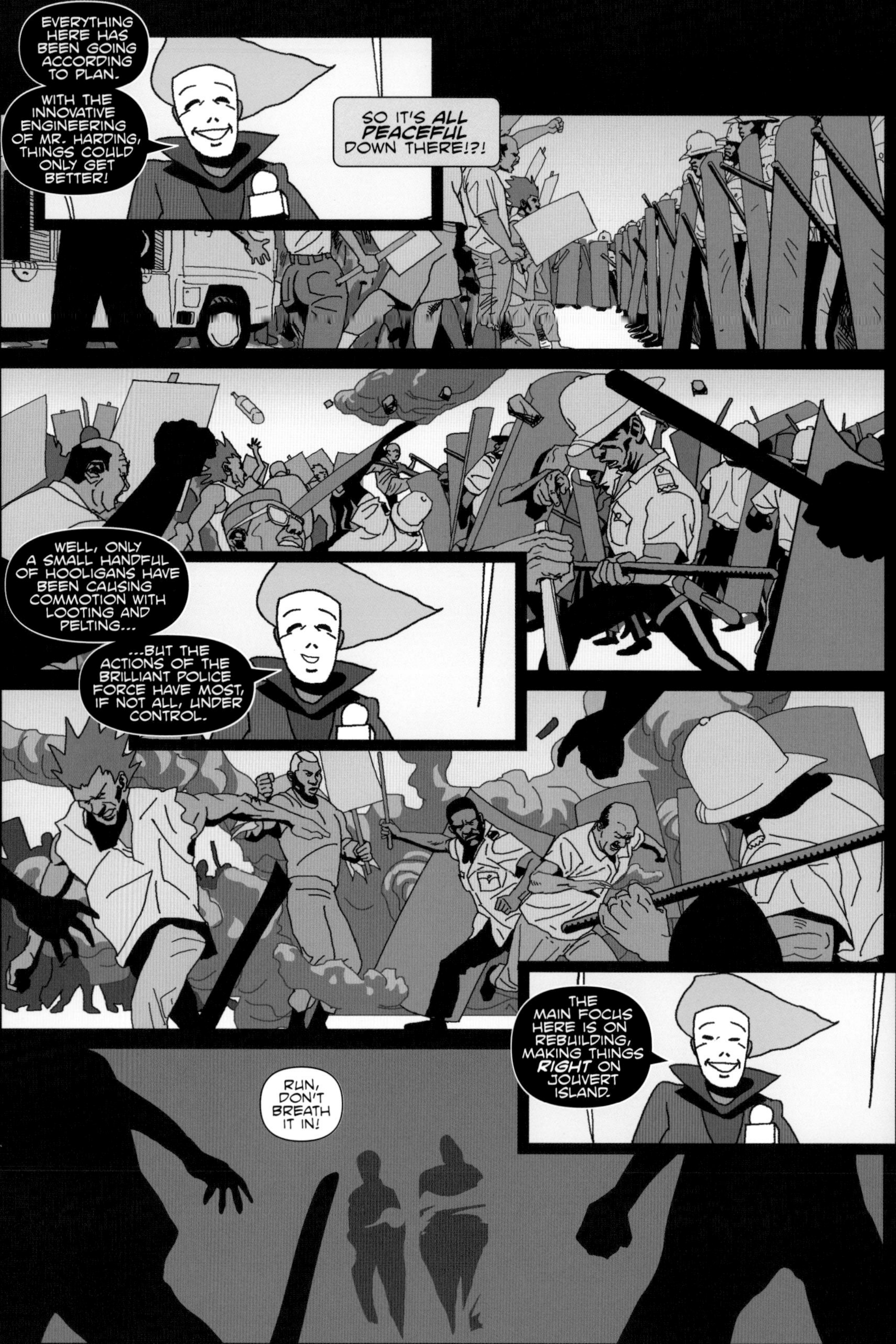
EVERYTHING HERE HAS BEEN GOING ACCORDING TO PLAN.
WITH THE INNOVATIVE ENGINEERING OF MR. HARDING, THINGS COULD ONLY GET BETTER!
SO IT'S ALL PEACEFUL DOWN THERE!?!
WELL, ONLY A SMALL HANDFUL OF HOOLIGANS HAVE BEEN CAUSING COMMOTION WITH LOOTING AND PELTING...
...BUT THE ACTIONS OF THE BRILLIANT POLICE FORCE HAVE MOST, IF NOT ALL, UNDER CONTROL.
THE MAIN FOCUS HERE IS ON REBUILDING, MAKING THINGS RIGHT ON JOUVERT ISLAND.
RUN, DON'T BREATH IT IN!

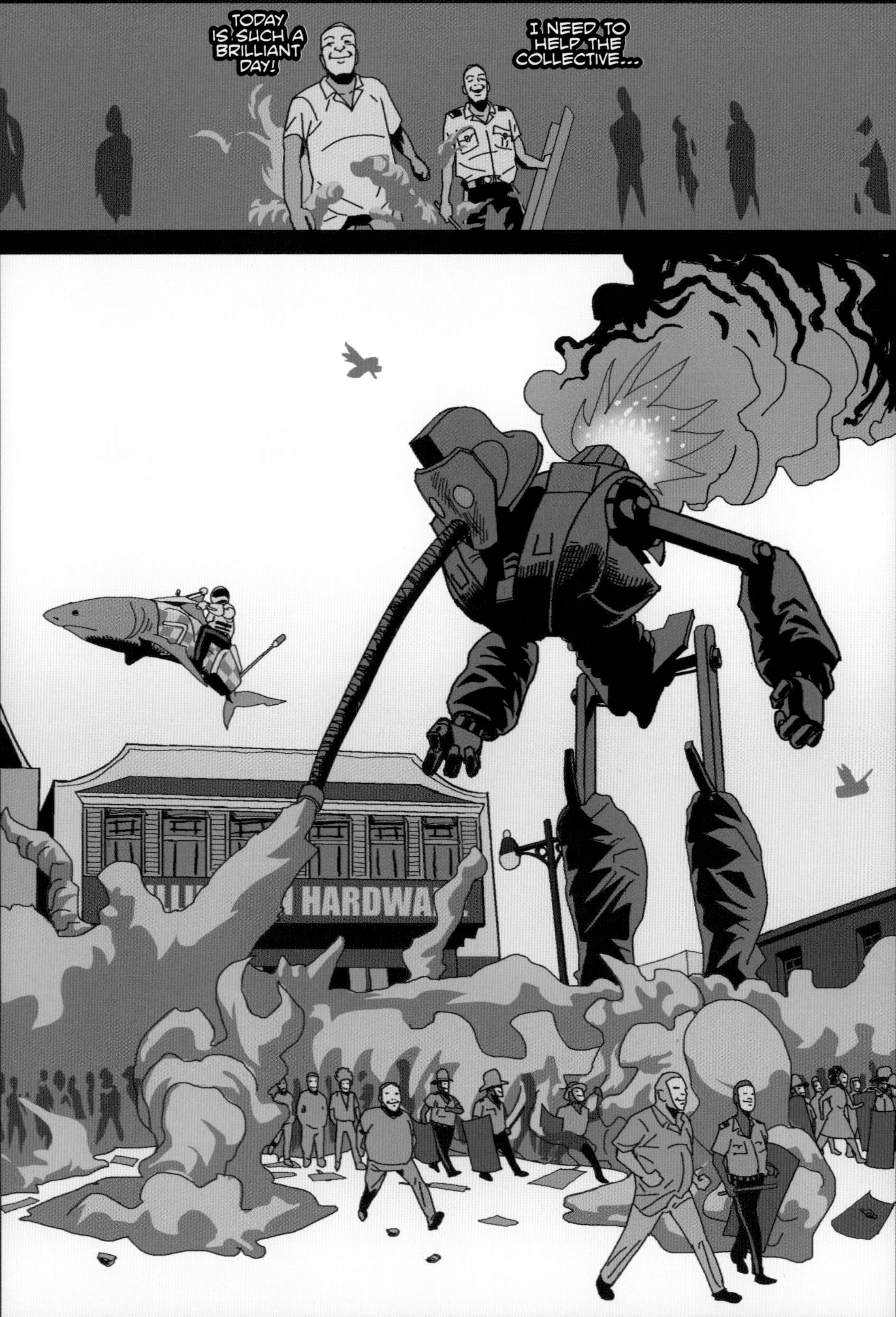
TODAY IS SUCH A BRILLIANT DAY!
I NEED TO HELP THE COLLECTIVE...

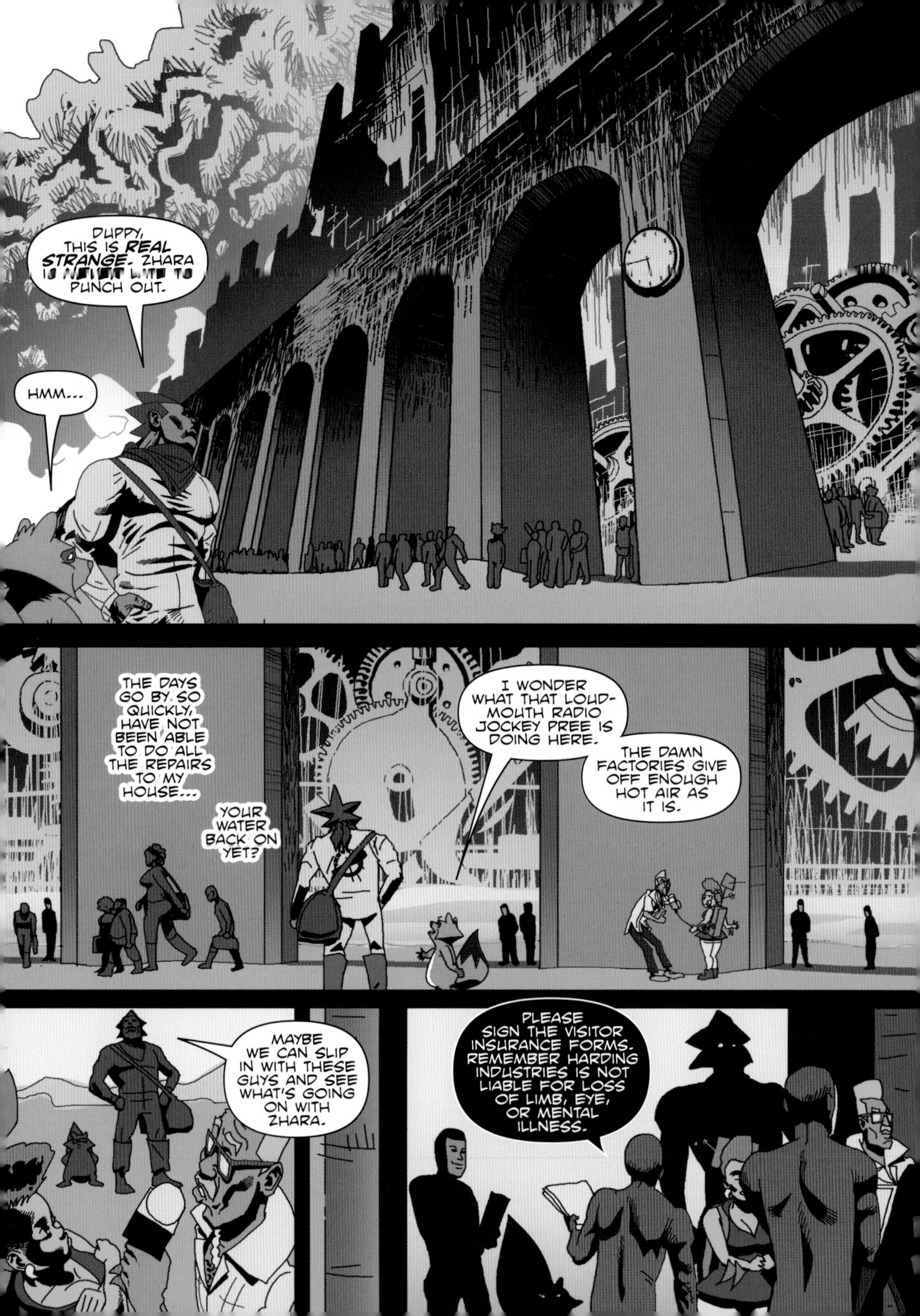
DUPPY, THIS IS **REAL STRANGE**. ZHARA
PUNCH OUT.
HMM...
THE DAYS GO BY SO QUICKLY, HAVE NOT BEEN ABLE TO DO ALL THE REPAIRS TO MY HOUSE...
YOUR WATER BACK ON YET?
I WONDER WHAT THAT LOUD-MOUTH RADIO JOCKEY PREE IS DOING HERE.
THE DAMN FACTORIES GIVE OFF ENOUGH HOT AIR AS IT IS.
MAYBE WE CAN SLIP IN WITH THESE GUYS AND SEE WHAT'S GOING ON WITH ZHARA.
PLEASE SIGN THE VISITOR INSURANCE FORMS. REMEMBER HARDING INDUSTRIES IS NOT LIABLE FOR LOSS OF LIMB, EYE, OR MENTAL ILLNESS.

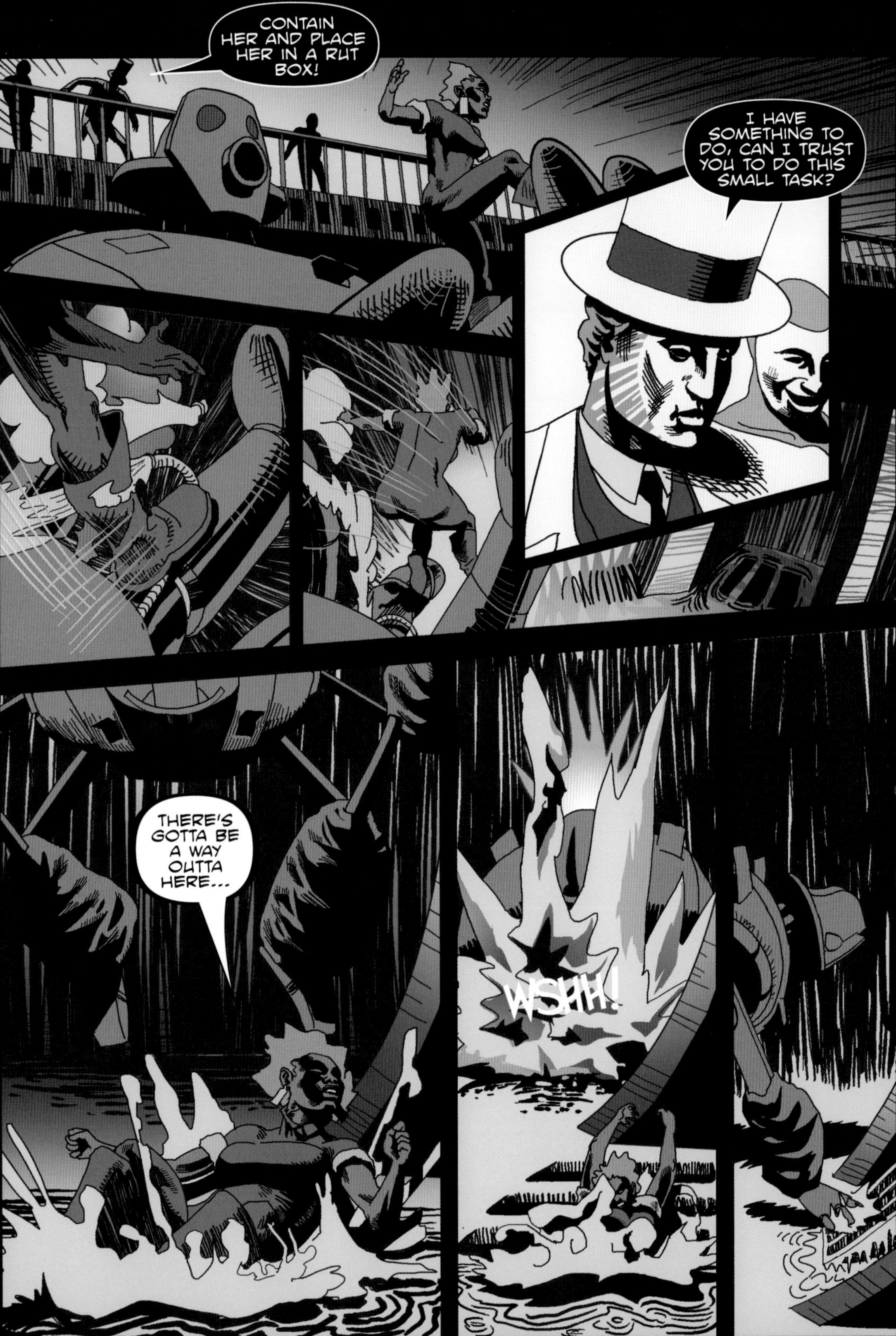
CONTAIN HER AND PLACE HER IN A RUT BOX!
I HAVE SOMETHING TO DO, CAN I TRUST YOU TO DO THIS SMALL TASK?
THERE'S GOTTA BE A WAY OUTTA HERE...
WSHH!

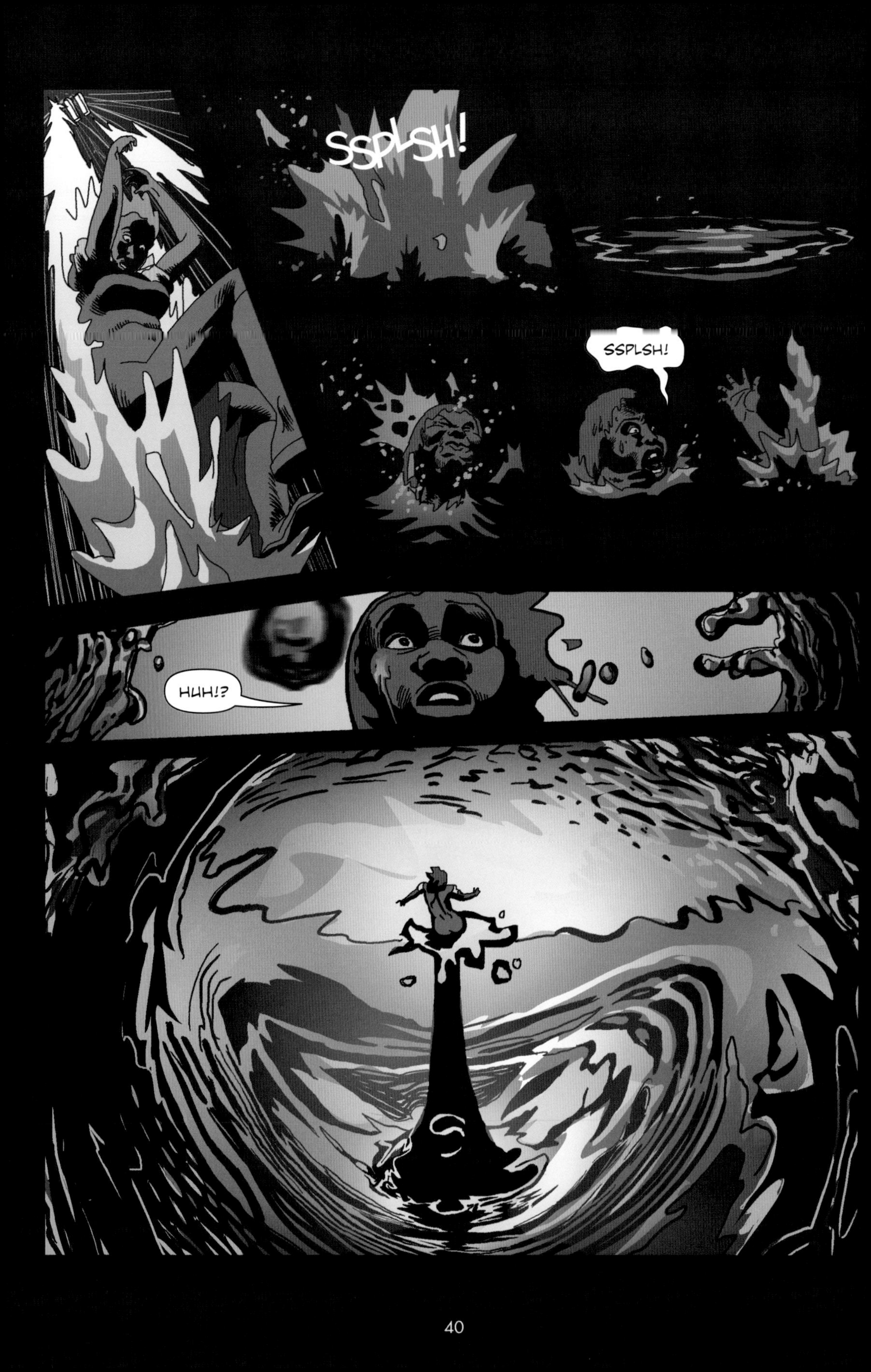
SSPLSH!
SSPLSH!
HUH!?

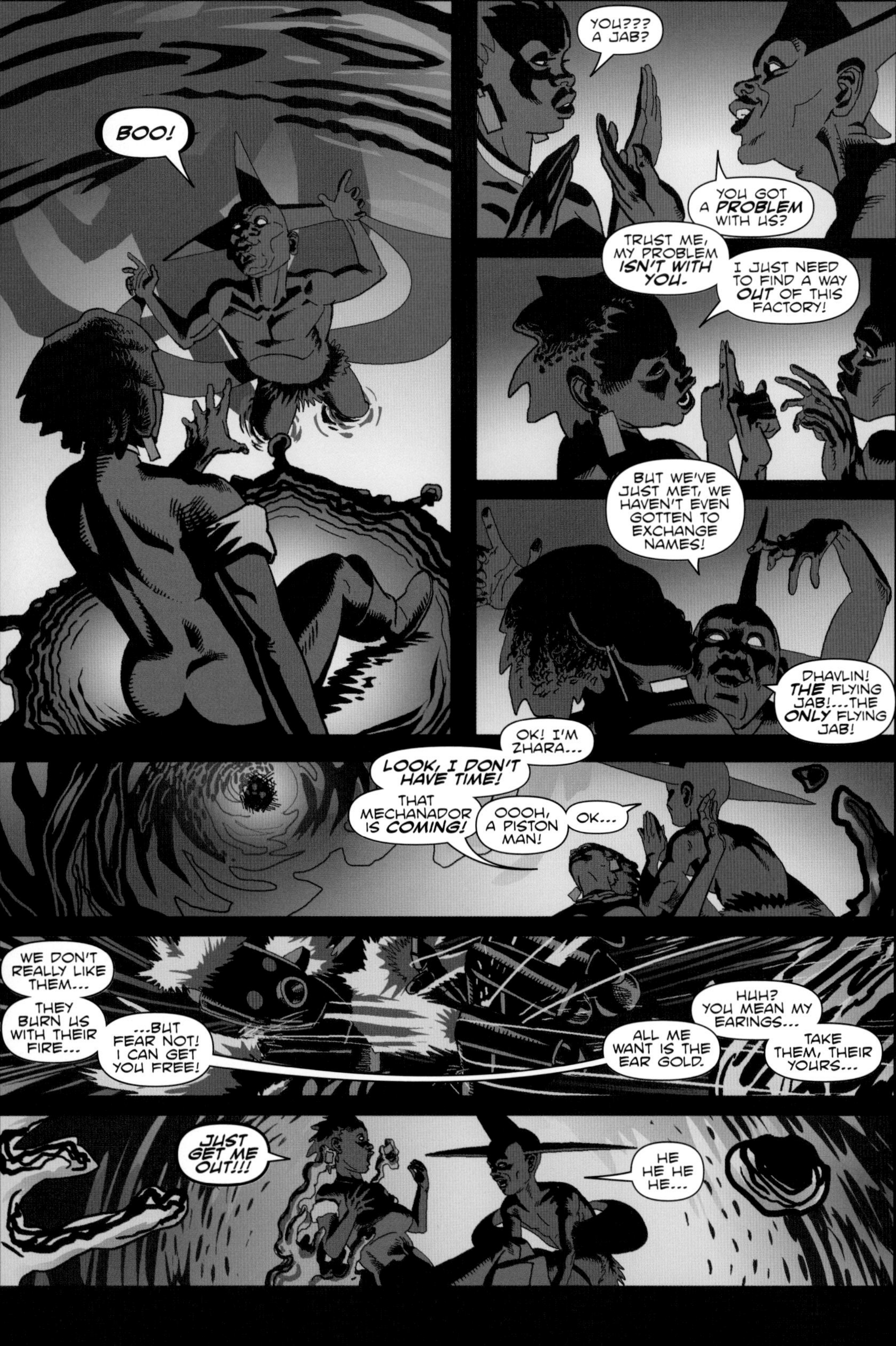
BOO!
YOU??? A JAB?
YOU GOT A PROBLEM WITH US?
TRUST ME, MY PROBLEM ISN'T WITH YOU.
I JUST NEED TO FIND A WAY OUT OF THIS FACTORY!
BUT WE'VE JUST MET, WE HAVEN'T EVEN GOTTEN TO EXCHANGE NAMES!
DHAVLIN! THE FLYING JAB!...THE ONLY FLYING JAB!
OK! I'M ZHARA...
LOOK, I DON'T HAVE TIME!
THAT MECHANADOR IS COMING!
OOOH, A PISTON MAN!
OK...
WE DON'T REALLY LIKE THEM...
THEY BURN US WITH THEIR FIRE...
...BUT FEAR NOT! I CAN GET YOU FREE!
ALL ME WANT IS THE EAR GOLD.
HUH? YOU MEAN MY EARINGS...
TAKE THEM, THEIR YOURS...
JUST GET ME OUT!!!
HE HE HE HE...

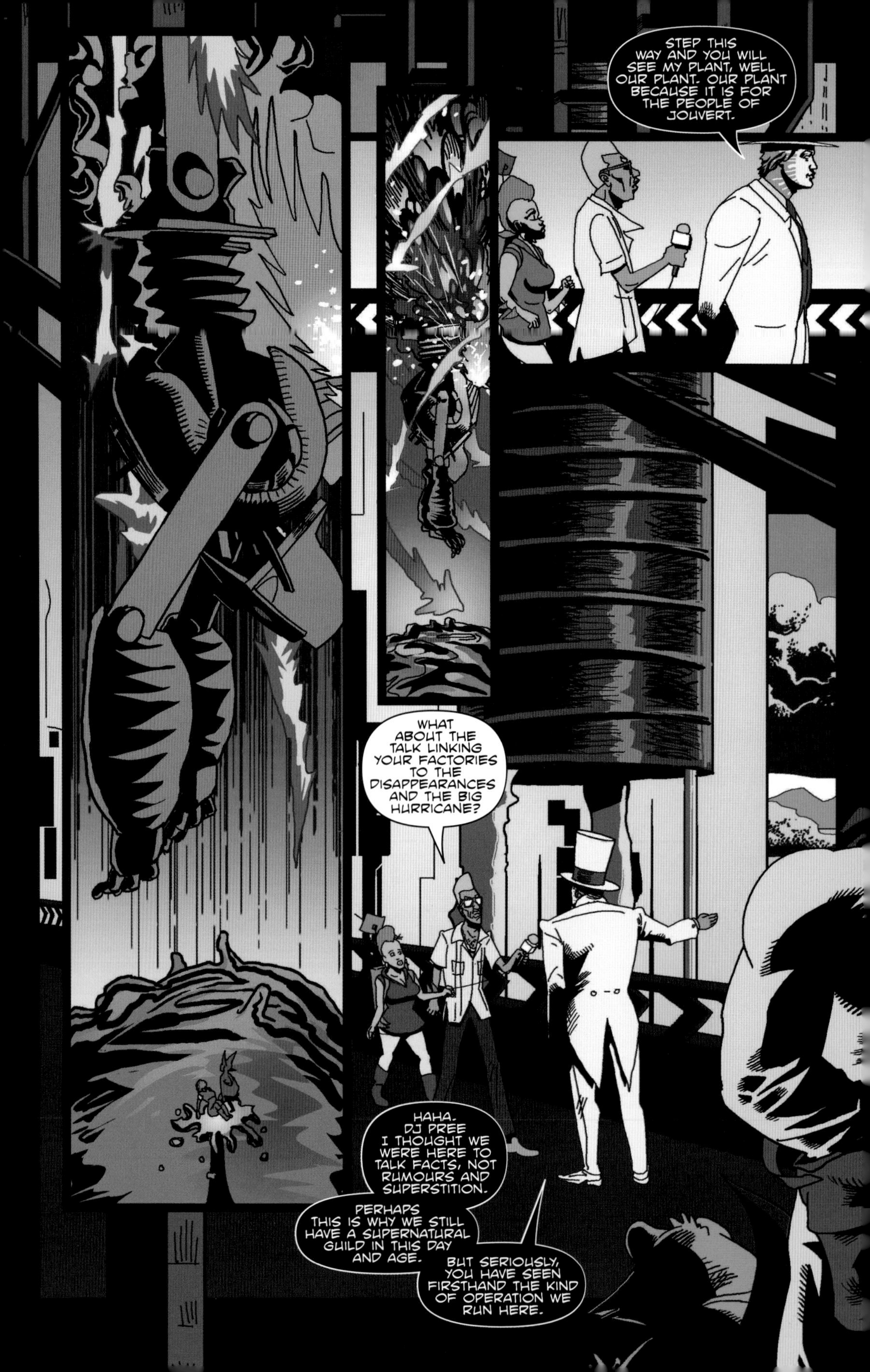
STEP THIS WAY AND YOU WILL SEE MY PLANT, WELL OUR PLANT. OUR PLANT BECAUSE IT IS FOR THE PEOPLE OF JOUVERT.
WHAT ABOUT THE TALK LINKING YOUR FACTORIES TO THE DISAPPEARANCES AND THE BIG HURRICANE?
HAHA. DJ PREE I THOUGHT WE WERE HERE TO TALK FACTS, NOT RUMOURS AND SUPERSTITION.
PERHAPS THIS IS WHY WE STILL HAVE A SUPERNATURAL GUILD IN THIS DAY AND AGE.
BUT SERIOUSLY, YOU HAVE SEEN FIRSTHAND THE KIND OF OPERATION WE RUN HERE.

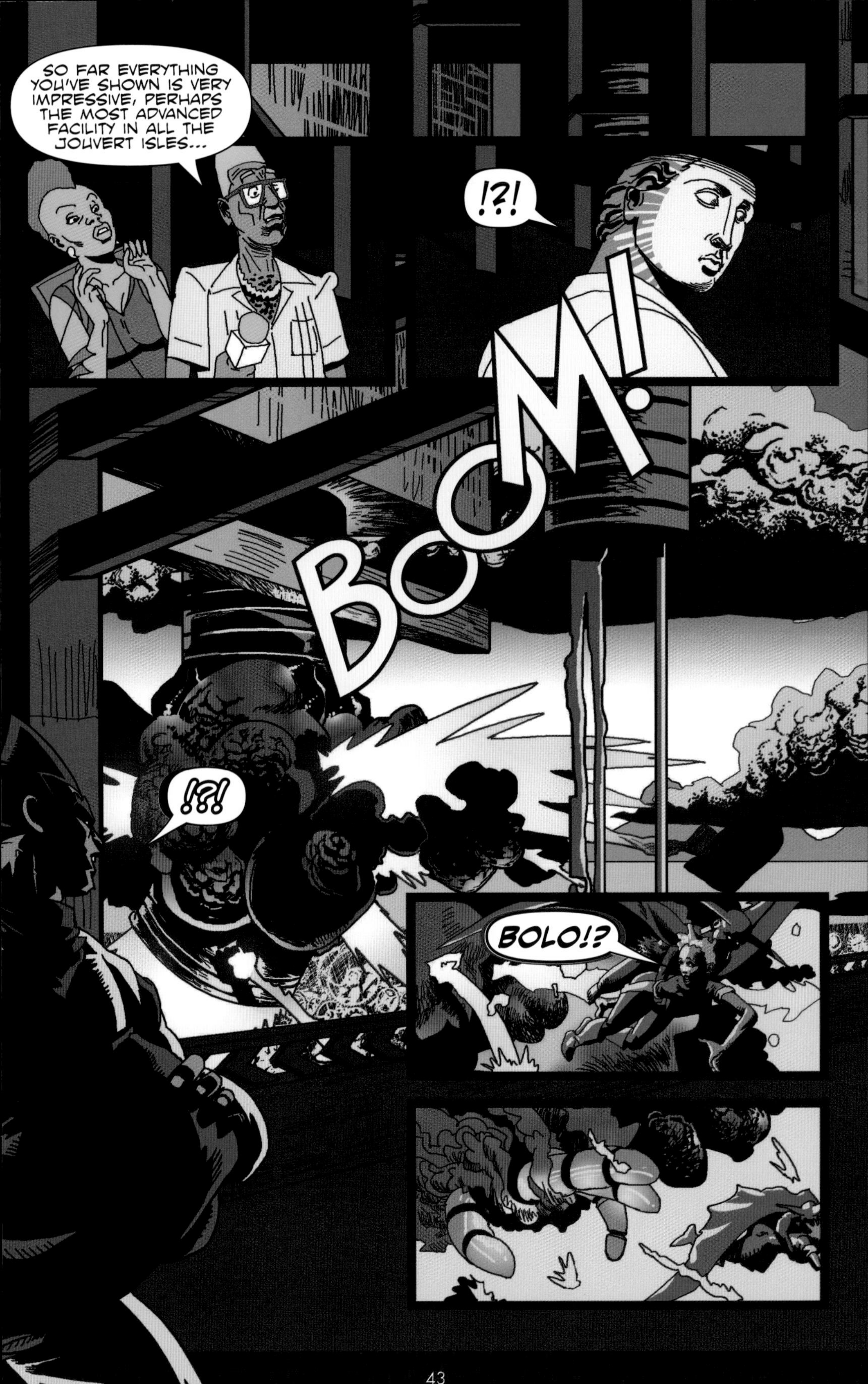
SO FAR EVERYTHING YOU'VE SHOWN IS VERY IMPRESSIVE, PERHAPS THE MOST ADVANCED FACILITY IN ALL THE JOUVERT ISLES...
!?!
BOOM!
!?!
BOLO!?

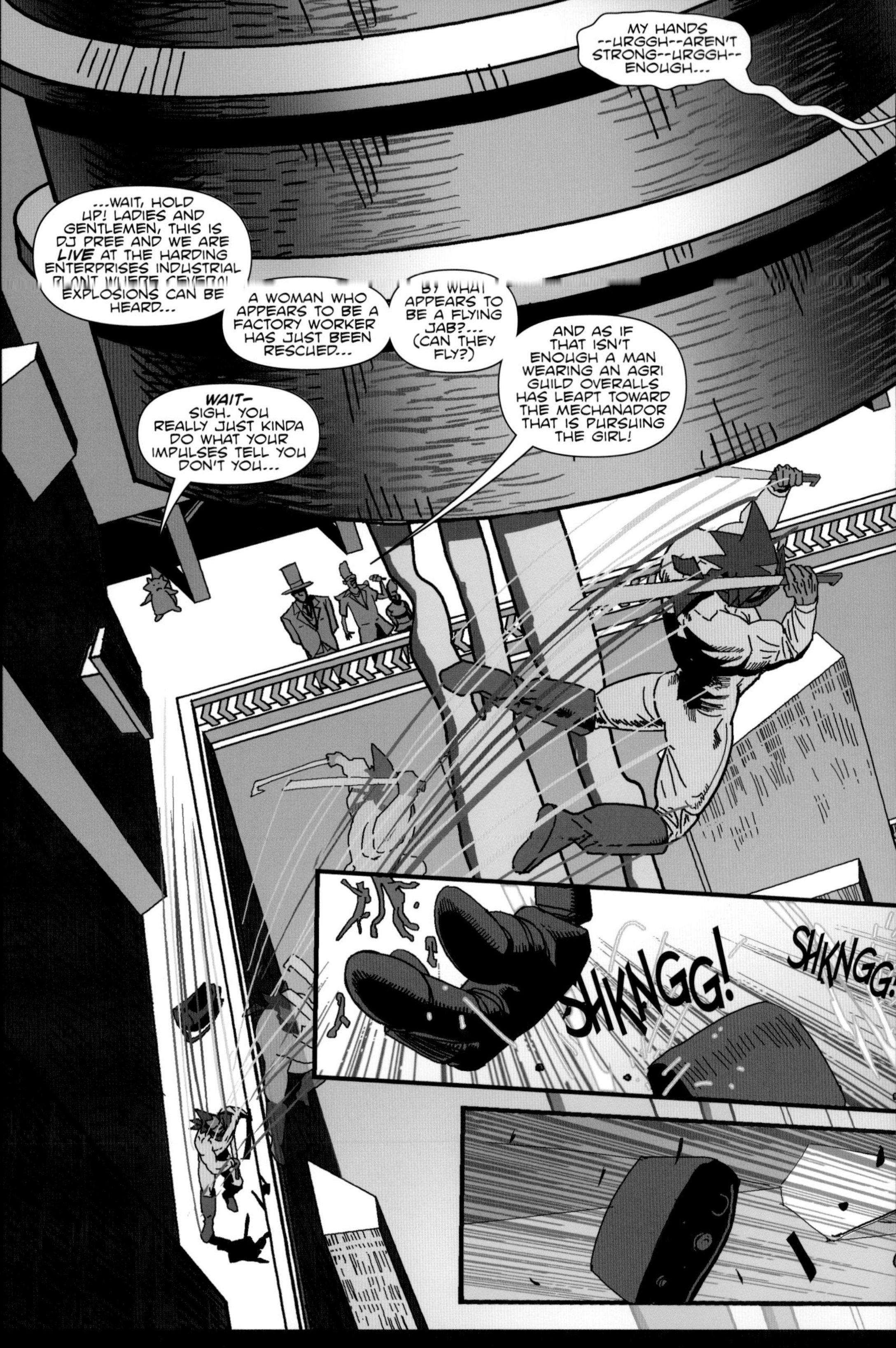
MY HANDS --URGGH--AREN'T STRONG--URGGH-- ENOUGH...
...WAIT, HOLD UP! LADIES AND GENTLEMEN, THIS IS DJ PREE AND WE ARE *LIVE* AT THE HARDING ENTERPRISES INDUSTRIAL PLANT WHERE SEVERAL EXPLOSIONS CAN BE HEARD...
A WOMAN WHO APPEARS TO BE A FACTORY WORKER HAS JUST BEEN RESCUED...
BY WHAT APPEARS TO BE A FLYING JAB?... (CAN THEY FLY?)
AND AS IF THAT ISN'T ENOUGH A MAN WEARING AN AGRI GUILD OVERALLS HAS LEAPT TOWARD THE MECHANADOR THAT IS PURSUING THE GIRL!
WAIT- SIGH. YOU REALLY JUST KINDA DO WHAT YOUR IMPULSES TELL YOU DON'T YOU...
SHKNGG!
SHKNGG!

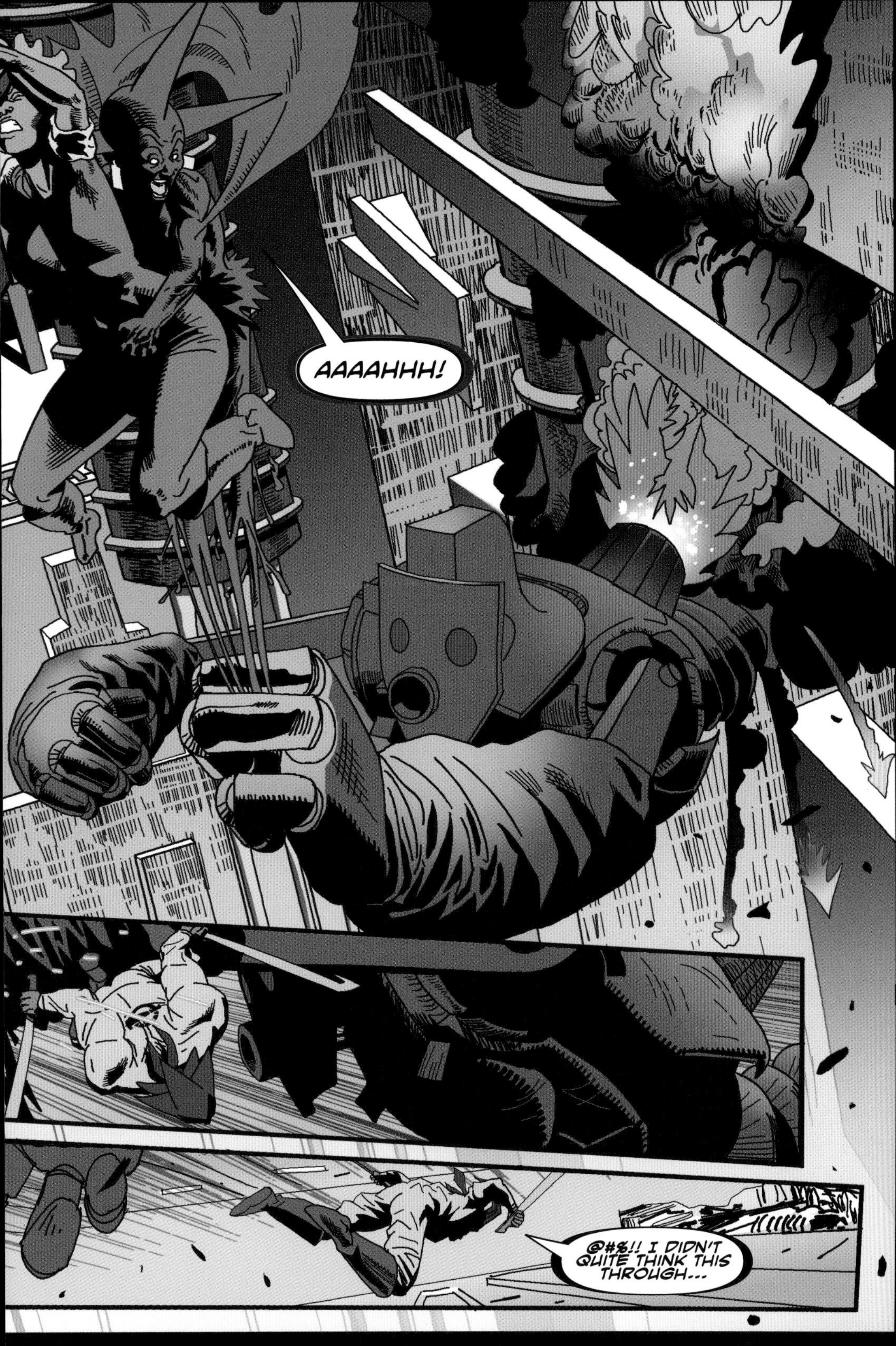
AAAAHHH!
@#$!! I DIDN'T QUITE THINK THIS THROUGH...

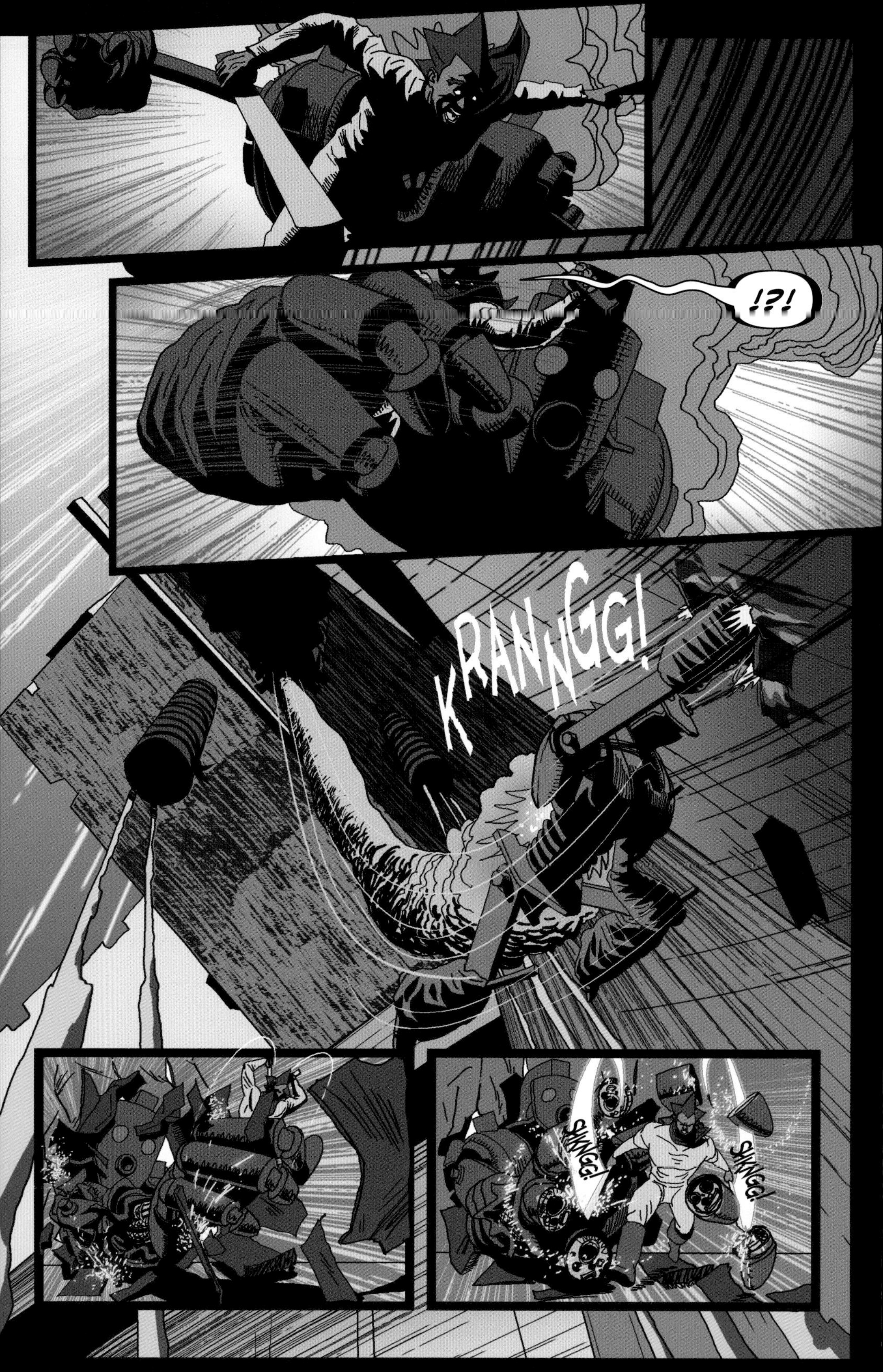
!?!
KRANNGG!
SHKNGG!
SHKNGG!

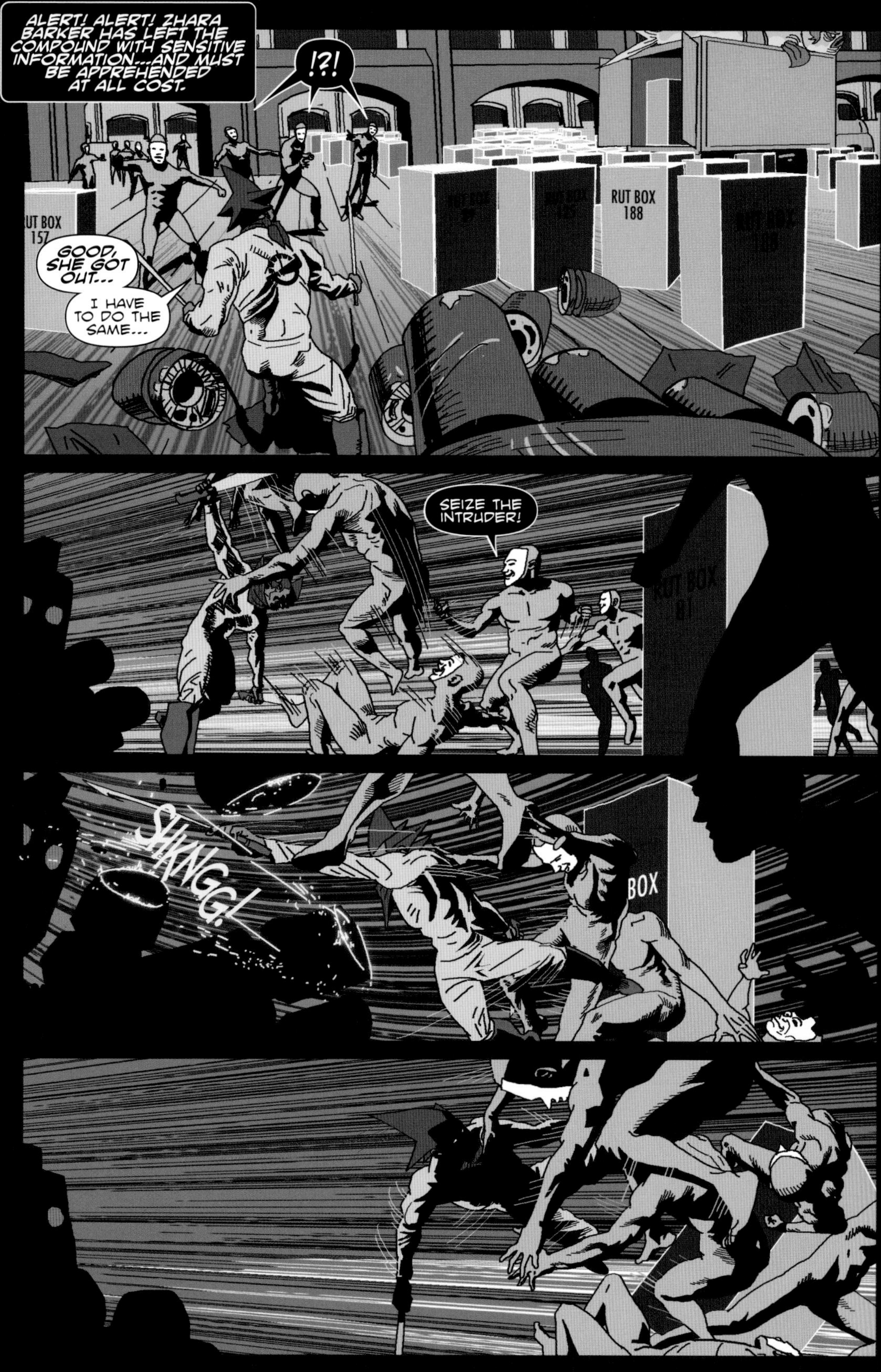
ALERT! ALERT! ZHARA BARKER HAS LEFT THE COMPOUND WITH SENSITIVE INFORMATION...AND MUST BE APPREHENDED AT ALL COST.
!?!
RUT BOX 157
RUT BOX 188
GOOD, SHE GOT OUT...
I HAVE TO DO THE SAME...
SEIZE THE INTRUDER!
RUT BOX 81
SHKNGG!
BOX

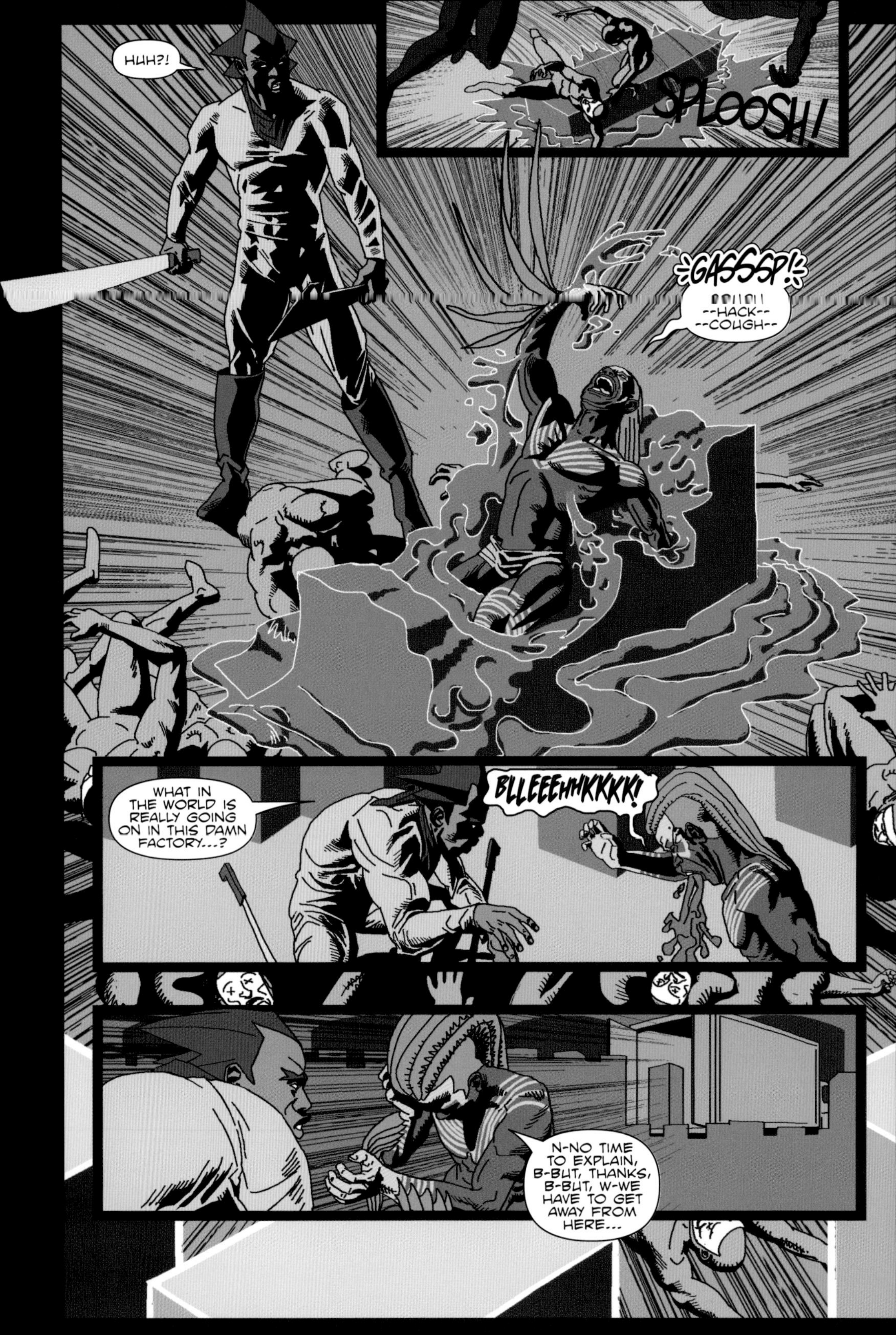
HUH?!
SPLOOSH!
GASSSP!
--HACK--
--COUGH--
WHAT IN THE WORLD IS REALLY GOING ON IN THIS DAMN FACTORY...?
BLLEEEHHKKKK!
N-NO TIME TO EXPLAIN, B-BUT, THANKS, B-BUT, W-WE HAVE TO GET AWAY FROM HERE...

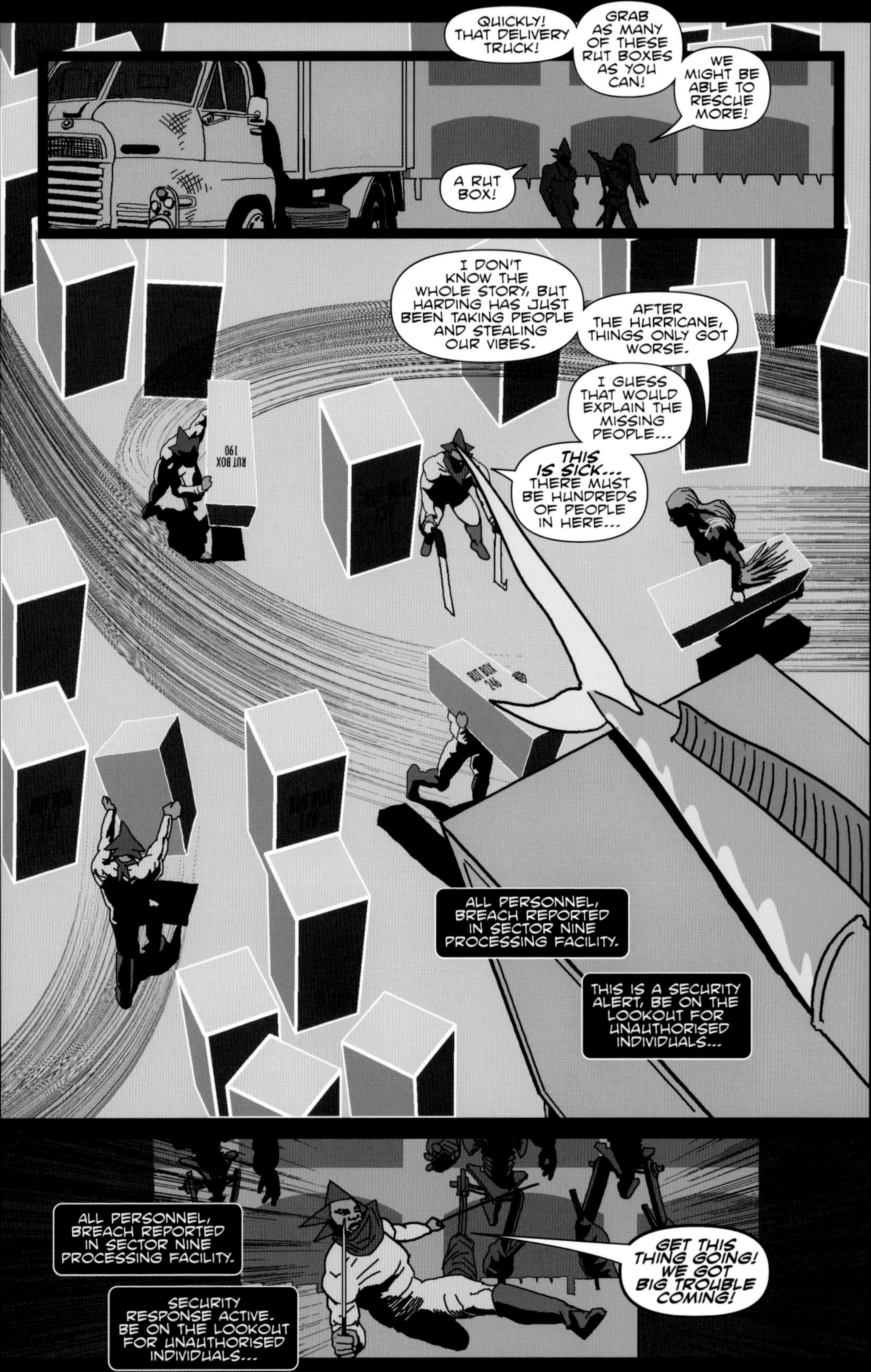
QUICKLY! THAT DELIVERY TRUCK!
GRAB AS MANY OF THESE RUT BOXES AS YOU CAN!
WE MIGHT BE ABLE TO RESCUE MORE!
A RUT BOX!
I DON'T KNOW THE WHOLE STORY, BUT HARDING HAS JUST BEEN TAKING PEOPLE AND STEALING OUR VIBES.
AFTER THE HURRICANE, THINGS ONLY GOT WORSE.
I GUESS THAT WOULD EXPLAIN THE MISSING PEOPLE...
RUT BOX 190
THIS IS SICK... THERE MUST BE HUNDREDS OF PEOPLE IN HERE...
RUT BOX 246
ALL PERSONNEL, BREACH REPORTED IN SECTOR NINE PROCESSING FACILITY.
THIS IS A SECURITY ALERT, BE ON THE LOOKOUT FOR UNAUTHORISED INDIVIDUALS...
ALL PERSONNEL, BREACH REPORTED IN SECTOR NINE PROCESSING FACILITY.
SECURITY RESPONSE ACTIVE. BE ON THE LOOKOUT FOR UNAUTHORISED INDIVIDUALS...
GET THIS THING GOING! WE GOT BIG TROUBLE COMING!

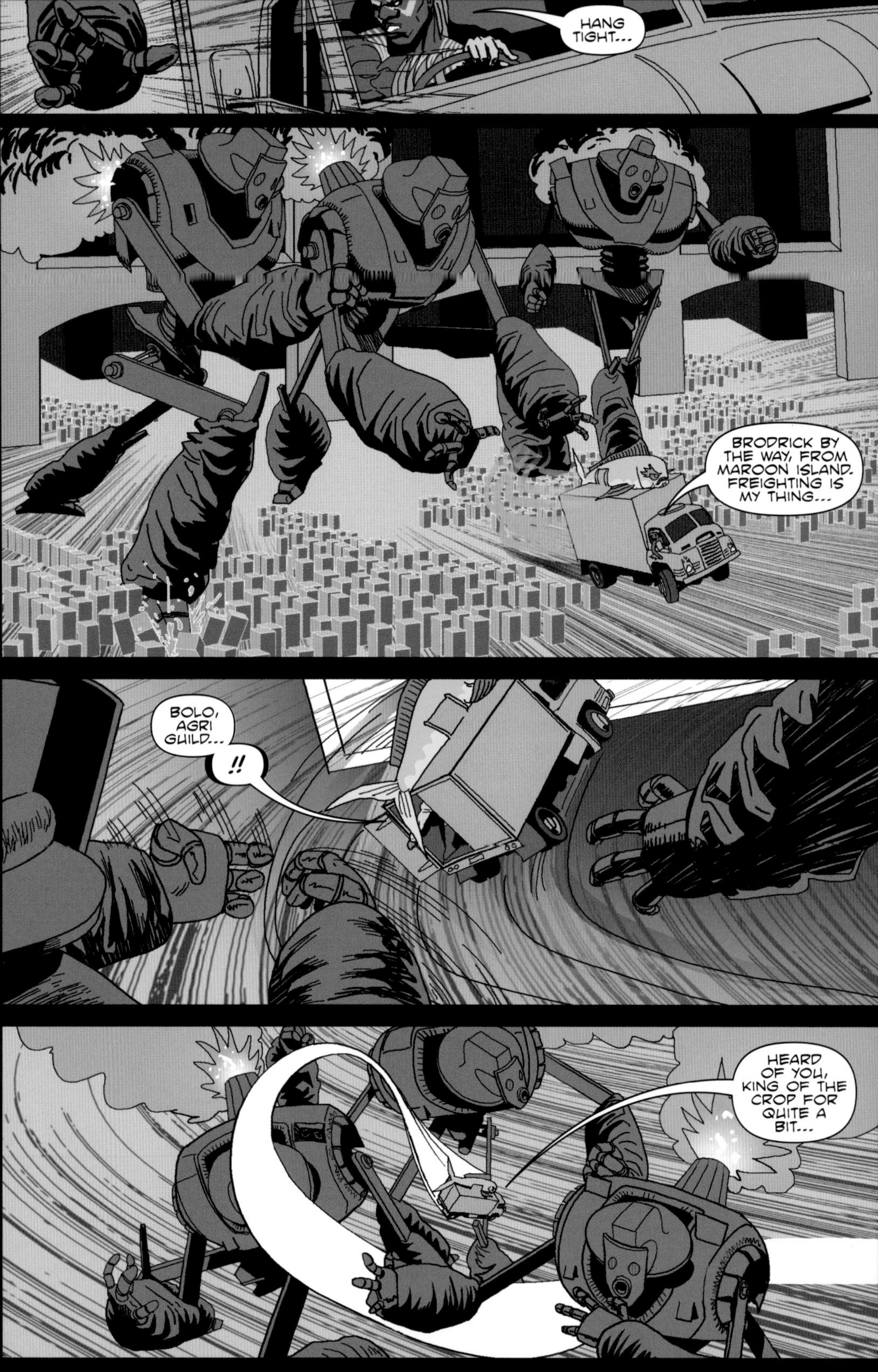
HANG TIGHT...
BRODRICK BY THE WAY, FROM MAROON ISLAND. FREIGHTING IS MY THING...
BOLO, AGRI GUILD...
!!
HEARD OF YOU, KING OF THE CROP FOR QUITE A BIT...

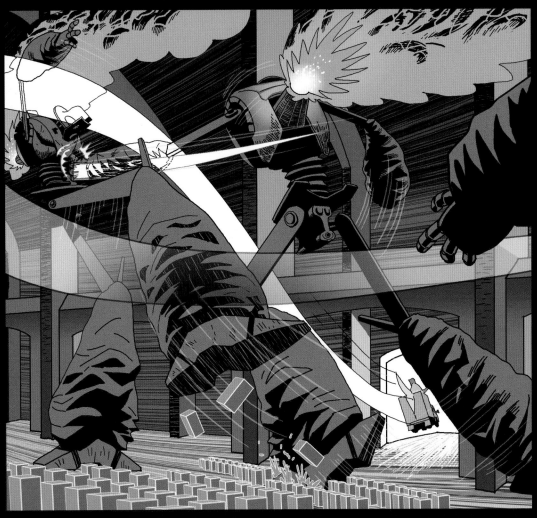

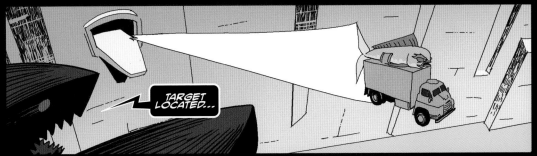

TARGET LOCATED...

OH #%!#%!

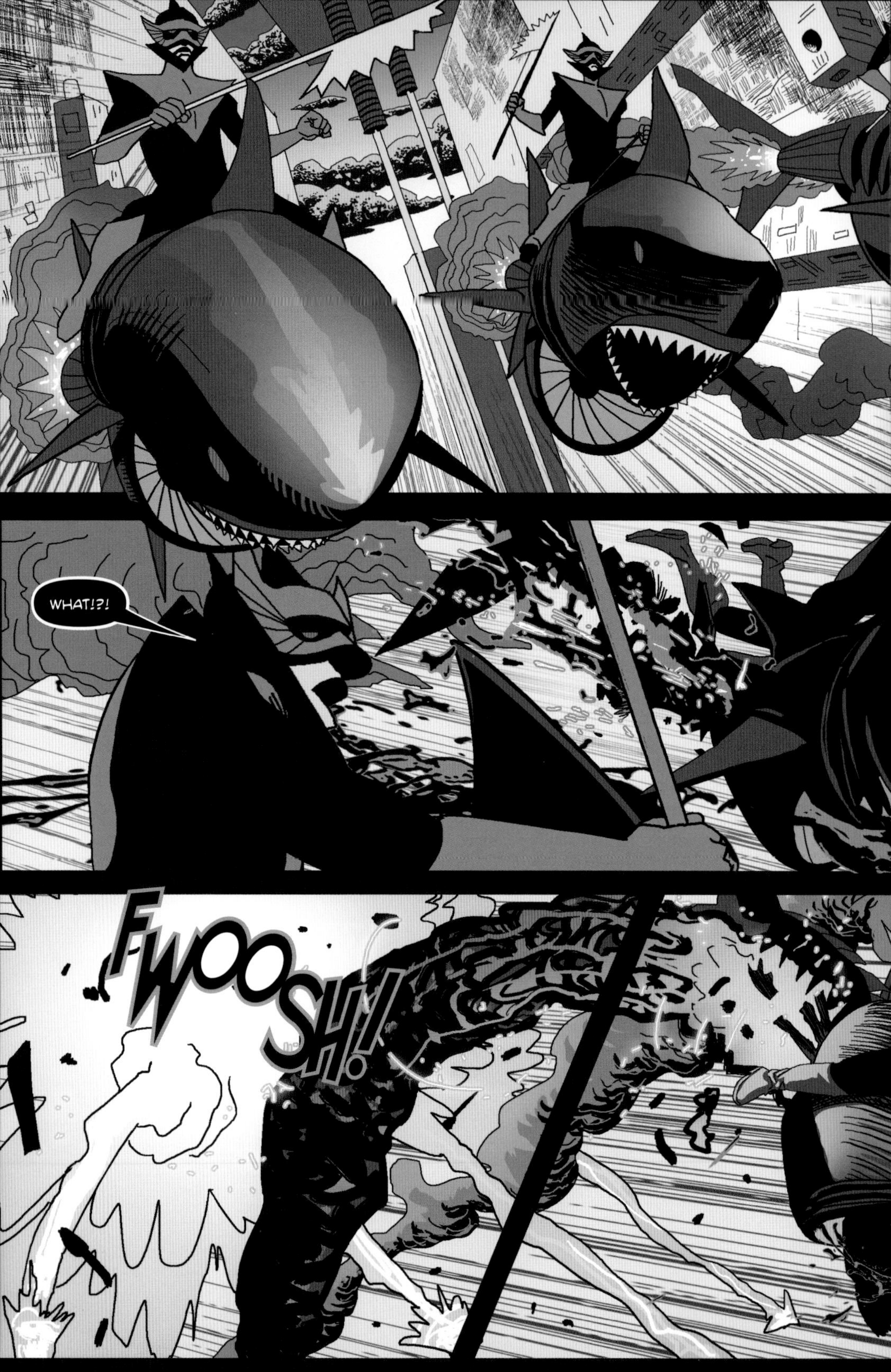
WHAT!?!
FWOOSH!!

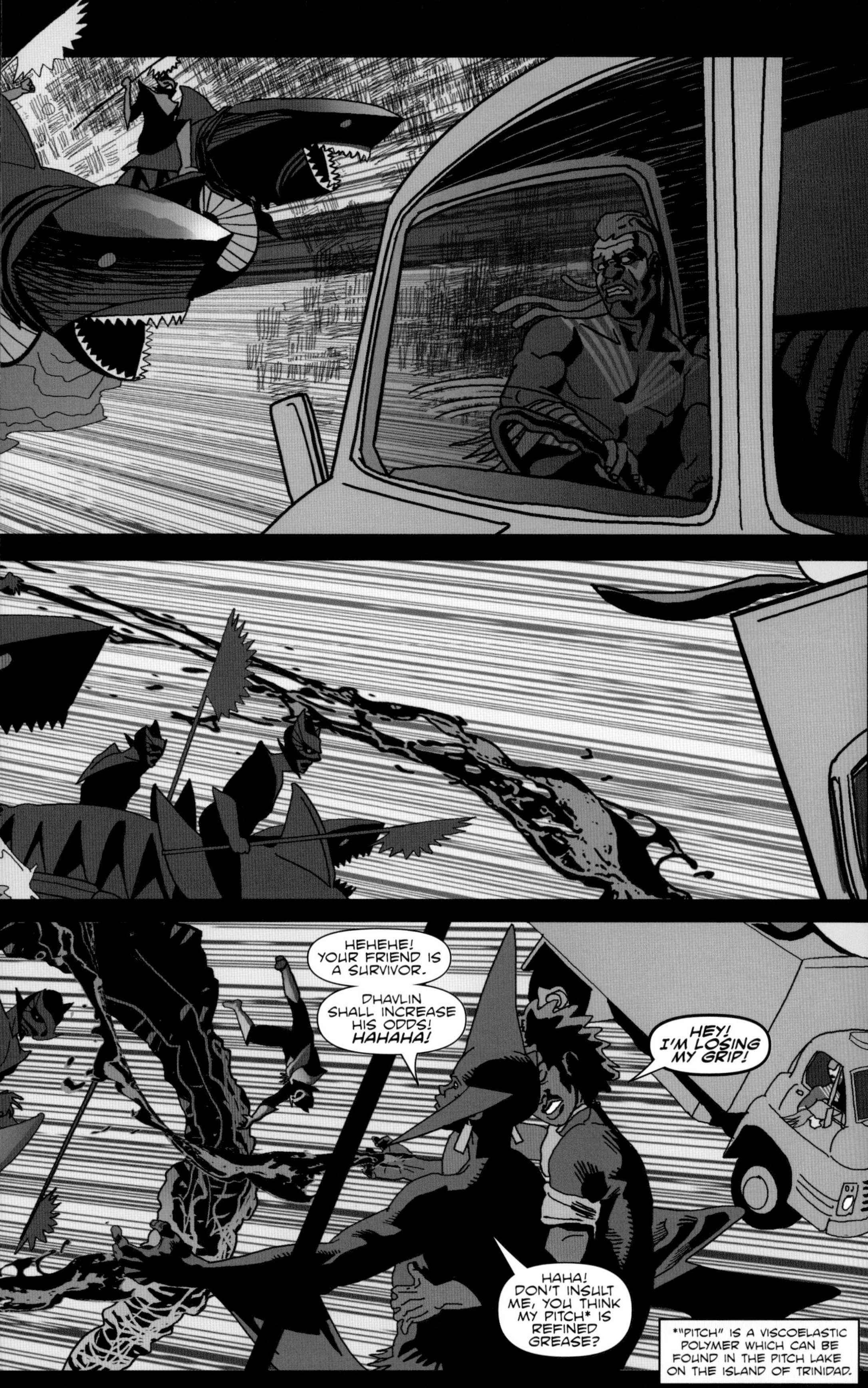
HEHEHE! YOUR FRIEND IS A SURVIVOR.
DHAVLIN SHALL INCREASE HIS ODDS! HAHAHA!
HEY! I'M LOSING MY GRIP!
HAHA! DON'T INSULT ME, YOU THINK MY PITCH* IS REFINED GREASE?
*"PITCH" IS A VISCOELASTIC POLYMER WHICH CAN BE FOUND IN THE PITCH LAKE ON THE ISLAND OF TRINIDAD.

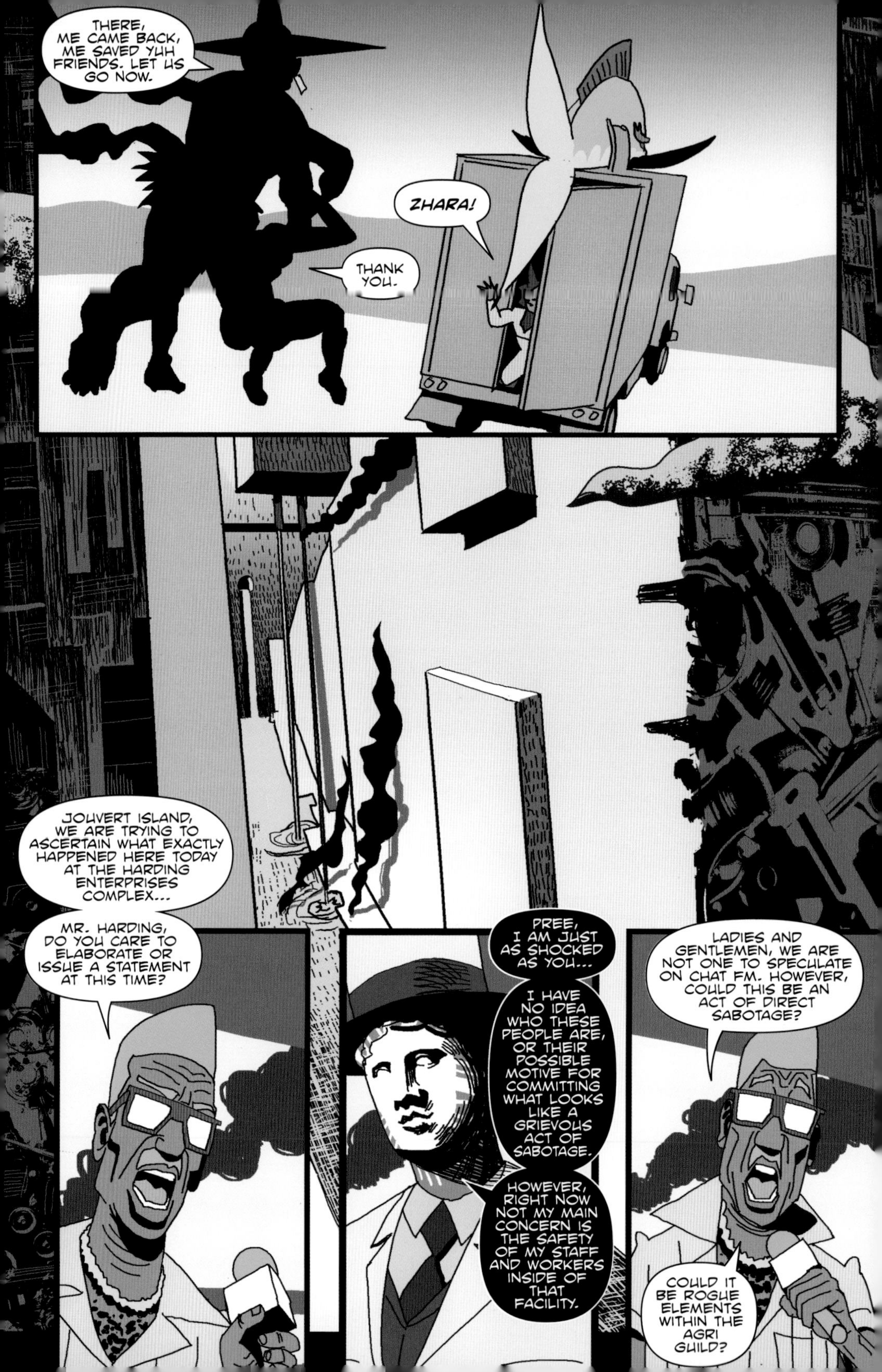
THERE, ME CAME BACK, ME SAVED YUH FRIENDS. LET US GO NOW.
ZHARA!
THANK YOU.
JOUVERT ISLAND, WE ARE TRYING TO ASCERTAIN WHAT EXACTLY HAPPENED HERE TODAY AT THE HARDING ENTERPRISES COMPLEX...
MR. HARDING, DO YOU CARE TO ELABORATE OR ISSUE A STATEMENT AT THIS TIME?
PREE, I AM JUST AS SHOCKED AS YOU...
I HAVE NO IDEA WHO THESE PEOPLE ARE, OR THEIR POSSIBLE MOTIVE FOR COMMITTING WHAT LOOKS LIKE A GRIEVOUS ACT OF SABOTAGE.
HOWEVER, RIGHT NOW NOT MY MAIN CONCERN IS THE SAFETY OF MY STAFF AND WORKERS INSIDE OF THAT FACILITY.
LADIES AND GENTLEMEN, WE ARE NOT ONE TO SPECULATE ON CHAT FM. HOWEVER, COULD THIS BE AN ACT OF DIRECT SABOTAGE?
COULD IT BE ROGUE ELEMENTS WITHIN THE AGRI GUILD?

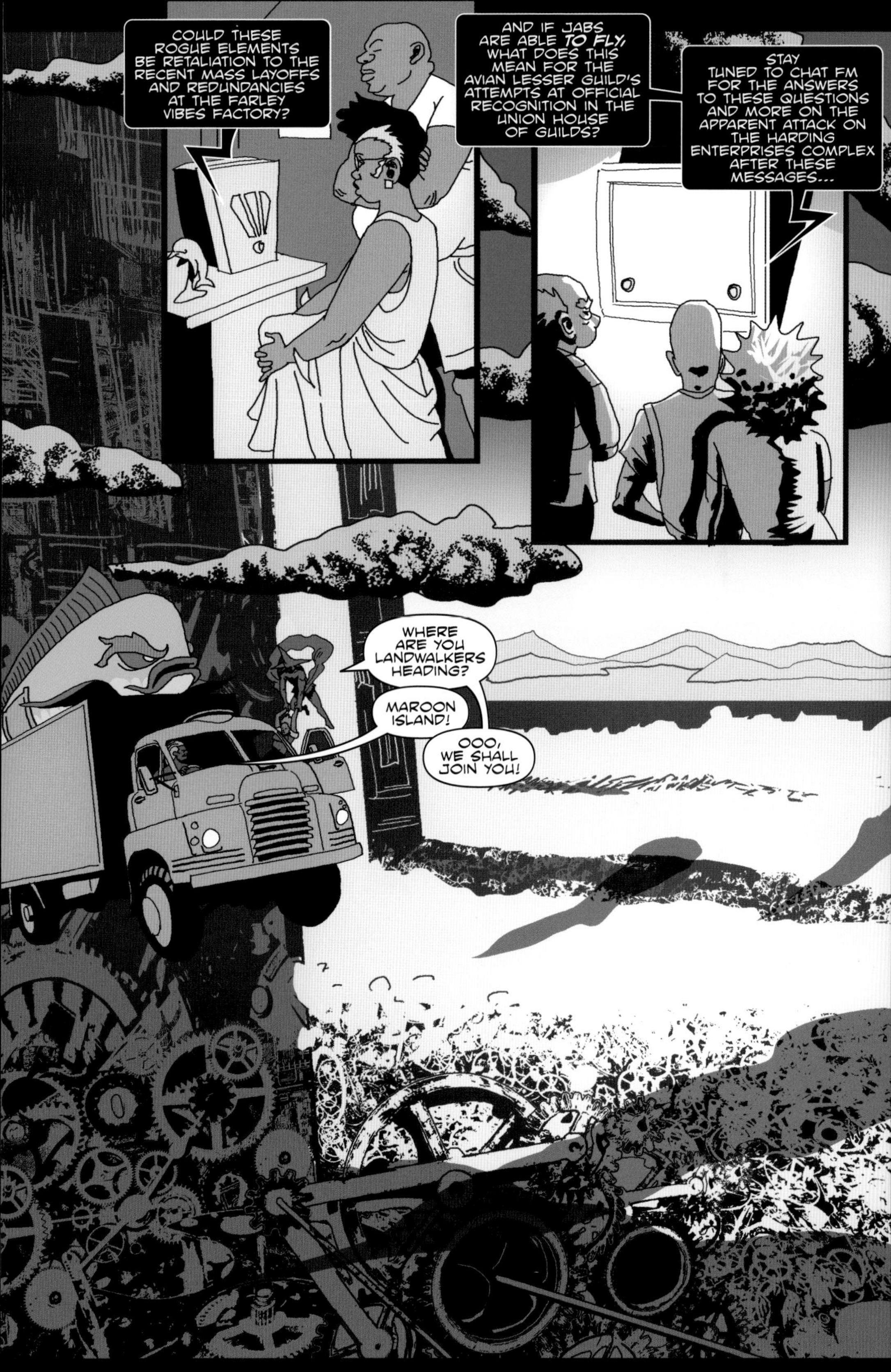
COULD THESE ROGUE ELEMENTS BE RETALIATION TO THE RECENT MASS LAYOFFS AND REDUNDANCIES AT THE FARLEY VIBES FACTORY?
AND IF JABS ARE ABLE TO FLY, WHAT DOES THIS MEAN FOR THE AVIAN LESSER GUILD'S ATTEMPTS AT OFFICIAL RECOGNITION IN THE UNION HOUSE OF GUILDS?
STAY TUNED TO CHAT FM FOR THE ANSWERS TO THESE QUESTIONS AND MORE ON THE APPARENT ATTACK ON THE HARDING ENTERPRISES COMPLEX AFTER THESE MESSAGES...
WHERE ARE YOU LANDWALKERS HEADING?
MAROON ISLAND!
OOO, WE SHALL JOIN YOU!

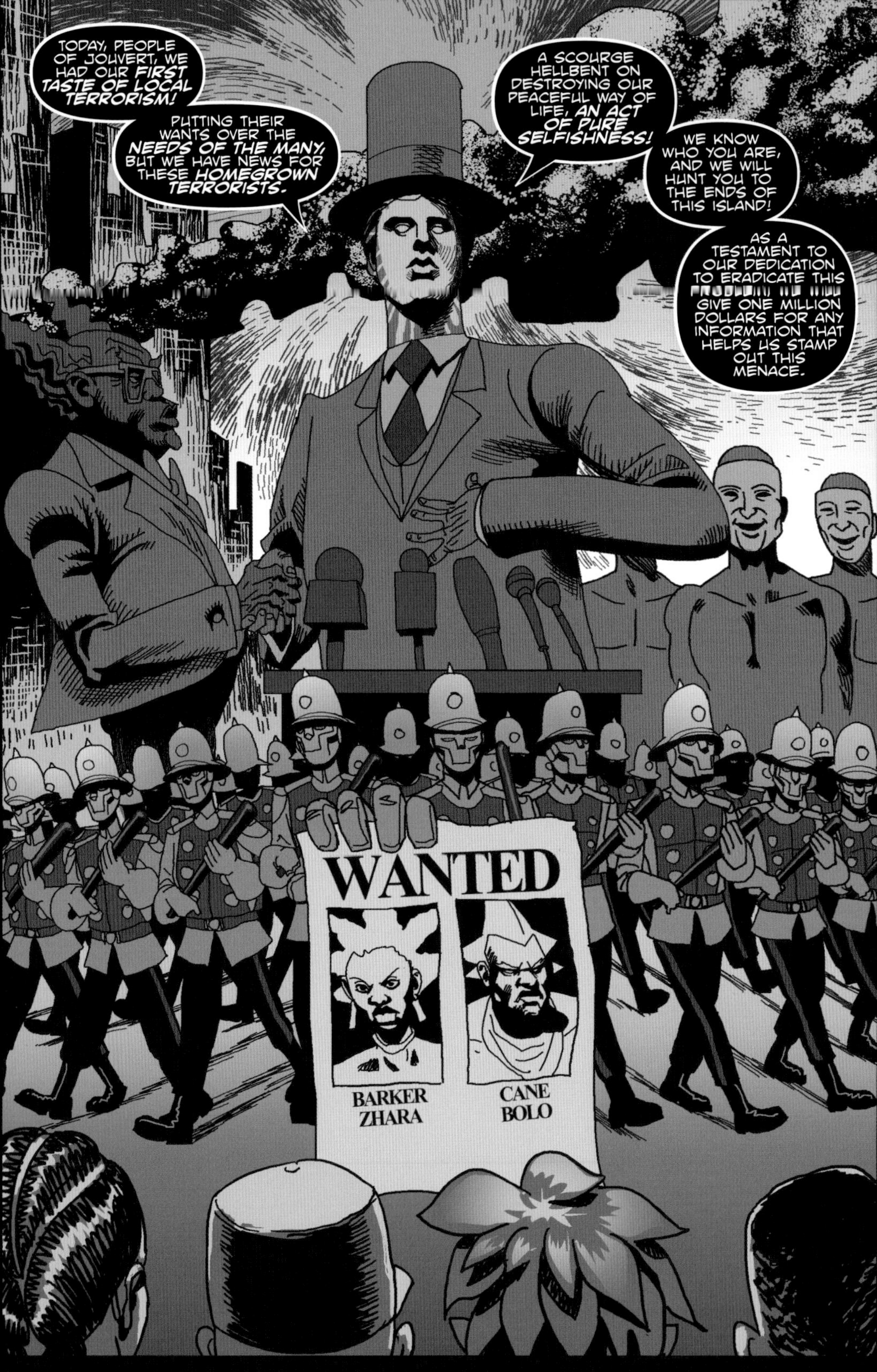
TODAY, PEOPLE OF JOUVERT, WE HAD OUR FIRST TASTE OF LOCAL TERRORISM!
PUTTING THEIR WANTS OVER THE NEEDS OF THE MANY, BUT WE HAVE NEWS FOR THESE HOMEGROWN TERRORISTS.
A SCOURGE HELLBENT ON DESTROYING OUR PEACEFUL WAY OF LIFE, AN ACT OF PURE SELFISHNESS!
WE KNOW WHO YOU ARE, AND WE WILL HUNT YOU TO THE ENDS OF THIS ISLAND!
AS A TESTAMENT TO OUR DEDICATION TO ERADICATE THIS
GIVE ONE MILLION DOLLARS FOR ANY INFORMATION THAT HELPS US STAMP OUT THIS MENACE.
WANTED
BARKER ZHARA
CANE BOLO

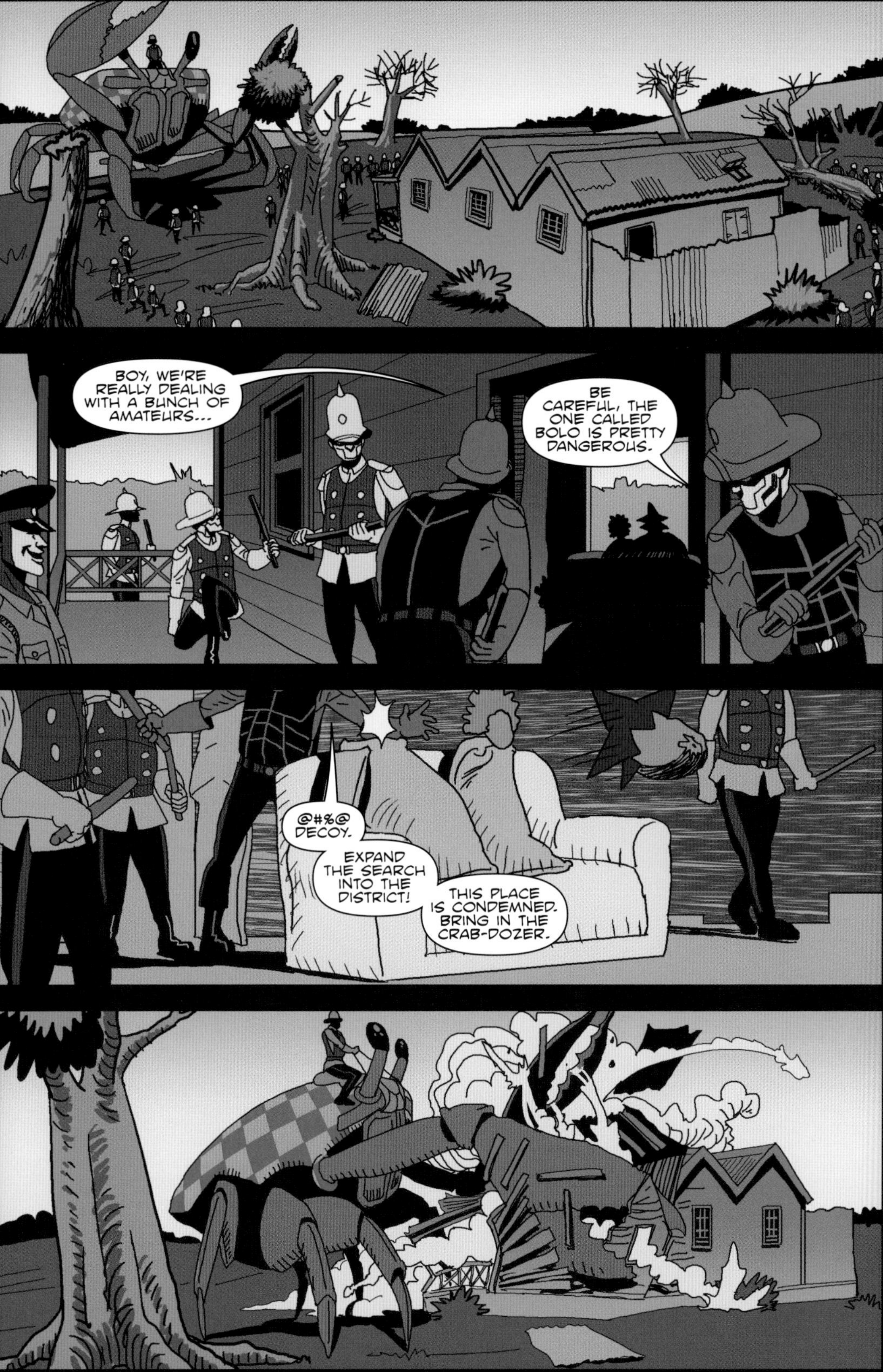
BOY, WE'RE REALLY DEALING WITH A BUNCH OF AMATEURS...
BE CAREFUL, THE ONE CALLED BOLO IS PRETTY DANGEROUS.
@#%@ DECOY.
EXPAND THE SEARCH INTO THE DISTRICT!
THIS PLACE IS CONDEMNED. BRING IN THE CRAB-DOZER.

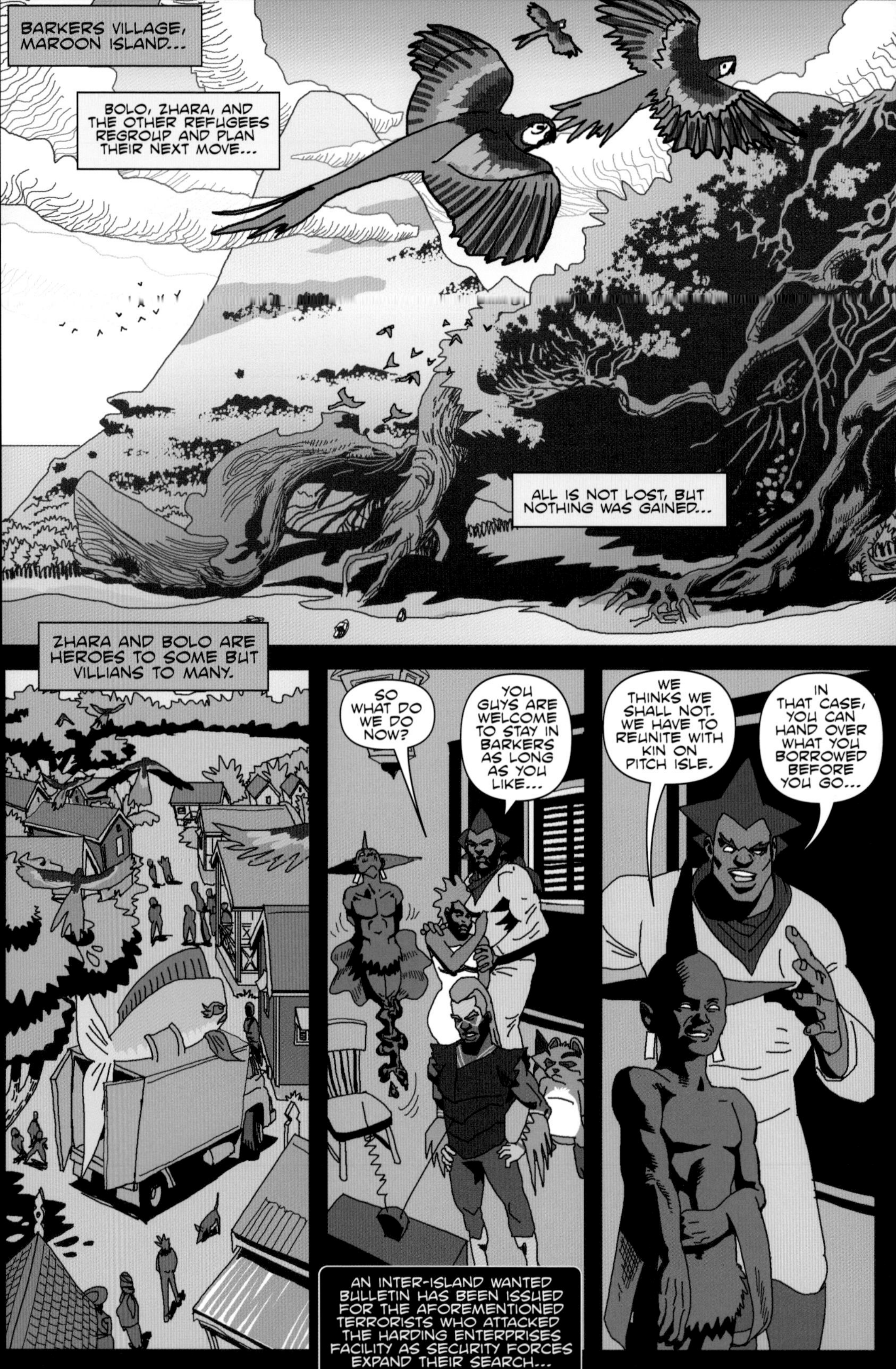
BARKERS VILLAGE, MAROON ISLAND...
BOLO, ZHARA, AND THE OTHER REFUGEES REGROUP AND PLAN THEIR NEXT MOVE...
ALL IS NOT LOST, BUT NOTHING WAS GAINED...
ZHARA AND BOLO ARE HEROES TO SOME BUT VILLIANS TO MANY.
SO WHAT DO WE DO NOW?
YOU GUYS ARE WELCOME TO STAY IN BARKERS AS LONG AS YOU LIKE...
AN INTER-ISLAND WANTED BULLETIN HAS BEEN ISSUED FOR THE AFOREMENTIONED TERRORISTS WHO ATTACKED THE HARDING ENTERPRISES FACILITY AS SECURITY FORCES EXPAND THEIR SEARCH...
WE THINKS WE SHALL NOT. WE HAVE TO REUNITE WITH KIN ON PITCH ISLE.
IN THAT CASE, YOU CAN HAND OVER WHAT YOU BORROWED BEFORE YOU GO...

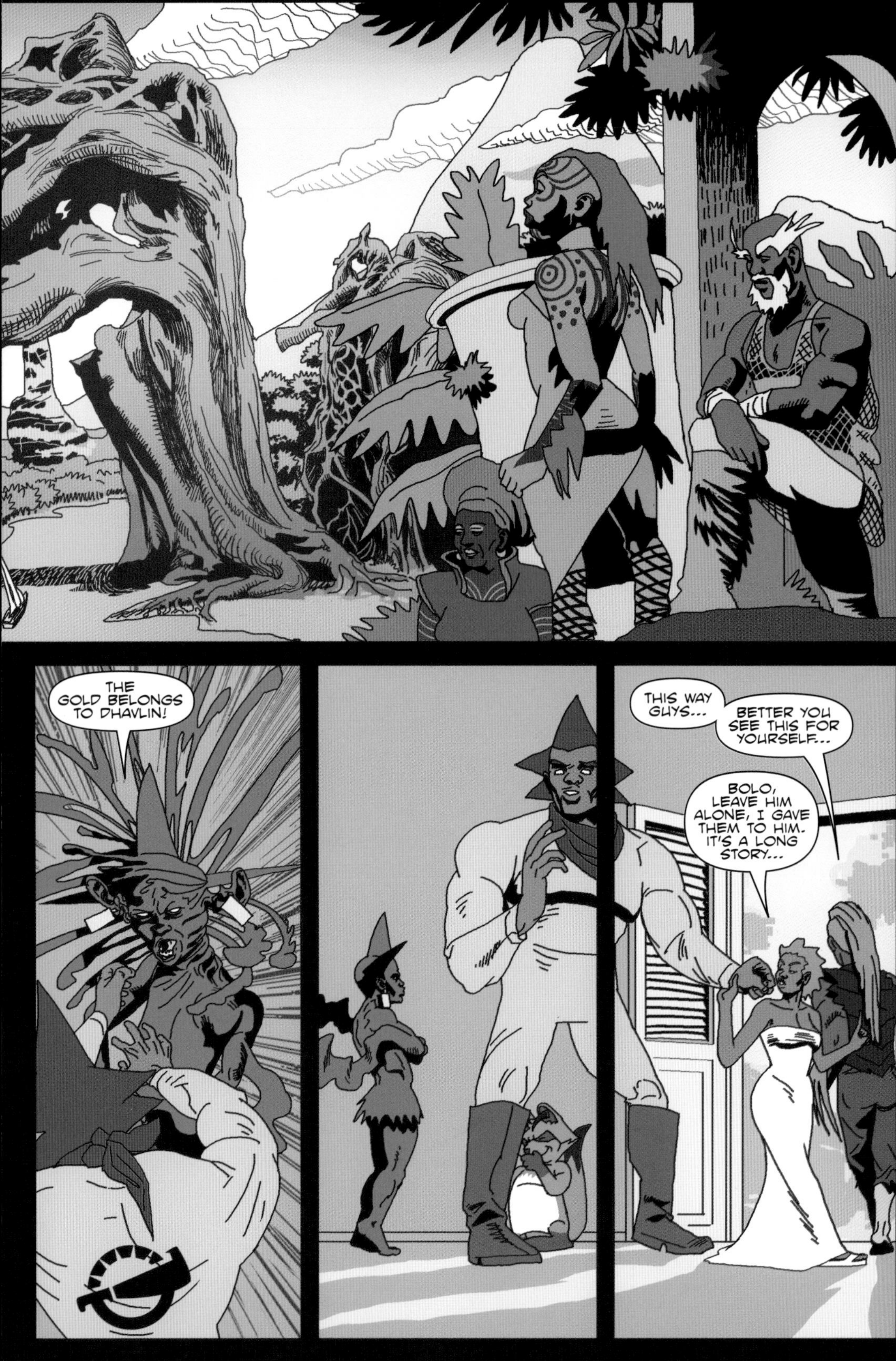
THE GOLD BELONGS TO DHAVLIN!
THIS WAY GUYS...
BETTER YOU SEE THIS FOR YOURSELF...
BOLO, LEAVE HIM ALONE, I GAVE THEM TO HIM. IT'S A LONG STORY...

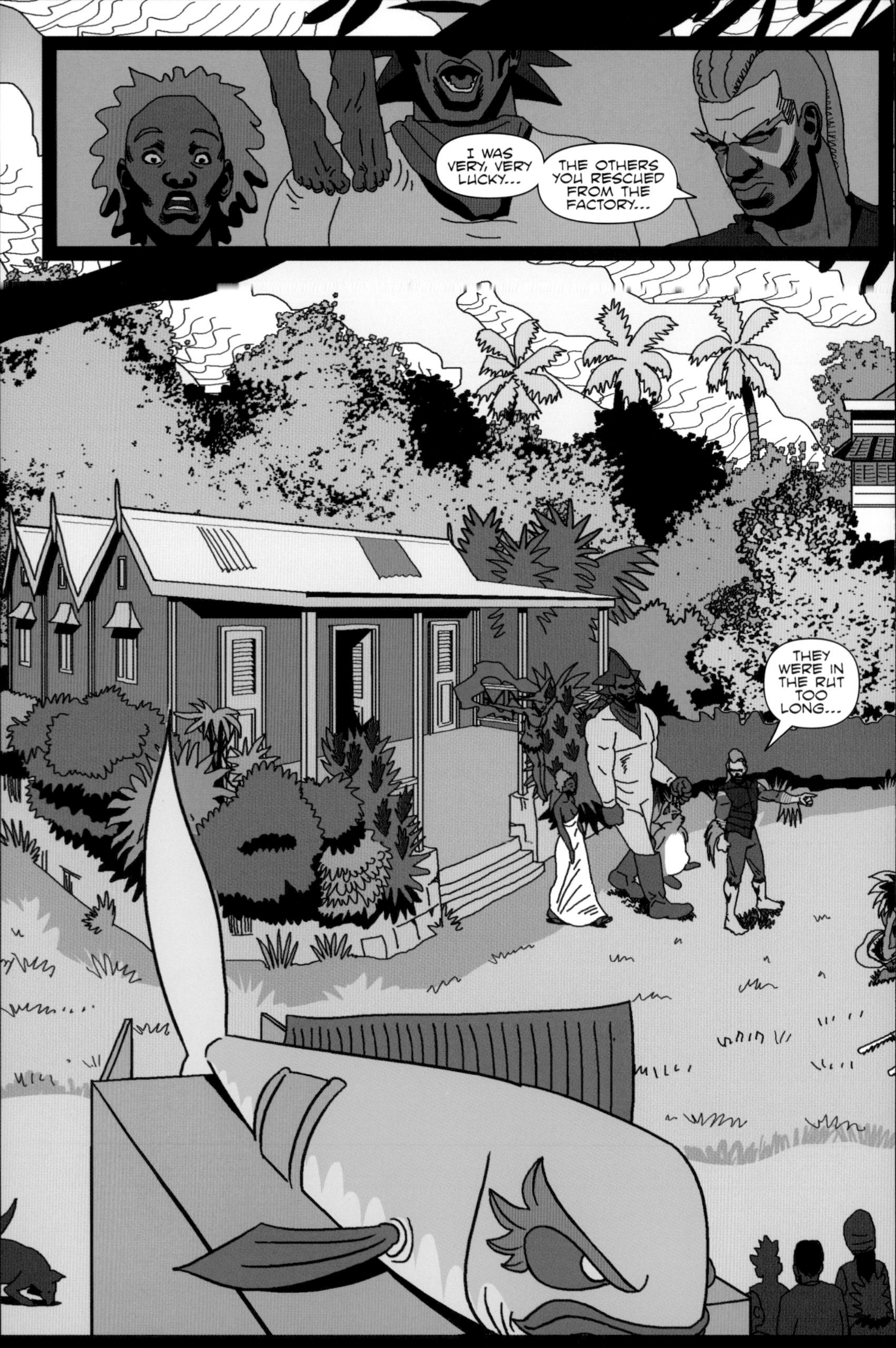
I WAS VERY, VERY LUCKY...
THE OTHERS YOU RESCUED FROM THE FACTORY...
THEY WERE IN THE RUT TOO LONG...

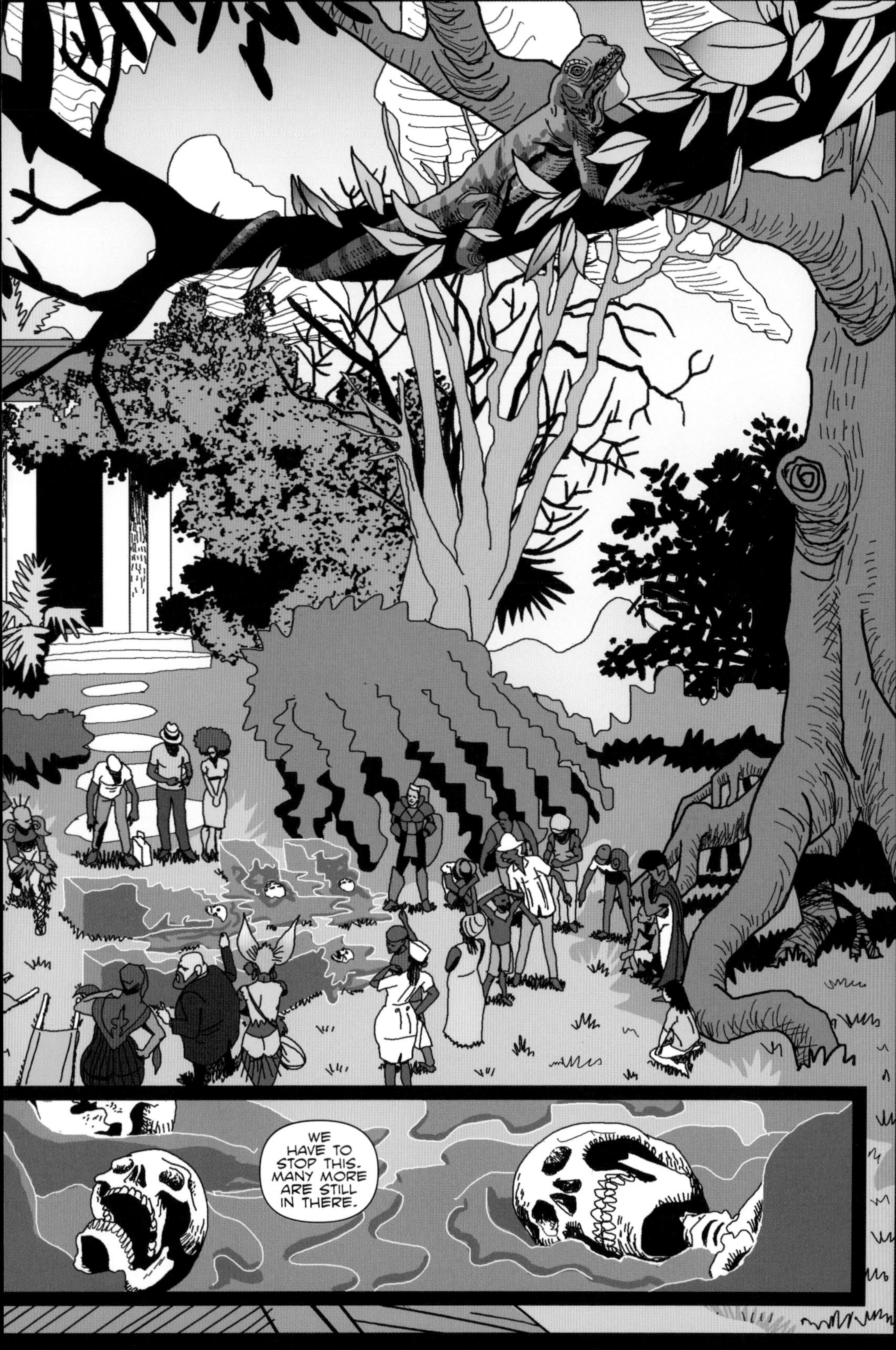
WE HAVE TO STOP THIS. MANY MORE ARE STILL IN THERE.

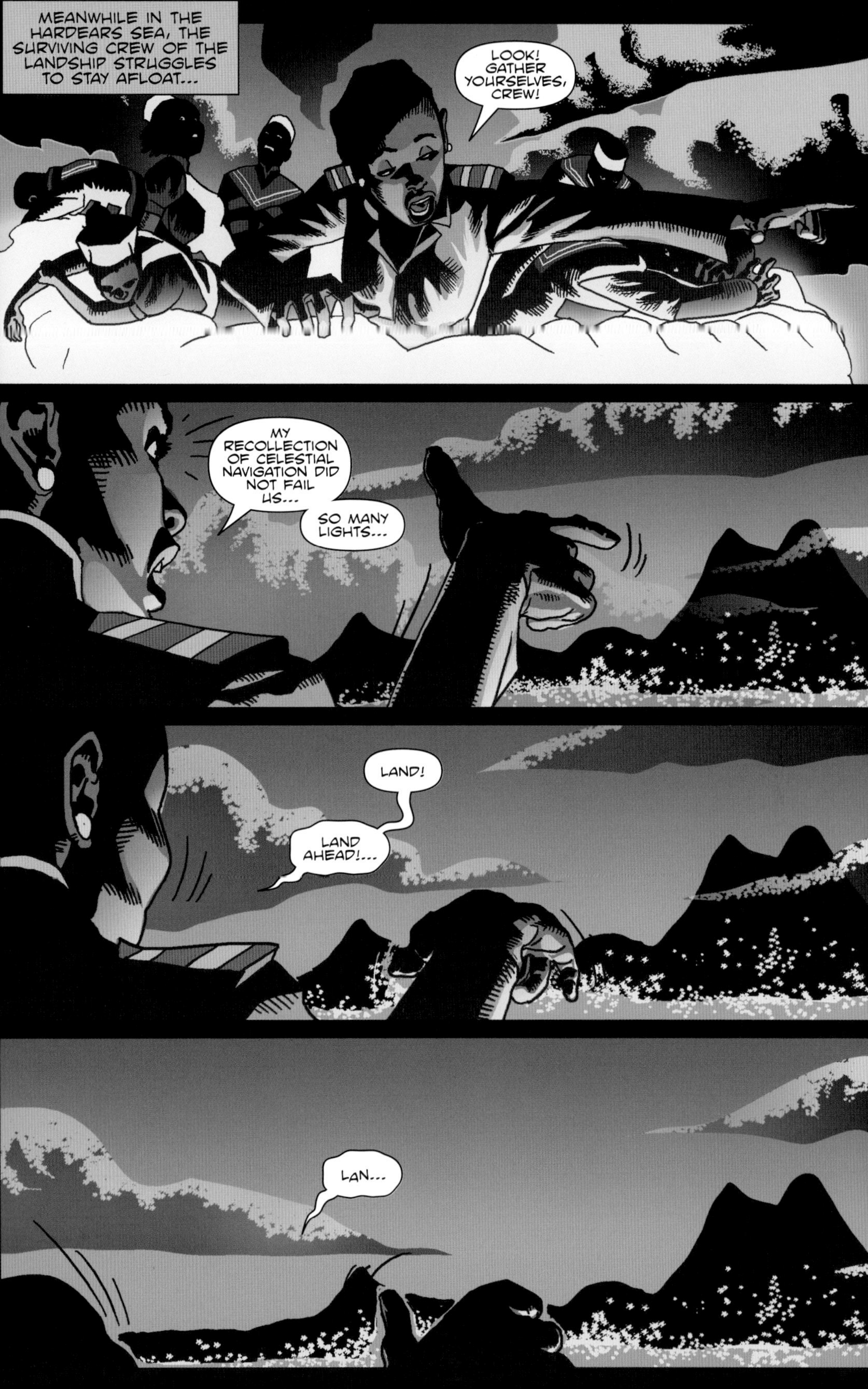
MEANWHILE IN THE HARDEARS SEA, THE SURVIVING CREW OF THE LANDSHIP STRUGGLES TO STAY AFLOAT...
LOOK! GATHER YOURSELVES, CREW!
MY RECOLLECTION OF CELESTIAL NAVIGATION DID NOT FAIL US...
SO MANY LIGHTS...
LAND!
LAND AHEAD!...
LAN...

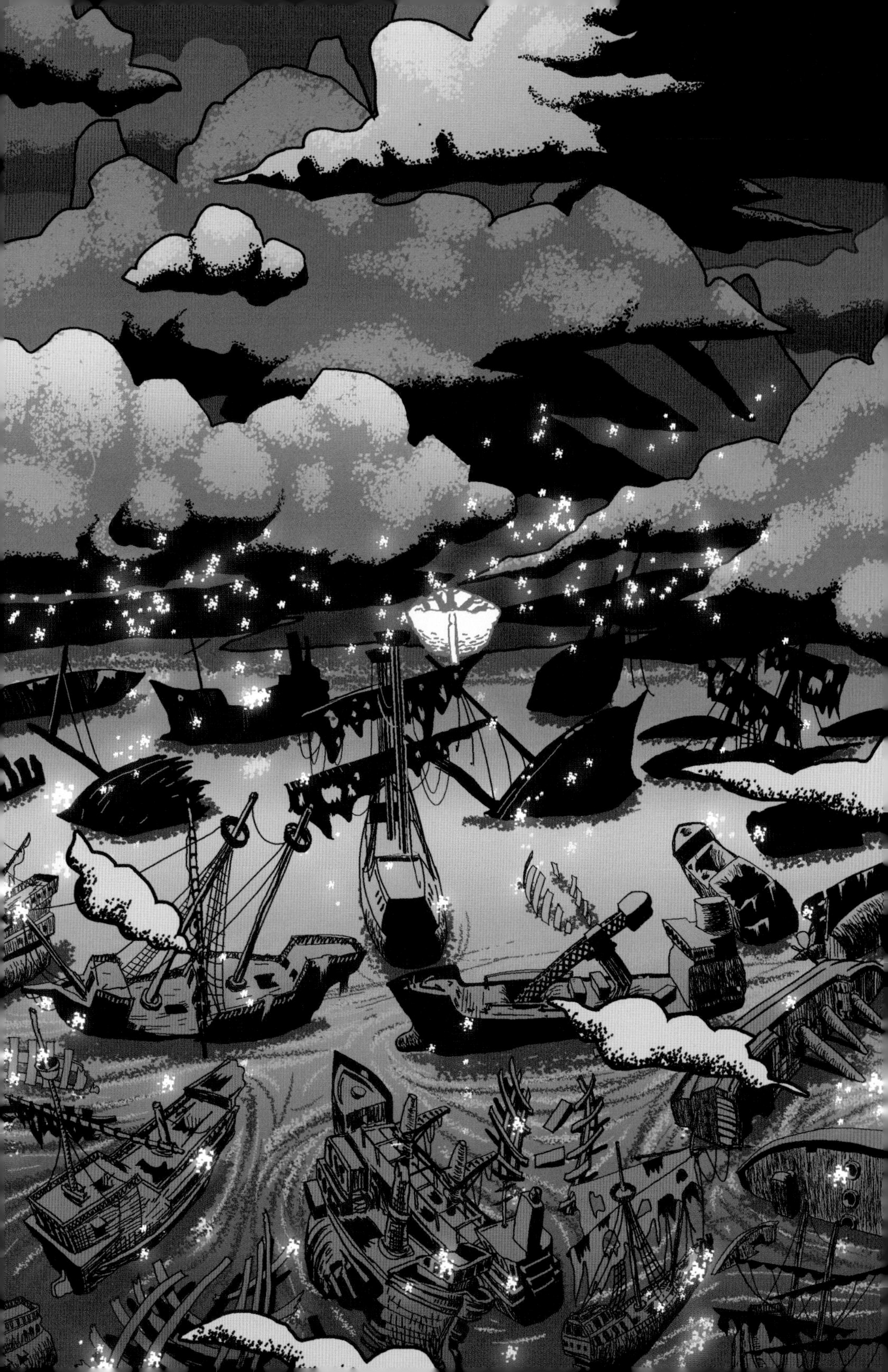

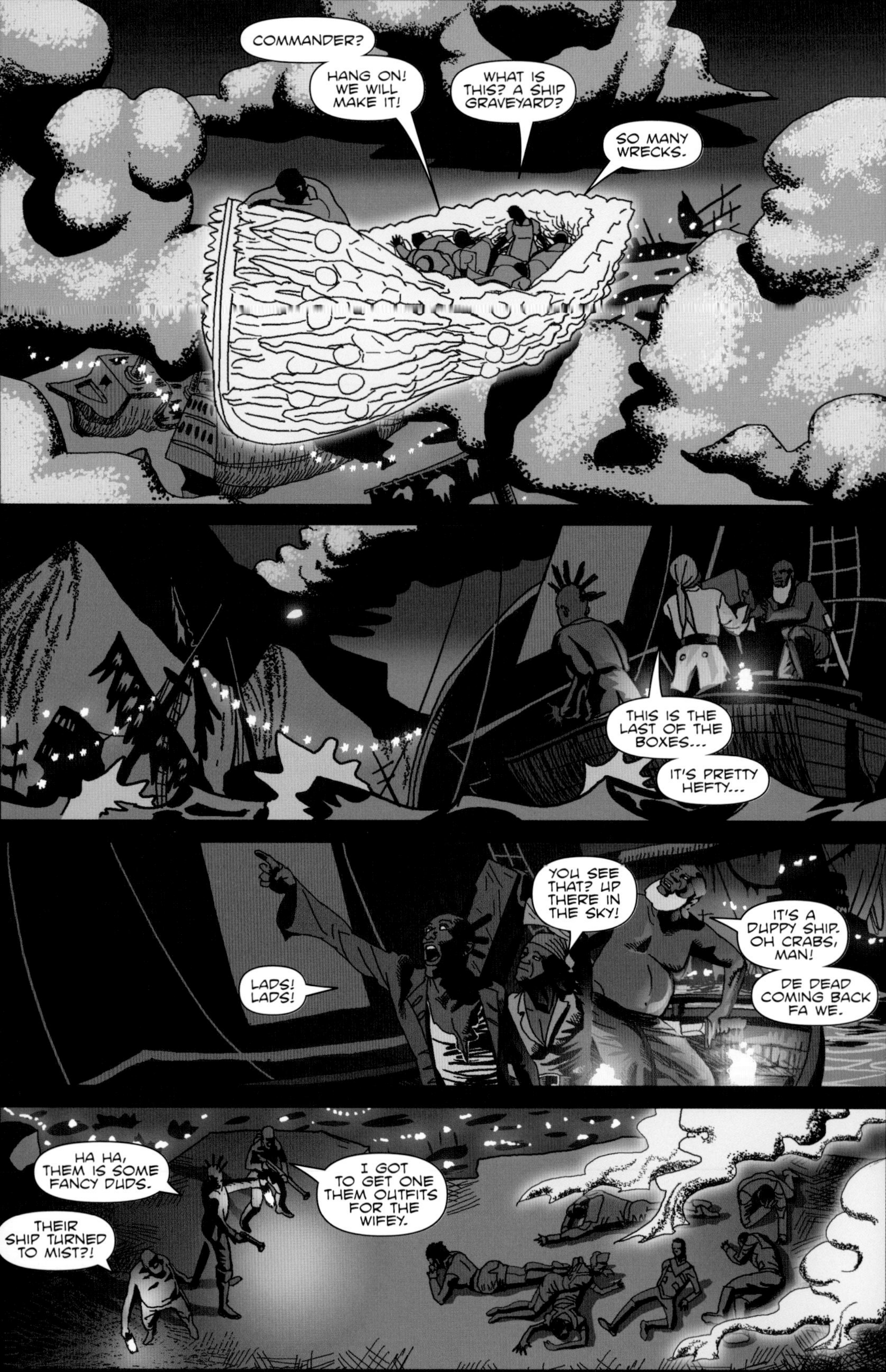
COMMANDER?
HANG ON! WE WILL MAKE IT!
WHAT IS THIS? A SHIP GRAVEYARD?
SO MANY WRECKS.
THIS IS THE LAST OF THE BOXES...
IT'S PRETTY HEFTY...
LADS! LADS!
YOU SEE THAT? UP THERE IN THE SKY!
IT'S A DUPPY SHIP. OH CRABS, MAN!
DE DEAD COMING BACK FA WE.
HA HA, THEM IS SOME FANCY DUDS.
THEIR SHIP TURNED TO MIST?!
I GOT TO GET ONE THEM OUTFITS FOR THE WIFEY.

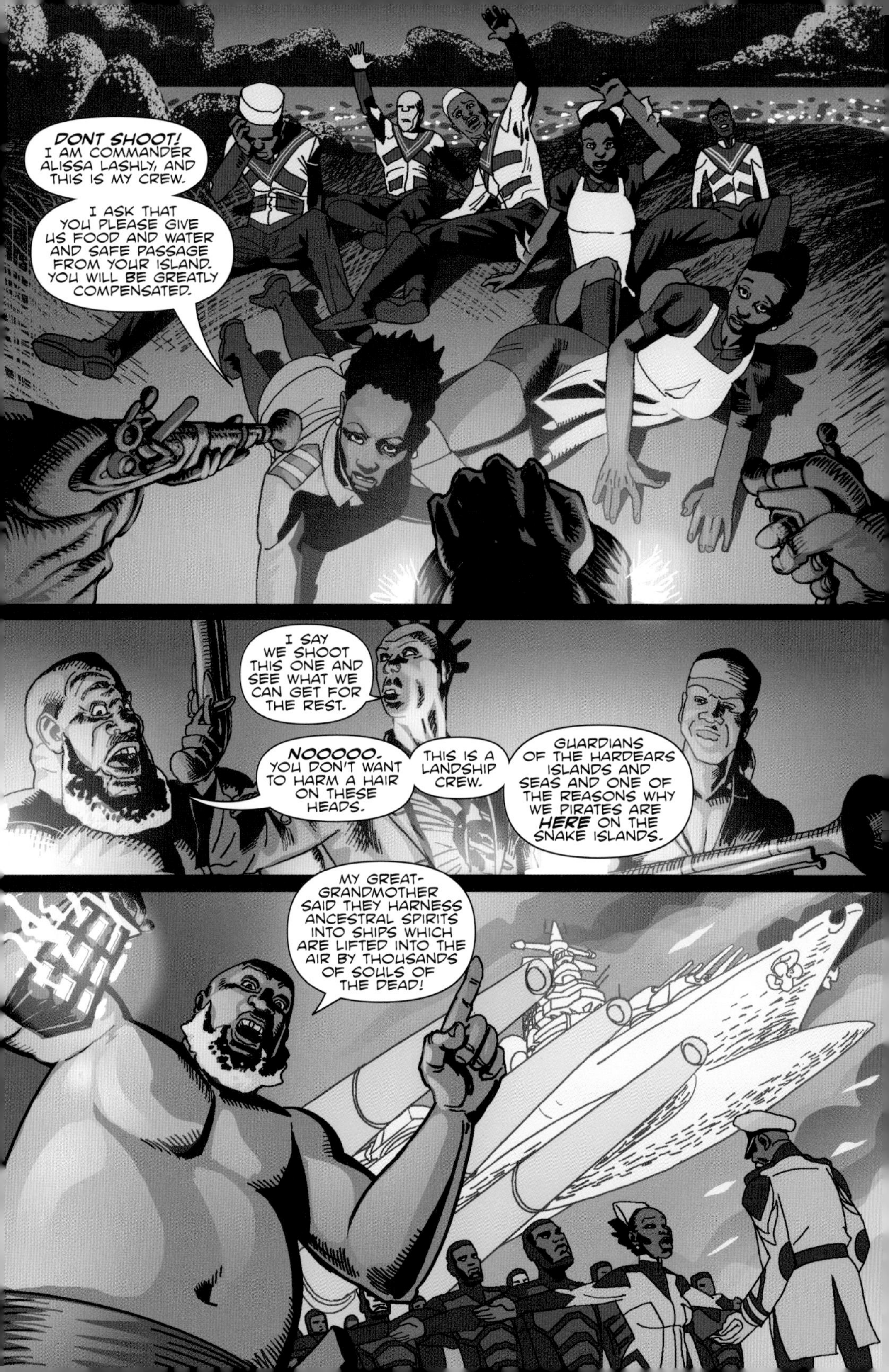
DONT SHOOT! I AM COMMANDER ALISSA LASHLY, AND THIS IS MY CREW.
I ASK THAT YOU PLEASE GIVE US FOOD AND WATER AND SAFE PASSAGE FROM YOUR ISLAND. YOU WILL BE GREATLY COMPENSATED.
I SAY WE SHOOT THIS ONE AND SEE WHAT WE CAN GET FOR THE REST.
NOOOOO. YOU DON'T WANT TO HARM A HAIR ON THESE HEADS.
THIS IS A LANDSHIP CREW.
GUARDIANS OF THE HARDEARS ISLANDS AND SEAS AND ONE OF THE REASONS WHY WE PIRATES ARE HERE ON THE SNAKE ISLANDS.
MY GREAT-GRANDMOTHER SAID THEY HARNESS ANCESTRAL SPIRITS INTO SHIPS WHICH ARE LIFTED INTO THE AIR BY THOUSANDS OF SOULS OF THE DEAD!

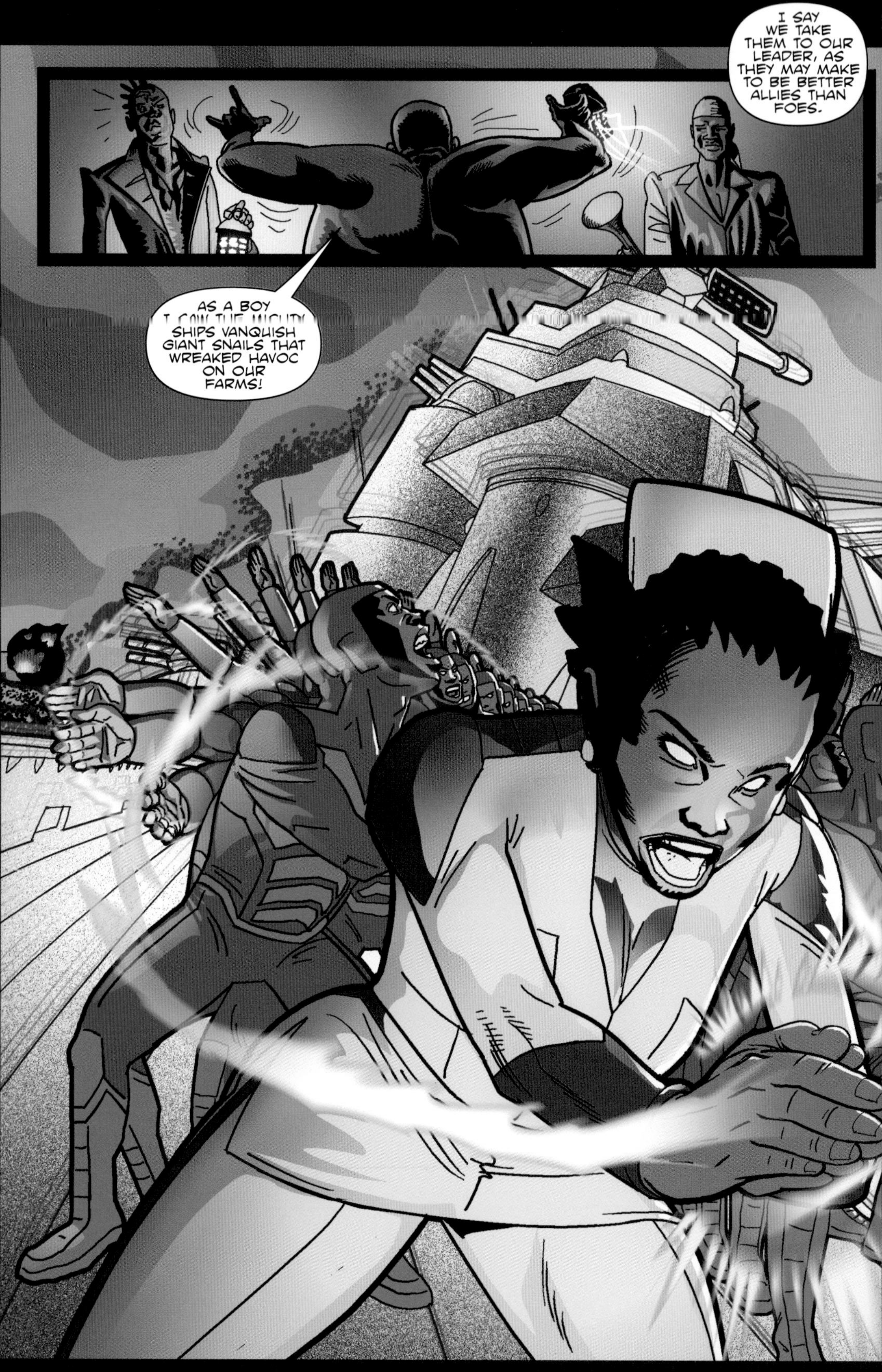
I SAY WE TAKE THEM TO OUR LEADER, AS THEY MAY MAKE TO BE BETTER ALLIES THAN FOES.
AS A BOY
SHIPS VANQUISH GIANT SNAILS THAT WREAKED HAVOC ON OUR FARMS!

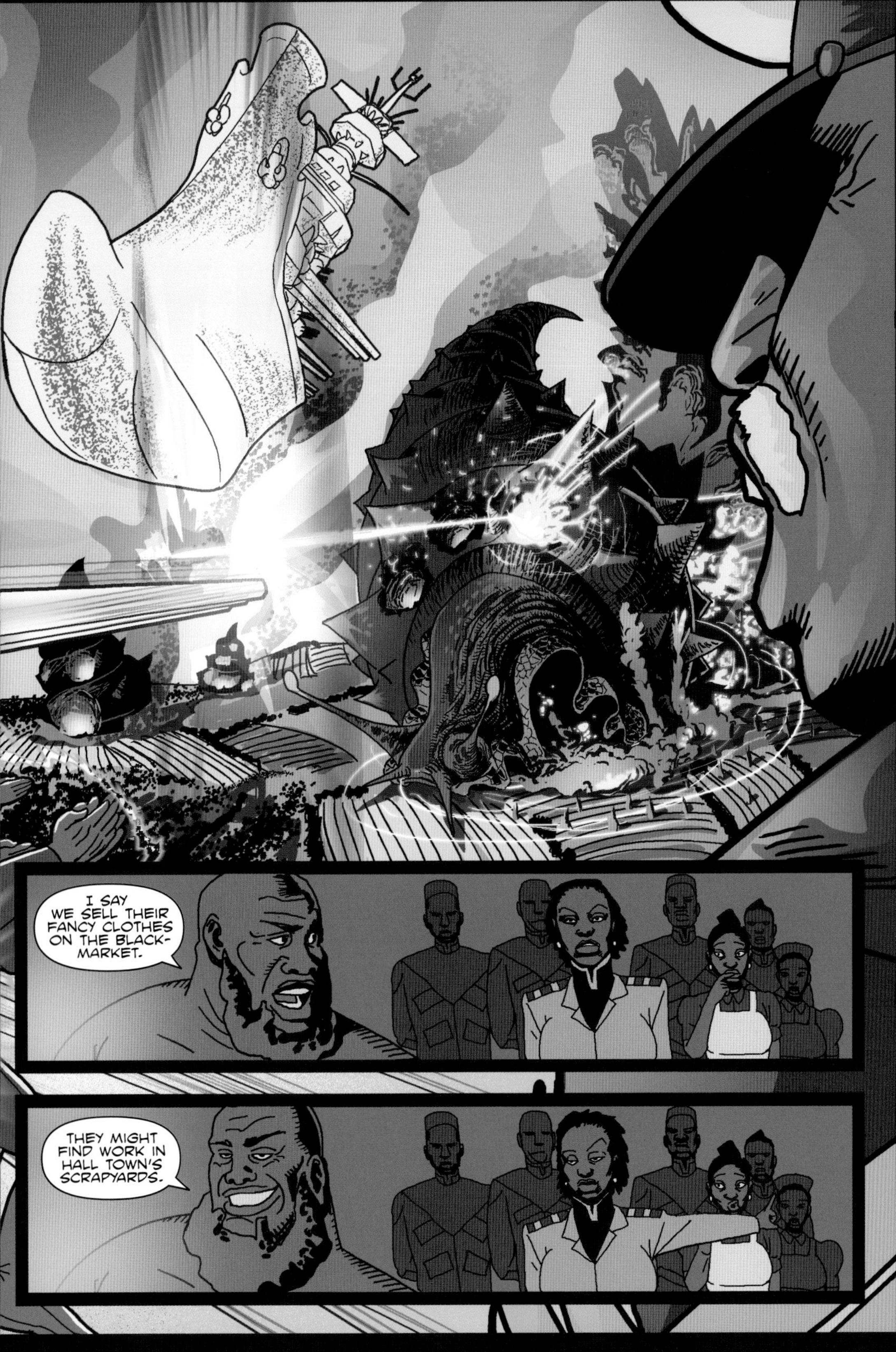
I SAY WE SELL THEIR FANCY CLOTHES ON THE BLACK-MARKET.
THEY MIGHT FIND WORK IN HALL TOWN'S SCRAPYARDS.

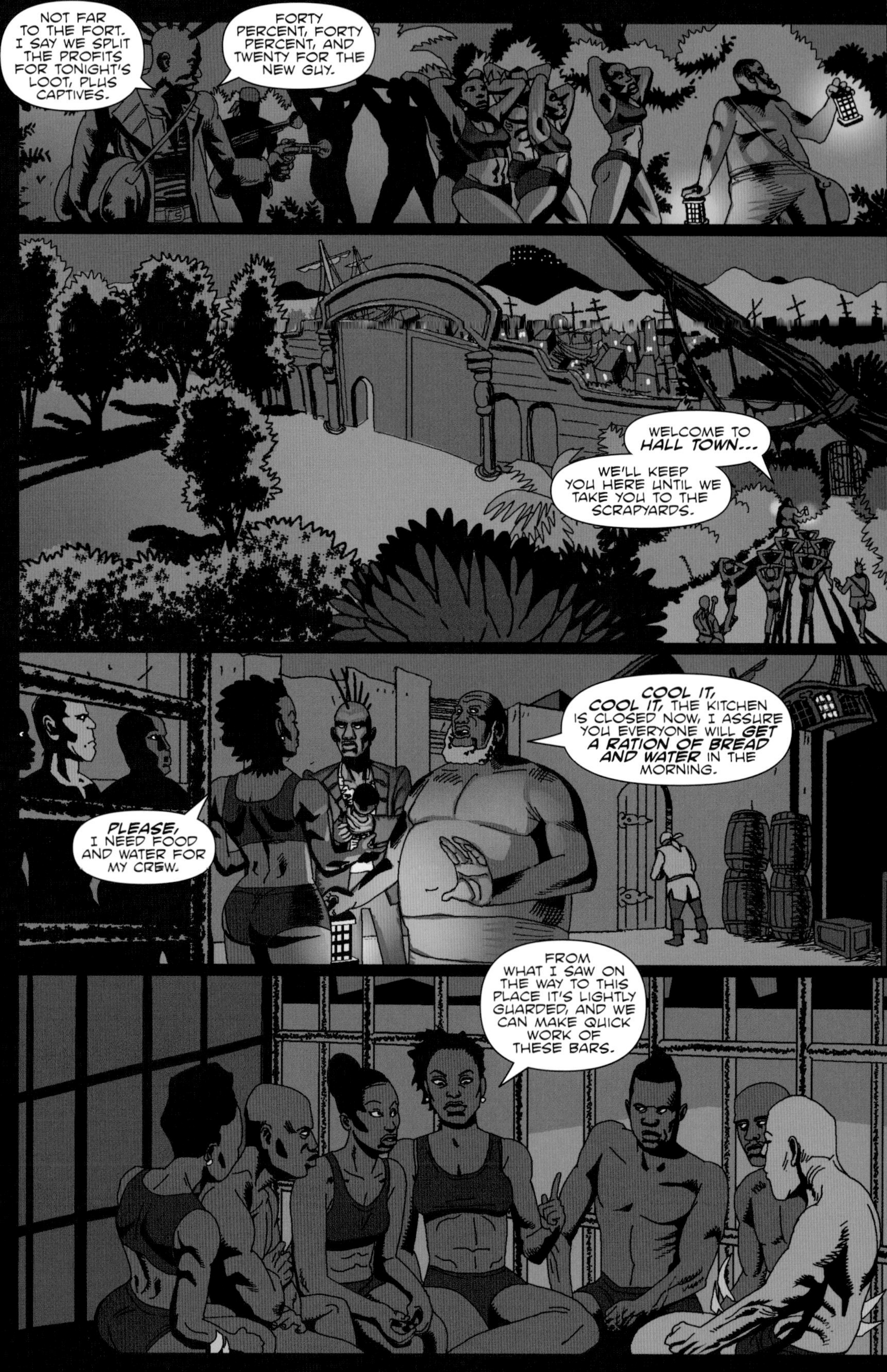
NOT FAR TO THE FORT. I SAY WE SPLIT THE PROFITS FOR TONIGHT'S LOOT, PLUS CAPTIVES.
FORTY PERCENT, FORTY PERCENT, AND TWENTY FOR THE NEW GUY.
WELCOME TO HALL TOWN...
WE'LL KEEP YOU HERE UNTIL WE TAKE YOU TO THE SCRAPYARDS.
PLEASE, I NEED FOOD AND WATER FOR MY CREW.
COOL IT, COOL IT, THE KITCHEN IS CLOSED NOW, I ASSURE YOU EVERYONE WILL GET A RATION OF BREAD AND WATER IN THE MORNING.
FROM WHAT I SAW ON THE WAY TO THIS PLACE IT'S LIGHTLY GUARDED, AND WE CAN MAKE QUICK WORK OF THESE BARS.

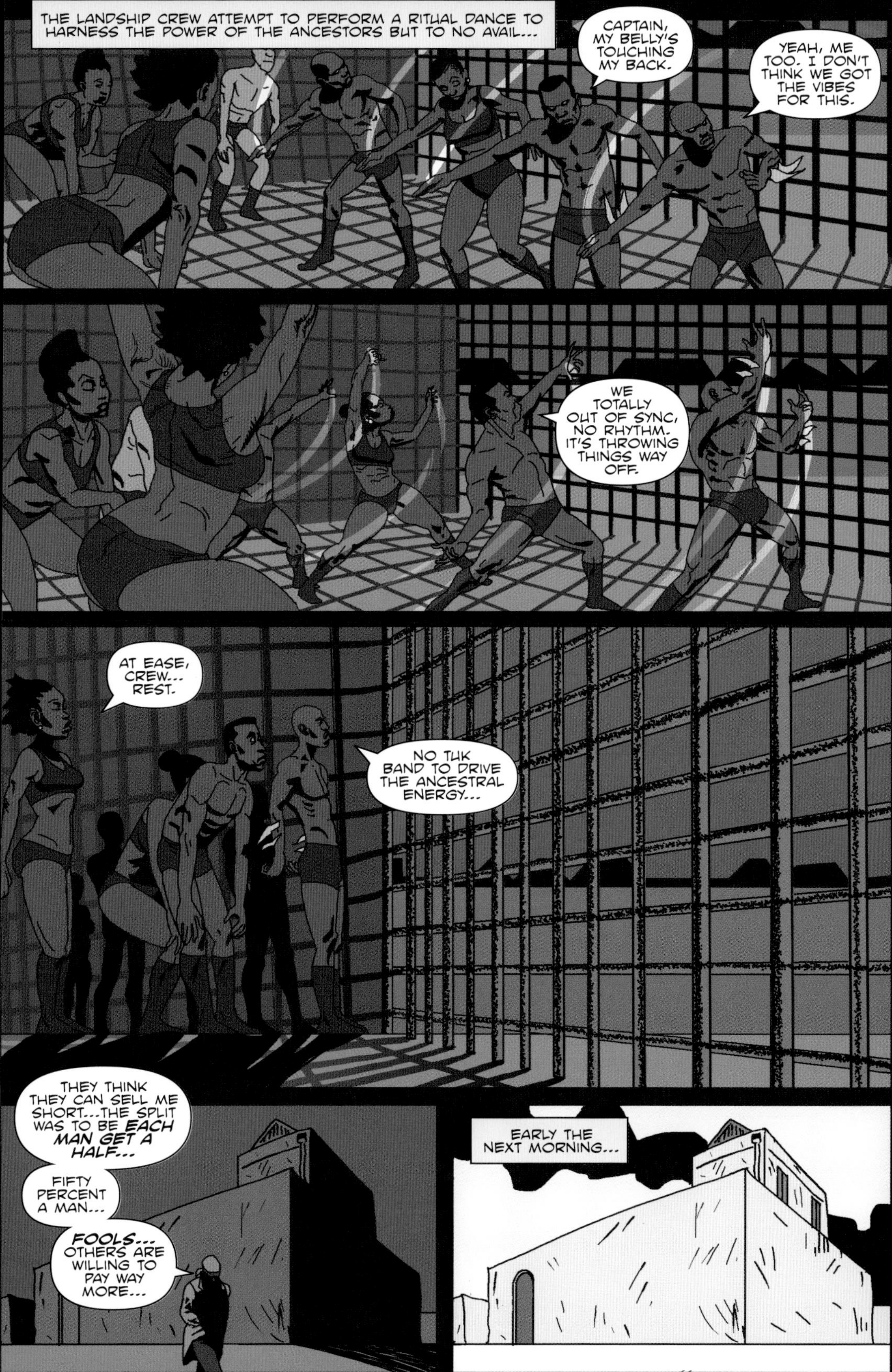
THE LANDSHIP CREW ATTEMPT TO PERFORM A RITUAL DANCE TO HARNESS THE POWER OF THE ANCESTORS BUT TO NO AVAIL...
CAPTAIN, MY BELLY'S TOUCHING MY BACK.
YEAH, ME TOO. I DON'T THINK WE GOT THE VIBES FOR THIS.
WE TOTALLY OUT OF SYNC, NO RHYTHM. IT'S THROWING THINGS WAY OFF.
AT EASE, CREW... REST.
NO TUK BAND TO DRIVE THE ANCESTRAL ENERGY...
THEY THINK THEY CAN SELL ME SHORT...THE SPLIT WAS TO BE EACH MAN GET A HALF...
FIFTY PERCENT A MAN...
FOOLS... OTHERS ARE WILLING TO PAY WAY MORE...
EARLY THE NEXT MORNING...

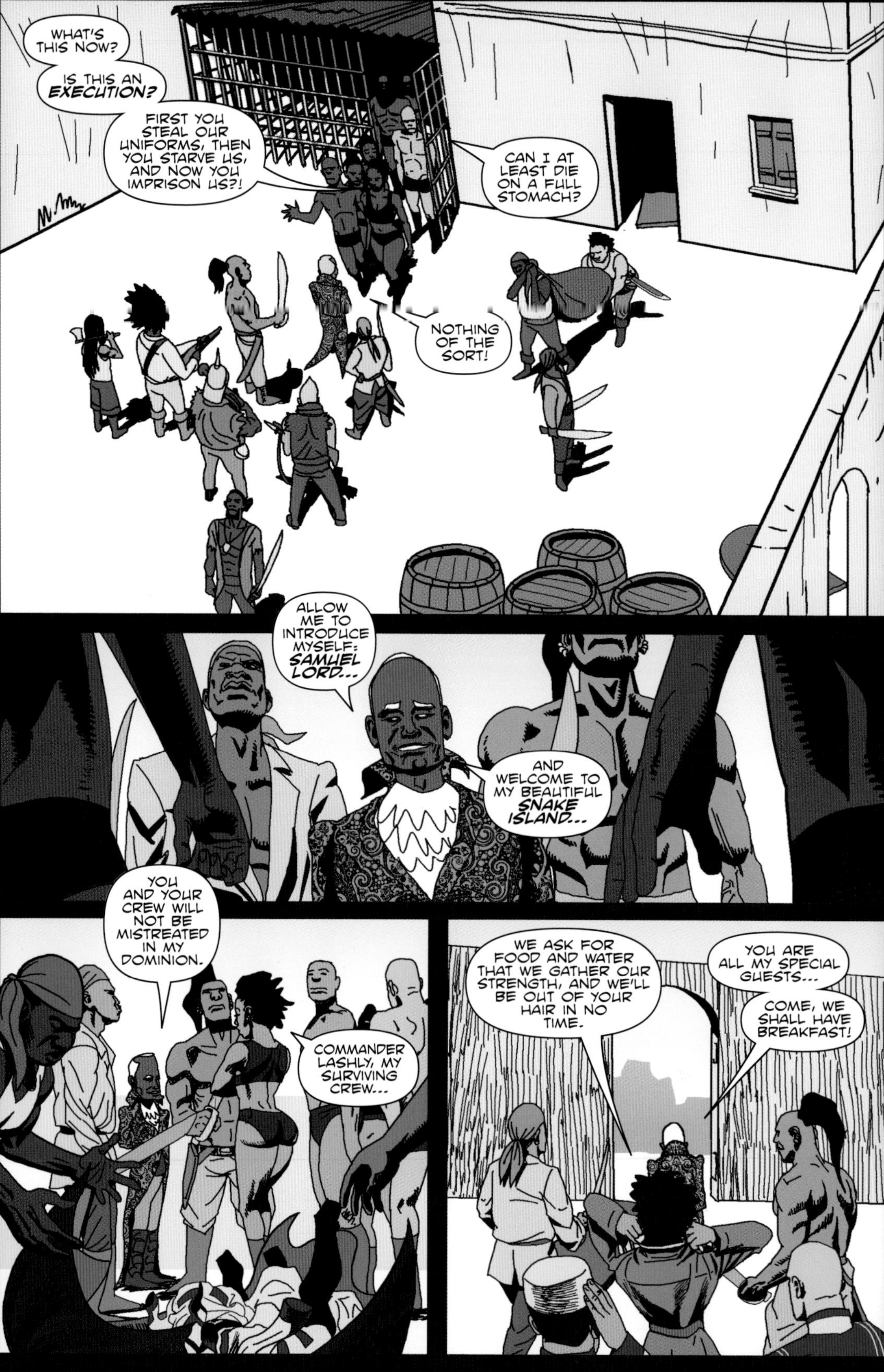
WHAT'S THIS NOW?
IS THIS AN EXECUTION?
FIRST YOU STEAL OUR UNIFORMS, THEN YOU STARVE US, AND NOW YOU IMPRISON US?!
CAN I AT LEAST DIE ON A FULL STOMACH?
NOTHING OF THE SORT!
ALLOW ME TO INTRODUCE MYSELF: SAMUEL LORD...
AND WELCOME TO MY BEAUTIFUL SNAKE ISLAND...
YOU AND YOUR CREW WILL NOT BE MISTREATED IN MY DOMINION.
COMMANDER LASHLY, MY SURVIVING CREW...
WE ASK FOR FOOD AND WATER THAT WE GATHER OUR STRENGTH, AND WE'LL BE OUT OF YOUR HAIR IN NO TIME.
YOU ARE ALL MY SPECIAL GUESTS...
COME, WE SHALL HAVE BREAKFAST!

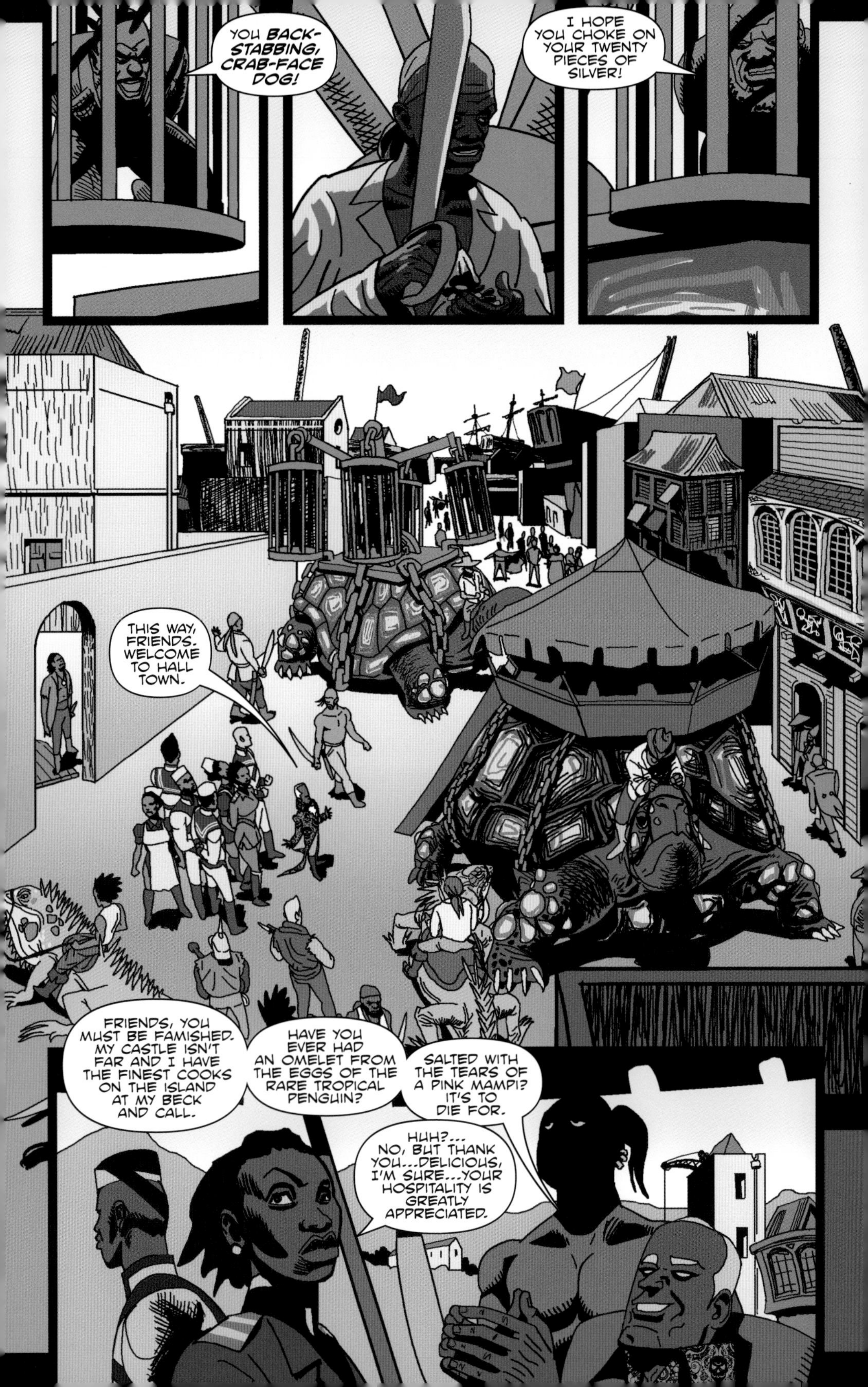
YOU BACK-STABBING, CRAB-FACE DOG!
I HOPE YOU CHOKE ON YOUR TWENTY PIECES OF SILVER!
THIS WAY, FRIENDS. WELCOME TO HALL TOWN.
FRIENDS, YOU MUST BE FAMISHED. MY CASTLE ISN'T FAR AND I HAVE THE FINEST COOKS ON THE ISLAND AT MY BECK AND CALL.
HAVE YOU EVER HAD AN OMELET FROM THE EGGS OF THE RARE TROPICAL PENGUIN?
SALTED WITH THE TEARS OF A PINK MAMPI? IT'S TO DIE FOR.
HUH?... NO, BUT THANK YOU...DELICIOUS, I'M SURE...YOUR HOSPITALITY IS GREATLY APPRECIATED.

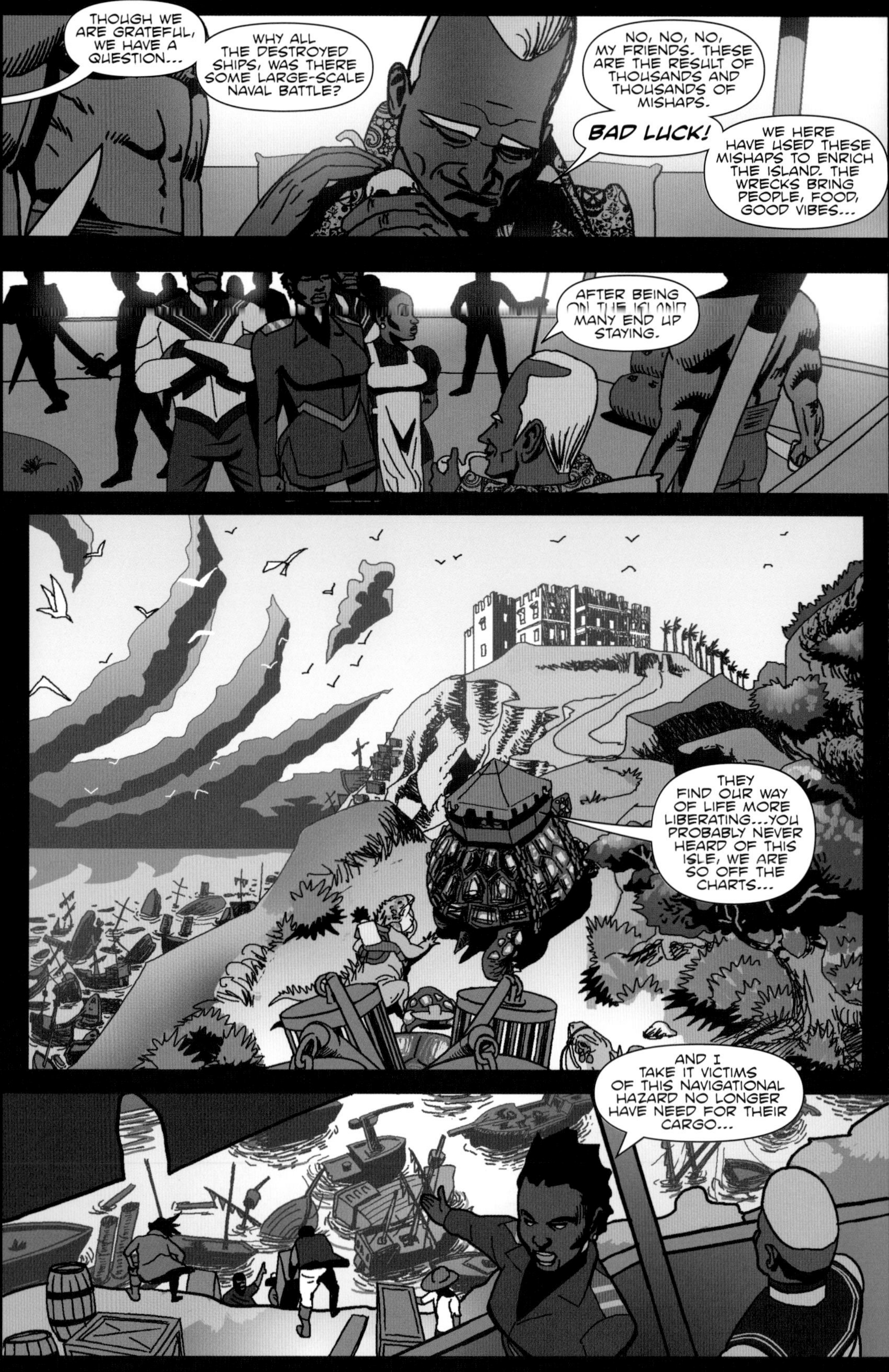
THOUGH WE ARE GRATEFUL, WE HAVE A QUESTION...
WHY ALL THE DESTROYED SHIPS, WAS THERE SOME LARGE-SCALE NAVAL BATTLE?
NO, NO, NO, MY FRIENDS. THESE ARE THE RESULT OF THOUSANDS AND THOUSANDS OF MISHAPS.
BAD LUCK!
WE HERE HAVE USED THESE MISHAPS TO ENRICH THE ISLAND. THE WRECKS BRING PEOPLE, FOOD, GOOD VIBES...
AFTER BEING ON THE ISLAND MANY END UP STAYING.
THEY FIND OUR WAY OF LIFE MORE LIBERATING...YOU PROBABLY NEVER HEARD OF THIS ISLE, WE ARE SO OFF THE CHARTS...
AND I TAKE IT VICTIMS OF THIS NAVIGATIONAL HAZARD NO LONGER HAVE NEED FOR THEIR CARGO...

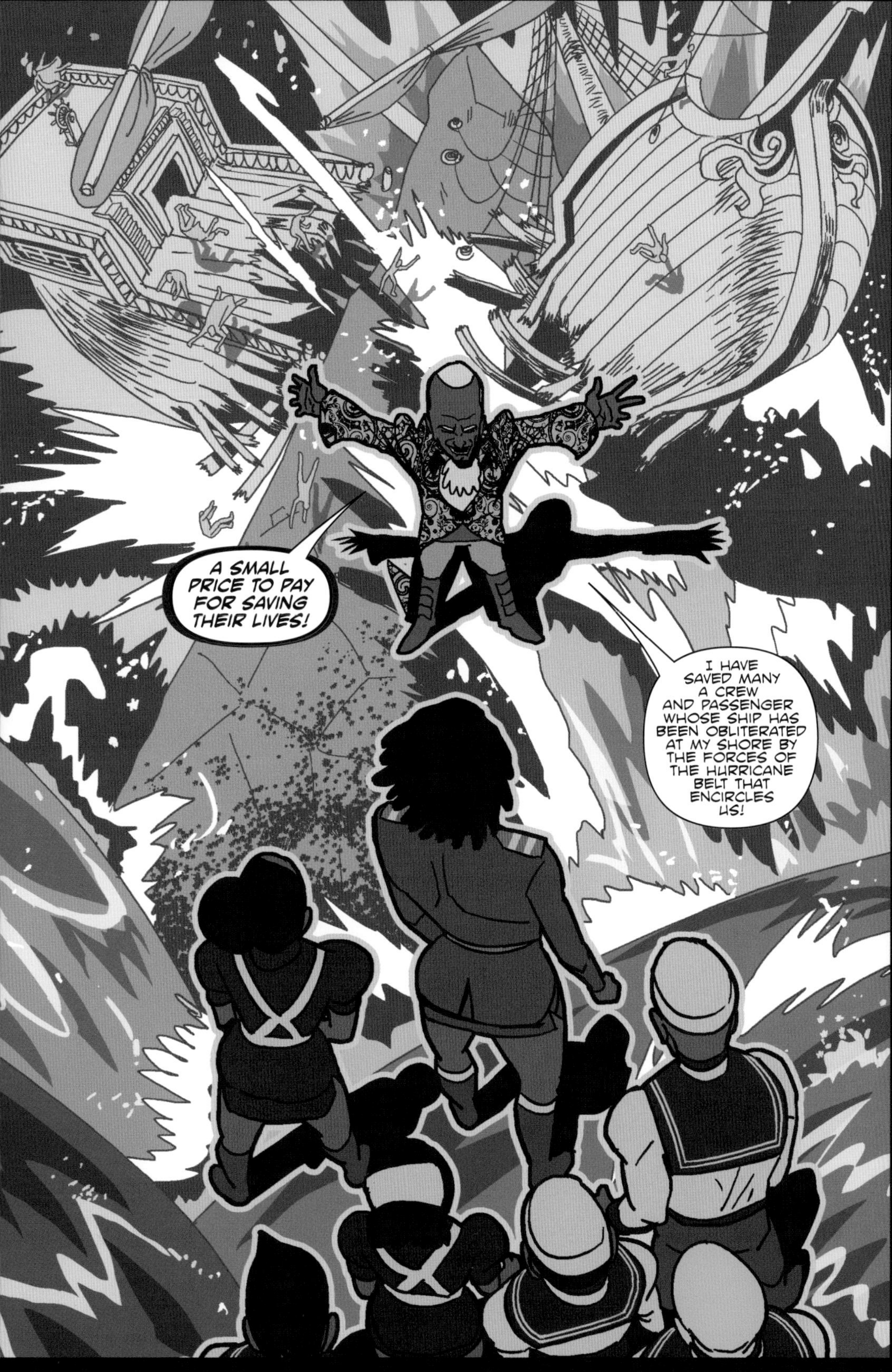
A SMALL PRICE TO PAY FOR SAVING THEIR LIVES!
I HAVE SAVED MANY A CREW AND PASSENGER WHOSE SHIP HAS BEEN OBLITERATED AT MY SHORE BY THE FORCES OF THE HURRICANE BELT THAT ENCIRCLES US!

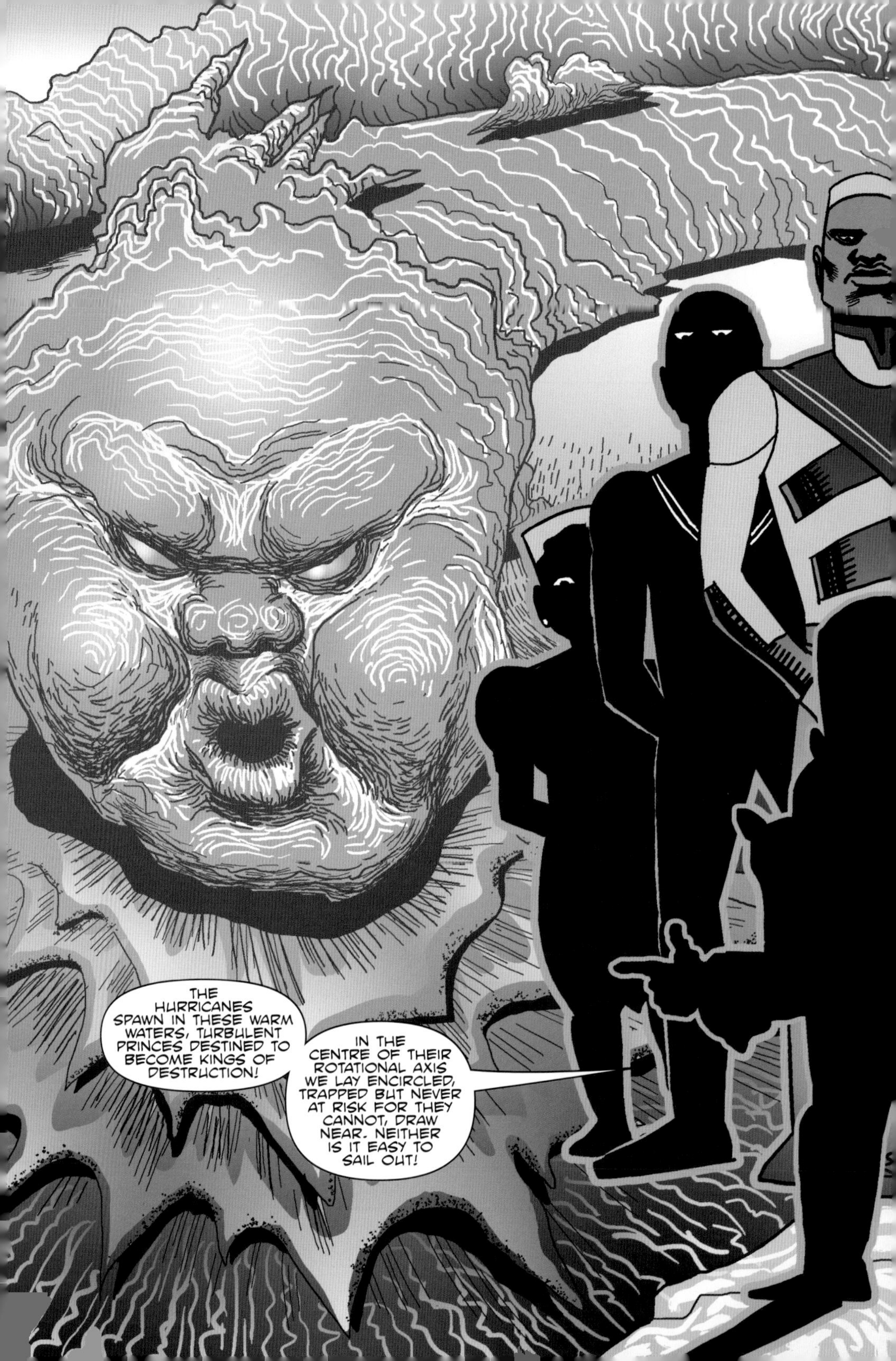
THE HURRICANES SPAWN IN THESE WARM WATERS, TURBULENT PRINCES DESTINED TO BECOME KINGS OF DESTRUCTION!
IN THE CENTRE OF THEIR ROTATIONAL AXIS WE LAY ENCIRCLED, TRAPPED BUT NEVER AT RISK FOR THEY CANNOT, DRAW NEAR. NEITHER IS IT EASY TO SAIL OUT!

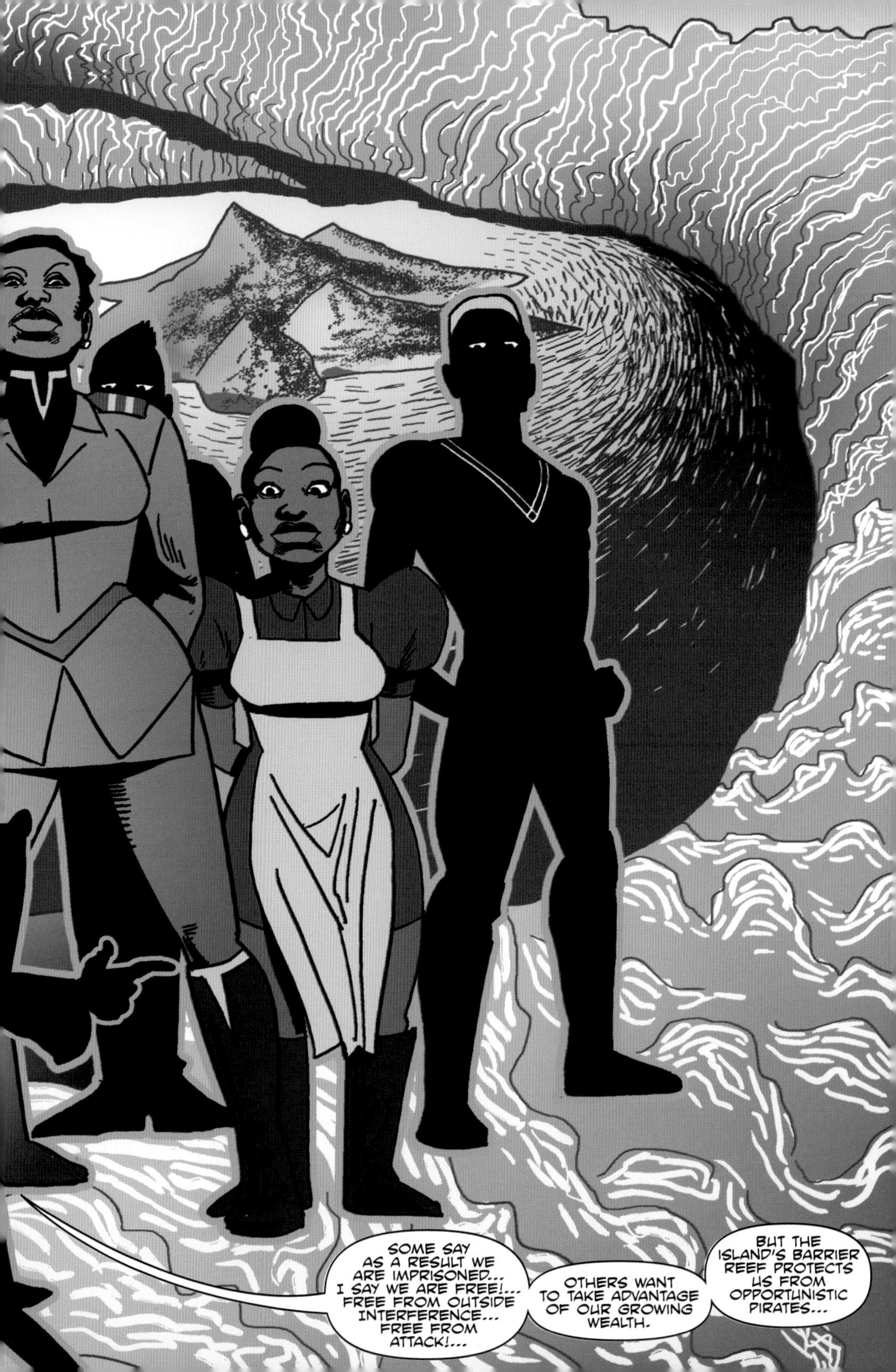
SOME SAY AS A RESULT WE ARE IMPRISONED... I SAY WE ARE FREE!... FREE FROM OUTSIDE INTERFERENCE... FREE FROM ATTACK!...
OTHERS WANT TO TAKE ADVANTAGE OF OUR GROWING WEALTH.
BUT THE ISLAND'S BARRIER REEF PROTECTS US FROM OPPORTUNISTIC PIRATES...

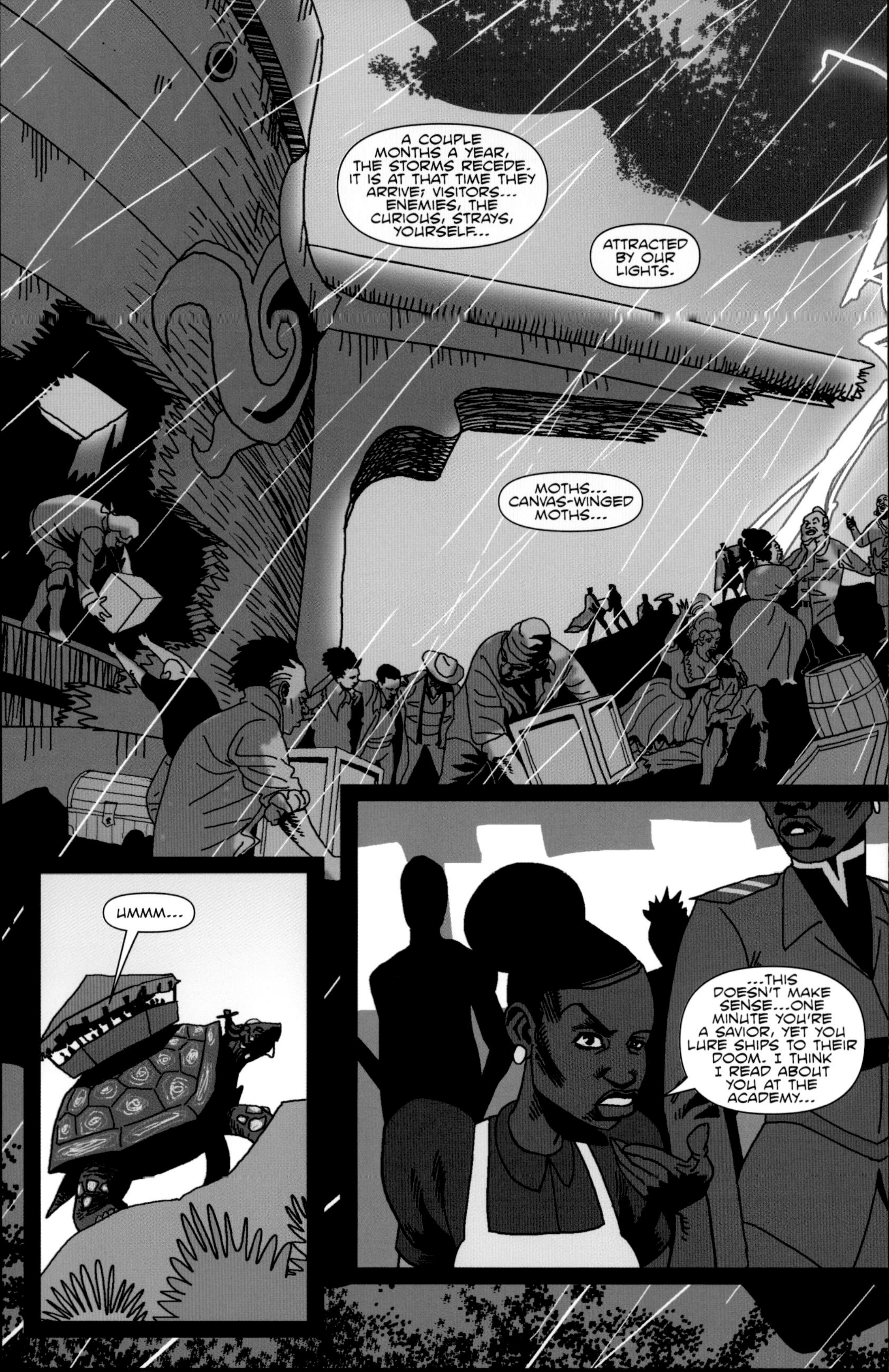
A COUPLE MONTHS A YEAR, THE STORMS RECEDE. IT IS AT THAT TIME THEY ARRIVE; VISITORS... ENEMIES, THE CURIOUS, STRAYS, YOURSELF...
ATTRACTED BY OUR LIGHTS.
MOTHS... CANVAS-WINGED MOTHS...
UMMM...
...THIS DOESN'T MAKE SENSE...ONE MINUTE YOU'RE A SAVIOR, YET YOU LURE SHIPS TO THEIR DOOM. I THINK I READ ABOUT YOU AT THE ACADEMY...

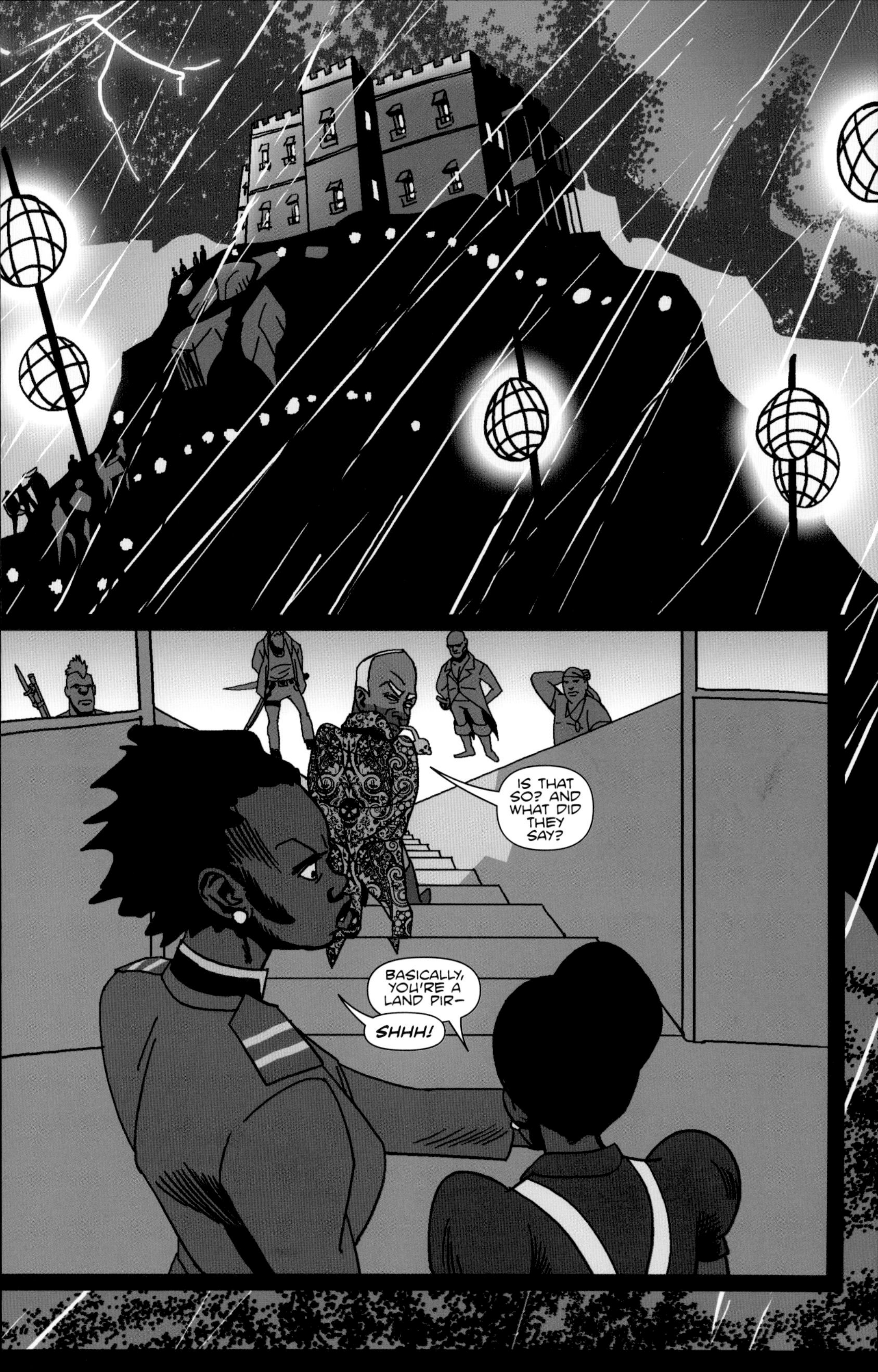
IS THAT SO? AND WHAT DID THEY SAY?
BASICALLY, YOU'RE A LAND PIR-
SHHH!

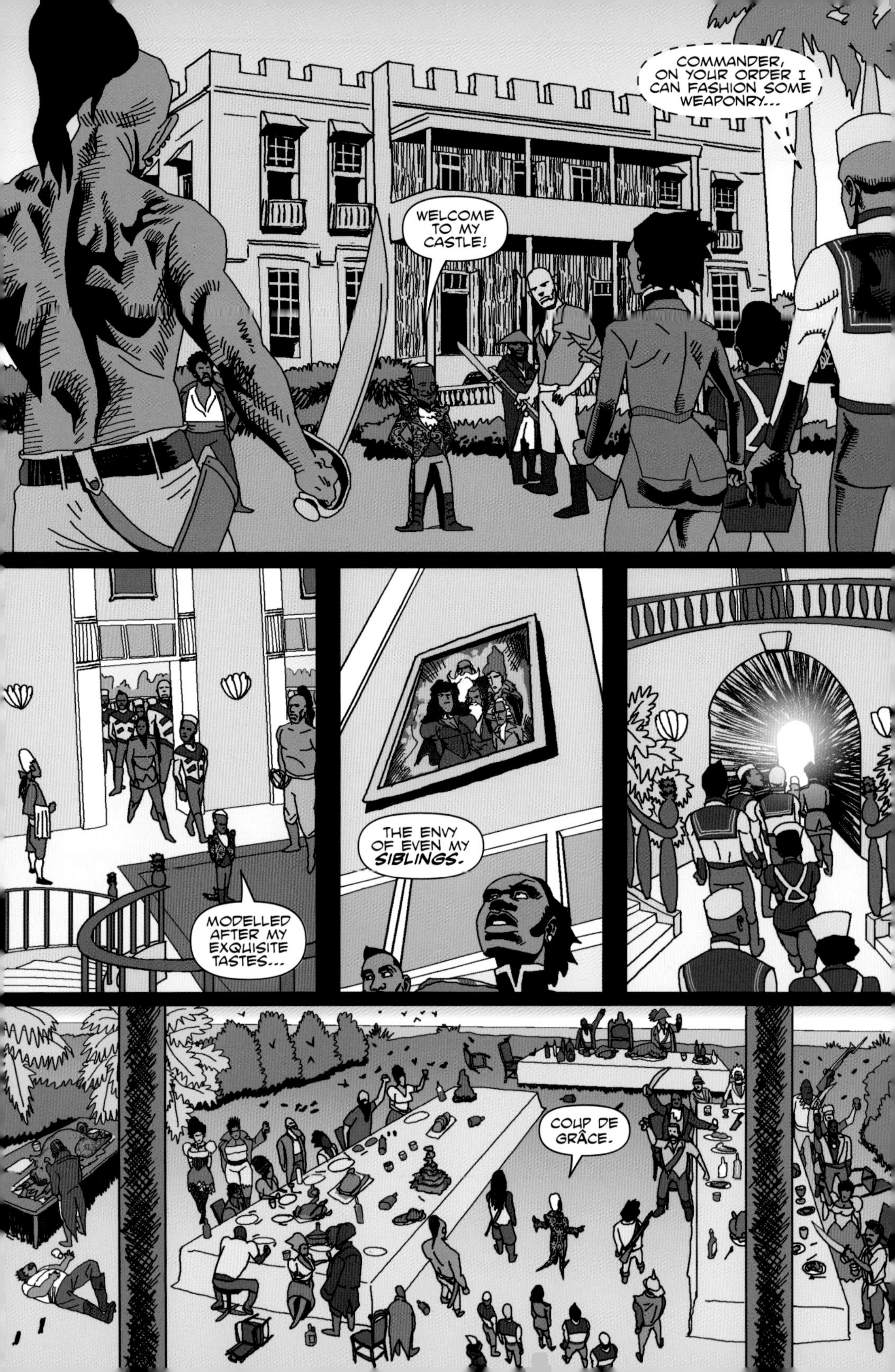

COMMANDER, ON YOUR ORDER I CAN FASHION SOME WEAPONRY...
WELCOME TO MY CASTLE!
MODELLED AFTER MY EXQUISITE TASTES...
THE ENVY OF EVEN MY *SIBLINGS*.
COUP DE GRÂCE.

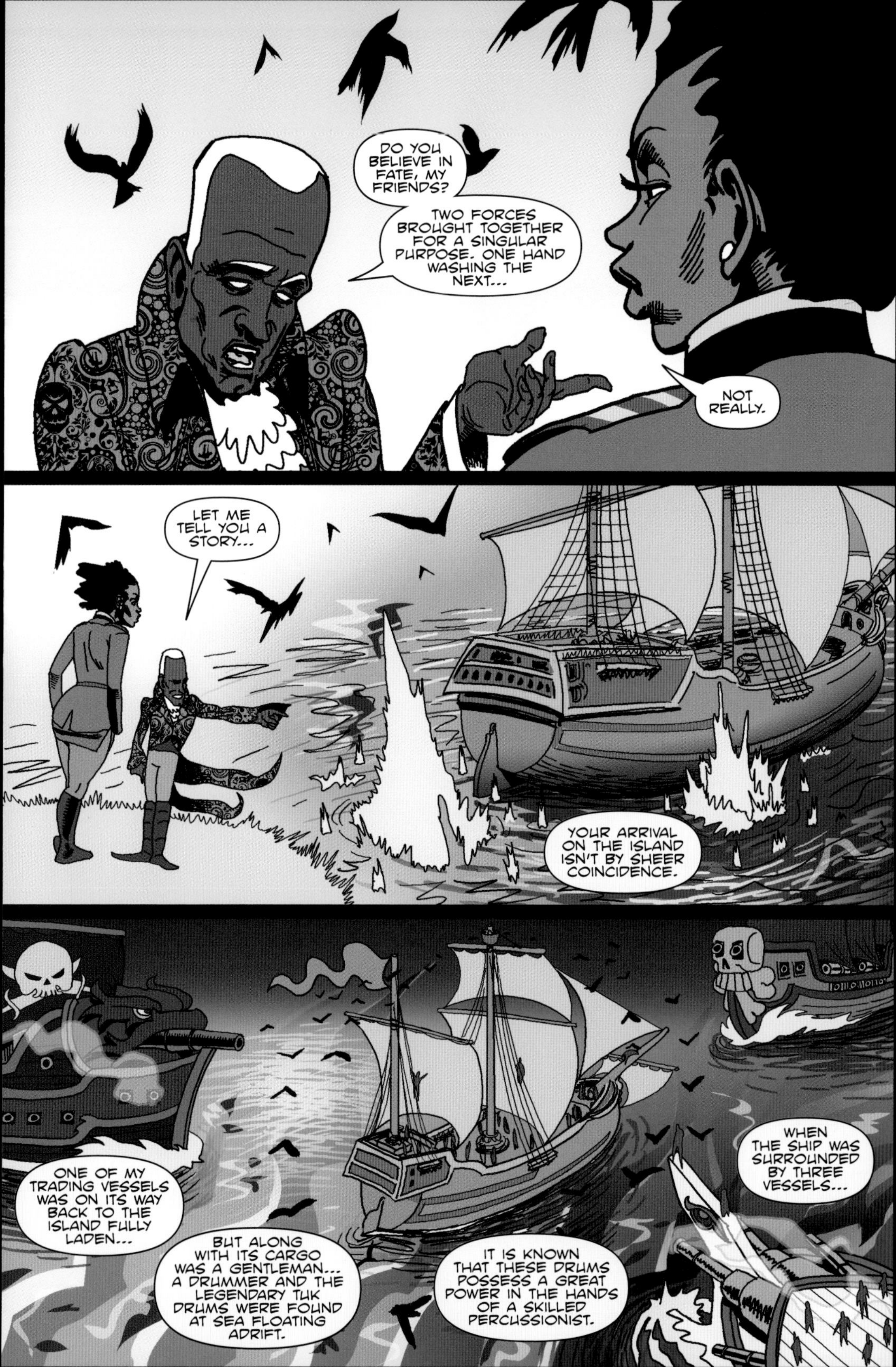

DO YOU BELIEVE IN FATE, MY FRIENDS?
TWO FORCES BROUGHT TOGETHER FOR A SINGULAR PURPOSE. ONE HAND WASHING THE NEXT...
NOT REALLY.
LET ME TELL YOU A STORY...
YOUR ARRIVAL ON THE ISLAND ISN'T BY SHEER COINCIDENCE.
ONE OF MY TRADING VESSELS WAS ON ITS WAY BACK TO THE ISLAND FULLY LADEN...
BUT ALONG WITH ITS CARGO WAS A GENTLEMAN... A DRUMMER AND THE LEGENDARY TUK DRUMS WERE FOUND AT SEA FLOATING ADRIFT.
IT IS KNOWN THAT THESE DRUMS POSSESS A GREAT POWER IN THE HANDS OF A SKILLED PERCUSSIONIST.
WHEN THE SHIP WAS SURROUNDED BY THREE VESSELS...

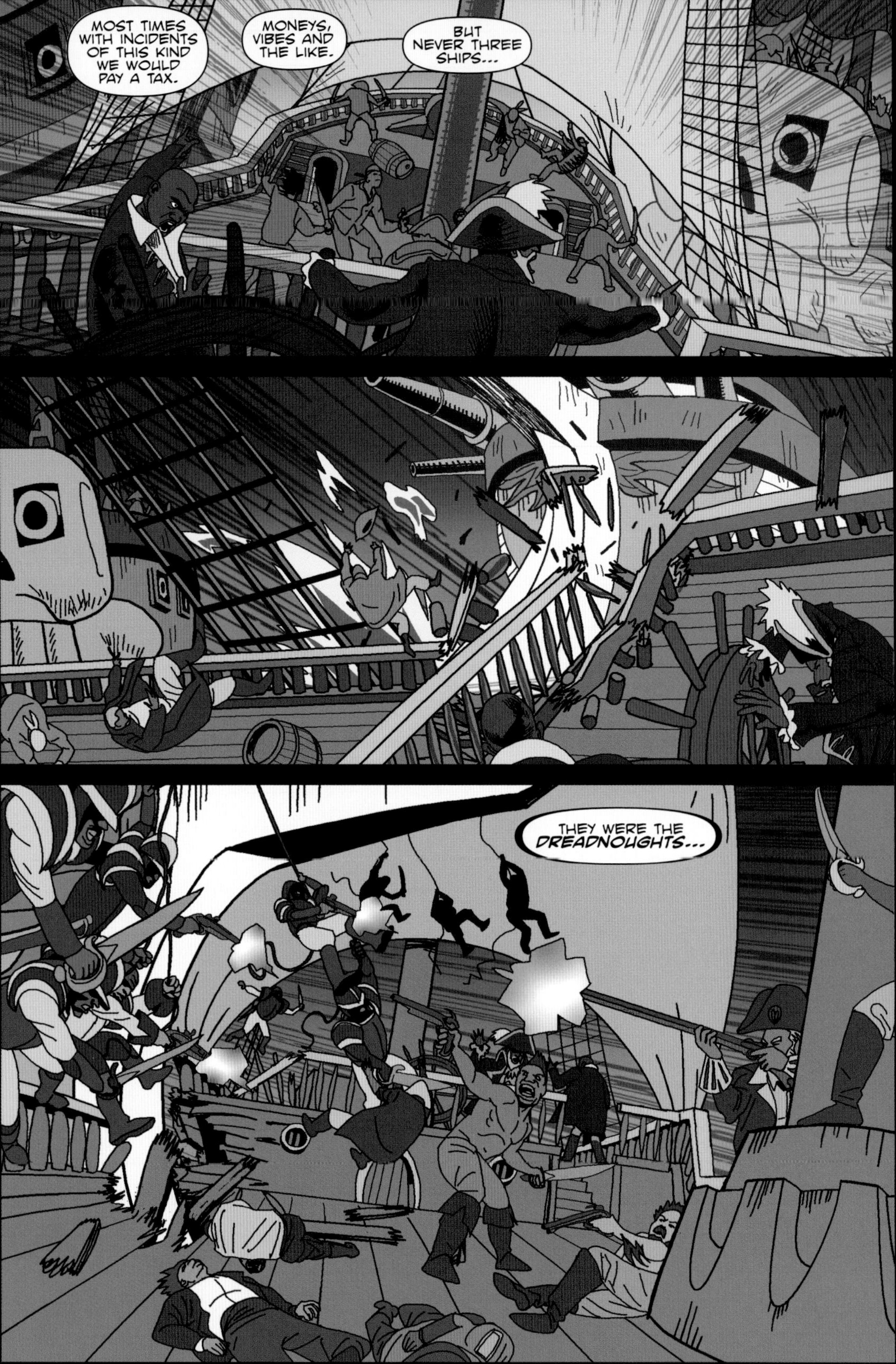
MOST TIMES WITH INCIDENTS OF THIS KIND WE WOULD PAY A TAX.
MONEYS, VIBES AND THE LIKE.
BUT NEVER THREE SHIPS...
THEY WERE THE *DREADNOUGHTS*...

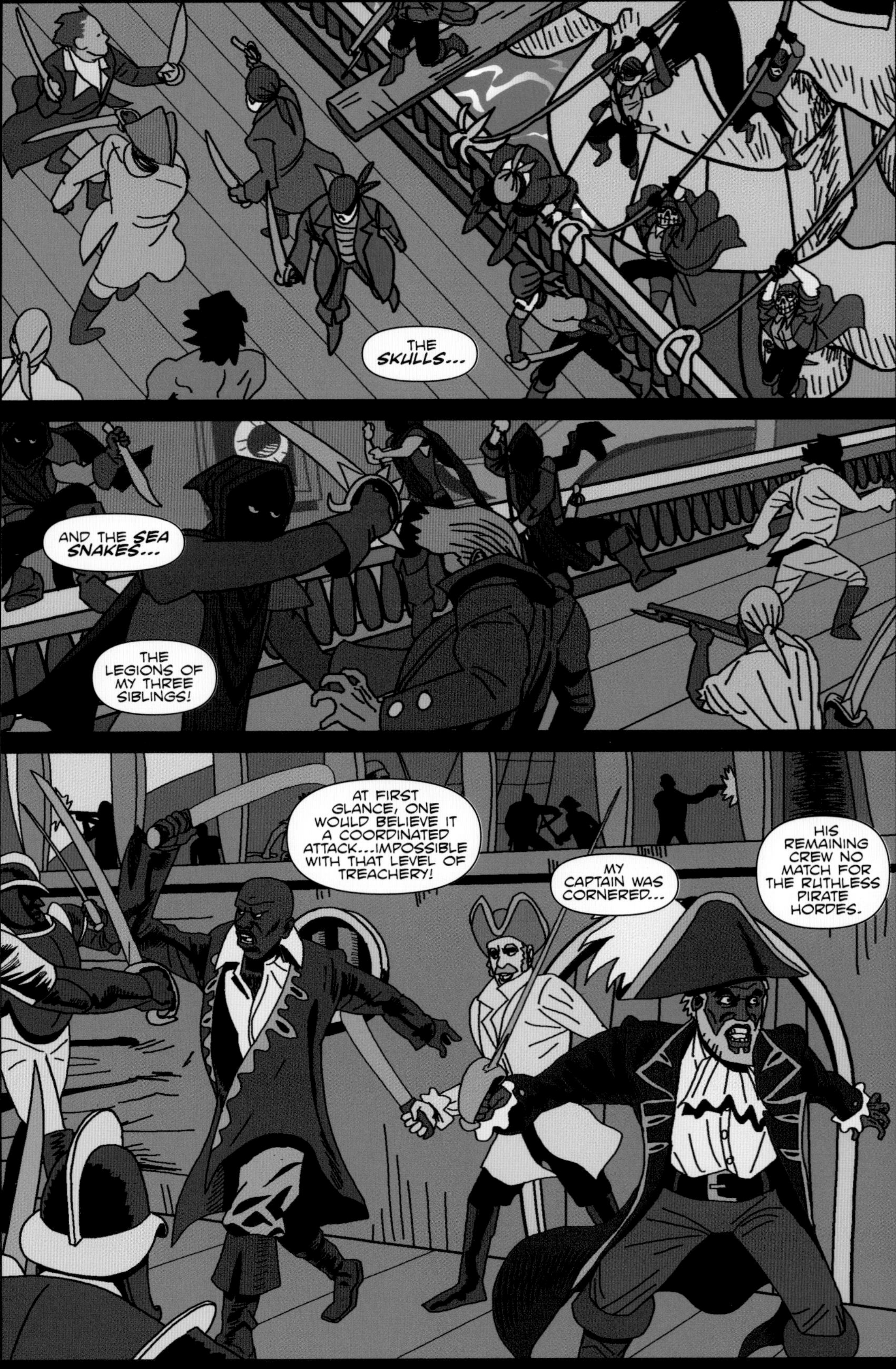
THE SKULLS...
AND THE SEA SNAKES...
THE LEGIONS OF MY THREE SIBLINGS!
AT FIRST GLANCE, ONE WOULD BELIEVE IT A COORDINATED ATTACK...IMPOSSIBLE WITH THAT LEVEL OF TREACHERY!
MY CAPTAIN WAS CORNERED...
HIS REMAINING CREW NO MATCH FOR THE RUTHLESS PIRATE HORDES.

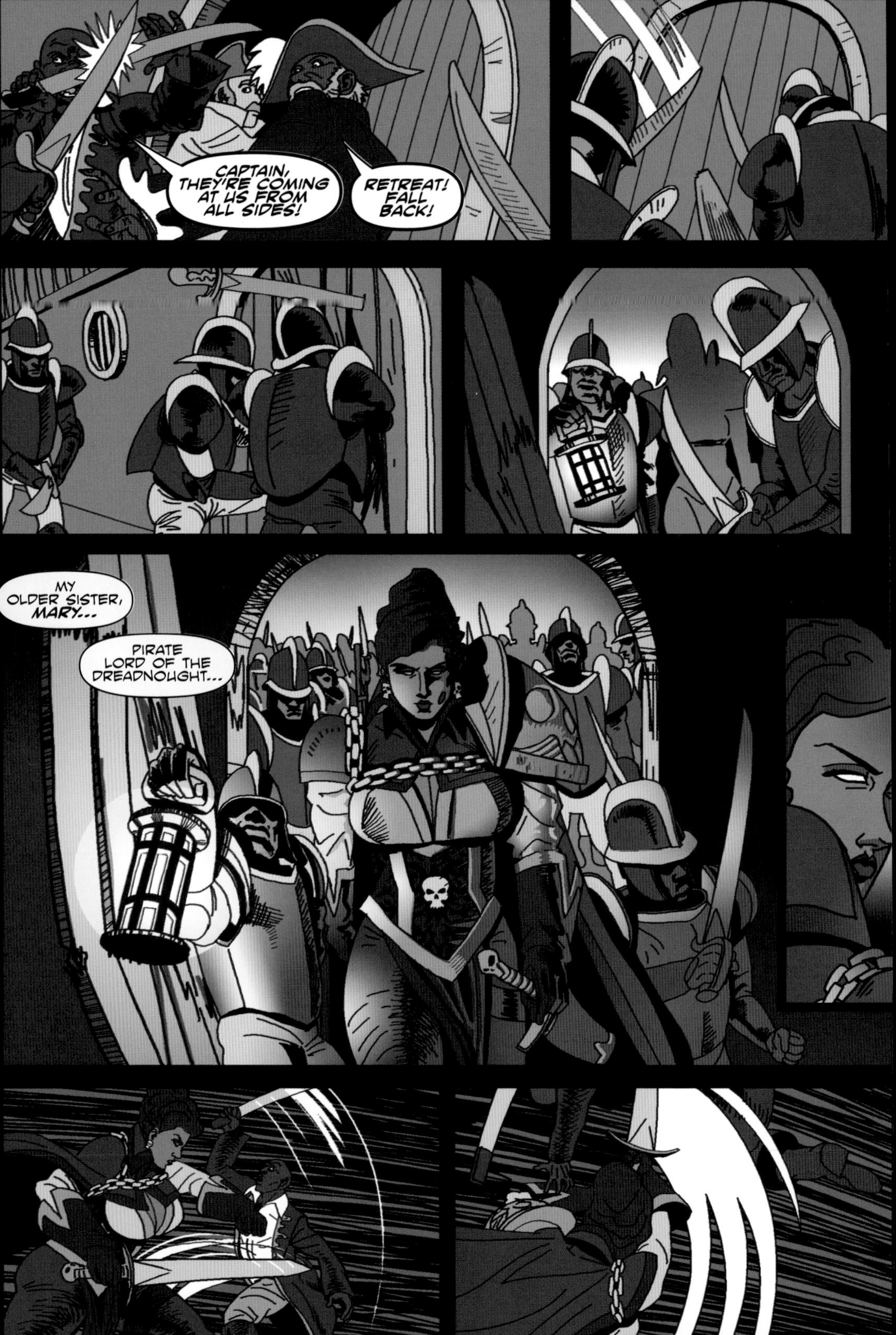
CAPTAIN, THEY'RE COMING AT US FROM ALL SIDES!
RETREAT! FALL BACK!
MY OLDER SISTER, MARY...
PIRATE LORD OF THE DREADNOUGHT...

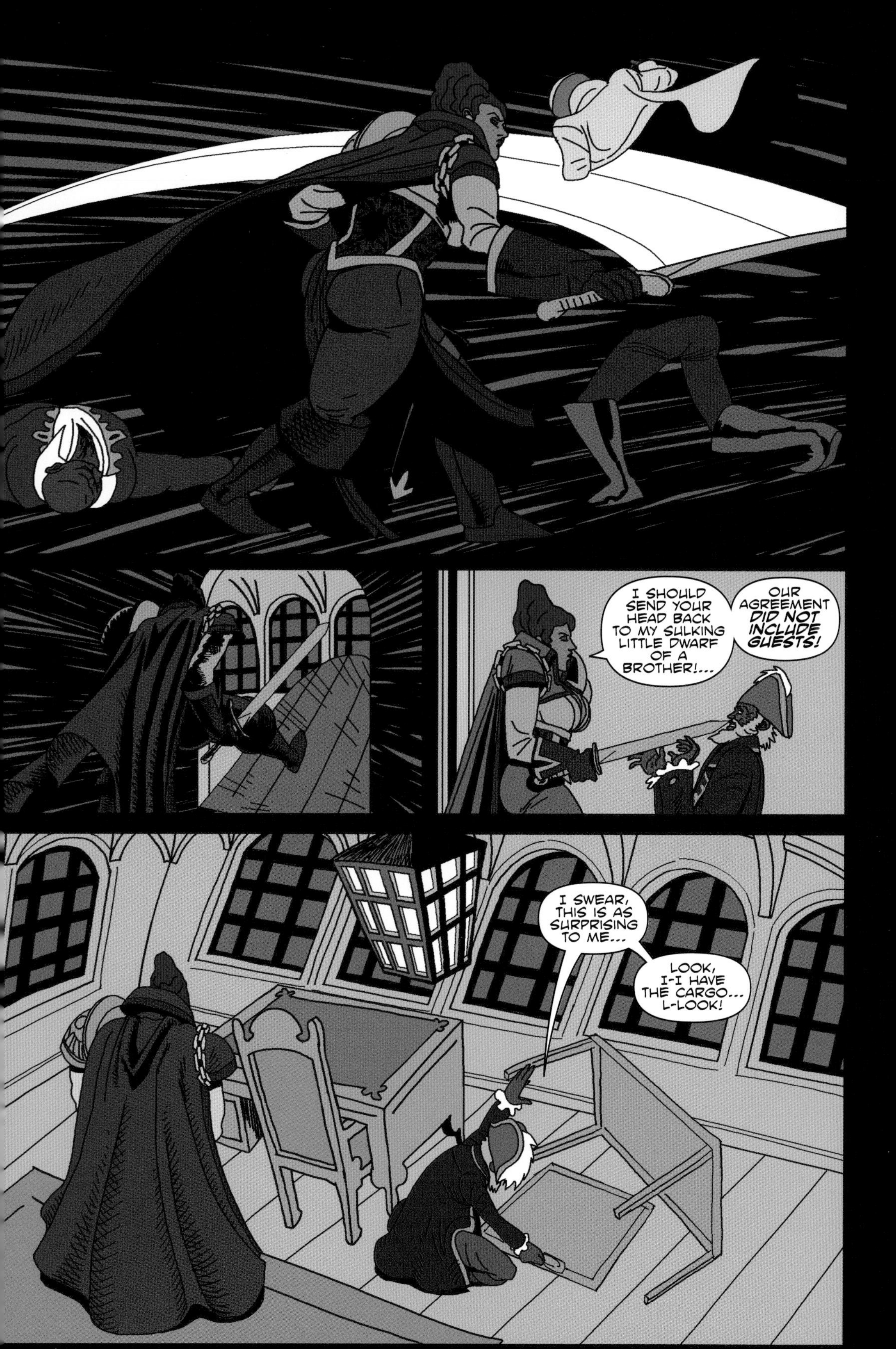
I SHOULD SEND YOUR HEAD BACK TO MY SULKING LITTLE DWARF OF A BROTHER!...
OUR AGREEMENT DID NOT INCLUDE GUESTS!
I SWEAR, THIS IS AS SURPRISING TO ME...
LOOK, I-I HAVE THE CARGO... L-LOOK!

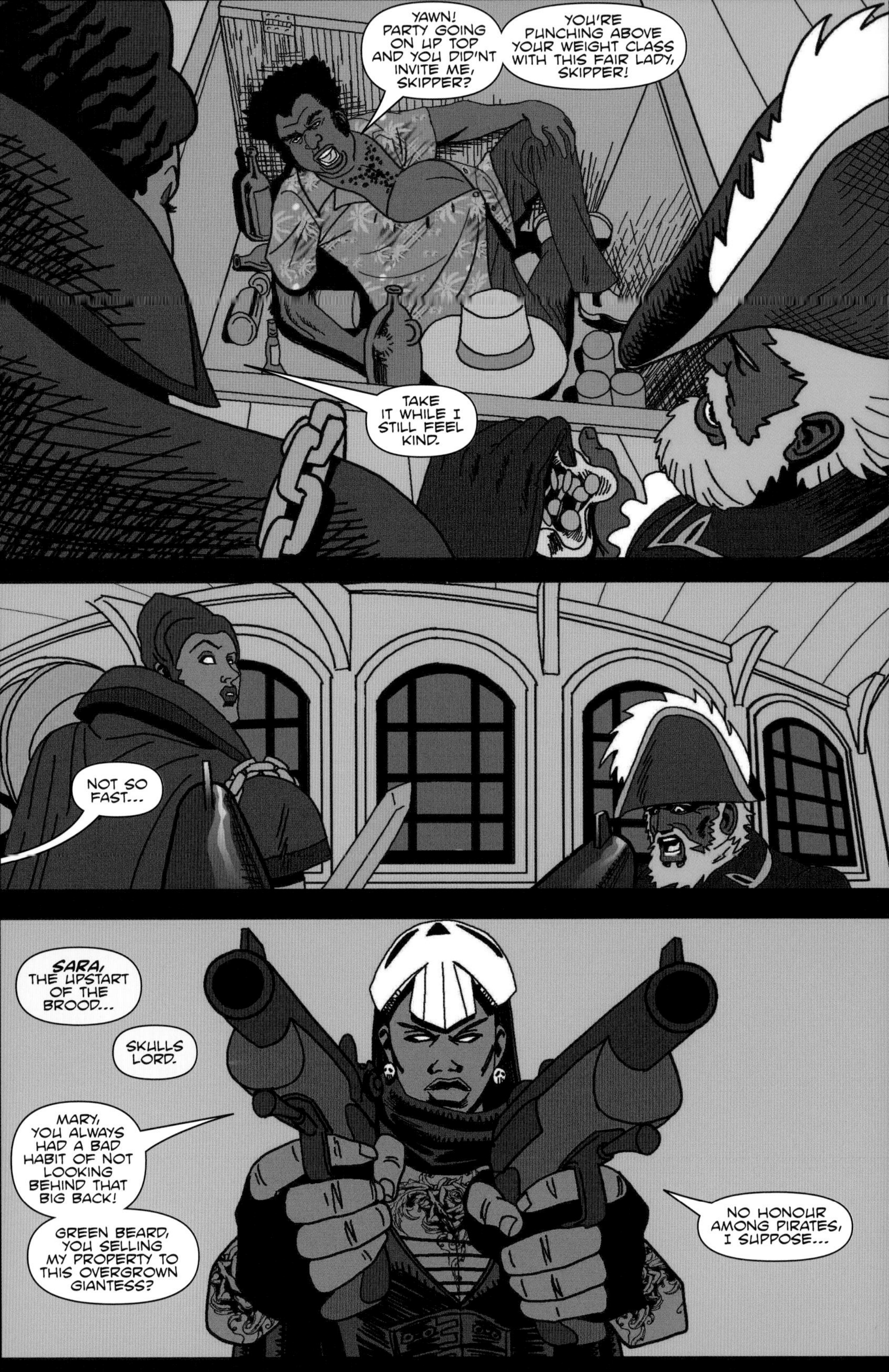
YAWN! PARTY GOING ON UP TOP AND YOU DIDN'T INVITE ME, SKIPPER?
YOU'RE PUNCHING ABOVE YOUR WEIGHT CLASS WITH THIS FAIR LADY, SKIPPER!
TAKE IT WHILE I STILL FEEL KIND.
NOT SO FAST...
SARA, THE UPSTART OF THE BROOD...
SKULLS LORD.
MARY, YOU ALWAYS HAD A BAD HABIT OF NOT LOOKING BEHIND THAT BIG BACK!
GREEN BEARD, YOU SELLING MY PROPERTY TO THIS OVERGROWN GIANTESS?
NO HONOUR AMONG PIRATES, I SUPPOSE...

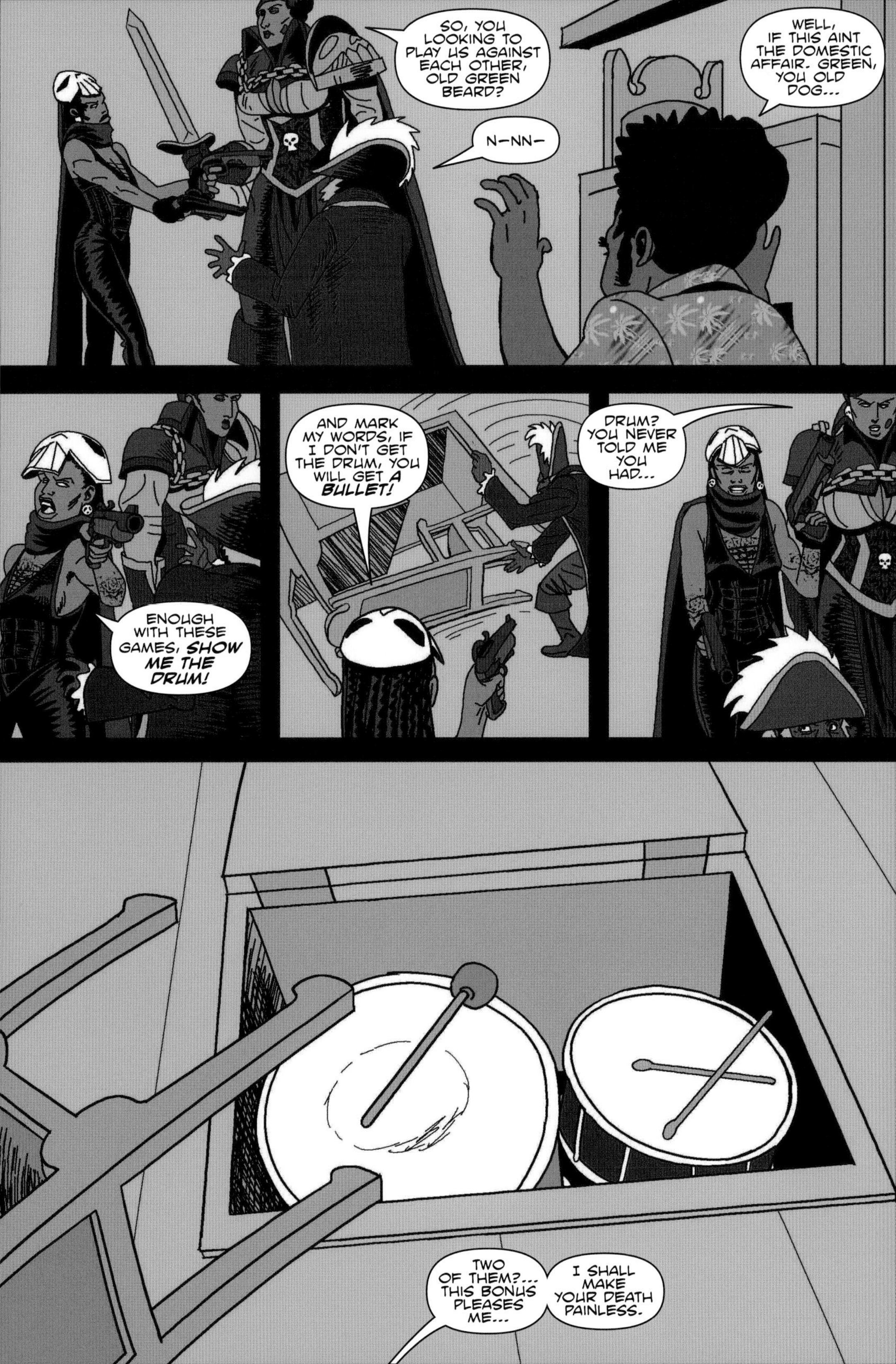
SO, YOU LOOKING TO PLAY US AGAINST EACH OTHER, OLD GREEN BEARD?
N-NN-
WELL, IF THIS AINT THE DOMESTIC AFFAIR. GREEN, YOU OLD DOG...
ENOUGH WITH THESE GAMES, SHOW ME THE DRUM!
AND MARK MY WORDS, IF I DON'T GET THE DRUM, YOU WILL GET A BULLET!
DRUM? YOU NEVER TOLD ME YOU HAD...
TWO OF THEM?... THIS BONUS PLEASES ME...
I SHALL MAKE YOUR DEATH PAINLESS.

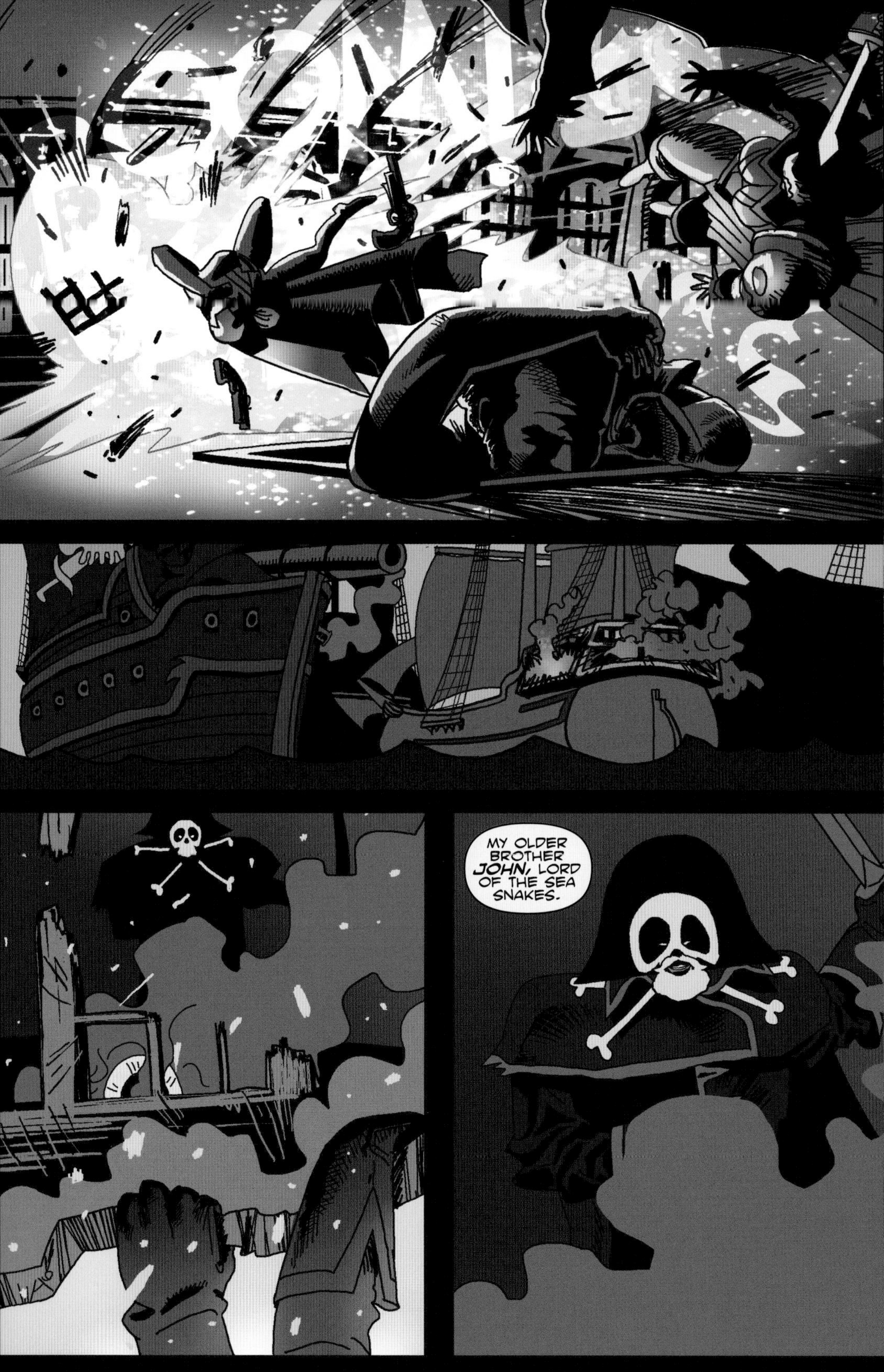
MY OLDER BROTHER JOHN, LORD OF THE SEA SNAKES.

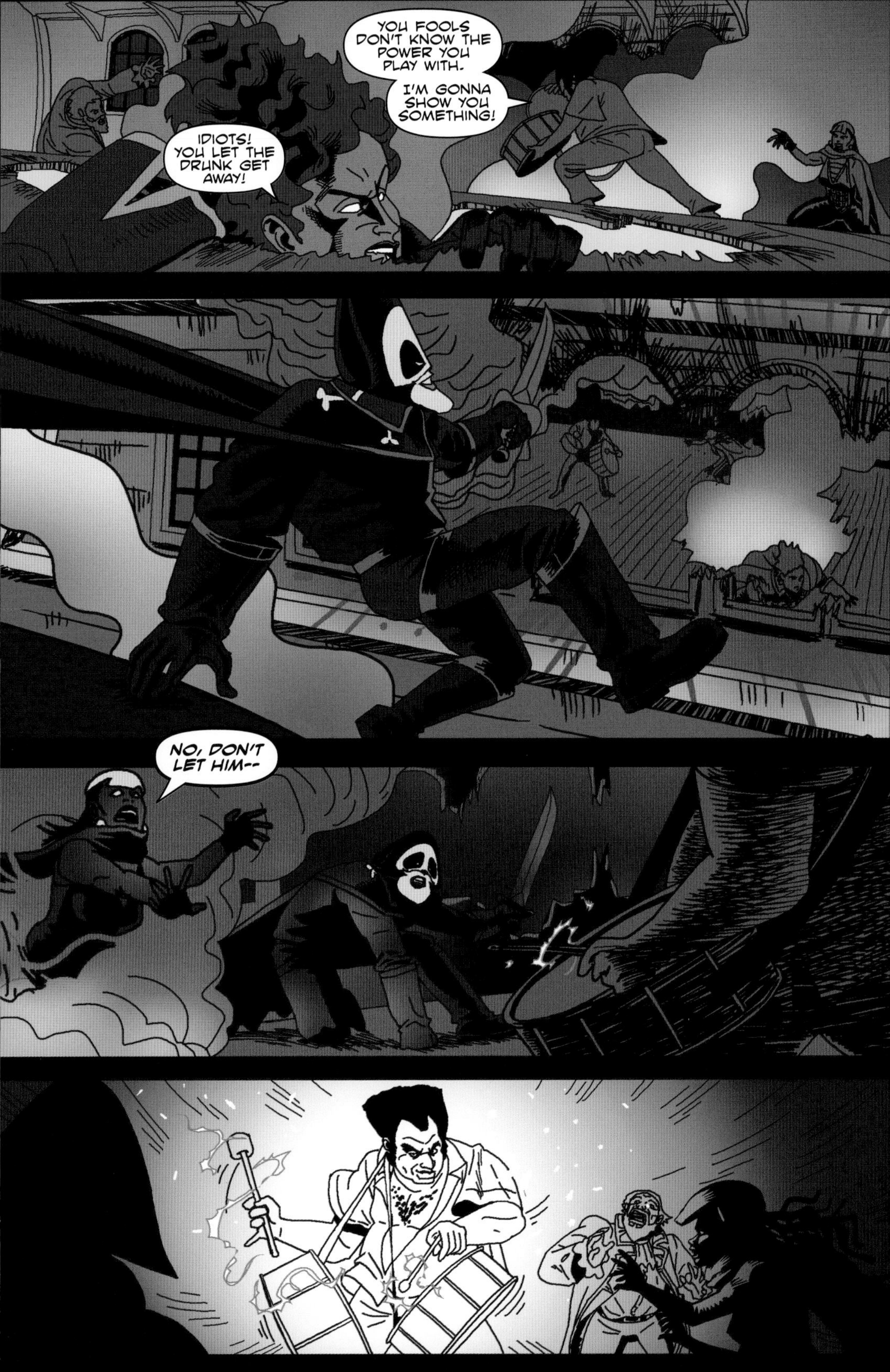
YOU FOOLS DON'T KNOW THE POWER YOU PLAY WITH.
I'M GONNA SHOW YOU SOMETHING!
IDIOTS! YOU LET THE DRUNK GET AWAY!
NO, DON'T LET HIM--

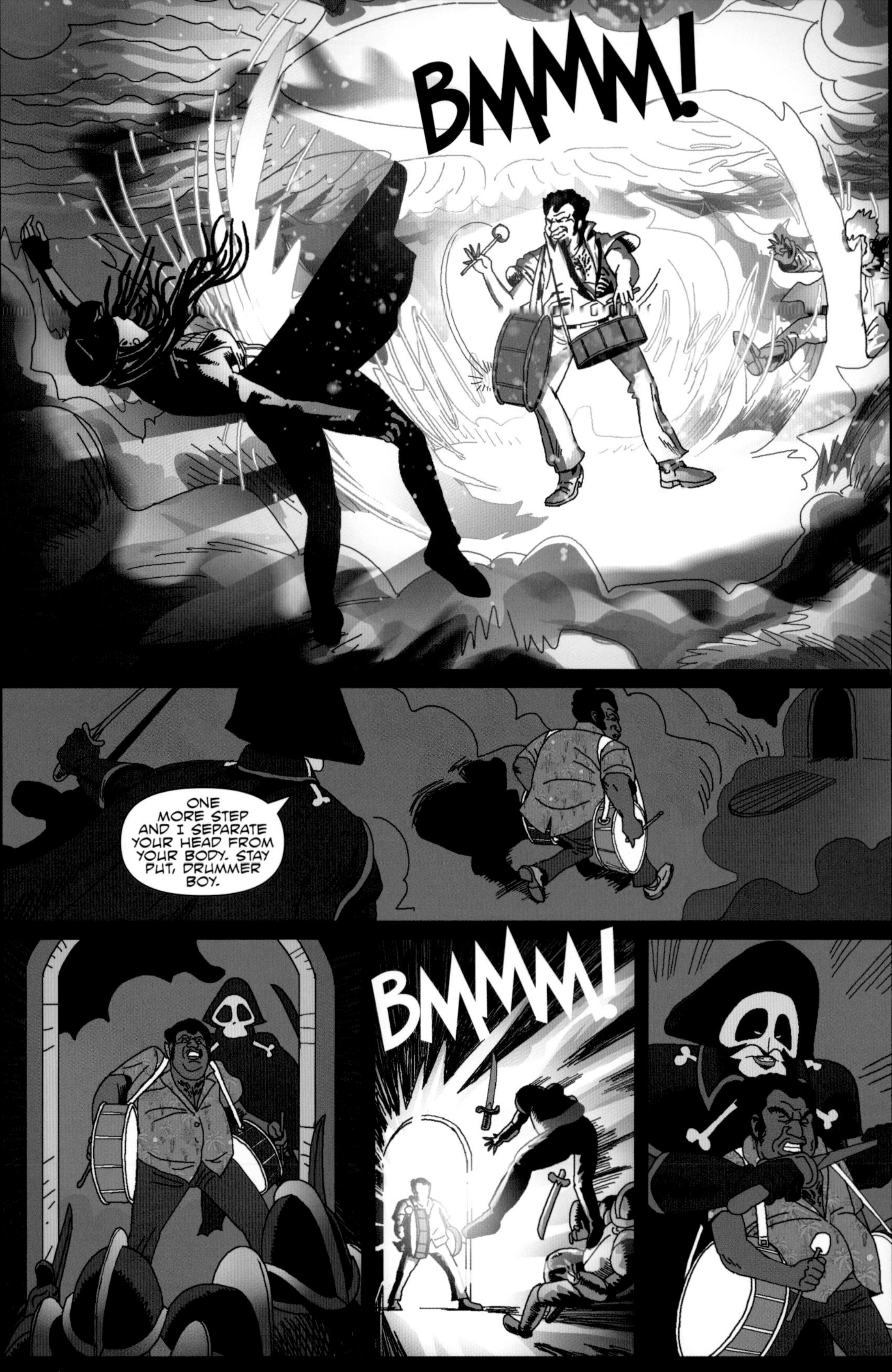
BMMM!
ONE MORE STEP AND I SEPARATE YOUR HEAD FROM YOUR BODY. STAY PUT, DRUMMER BOY.
BMMM!

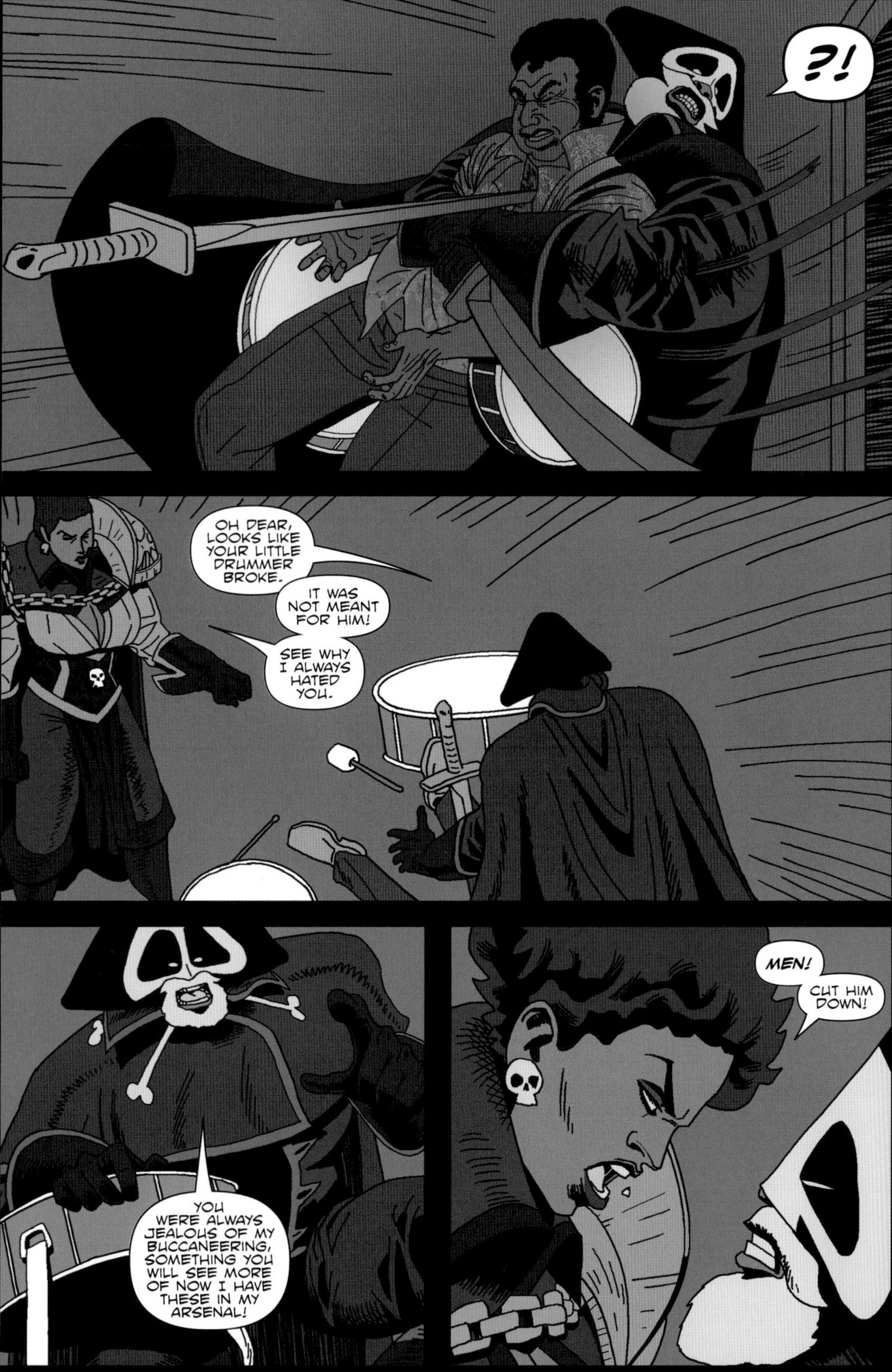
?!
OH DEAR, LOOKS LIKE YOUR LITTLE DRUMMER BROKE.
IT WAS NOT MEANT FOR HIM!
SEE WHY I ALWAYS HATED YOU.
YOU WERE ALWAYS JEALOUS OF MY BUCCANEERING, SOMETHING YOU WILL SEE MORE OF NOW I HAVE THESE IN MY ARSENAL!
MEN!
CUT HIM DOWN!

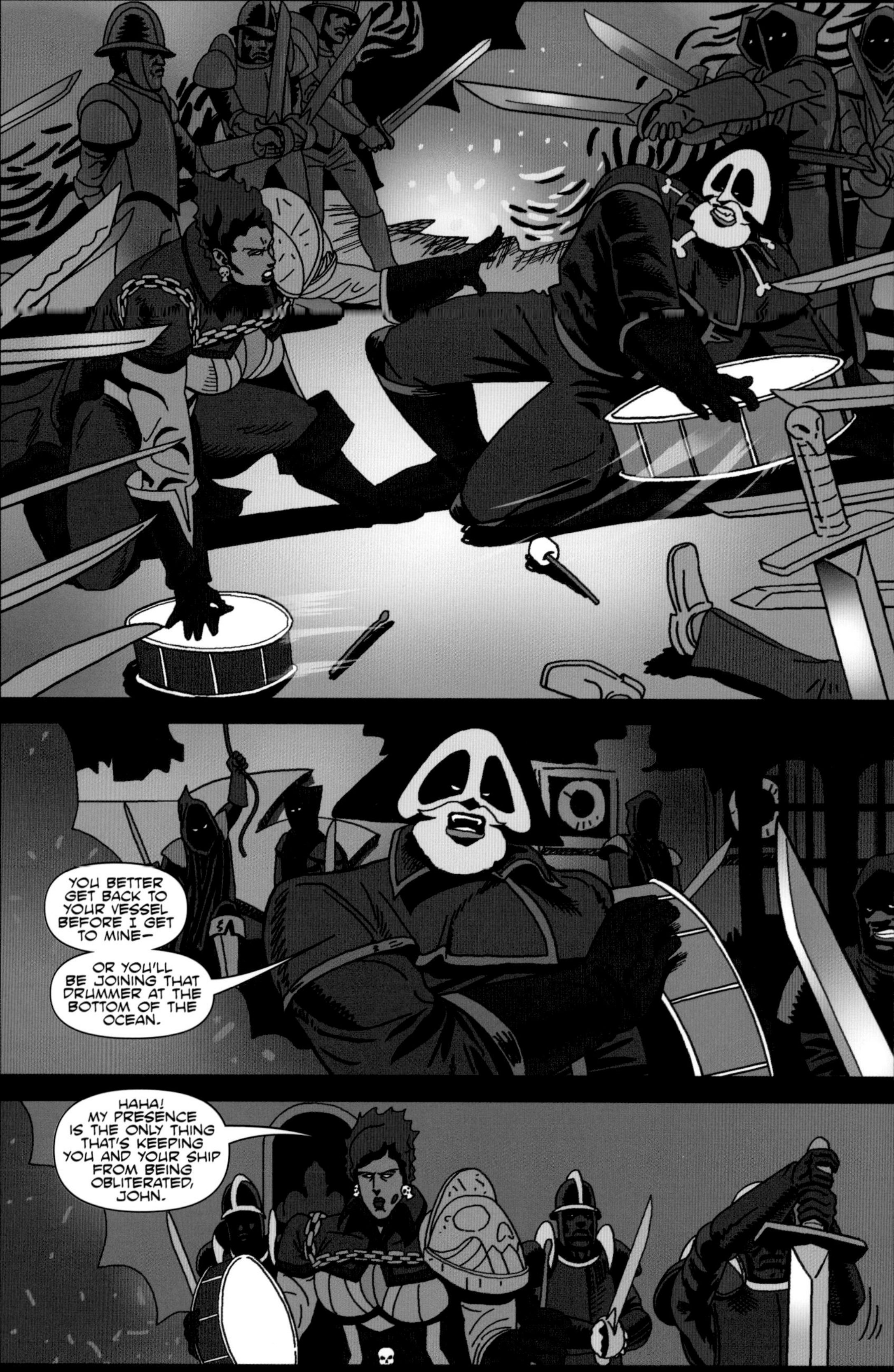
YOU BETTER GET BACK TO YOUR VESSEL BEFORE I GET TO MINE—
OR YOU'LL BE JOINING THAT DRUMMER AT THE BOTTOM OF THE OCEAN.
HAHA! MY PRESENCE IS THE ONLY THING THAT'S KEEPING YOU AND YOUR SHIP FROM BEING OBLITERATED, JOHN.

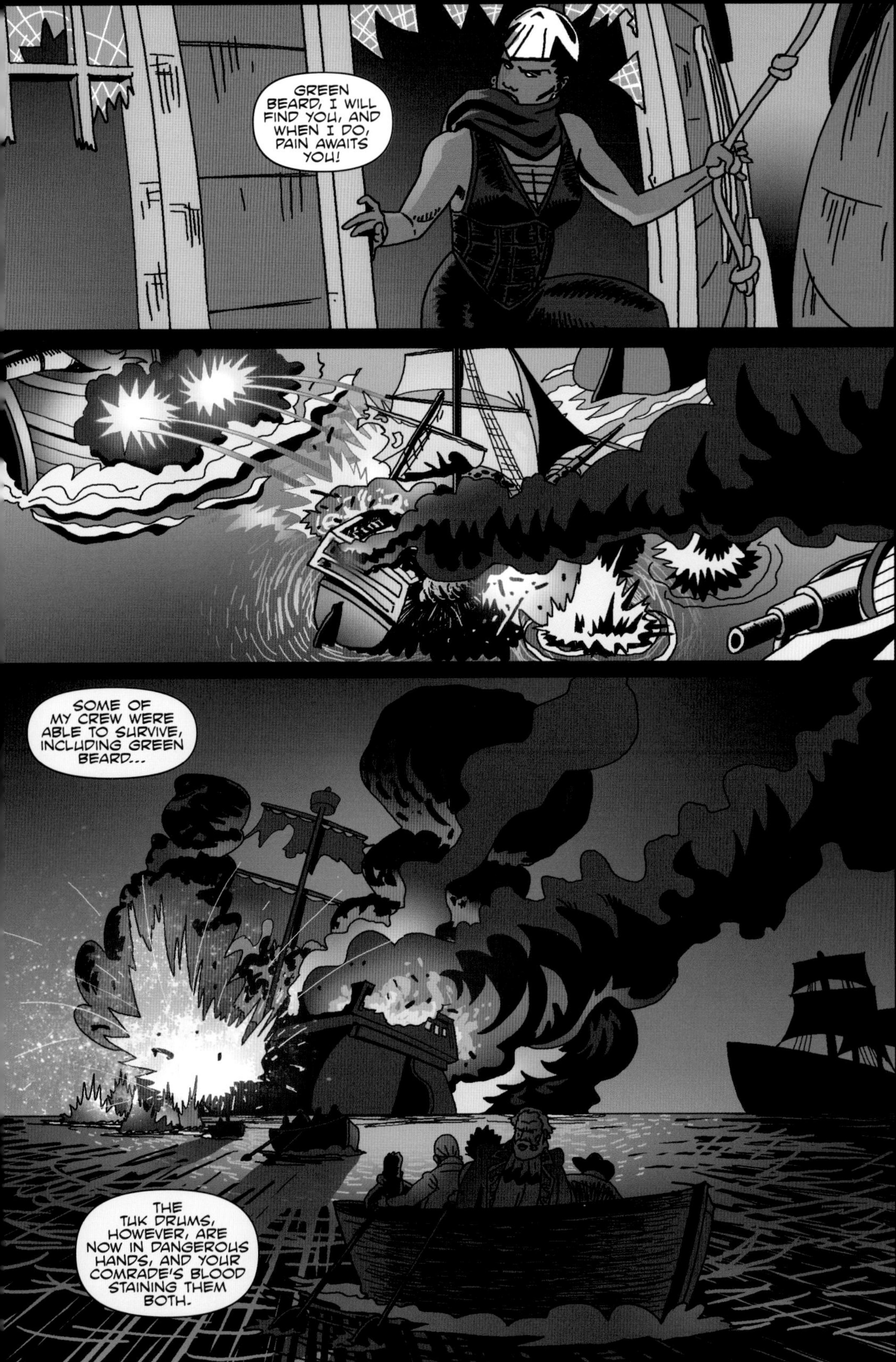
GREEN BEARD, I WILL FIND YOU, AND WHEN I DO, PAIN AWAITS YOU!
SOME OF MY CREW WERE ABLE TO SURVIVE, INCLUDING GREEN BEARD...
THE TUK DRUMS, HOWEVER, ARE NOW IN DANGEROUS HANDS, AND YOUR COMRADE'S BLOOD STAINING THEM BOTH.

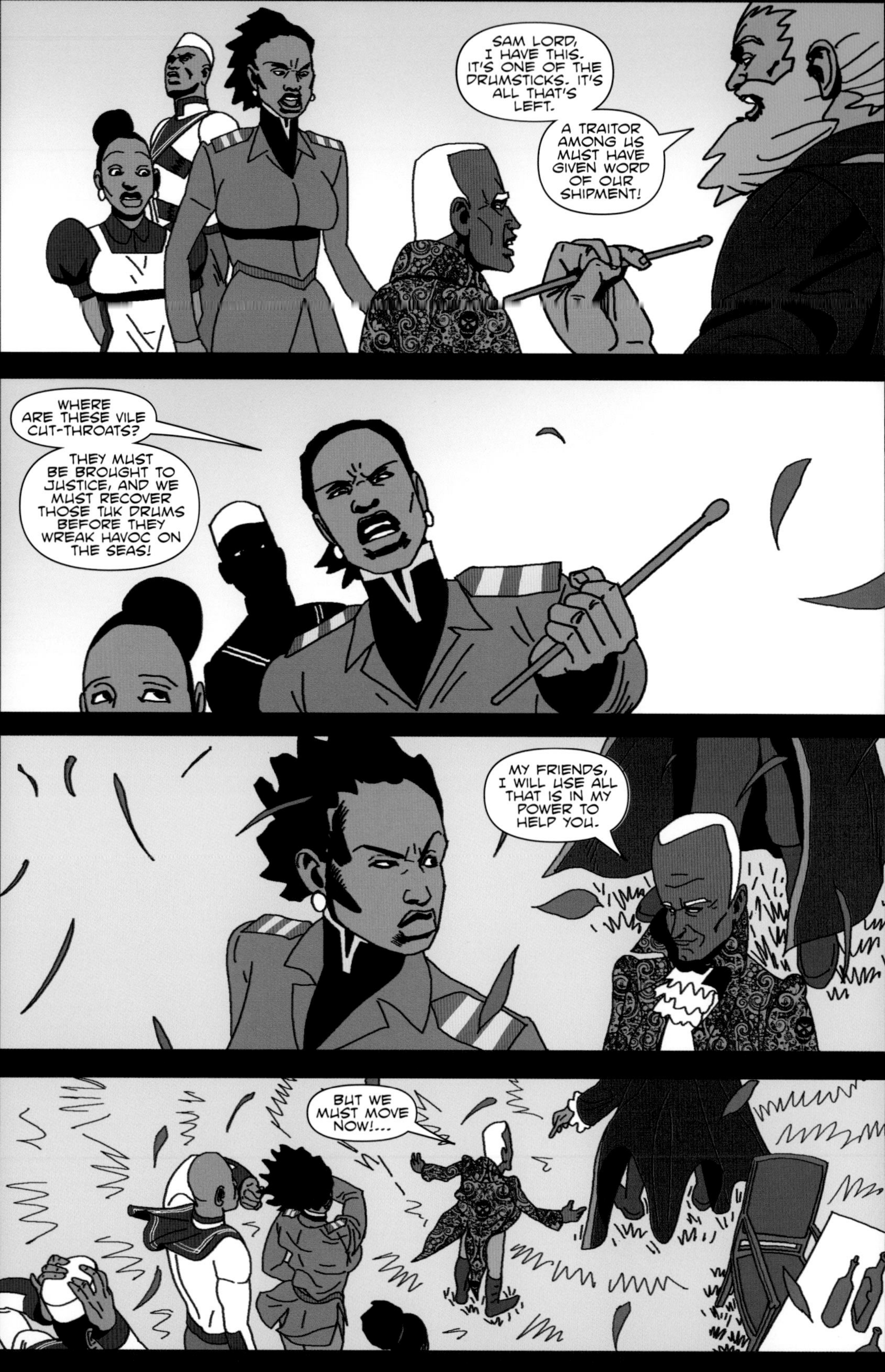
SAM LORD, I HAVE THIS. IT'S ONE OF THE DRUMSTICKS. IT'S ALL THAT'S LEFT.
A TRAITOR AMONG US MUST HAVE GIVEN WORD OF OUR SHIPMENT!
WHERE ARE THESE VILE CUT-THROATS?
THEY MUST BE BROUGHT TO JUSTICE, AND WE MUST RECOVER THOSE TUK DRUMS BEFORE THEY WREAK HAVOC ON THE SEAS!
MY FRIENDS, I WILL USE ALL THAT IS IN MY POWER TO HELP YOU.
BUT WE MUST MOVE NOW!...

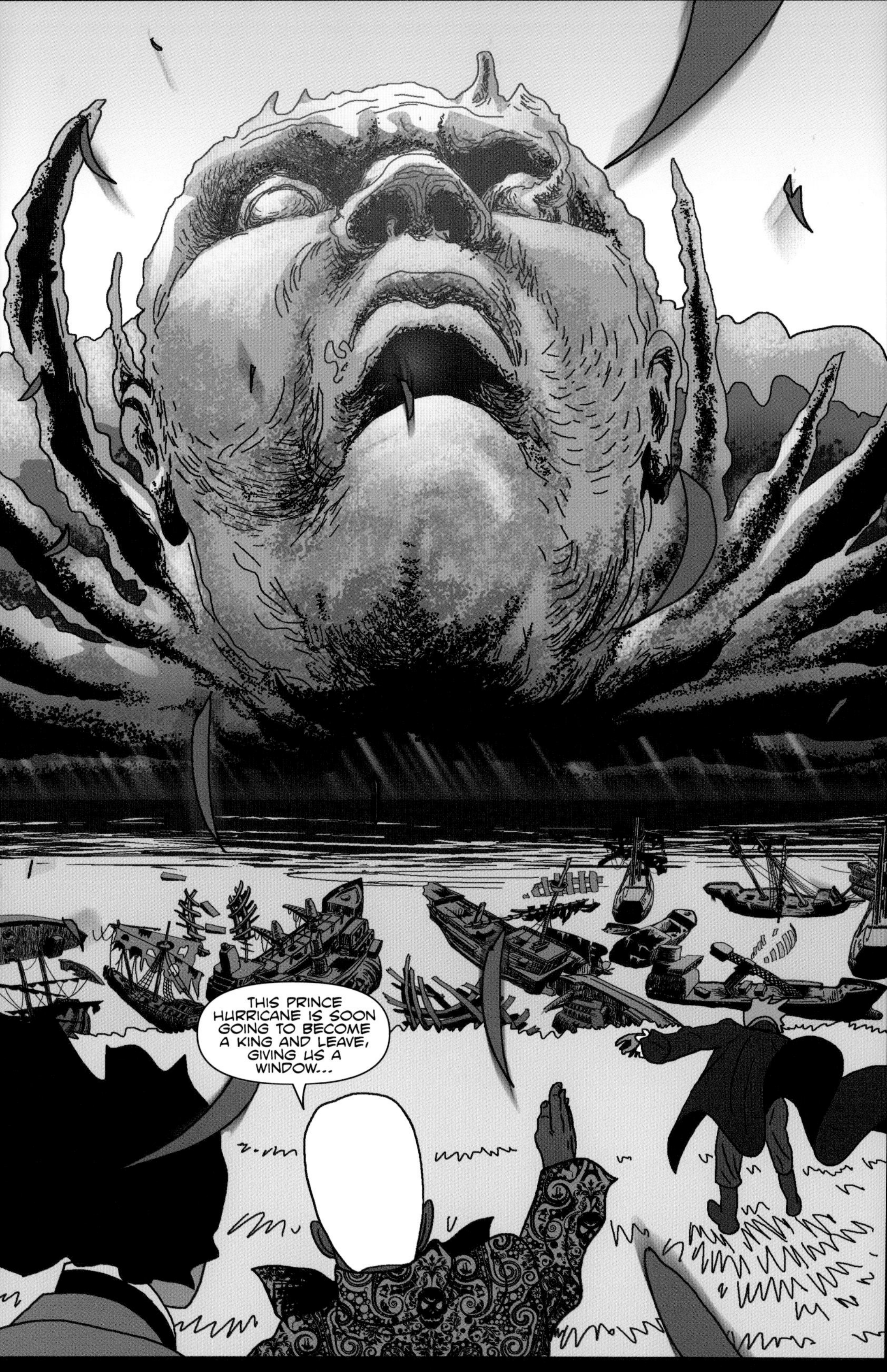
THIS PRINCE HURRICANE IS SOON GOING TO BECOME A KING AND LEAVE, GIVING US A WINDOW...

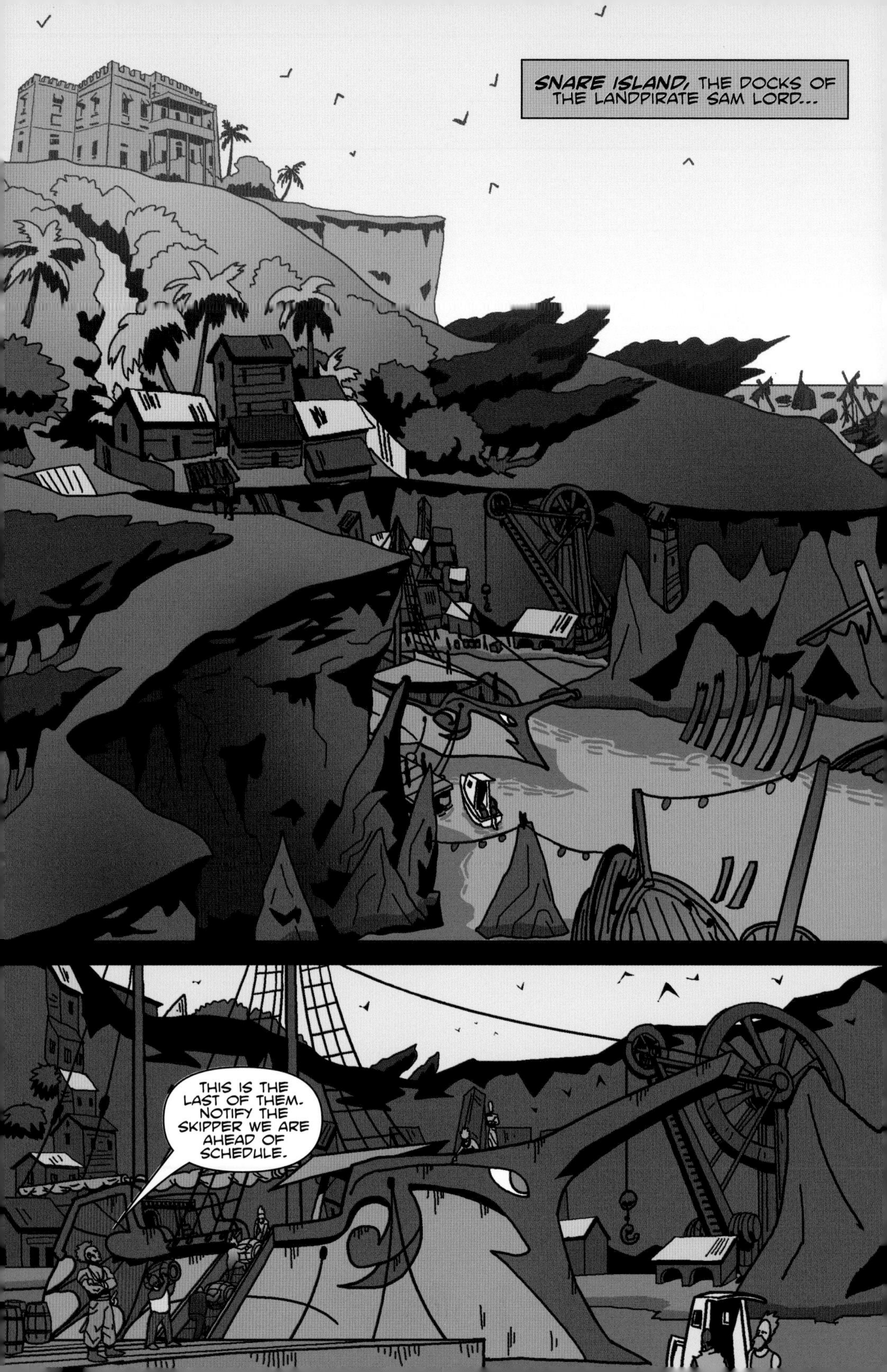
SNARE ISLAND, THE DOCKS OF THE LANDPIRATE SAM LORD...
THIS IS THE LAST OF THEM. NOTIFY THE SKIPPER WE ARE AHEAD OF SCHEDULE.

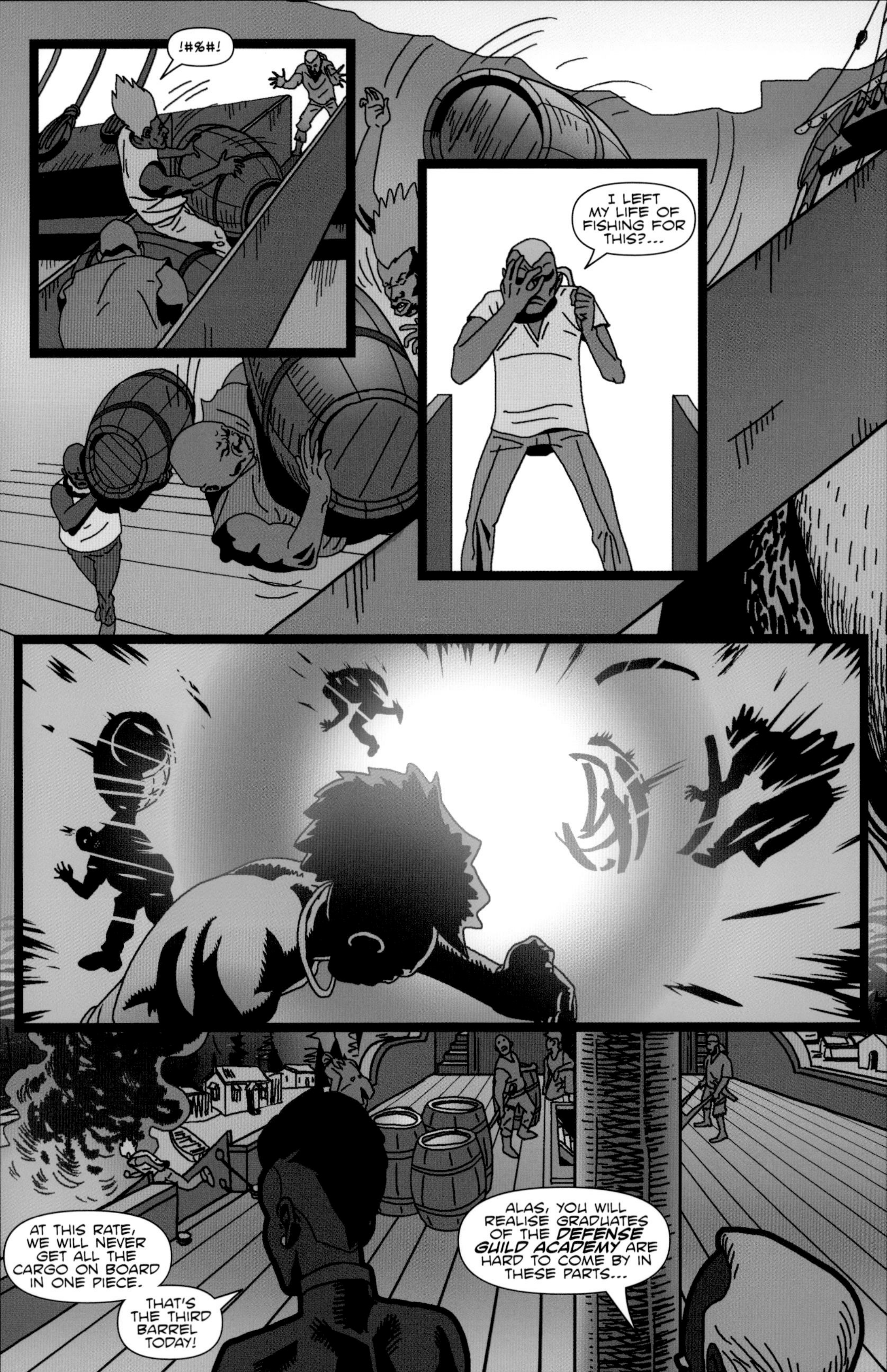
!#%#!
I LEFT MY LIFE OF FISHING FOR THIS?...
AT THIS RATE, WE WILL NEVER GET ALL THE CARGO ON BOARD IN ONE PIECE.
THAT'S THE THIRD BARREL TODAY!
ALAS, YOU WILL REALISE GRADUATES OF THE DEFENSE GUILD ACADEMY ARE HARD TO COME BY IN THESE PARTS...

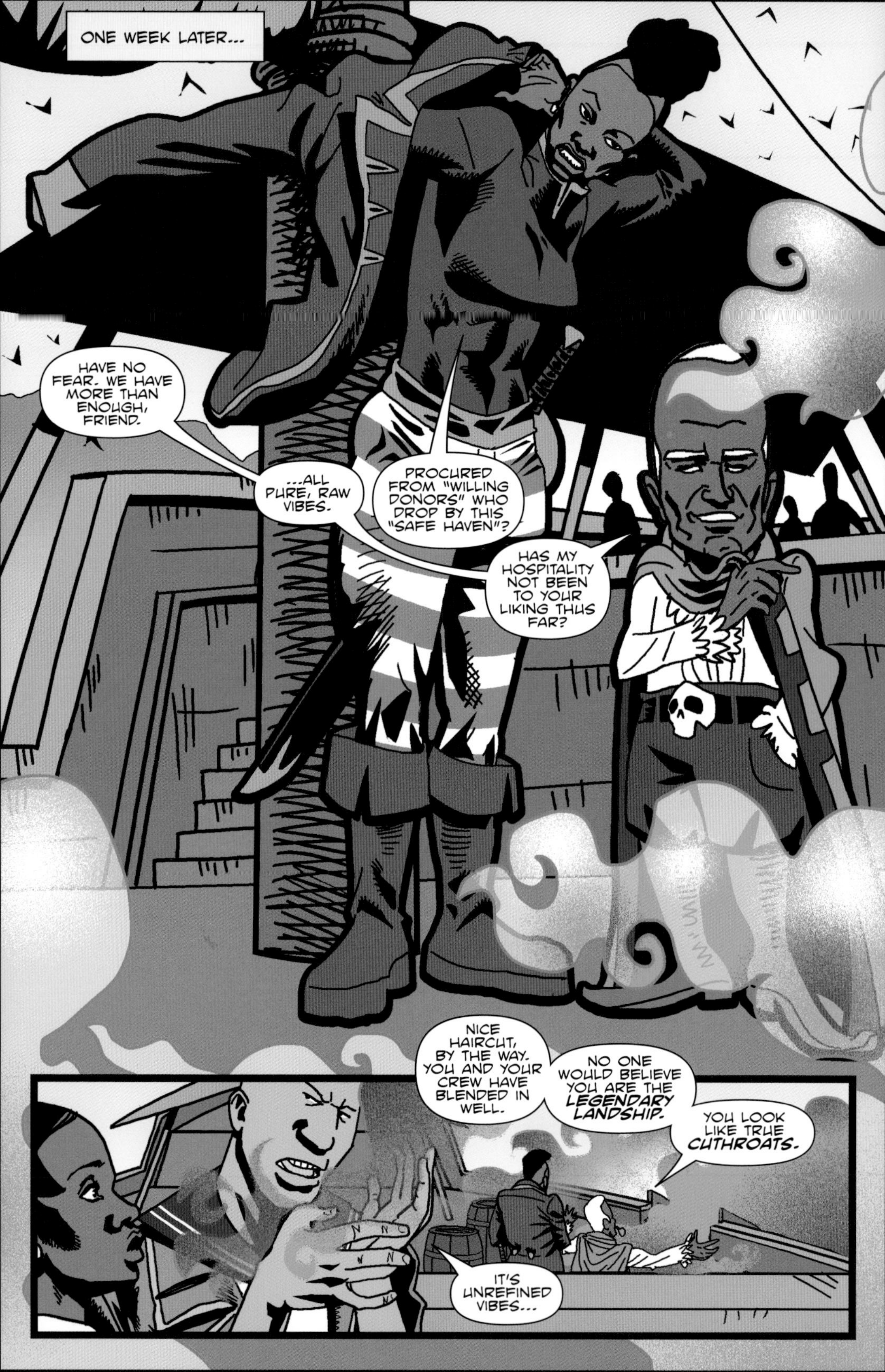
ONE WEEK LATER...
PROCURED FROM "WILLING DONORS" WHO DROP BY THIS "SAFE HAVEN"?
HAS MY HOSPITALITY NOT BEEN TO YOUR LIKING THUS FAR?
HAVE NO FEAR. WE HAVE MORE THAN ENOUGH, FRIEND.
...ALL PURE, RAW VIBES.
NICE HAIRCUT, BY THE WAY. YOU AND YOUR CREW HAVE BLENDED IN WELL.
NO ONE WOULD BELIEVE YOU ARE THE *LEGENDARY LANDSHIP.*
YOU LOOK LIKE TRUE *CUTHROATS.*
IT'S UNREFINED VIBES...

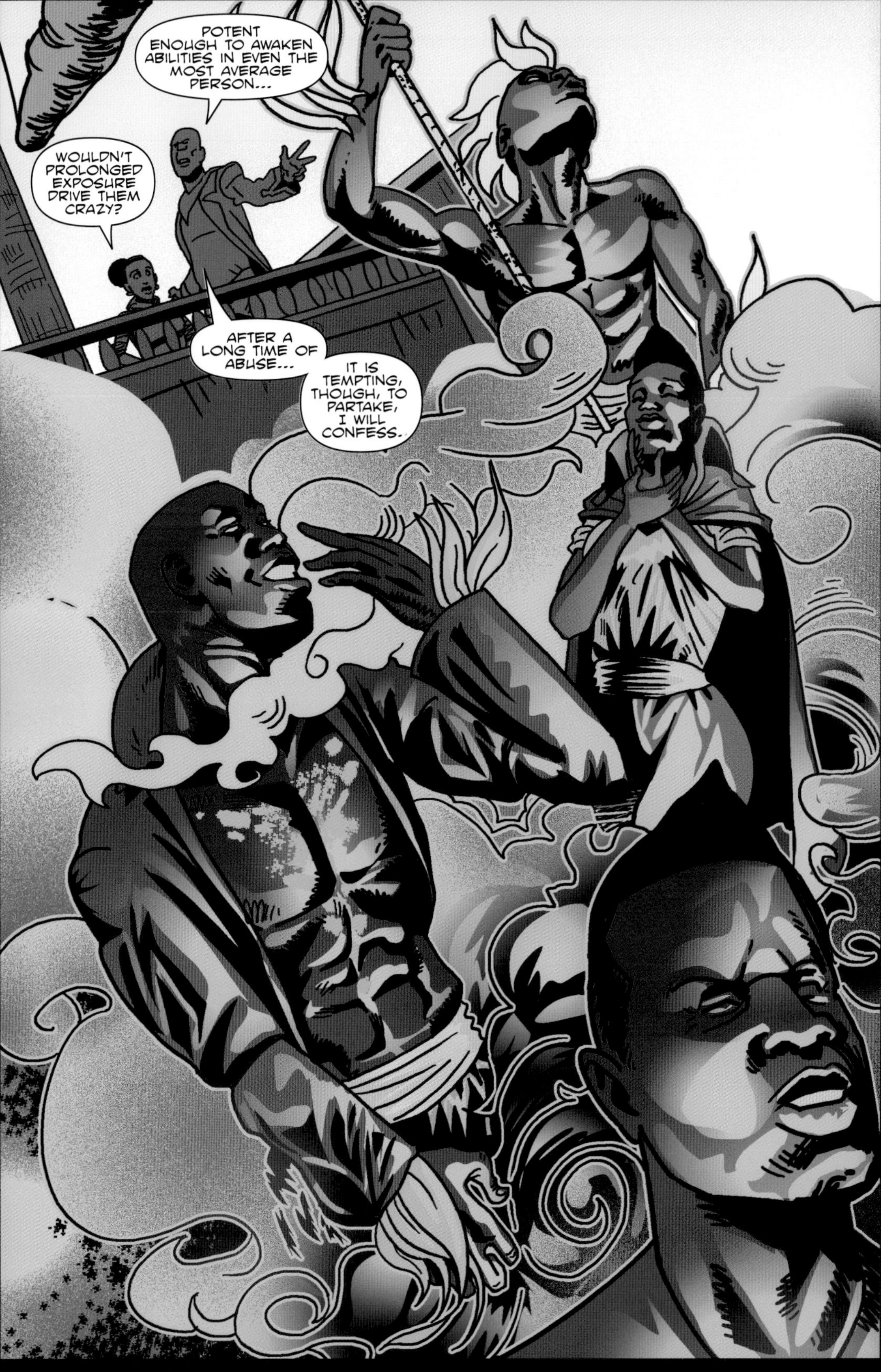
POTENT ENOUGH TO AWAKEN ABILITIES IN EVEN THE MOST AVERAGE PERSON...
WOULDN'T PROLONGED EXPOSURE DRIVE THEM CRAZY?
AFTER A LONG TIME OF ABUSE...
IT IS TEMPTING, THOUGH, TO PARTAKE, I WILL CONFESS.

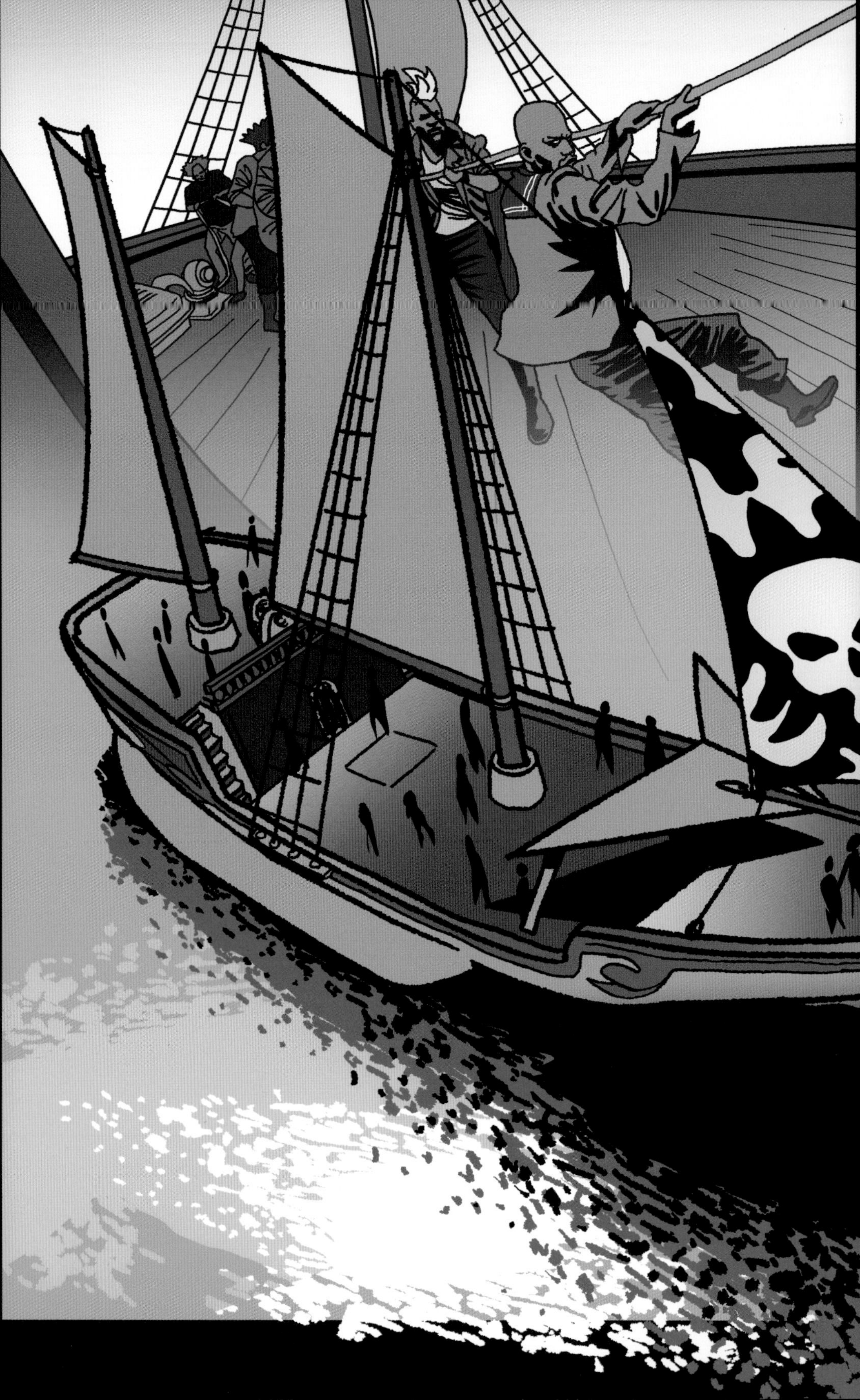

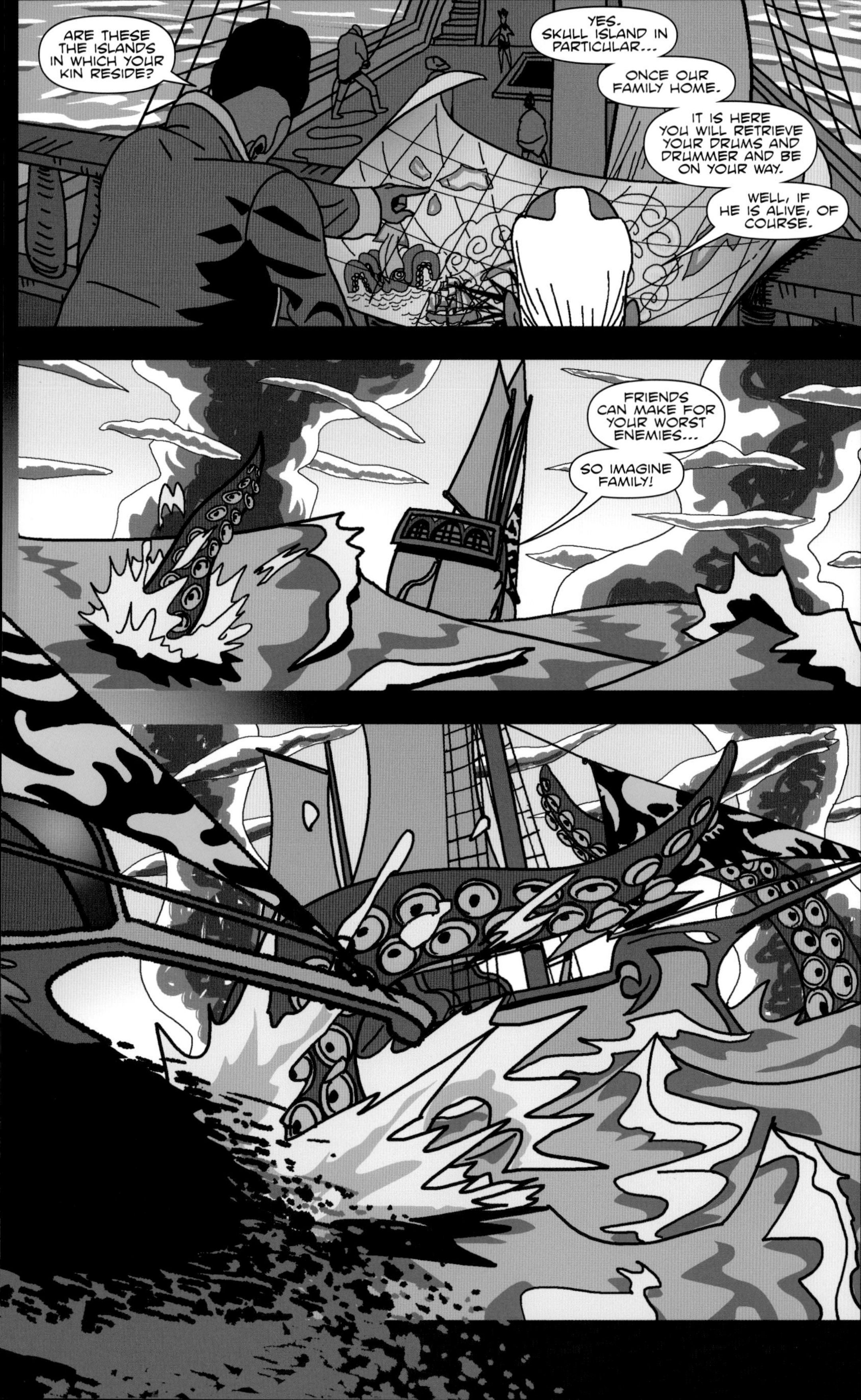
ARE THESE THE ISLANDS IN WHICH YOUR KIN RESIDE?
YES. SKULL ISLAND IN PARTICULAR...
ONCE OUR FAMILY HOME.
IT IS HERE YOU WILL RETRIEVE YOUR DRUMS AND DRUMMER AND BE ON YOUR WAY.
WELL, IF HE IS ALIVE, OF COURSE.
FRIENDS CAN MAKE FOR YOUR WORST ENEMIES...
SO IMAGINE FAMILY!

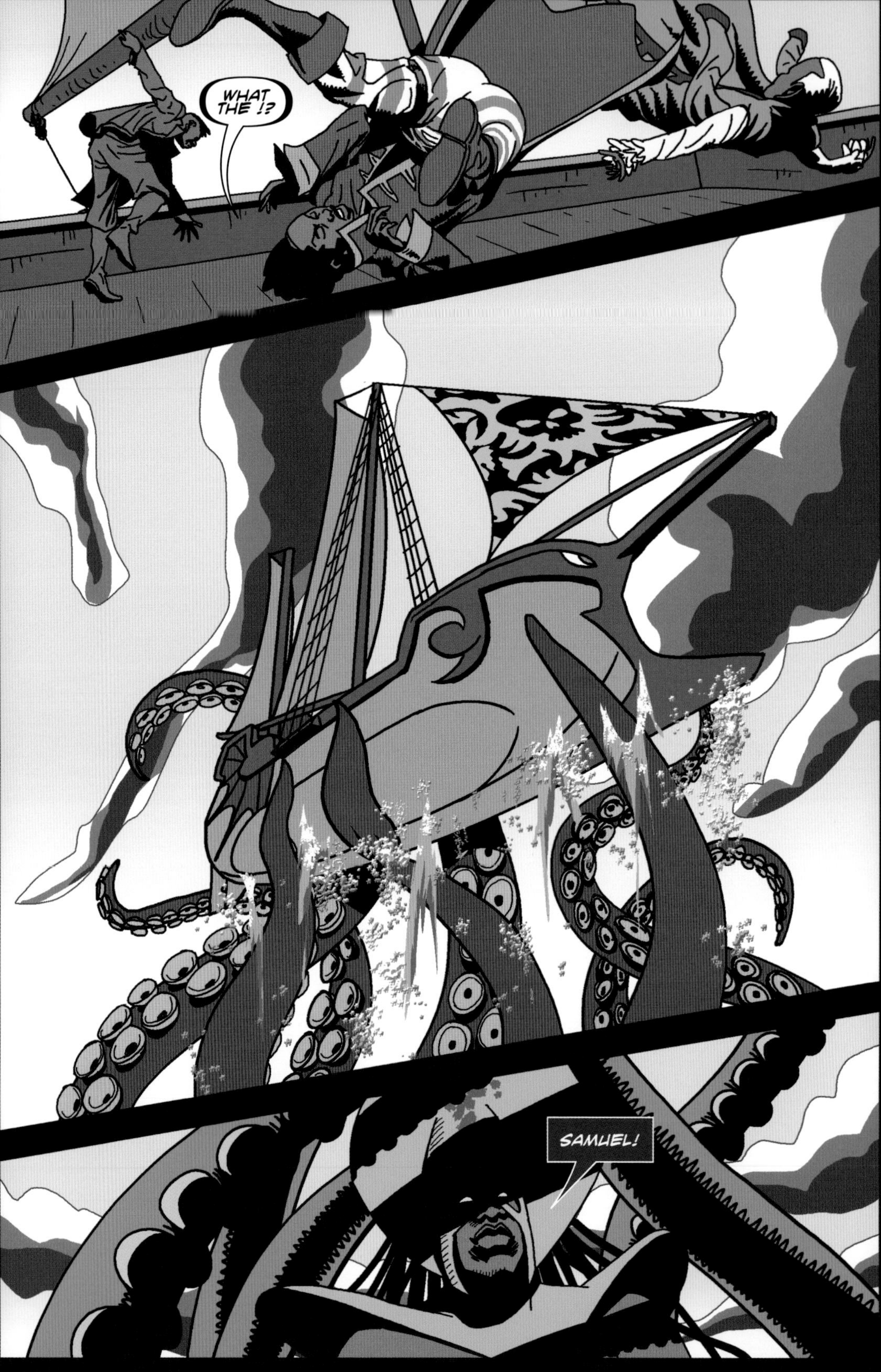
WHAT THE !?
SAMUEL!

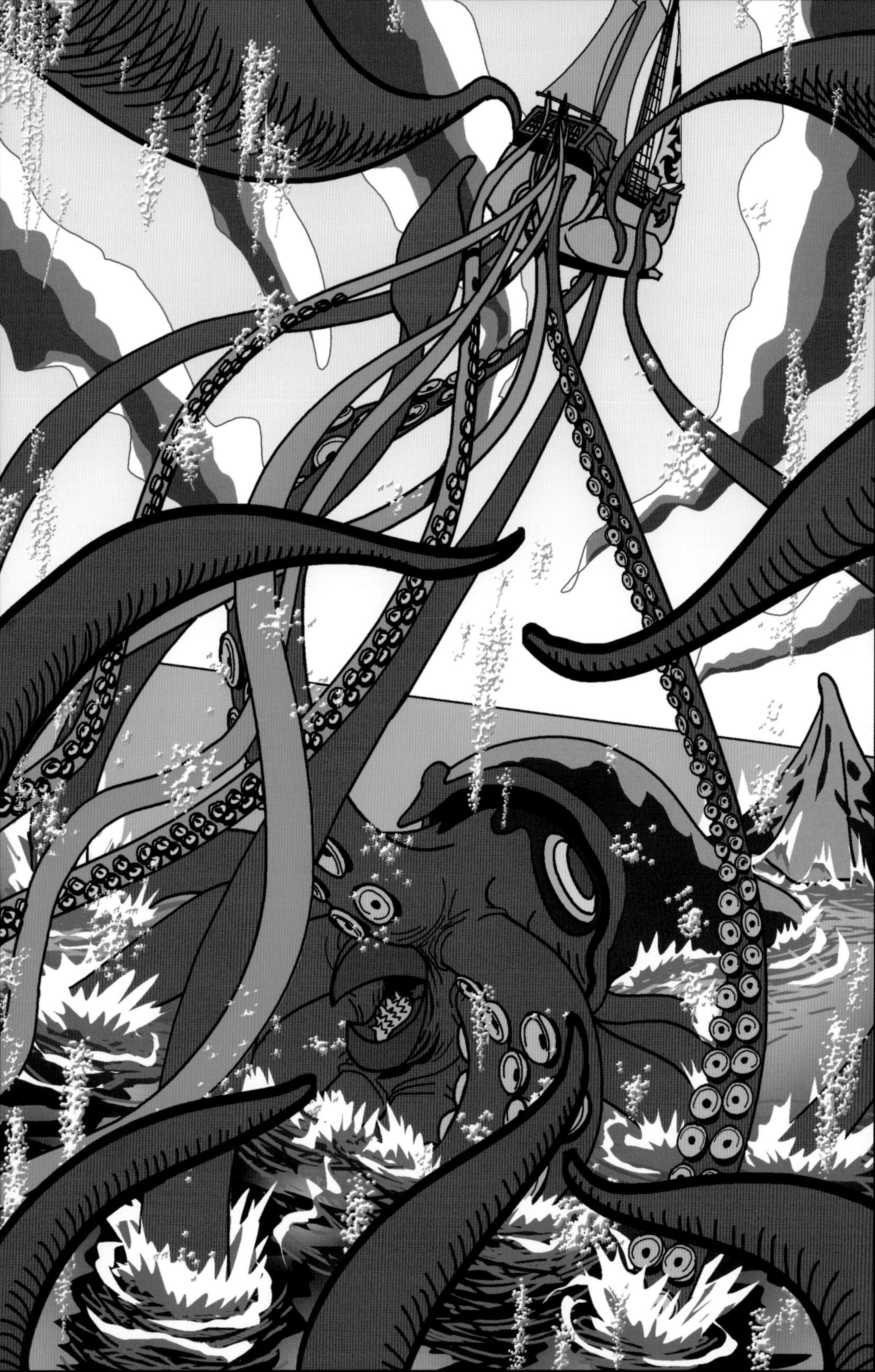

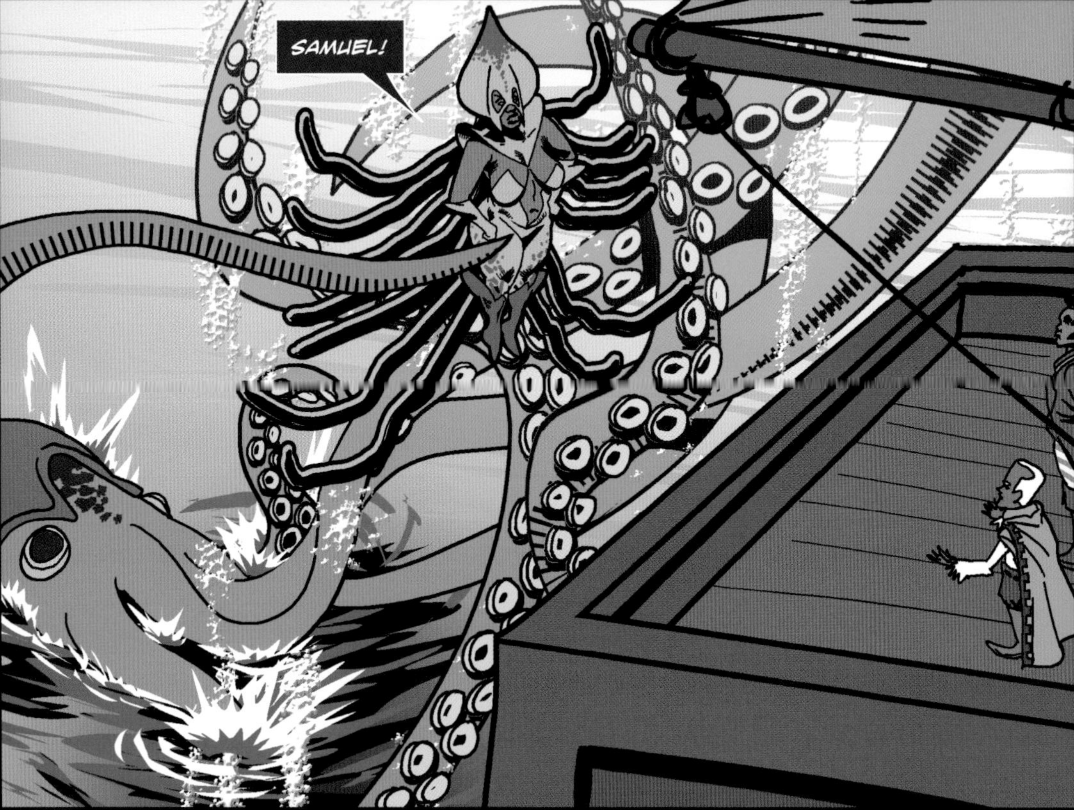
SAMUEL!

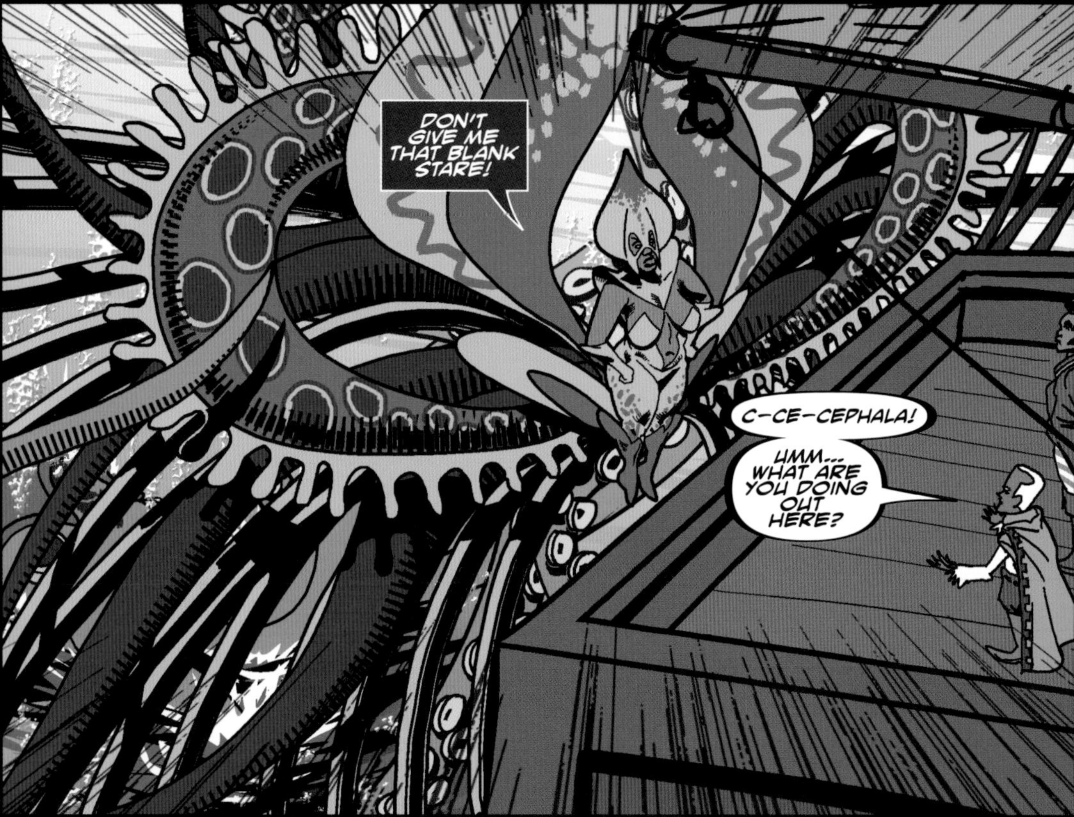
DON'T GIVE ME THAT BLANK STARE!
C-CE-CEPHALA!
UMM... WHAT ARE YOU DOING OUT HERE?

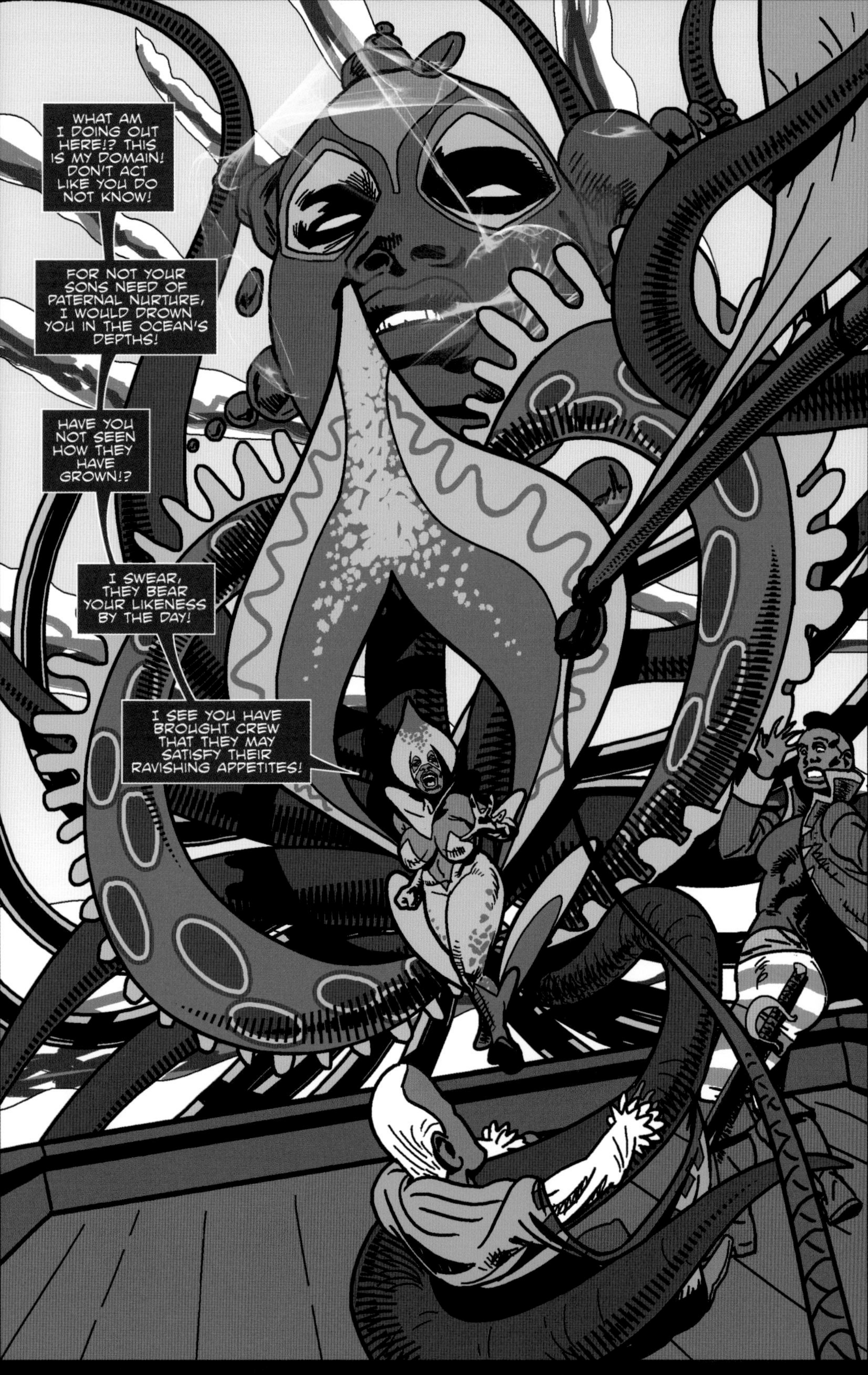
WHAT AM I DOING OUT HERE!? THIS IS MY DOMAIN! DON'T ACT LIKE YOU DO NOT KNOW!
FOR NOT YOUR SONS NEED OF PATERNAL NURTURE, I WOULD DROWN YOU IN THE OCEAN'S DEPTHS!
HAVE YOU NOT SEEN HOW THEY HAVE GROWN!?
I SWEAR, THEY BEAR YOUR LIKENESS BY THE DAY!
I SEE YOU HAVE BROUGHT CREW THAT THEY MAY SATISFY THEIR RAVISHING APPETITES!

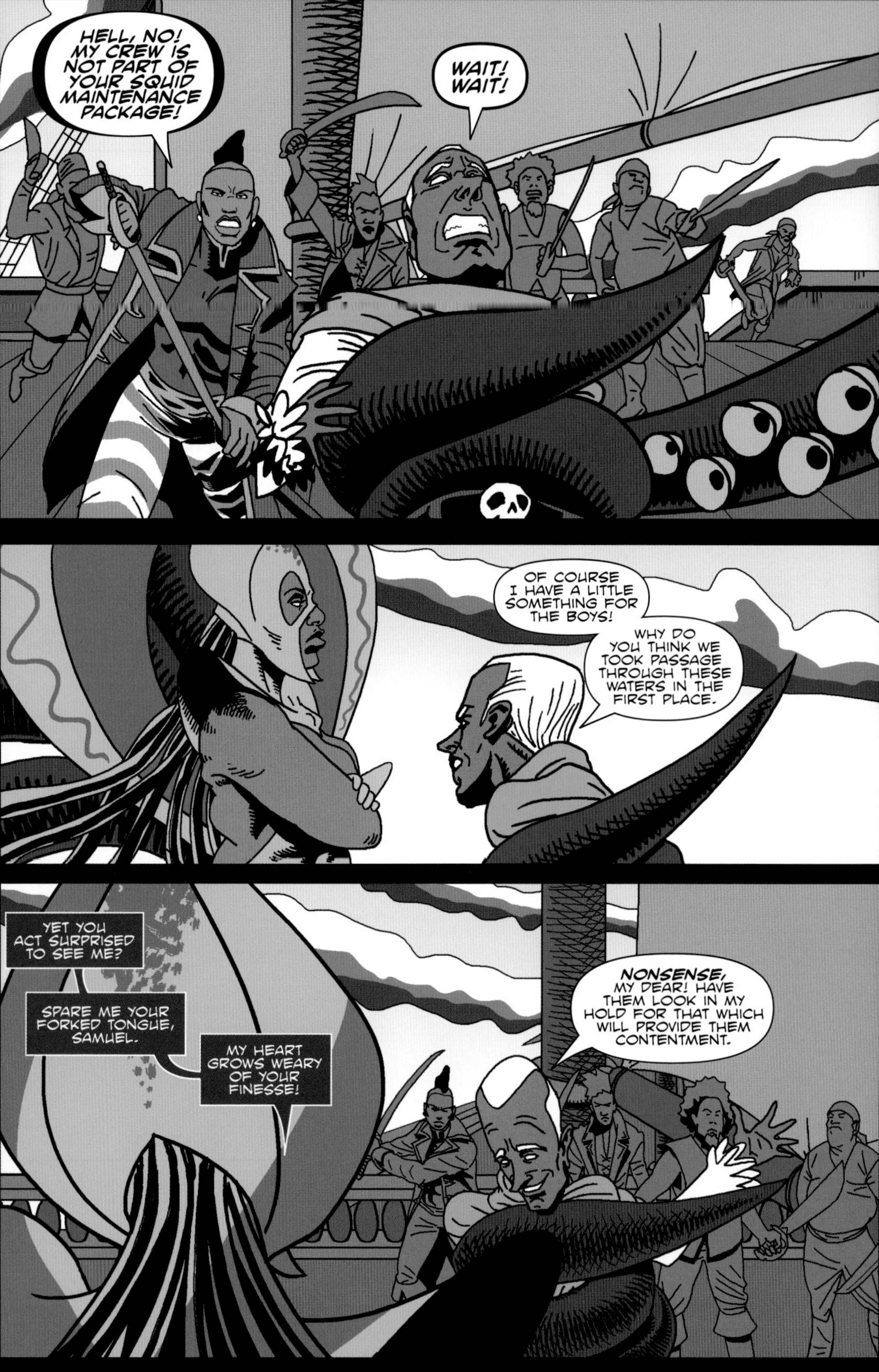

HELL, NO! MY CREW IS NOT PART OF YOUR SQUID MAINTENANCE PACKAGE!
WAIT! WAIT!
OF COURSE I HAVE A LITTLE SOMETHING FOR THE BOYS!
WHY DO YOU THINK WE TOOK PASSAGE THROUGH THESE WATERS IN THE FIRST PLACE.
YET YOU ACT SURPRISED TO SEE ME?
SPARE ME YOUR FORKED TONGUE, SAMUEL.
MY HEART GROWS WEARY OF YOUR FINESSE!
NONSENSE, MY DEAR! HAVE THEM LOOK IN MY HOLD FOR THAT WHICH WILL PROVIDE THEM CONTENTMENT.

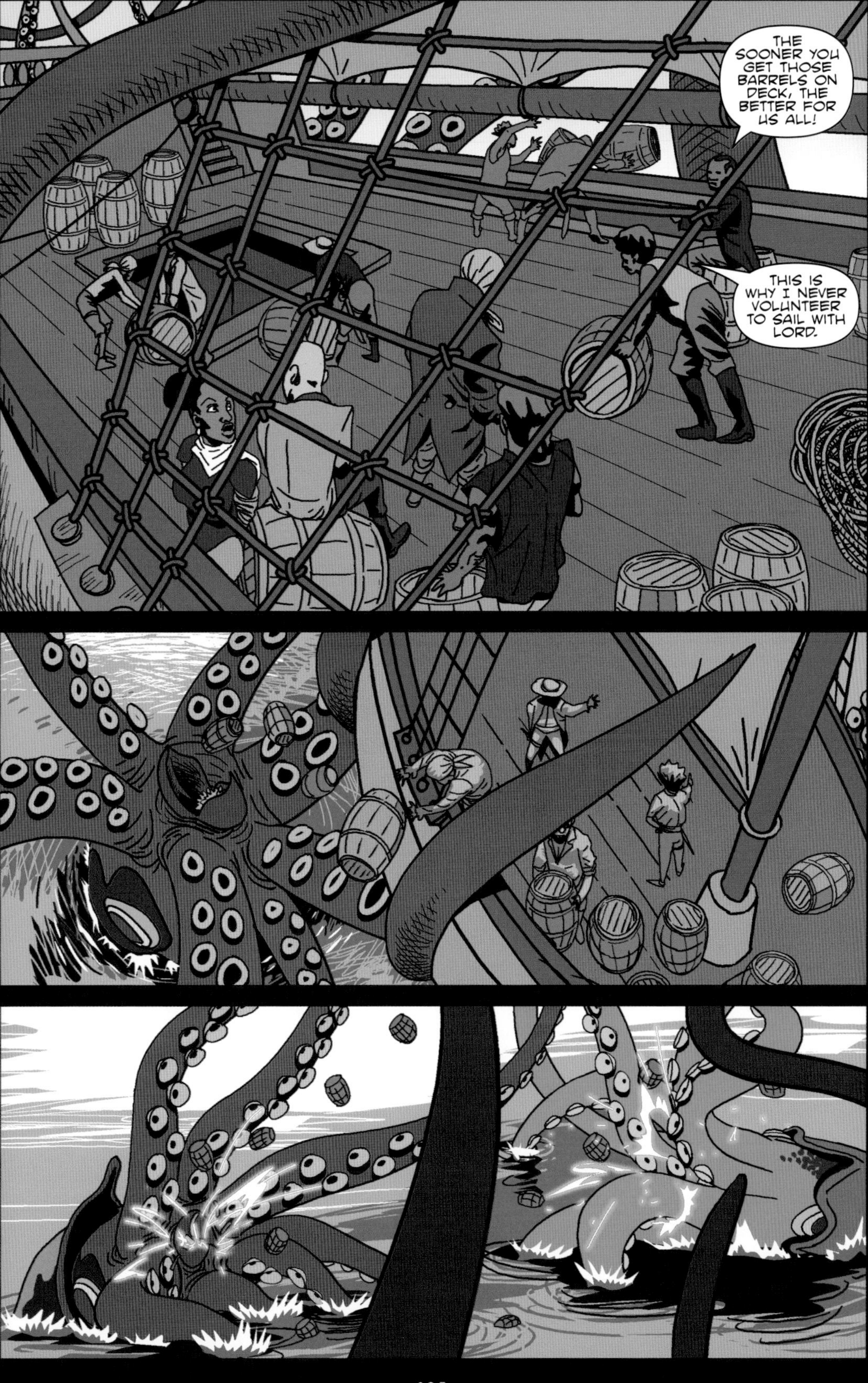
THE SOONER YOU GET THOSE BARRELS ON DECK, THE BETTER FOR US ALL!
THIS IS WHY I NEVER VOLUNTEER TO SAIL WITH LORD.

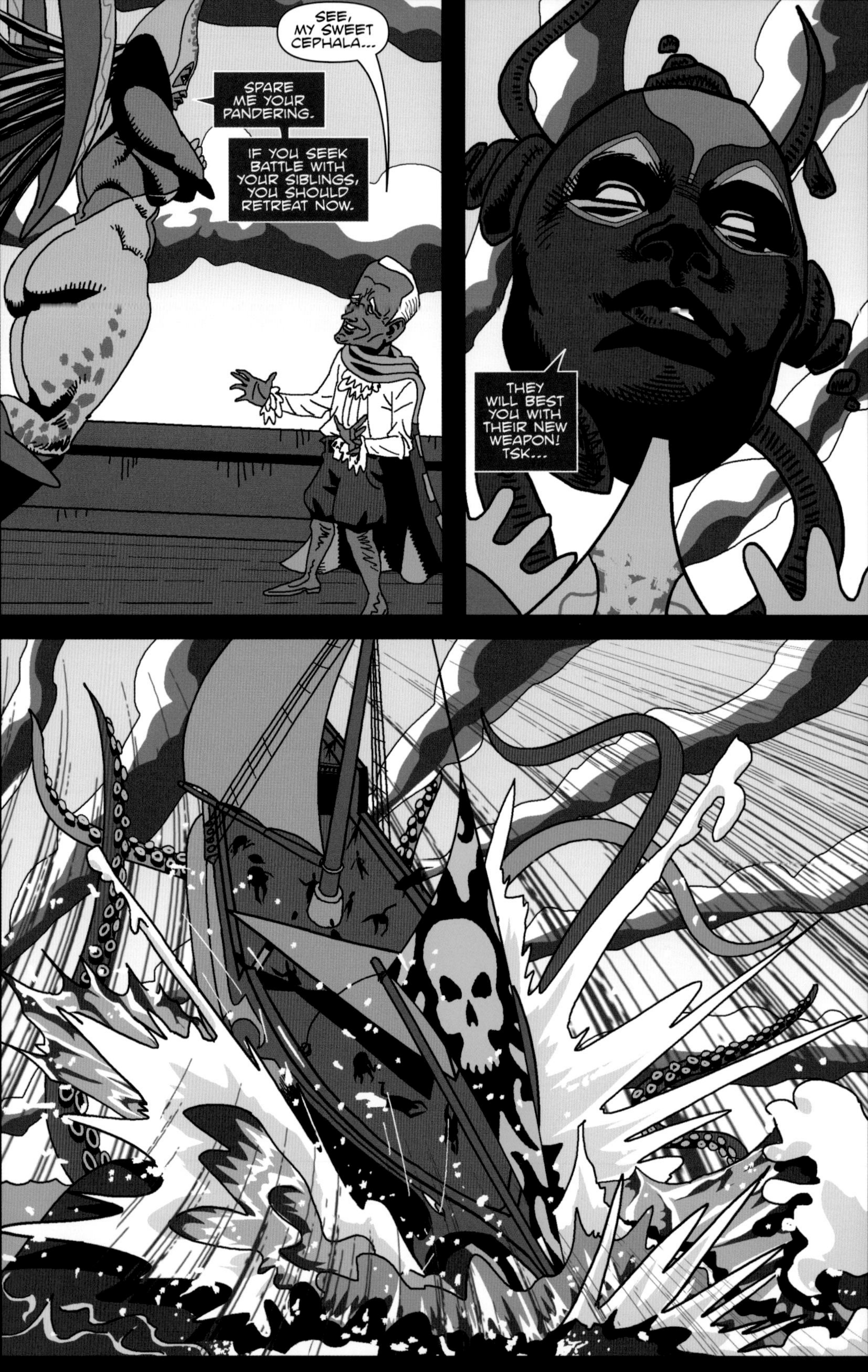
SEE, MY SWEET CEPHALA...
SPARE ME YOUR PANDERING.
IF YOU SEEK BATTLE WITH YOUR SIBLINGS, YOU SHOULD RETREAT NOW.
THEY WILL BEST YOU WITH THEIR NEW WEAPON! TSK...

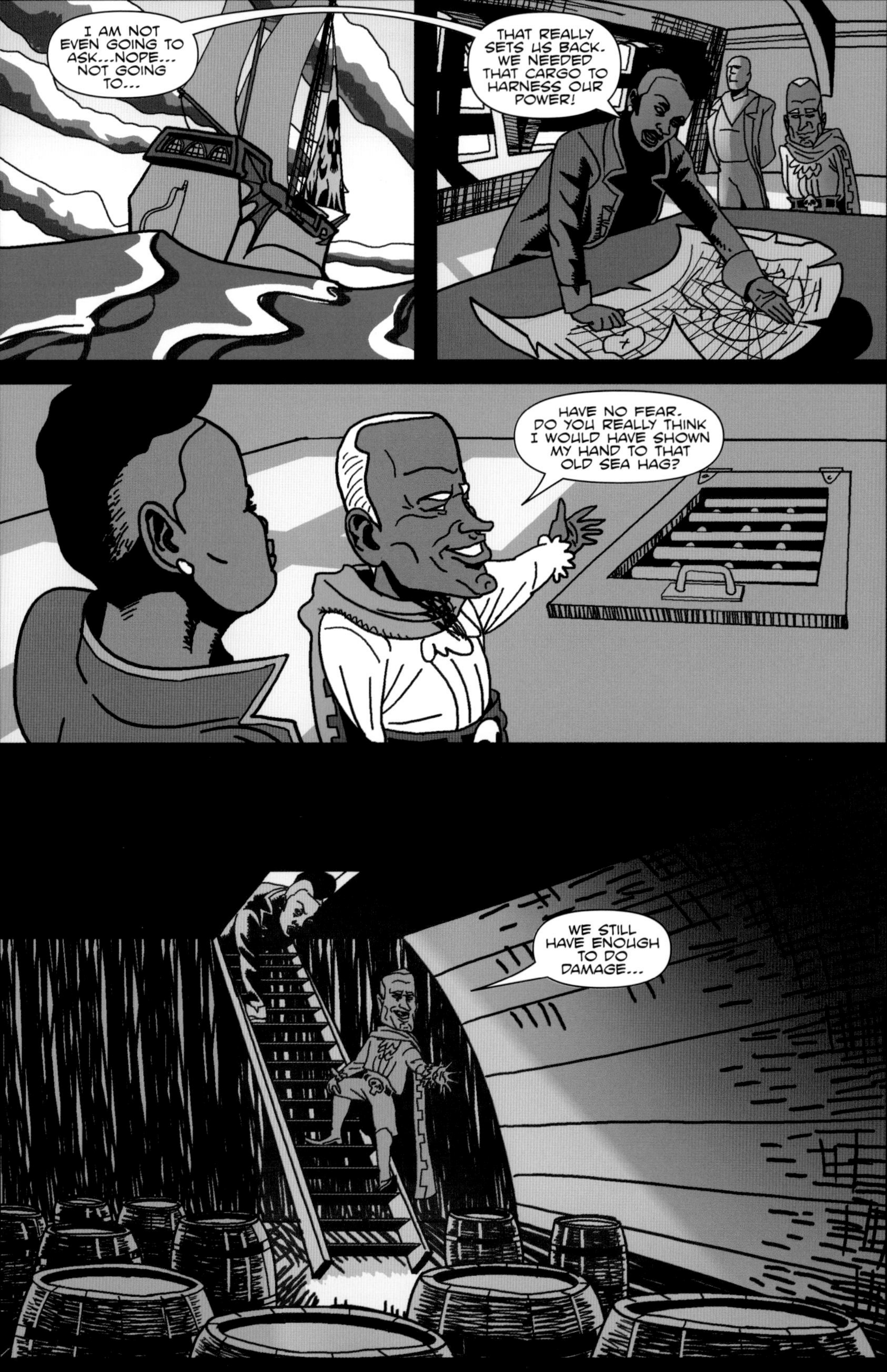
I AM NOT EVEN GOING TO ASK...NOPE... NOT GOING TO...
THAT REALLY SETS US BACK. WE NEEDED THAT CARGO TO HARNESS OUR POWER!
HAVE NO FEAR. DO YOU REALLY THINK I WOULD HAVE SHOWN MY HAND TO THAT OLD SEA HAG?
WE STILL HAVE ENOUGH TO DO DAMAGE...

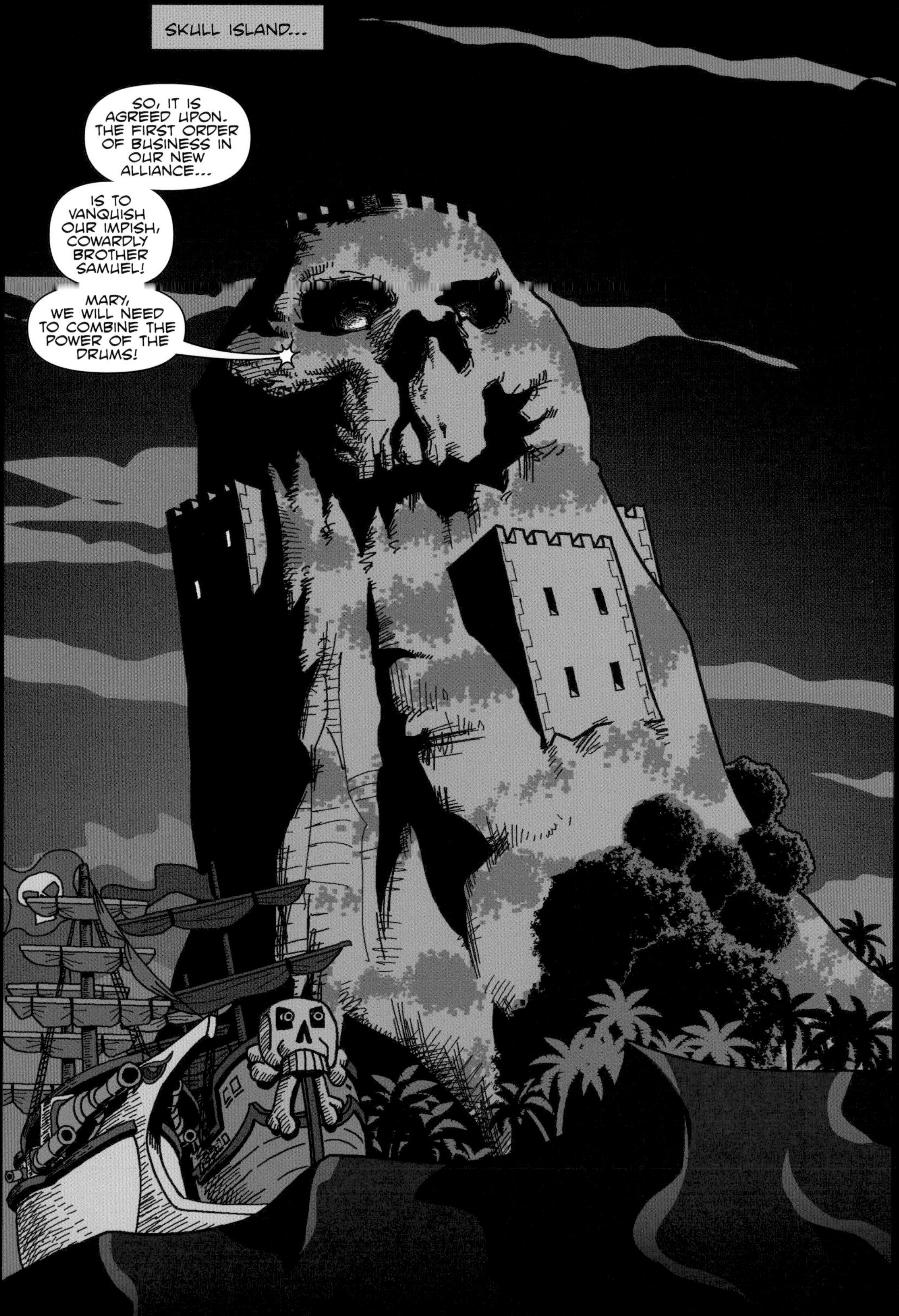
SKULL ISLAND...
SO, IT IS AGREED UPON. THE FIRST ORDER OF BUSINESS IN OUR NEW ALLIANCE...
IS TO VANQUISH OUR IMPISH, COWARDLY BROTHER SAMUEL!
MARY, WE WILL NEED TO COMBINE THE POWER OF THE DRUMS!

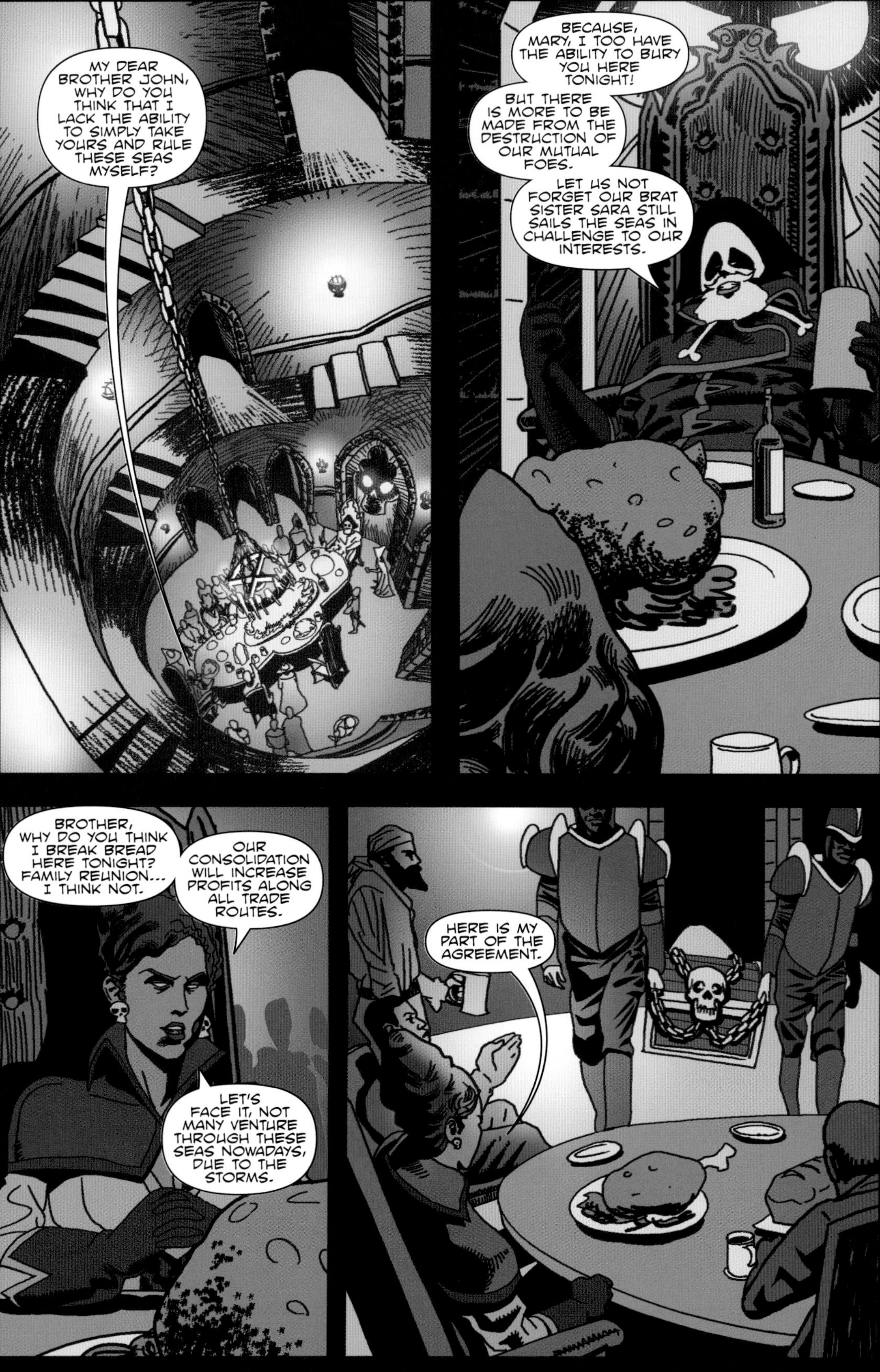
MY DEAR BROTHER JOHN, WHY DO YOU THINK THAT I LACK THE ABILITY TO SIMPLY TAKE YOURS AND RULE THESE SEAS MYSELF?
BECAUSE, MARY, I TOO HAVE THE ABILITY TO BURY YOU HERE TONIGHT!
BUT THERE IS MORE TO BE MADE FROM THE DESTRUCTION OF OUR MUTUAL FOES.
LET US NOT FORGET OUR BRAT SISTER SARA STILL SAILS THE SEAS IN CHALLENGE TO OUR INTERESTS.
BROTHER, WHY DO YOU THINK I BREAK BREAD HERE TONIGHT? FAMILY REUNION... I THINK NOT.
OUR CONSOLIDATION WILL INCREASE PROFITS ALONG ALL TRADE ROUTES.
LET'S FACE IT, NOT MANY VENTURE THROUGH THESE SEAS NOWADAYS, DUE TO THE STORMS.
HERE IS MY PART OF THE AGREEMENT.

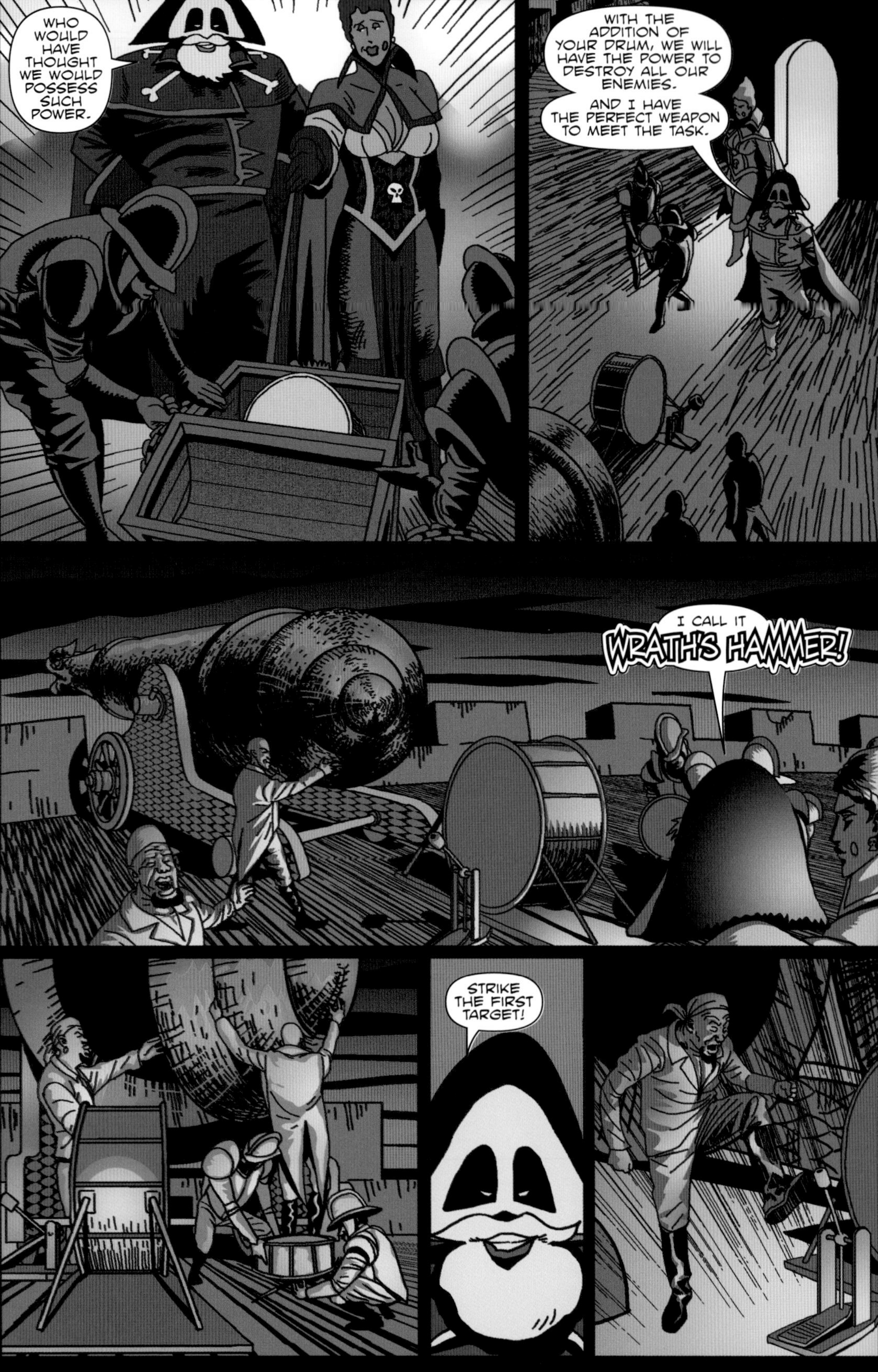
WHO WOULD HAVE THOUGHT WE WOULD POSSESS SUCH POWER.
WITH THE ADDITION OF YOUR DRUM, WE WILL HAVE THE POWER TO DESTROY ALL OUR ENEMIES.
AND I HAVE THE PERFECT WEAPON TO MEET THE TASK.
I CALL IT
WRATH'S HAMMER!
STRIKE THE FIRST TARGET!

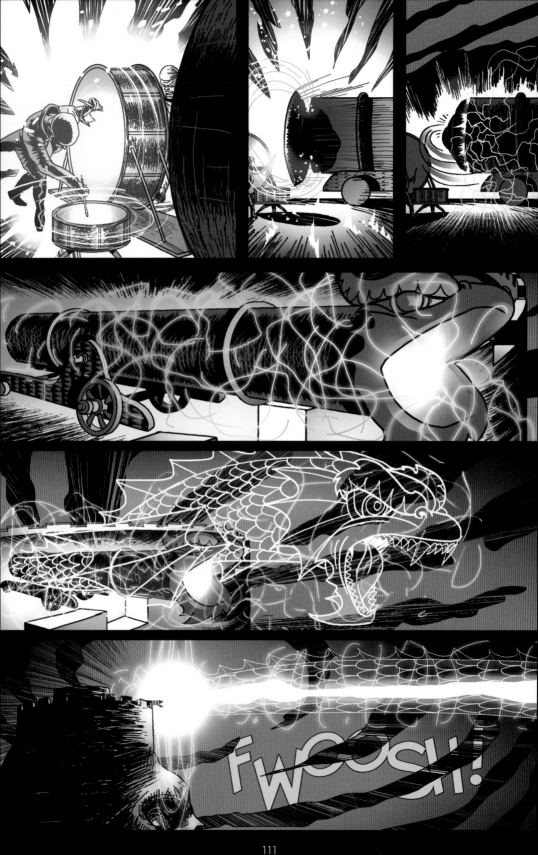

FWOOSH!

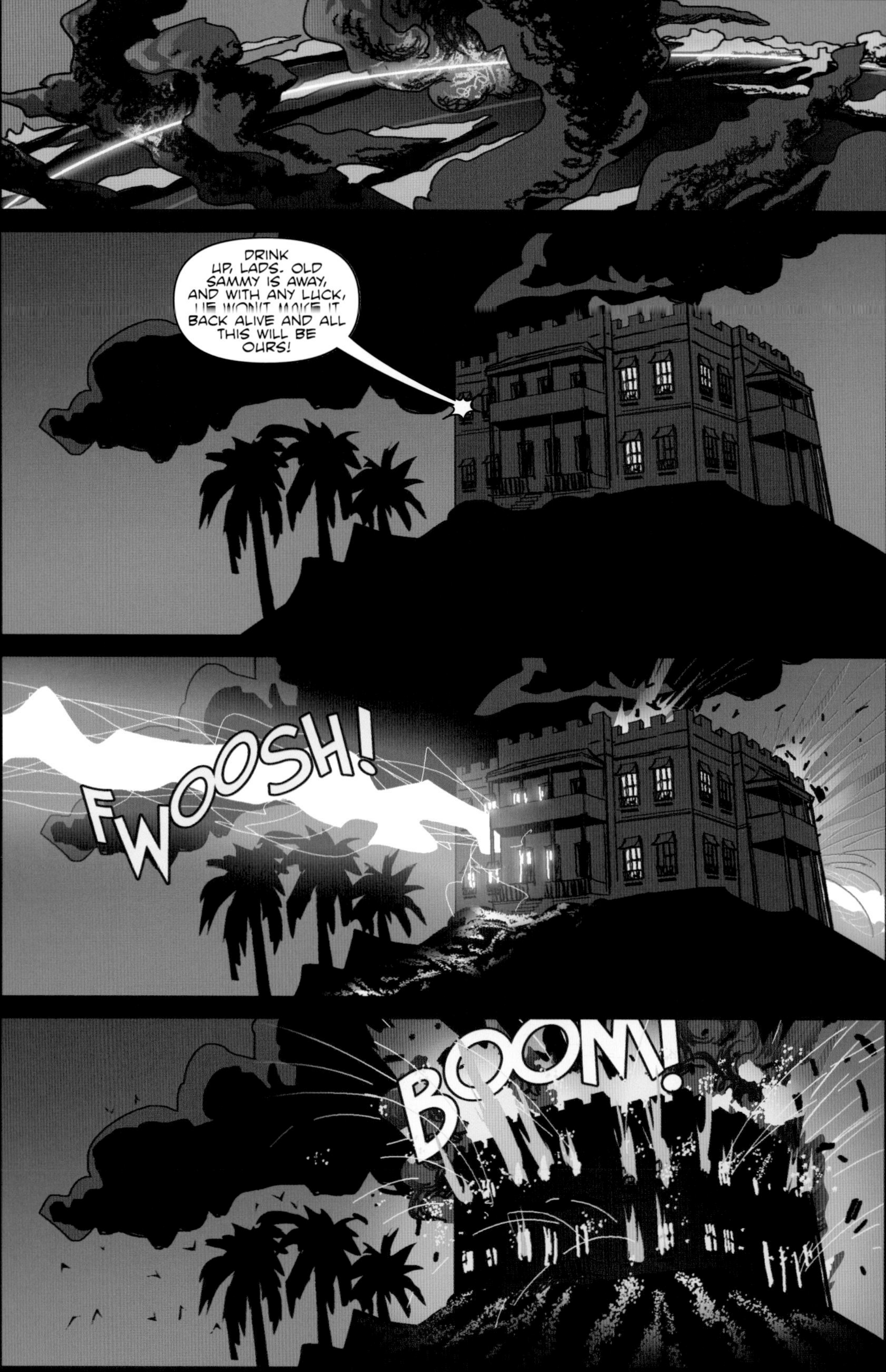
DRINK UP, LADS. OLD SAMMY IS AWAY, AND WITH ANY LUCK, HE WON'T MAKE IT BACK ALIVE AND ALL THIS WILL BE OURS!
FWOOSH!
BOOM!

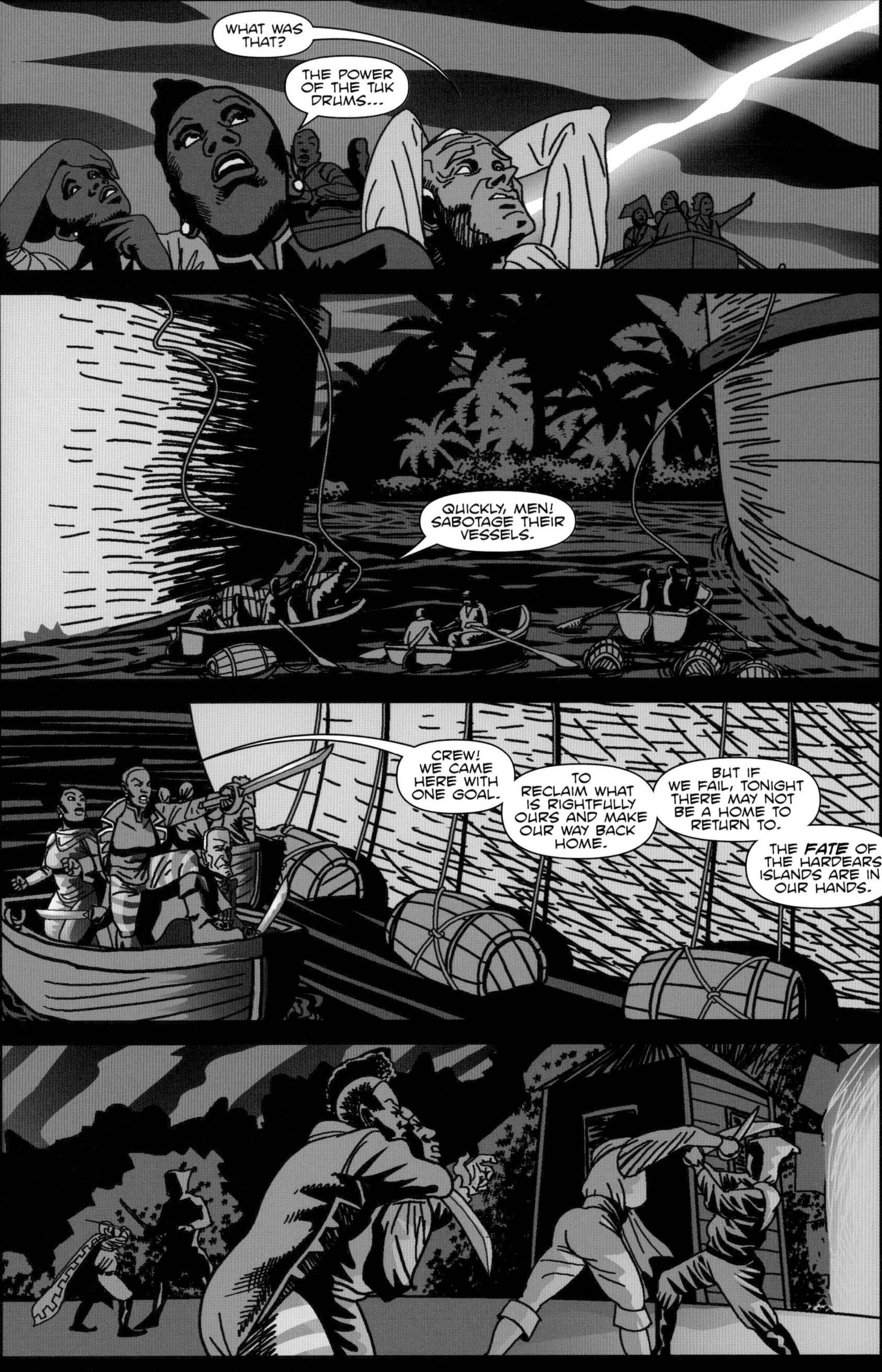
WHAT WAS THAT?
THE POWER OF THE TUK DRUMS...
QUICKLY, MEN! SABOTAGE THEIR VESSELS.
CREW! WE CAME HERE WITH ONE GOAL.
TO RECLAIM WHAT IS RIGHTFULLY OURS AND MAKE OUR WAY BACK HOME.
BUT IF WE FAIL, TONIGHT THERE MAY NOT BE A HOME TO RETURN TO.
THE FATE OF THE HARDEARS ISLANDS ARE IN OUR HANDS.

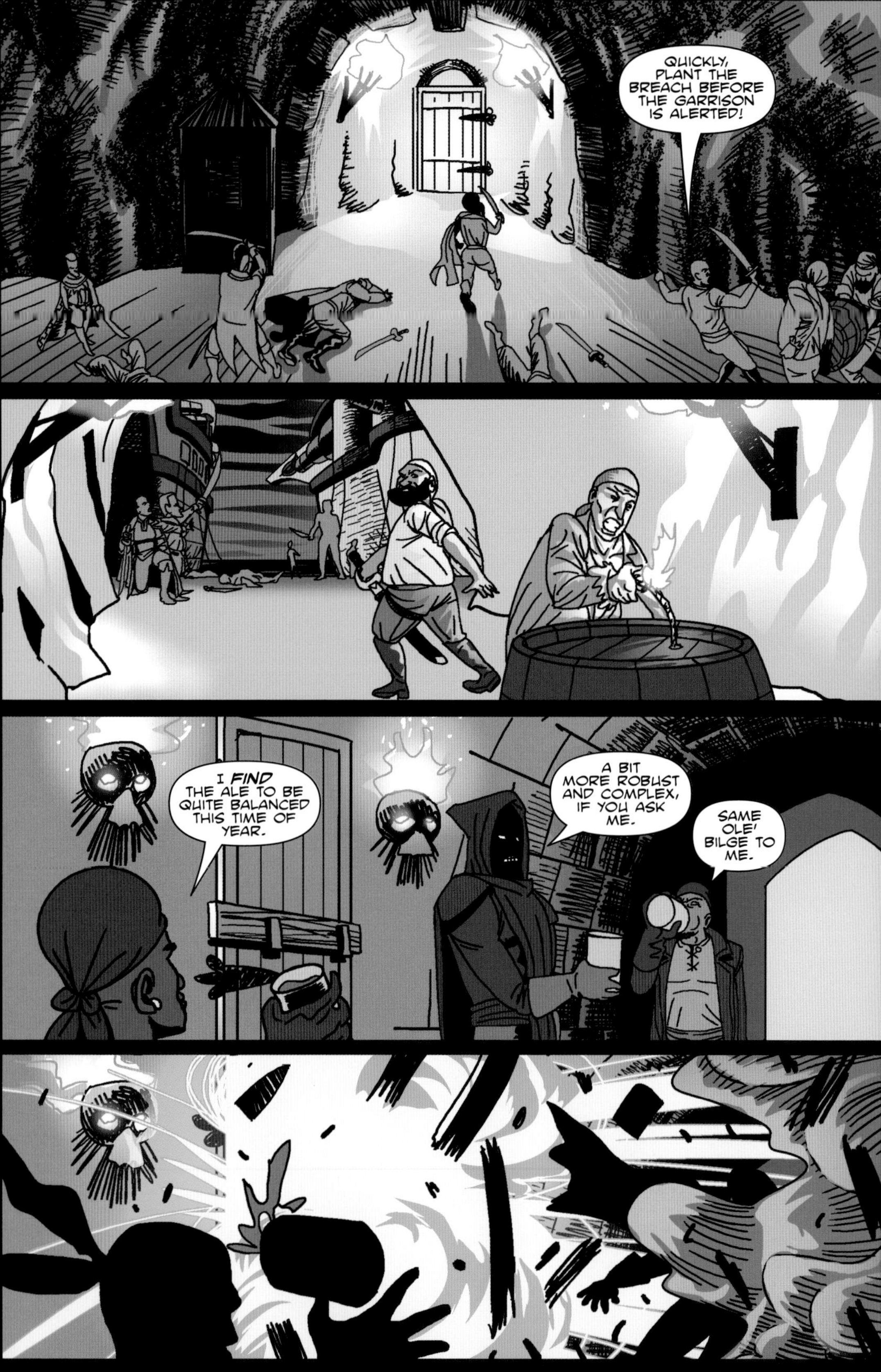
QUICKLY, PLANT THE BREACH BEFORE THE GARRISON IS ALERTED!
I *FIND* THE ALE TO BE QUITE BALANCED THIS TIME OF YEAR.
A BIT MORE ROBUST AND COMPLEX, IF YOU ASK ME.
SAME OLE' BILGE TO ME.

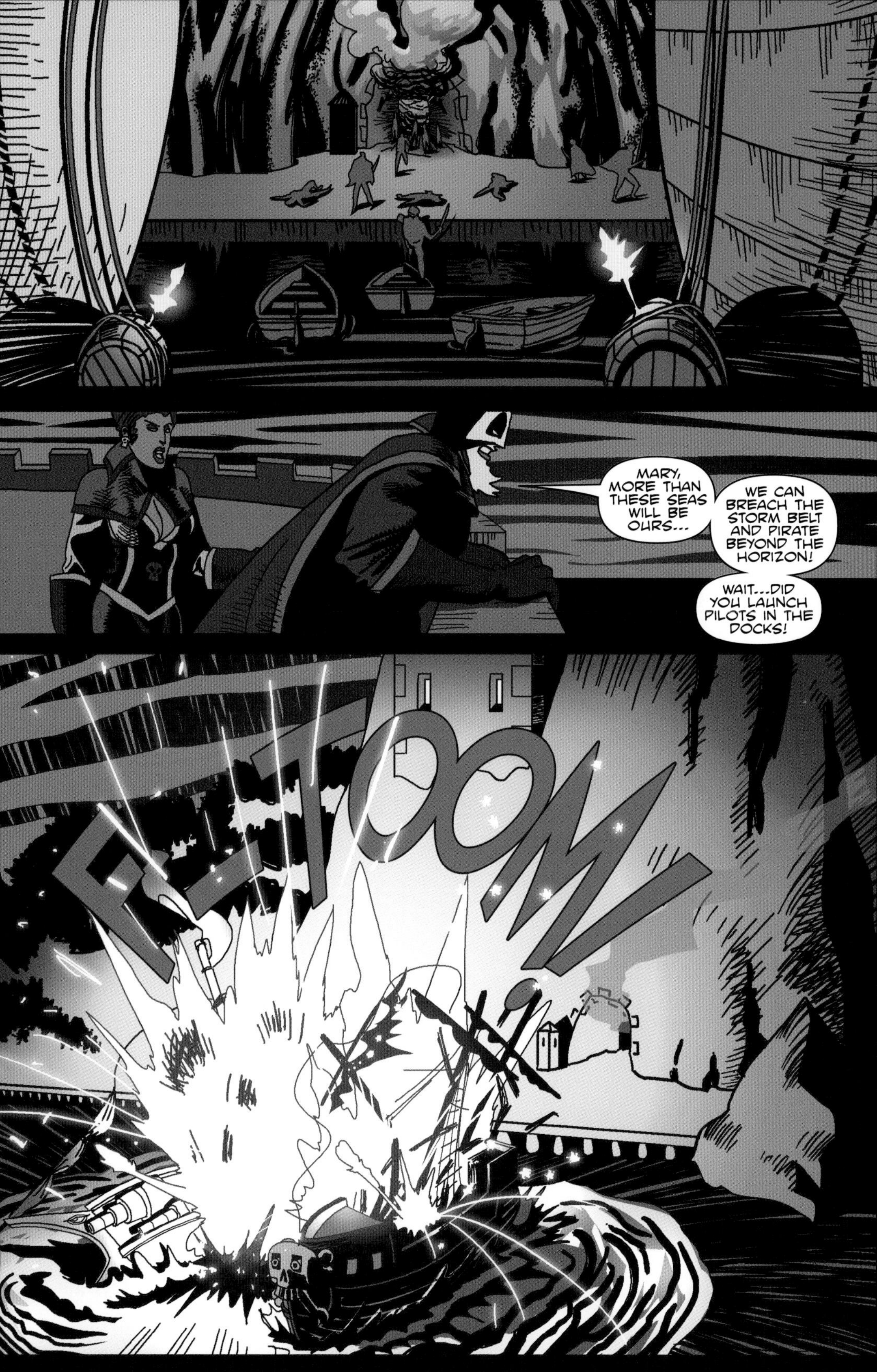
MARY, MORE THAN THESE SEAS WILL BE OURS...
WE CAN BREACH THE STORM BELT AND PIRATE BEYOND THE HORIZON!
WAIT...DID YOU LAUNCH PILOTS IN THE DOCKS!
F-TOOM!

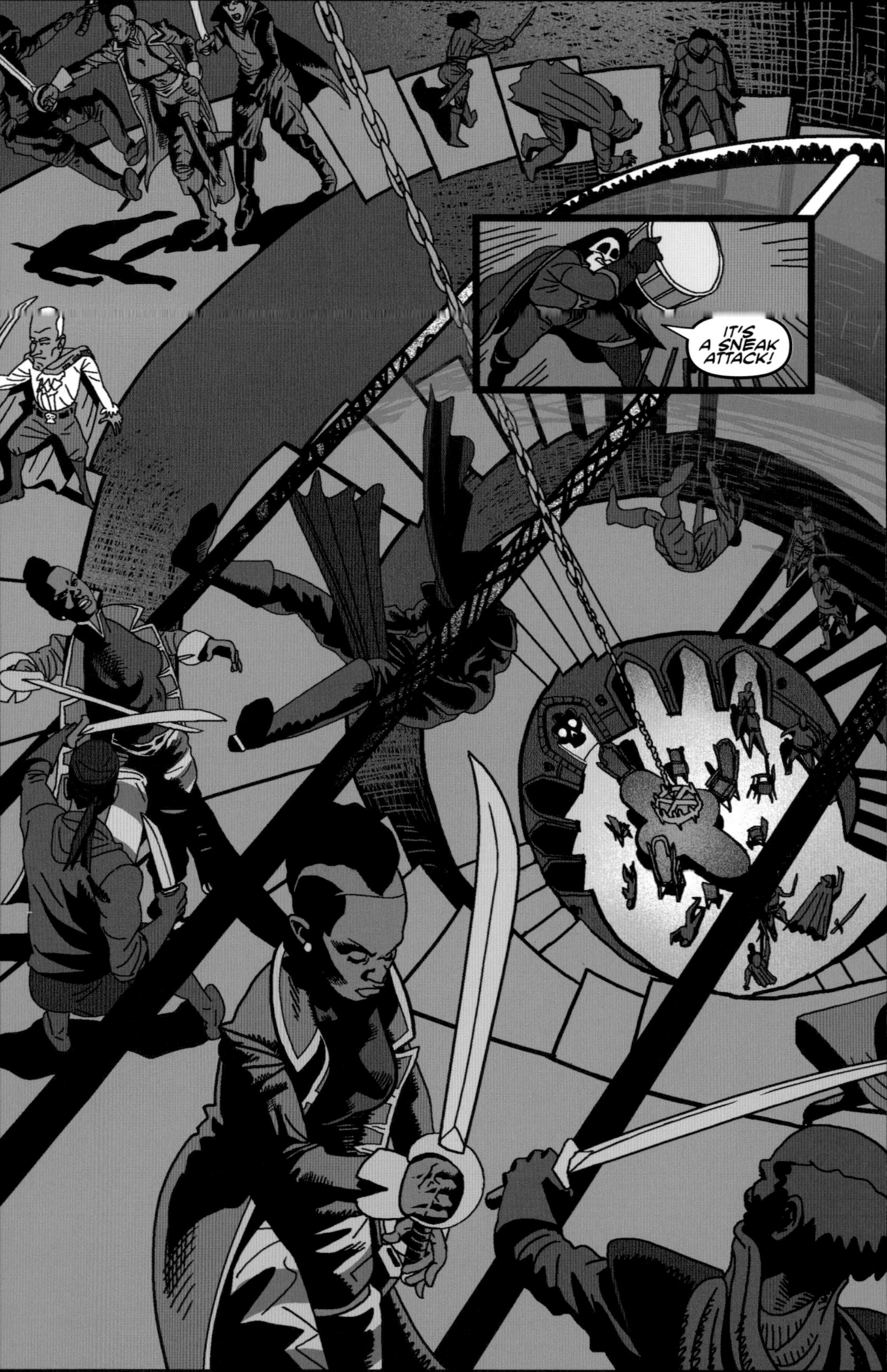
IT'S A SNEAK ATTACK!

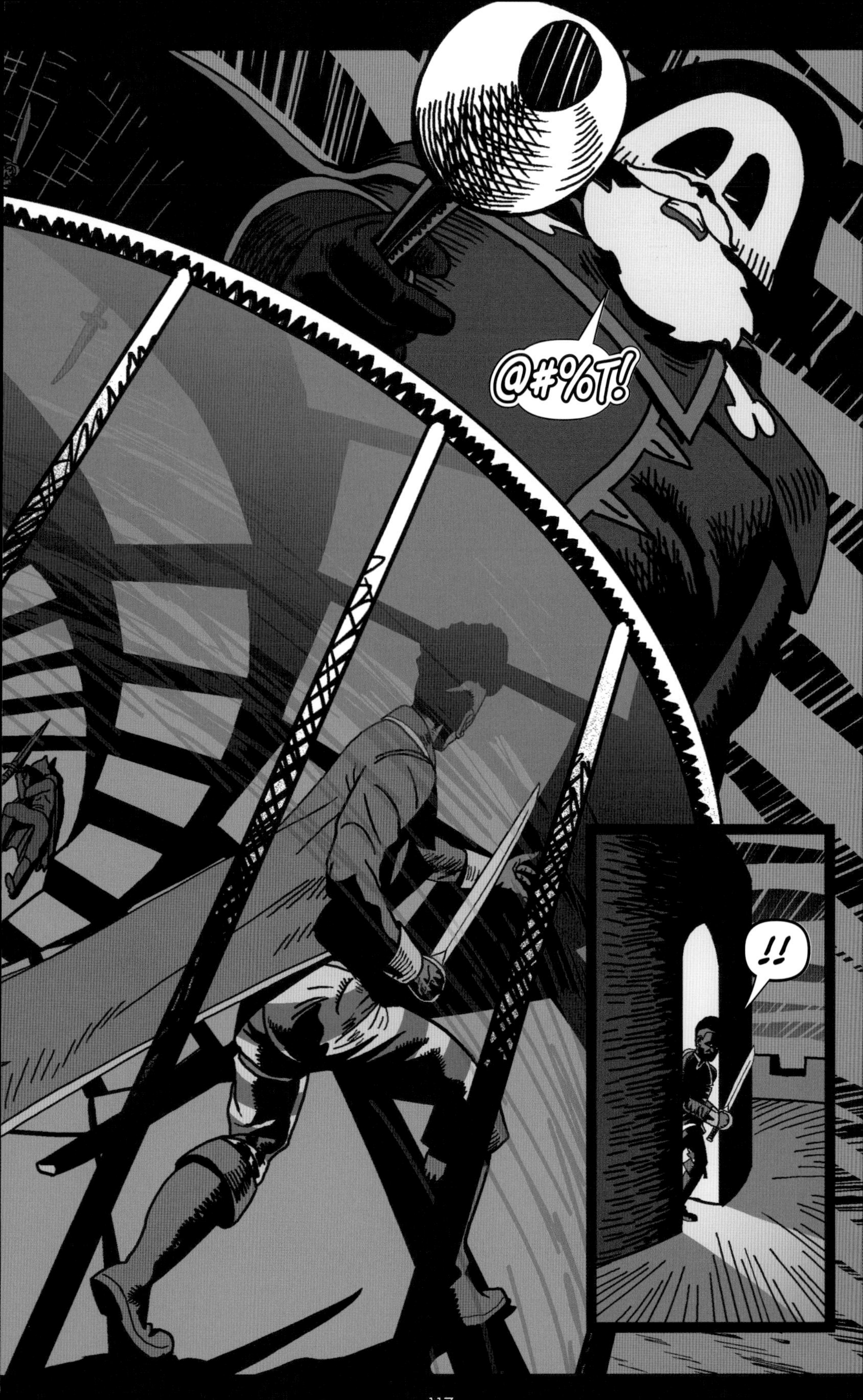
@#%T!
!!

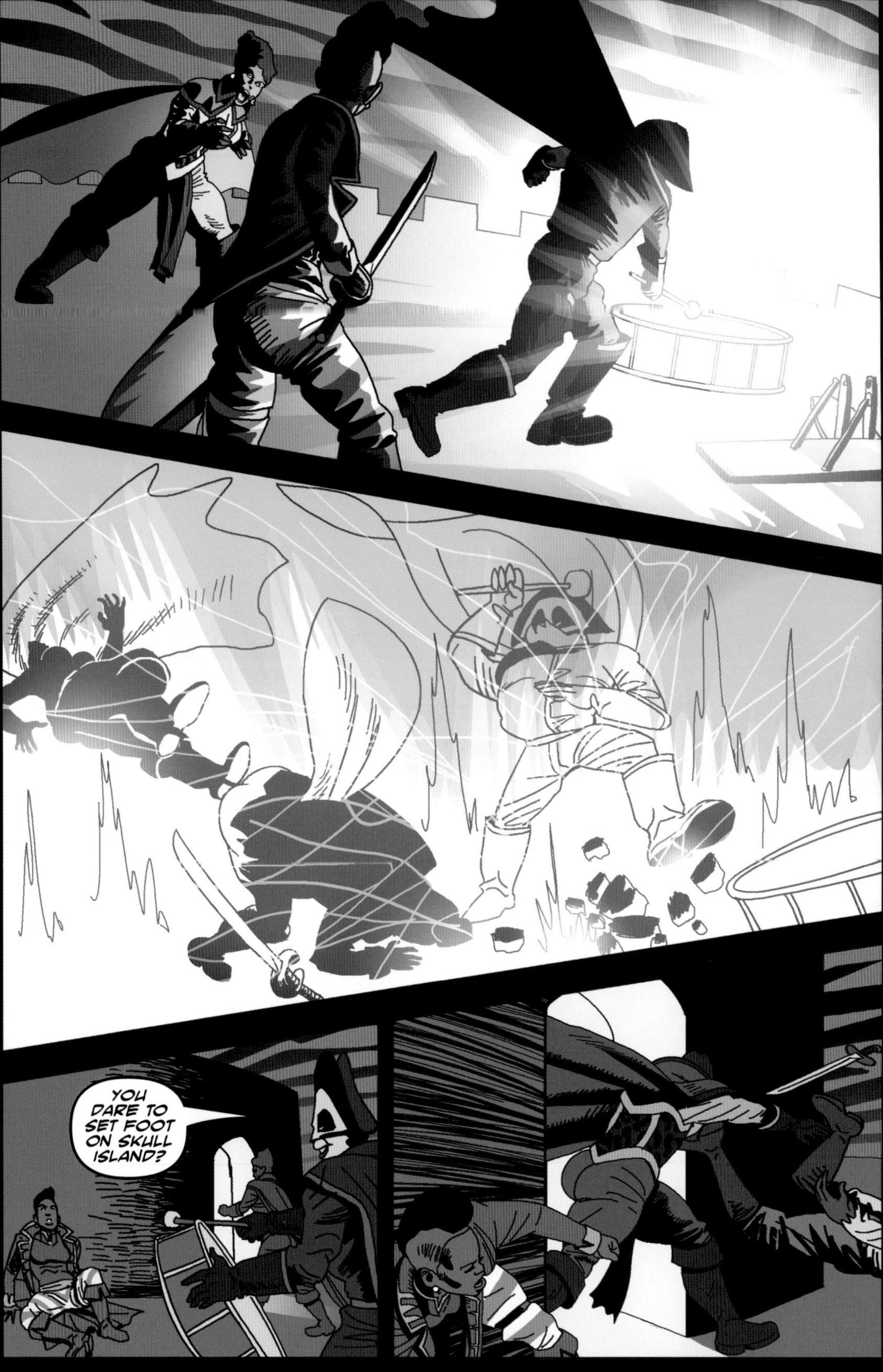
YOU DARE TO SET FOOT ON SKULL ISLAND?

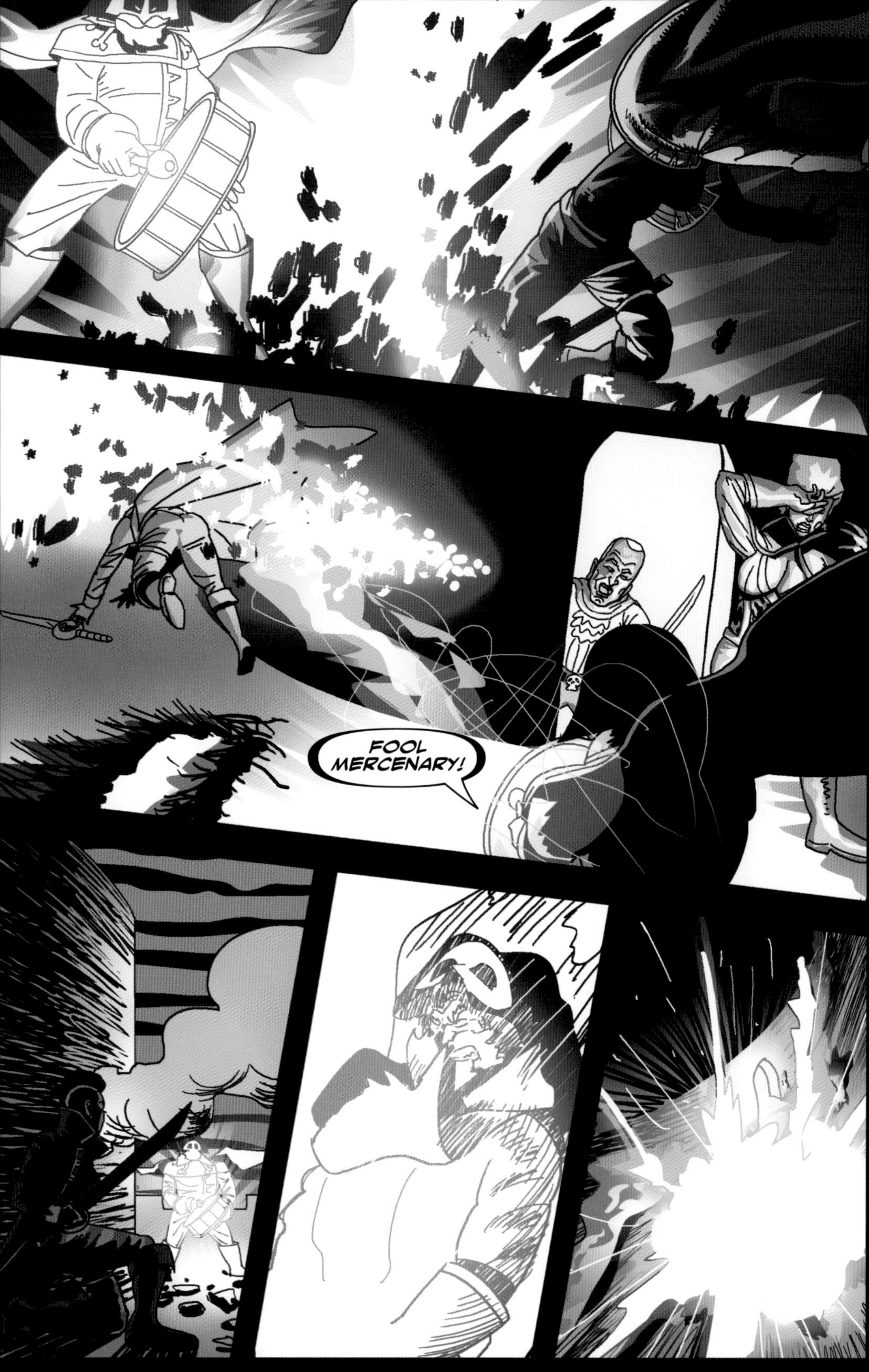
FOOL MERCENARY!

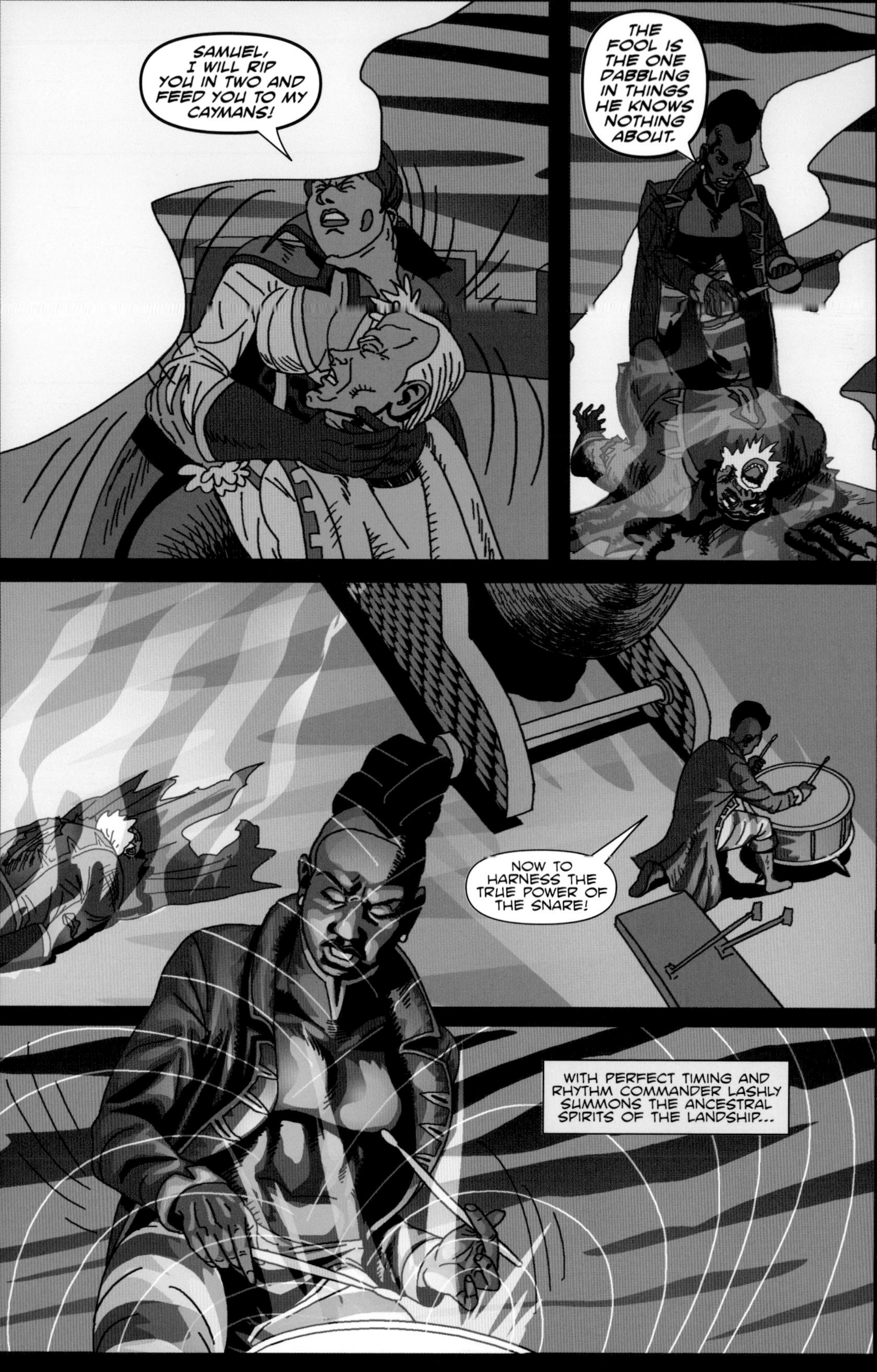
SAMUEL, I WILL RIP YOU IN TWO AND FEED YOU TO MY CAYMANS!
THE FOOL IS THE ONE DABBLING IN THINGS HE KNOWS NOTHING ABOUT.
NOW TO HARNESS THE TRUE POWER OF THE SNARE!
WITH PERFECT TIMING AND RHYTHM COMMANDER LASHLY SUMMONS THE ANCESTRAL SPIRITS OF THE LANDSHIP...

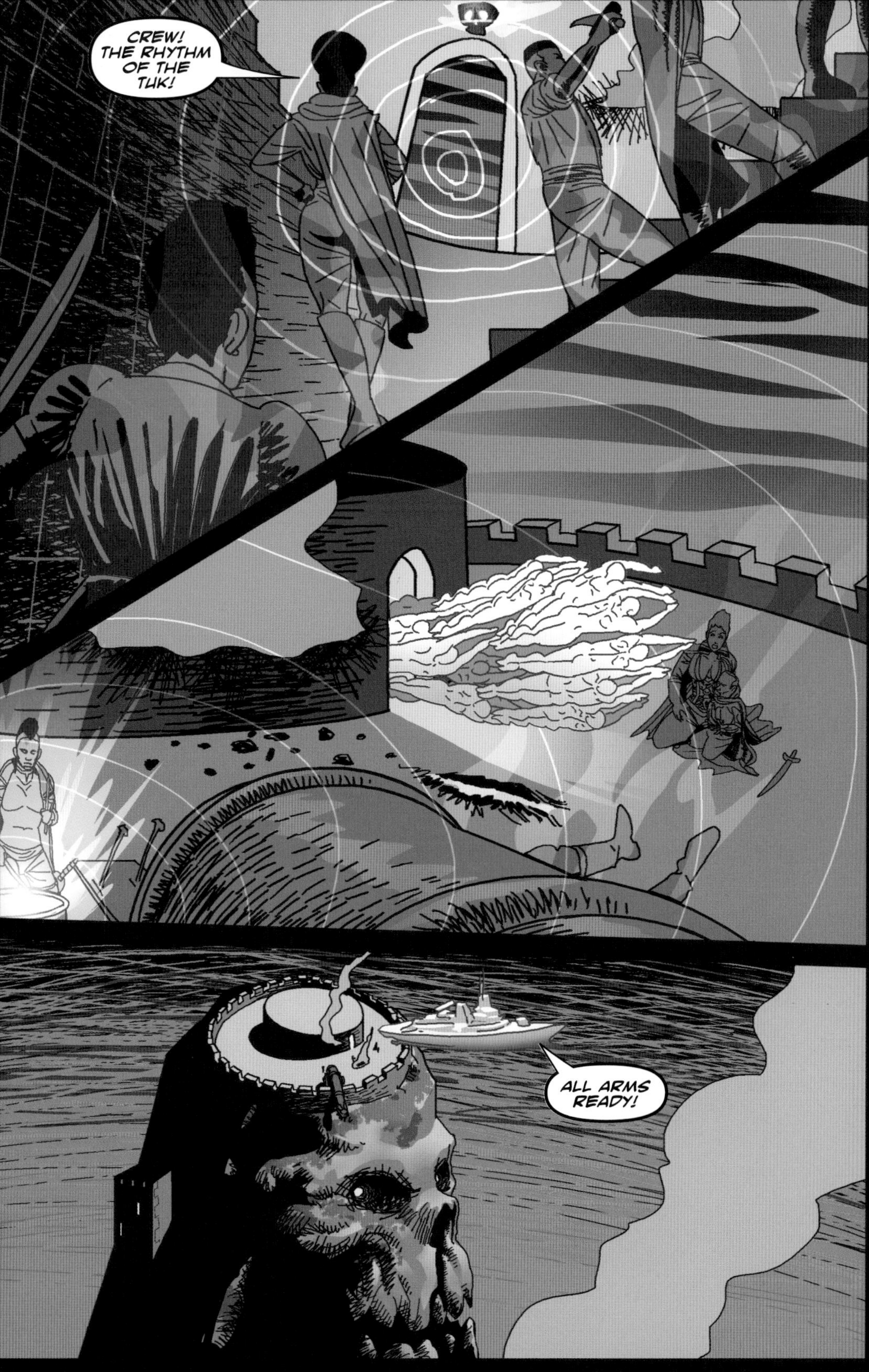
CREW! THE RHYTHM OF THE TUK!
ALL ARMS READY!

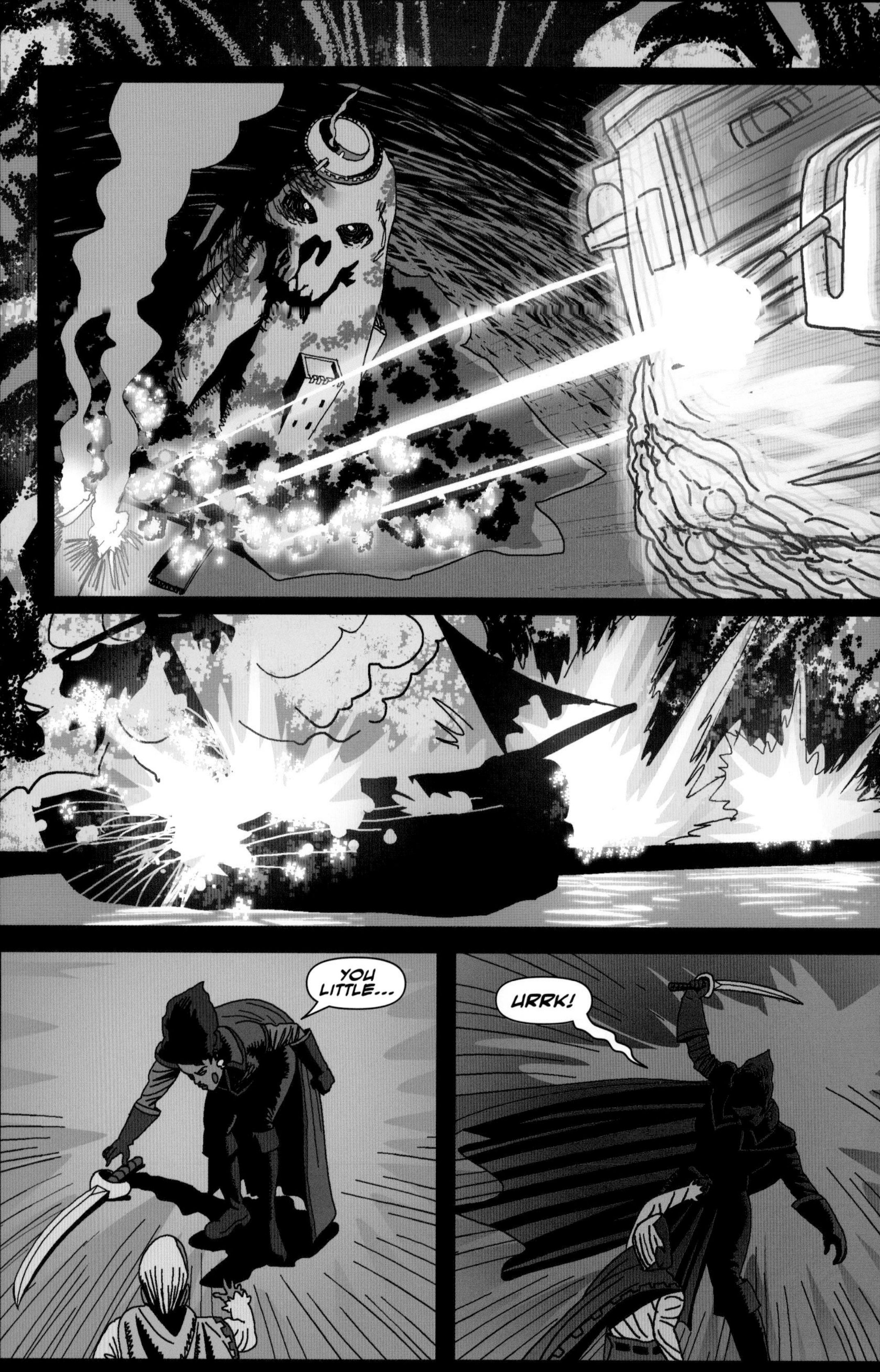
YOU LITTLE...
URRK!

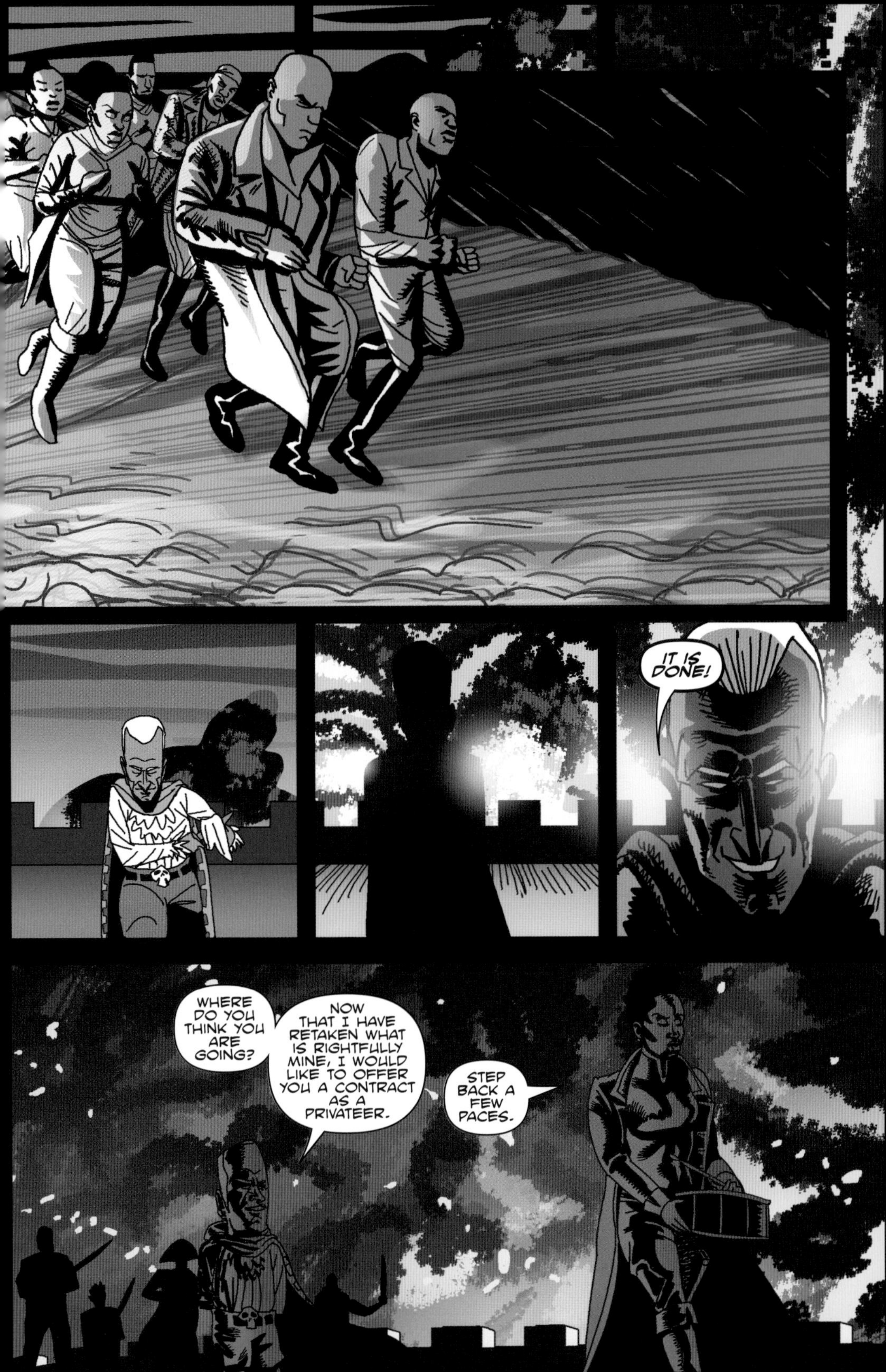
IT IS DONE!
WHERE DO YOU THINK YOU ARE GOING?
NOW THAT I HAVE RETAKEN WHAT IS RIGHTFULLY MINE, I WOULD LIKE TO OFFER YOU A CONTRACT AS A PRIVATEER.
STEP BACK A FEW PACES.

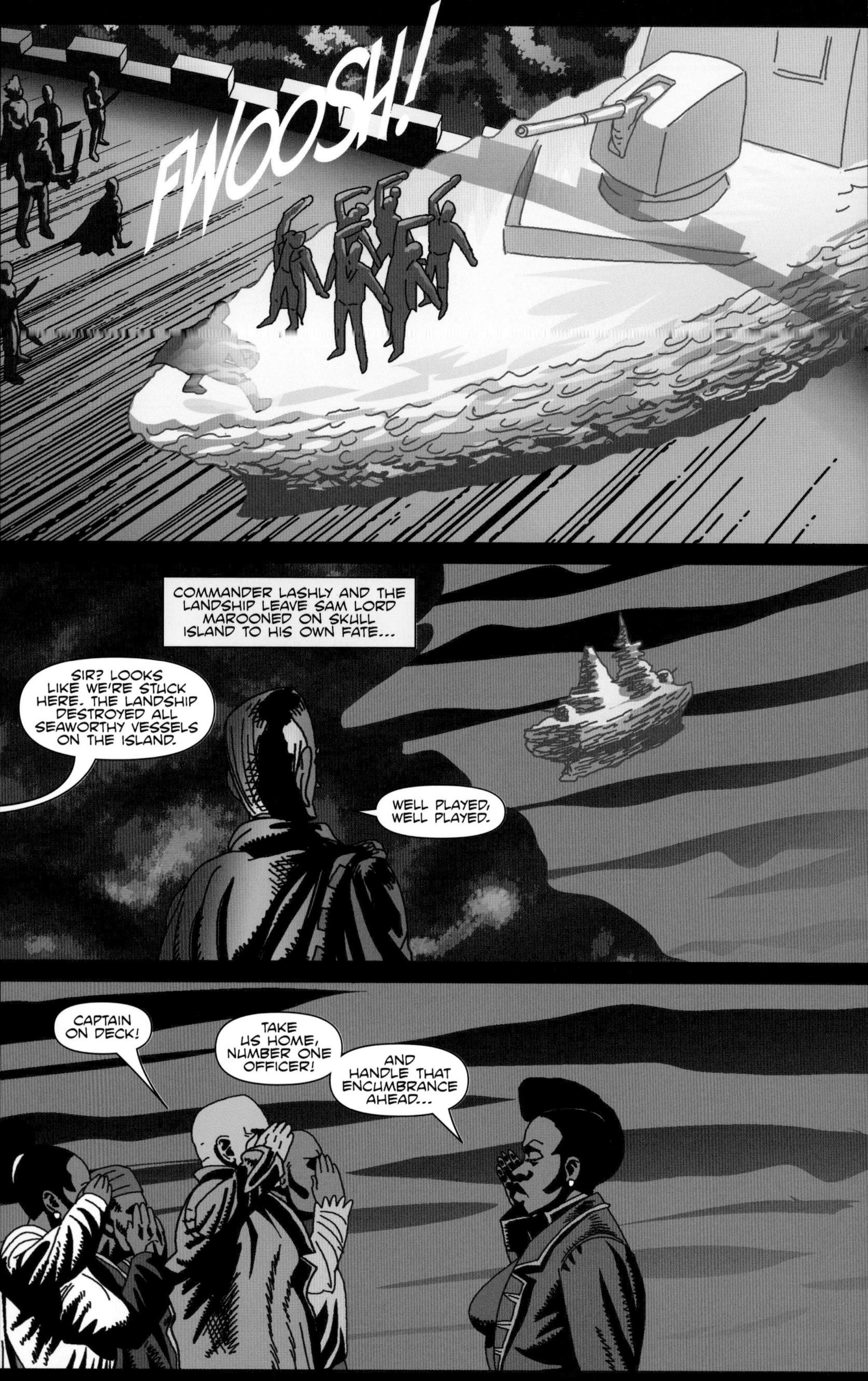
FWOOSH!
COMMANDER LASHLY AND THE LANDSHIP LEAVE SAM LORD MAROONED ON SKULL ISLAND TO HIS OWN FATE...
SIR? LOOKS LIKE WE'RE STUCK HERE. THE LANDSHIP DESTROYED ALL SEAWORTHY VESSELS ON THE ISLAND.
WELL PLAYED, WELL PLAYED.
CAPTAIN ON DECK!
TAKE US HOME, NUMBER ONE OFFICER!
AND HANDLE THAT ENCUMBRANCE AHEAD...

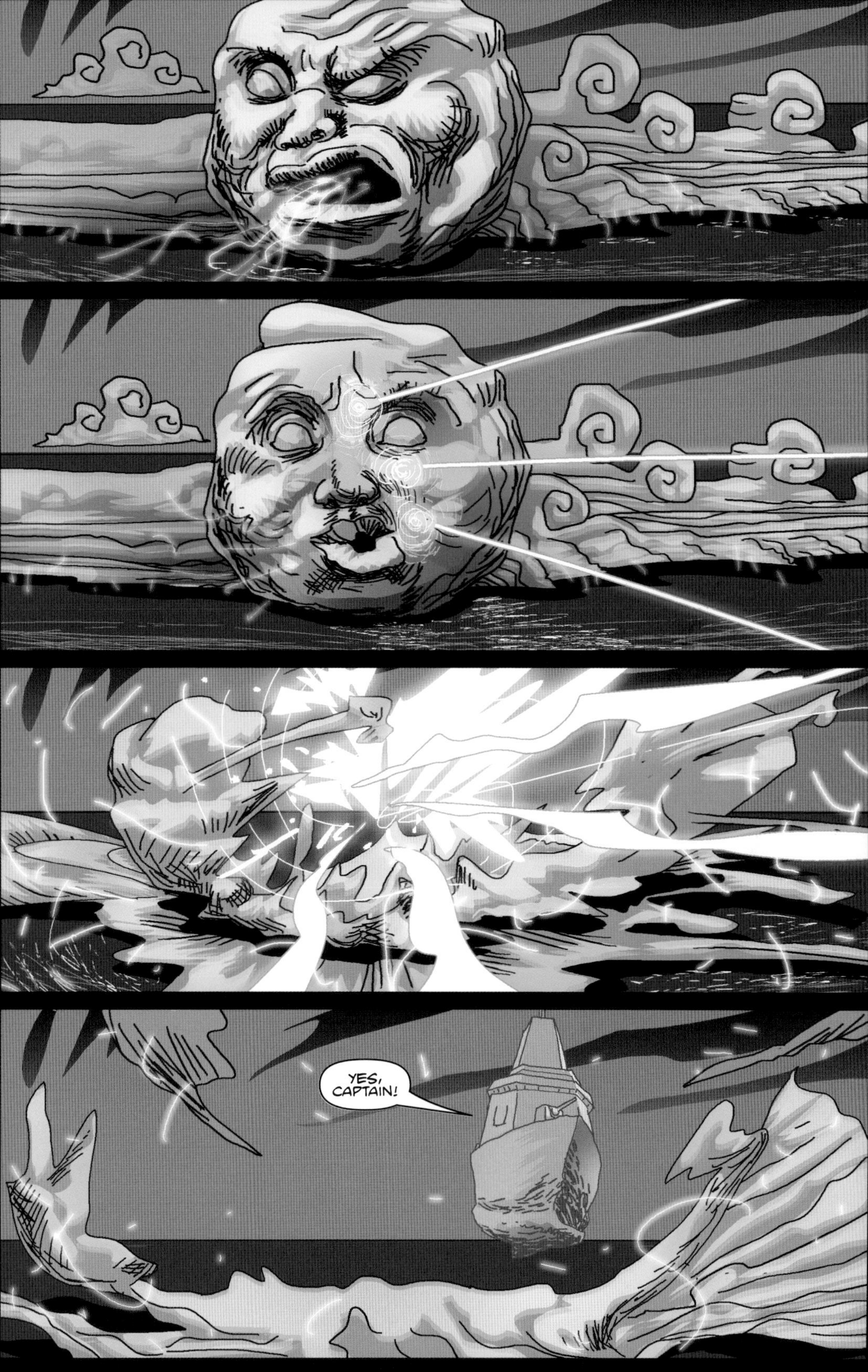
YES, CAPTAIN!

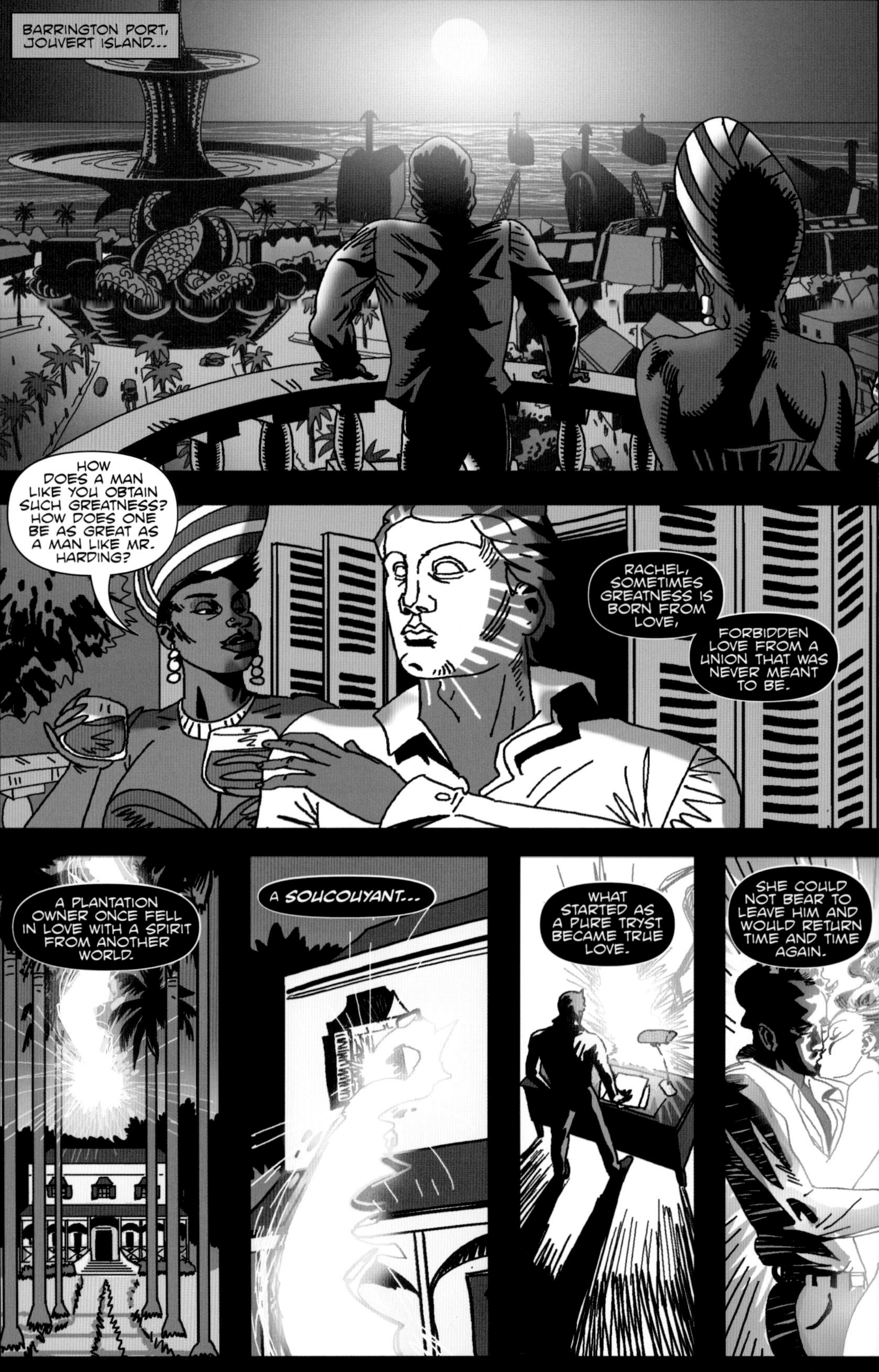
BARRINGTON PORT, JOUVERT ISLAND...
HOW DOES A MAN LIKE YOU OBTAIN SUCH GREATNESS? HOW DOES ONE BE AS GREAT AS A MAN LIKE MR. HARDING?
RACHEL, SOMETIMES GREATNESS IS BORN FROM LOVE,
FORBIDDEN LOVE FROM A UNION THAT WAS NEVER MEANT TO BE.
A PLANTATION OWNER ONCE FELL IN LOVE WITH A SPIRIT FROM ANOTHER WORLD.
A SOUCOUYANT...
WHAT STARTED AS A PURE TRYST BECAME TRUE LOVE.
SHE COULD NOT BEAR TO LEAVE HIM AND WOULD RETURN TIME AND TIME AGAIN.

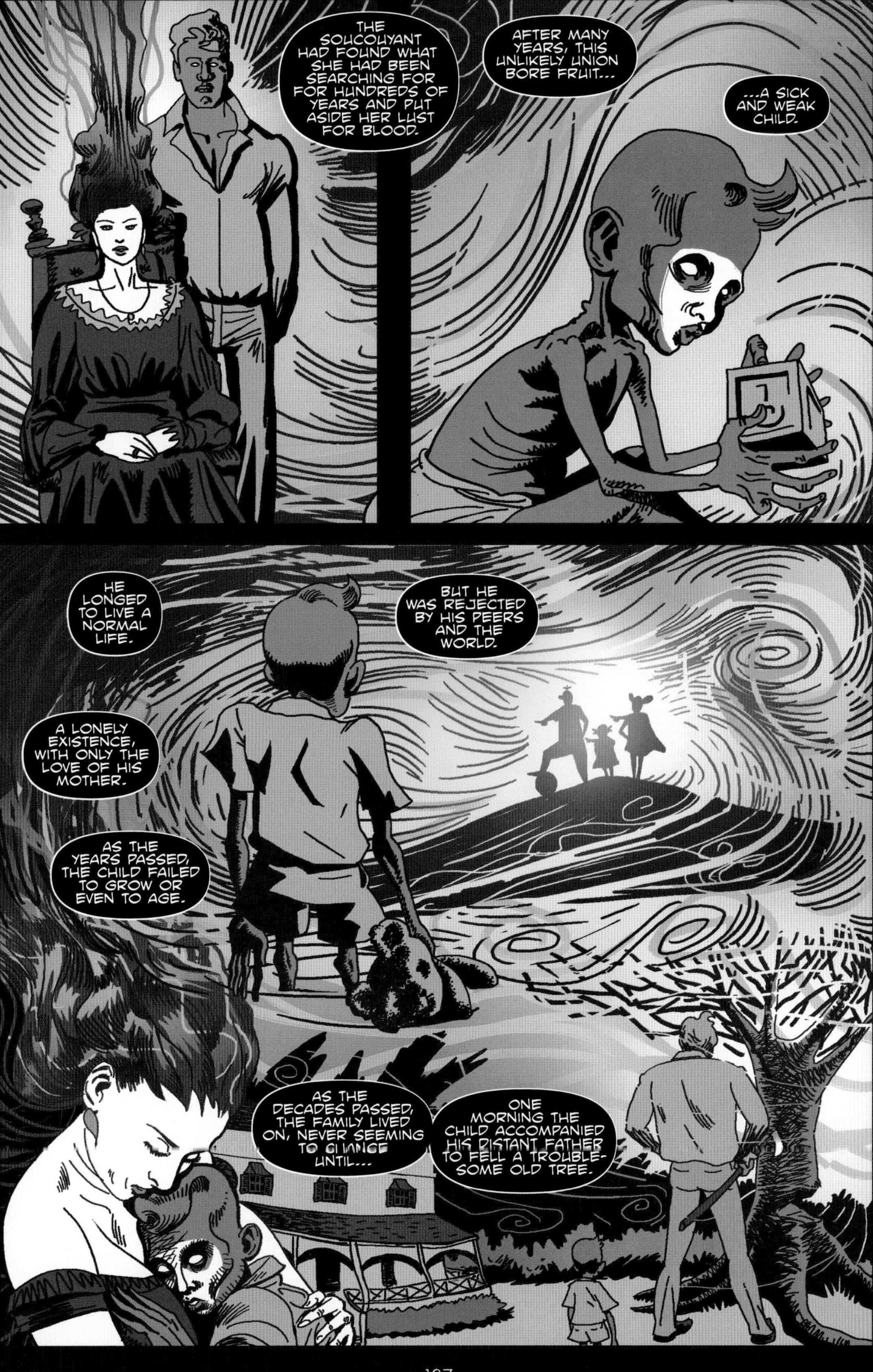
THE SOUCOUYANT HAD FOUND WHAT SHE HAD BEEN SEARCHING FOR FOR HUNDREDS OF YEARS AND PUT ASIDE HER LUST FOR BLOOD.
AFTER MANY YEARS, THIS UNLIKELY UNION BORE FRUIT...
...A SICK AND WEAK CHILD.
HE LONGED TO LIVE A NORMAL LIFE.
BUT HE WAS REJECTED BY HIS PEERS AND THE WORLD.
A LONELY EXISTENCE, WITH ONLY THE LOVE OF HIS MOTHER.
AS THE YEARS PASSED, THE CHILD FAILED TO GROW OR EVEN TO AGE.
AS THE DECADES PASSED, THE FAMILY LIVED ON, NEVER SEEMING TO CHANGE UNTIL...
ONE MORNING THE CHILD ACCOMPANIED HIS DISTANT FATHER TO FELL A TROUBLE-SOME OLD TREE.

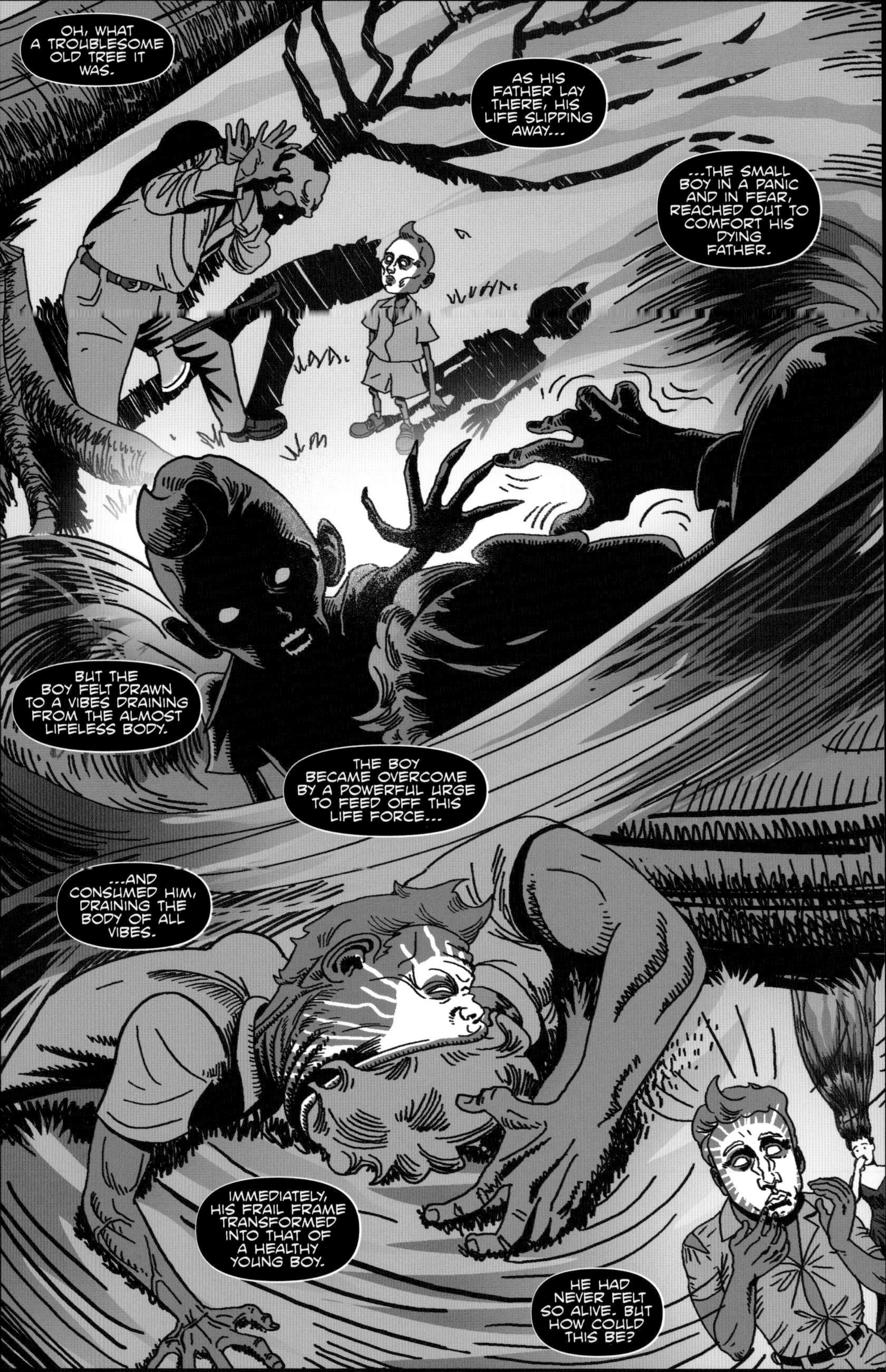
OH, WHAT A TROUBLESOME OLD TREE IT WAS.
AS HIS FATHER LAY THERE, HIS LIFE SLIPPING AWAY...
...THE SMALL BOY IN A PANIC AND IN FEAR, REACHED OUT TO COMFORT HIS DYING FATHER.
BUT THE BOY FELT DRAWN TO A VIBES DRAINING FROM THE ALMOST LIFELESS BODY.
THE BOY BECAME OVERCOME BY A POWERFUL URGE TO FEED OFF THIS LIFE FORCE...
...AND CONSUMED HIM, DRAINING THE BODY OF ALL VIBES.
IMMEDIATELY, HIS FRAIL FRAME TRANSFORMED INTO THAT OF A HEALTHY YOUNG BOY.
HE HAD NEVER FELT SO ALIVE. BUT HOW COULD THIS BE?

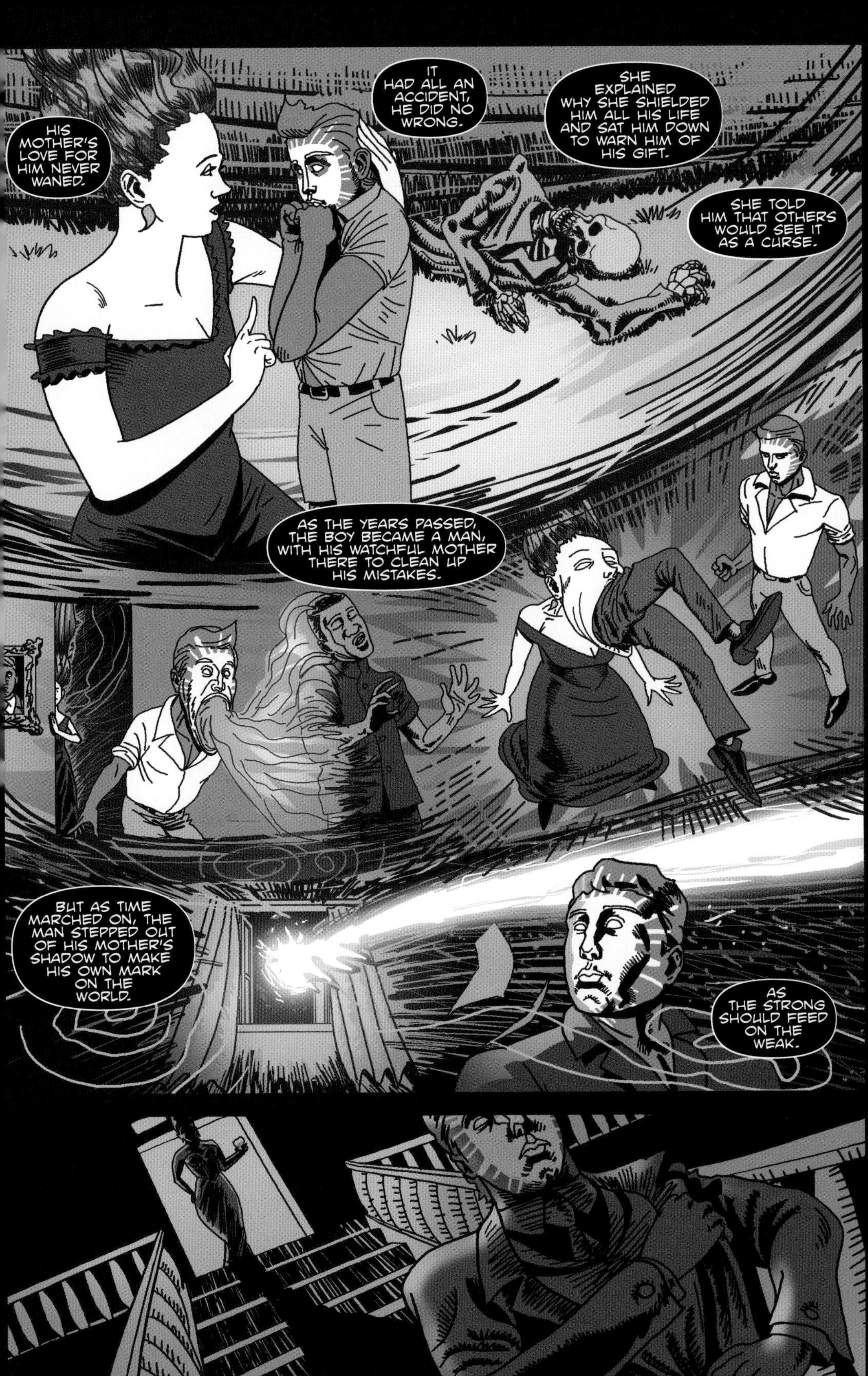
HIS MOTHER'S LOVE FOR HIM NEVER WANED.
IT HAD ALL AN ACCIDENT, HE DID NO WRONG.
SHE EXPLAINED WHY SHE SHIELDED HIM ALL HIS LIFE AND SAT HIM DOWN TO WARN HIM OF HIS GIFT.
SHE TOLD HIM THAT OTHERS WOULD SEE IT AS A CURSE.
AS THE YEARS PASSED, THE BOY BECAME A MAN, WITH HIS WATCHFUL MOTHER THERE TO CLEAN UP HIS MISTAKES.
BUT AS TIME MARCHED ON, THE MAN STEPPED OUT OF HIS MOTHER'S SHADOW TO MAKE HIS OWN MARK ON THE WORLD.
AS THE STRONG SHOULD FEED ON THE WEAK.

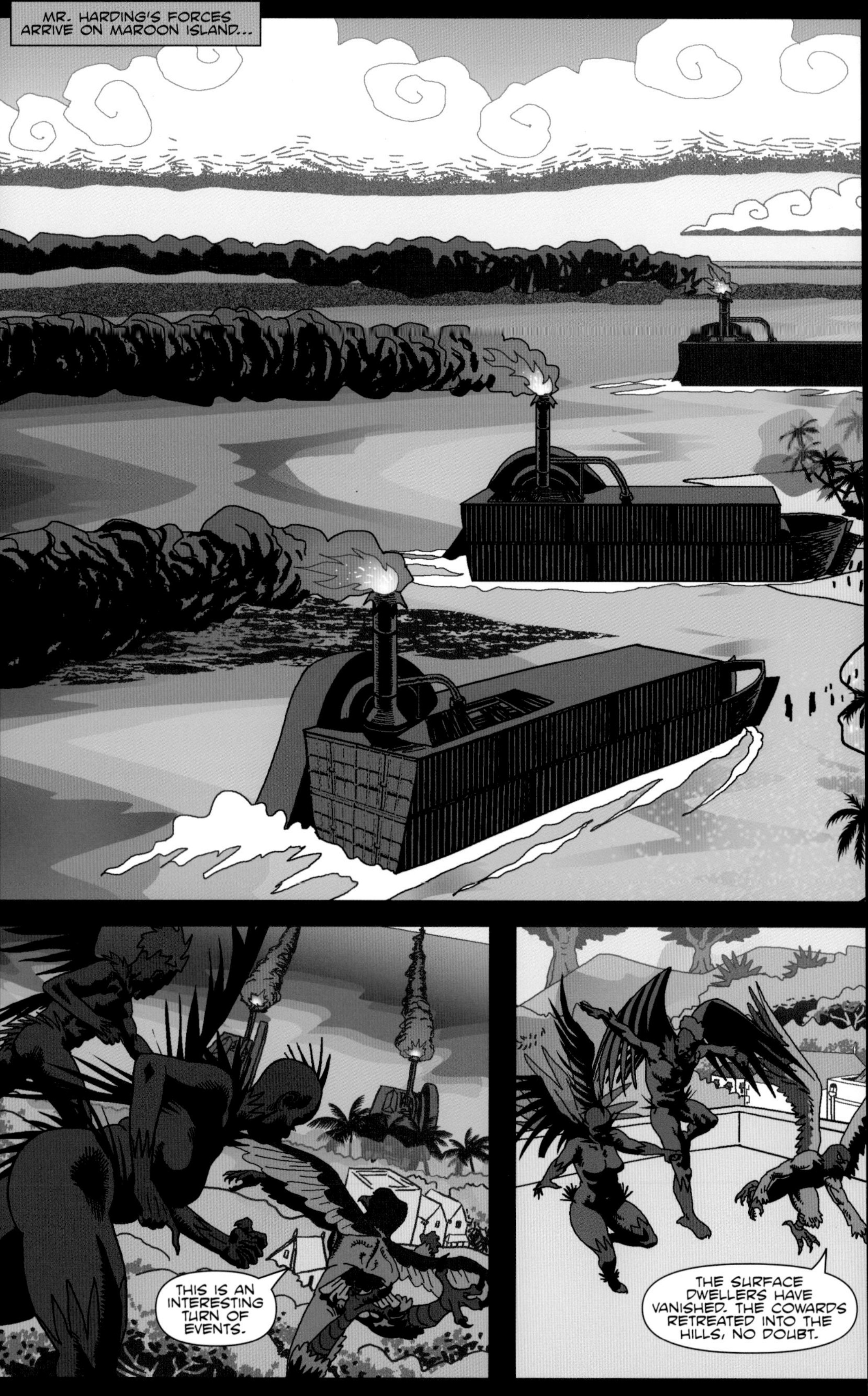
MR. HARDING'S FORCES ARRIVE ON MAROON ISLAND...
THIS IS AN INTERESTING TURN OF EVENTS.
THE SURFACE DWELLERS HAVE VANISHED. THE COWARDS RETREATED INTO THE HILLS, NO DOUBT.

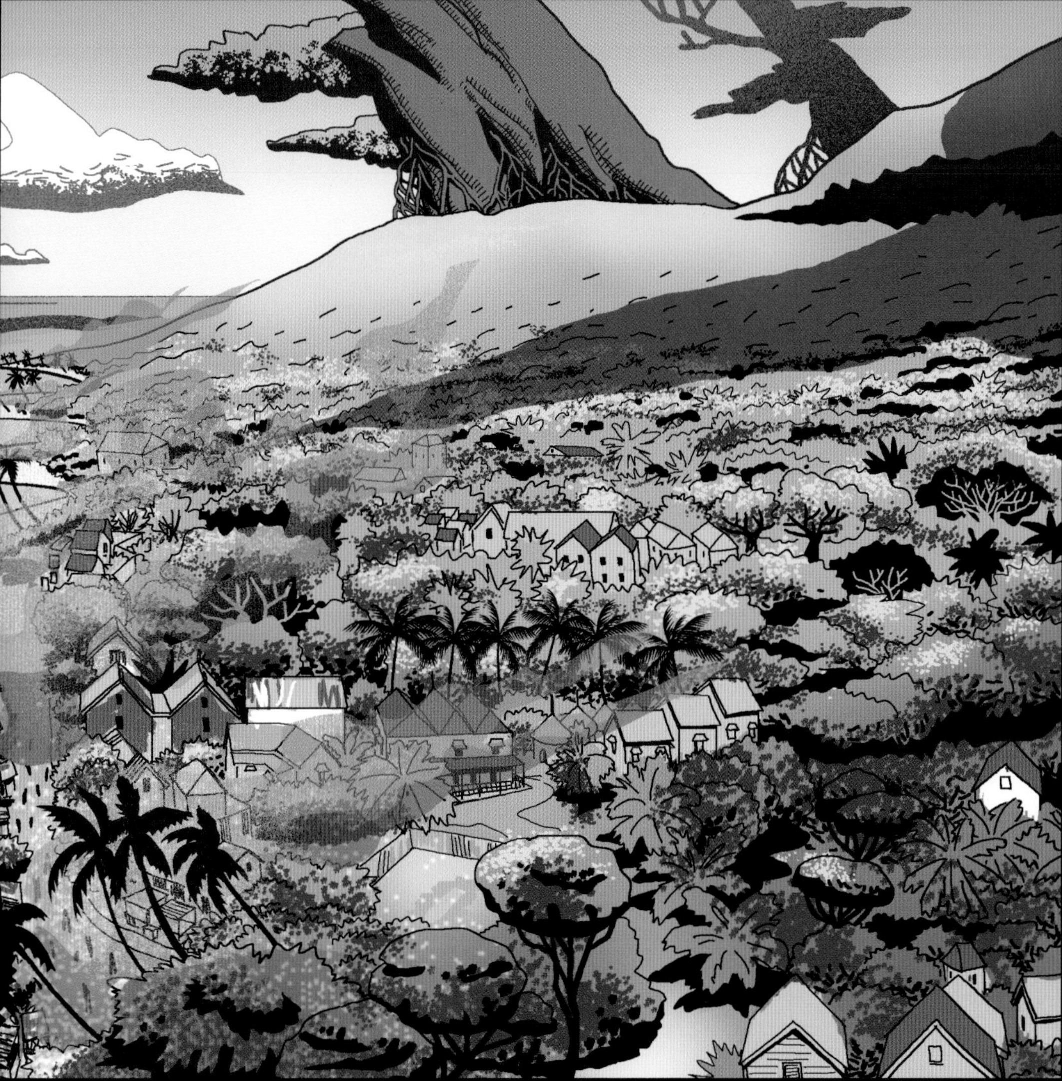

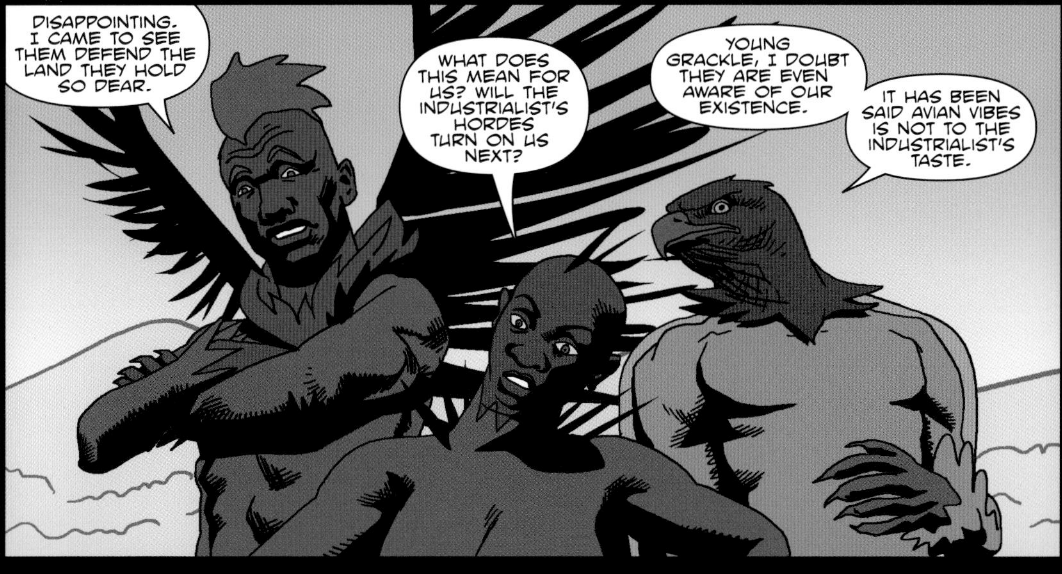

DISAPPOINTING. I CAME TO SEE THEM DEFEND THE LAND THEY HOLD SO DEAR.
WHAT DOES THIS MEAN FOR US? WILL THE INDUSTRIALIST'S HORDES TURN ON US NEXT?
YOUNG GRACKLE, I DOUBT THEY ARE EVEN AWARE OF OUR EXISTENCE.
IT HAS BEEN SAID AVIAN VIBES IS NOT TO THE INDUSTRIALIST'S TASTE.

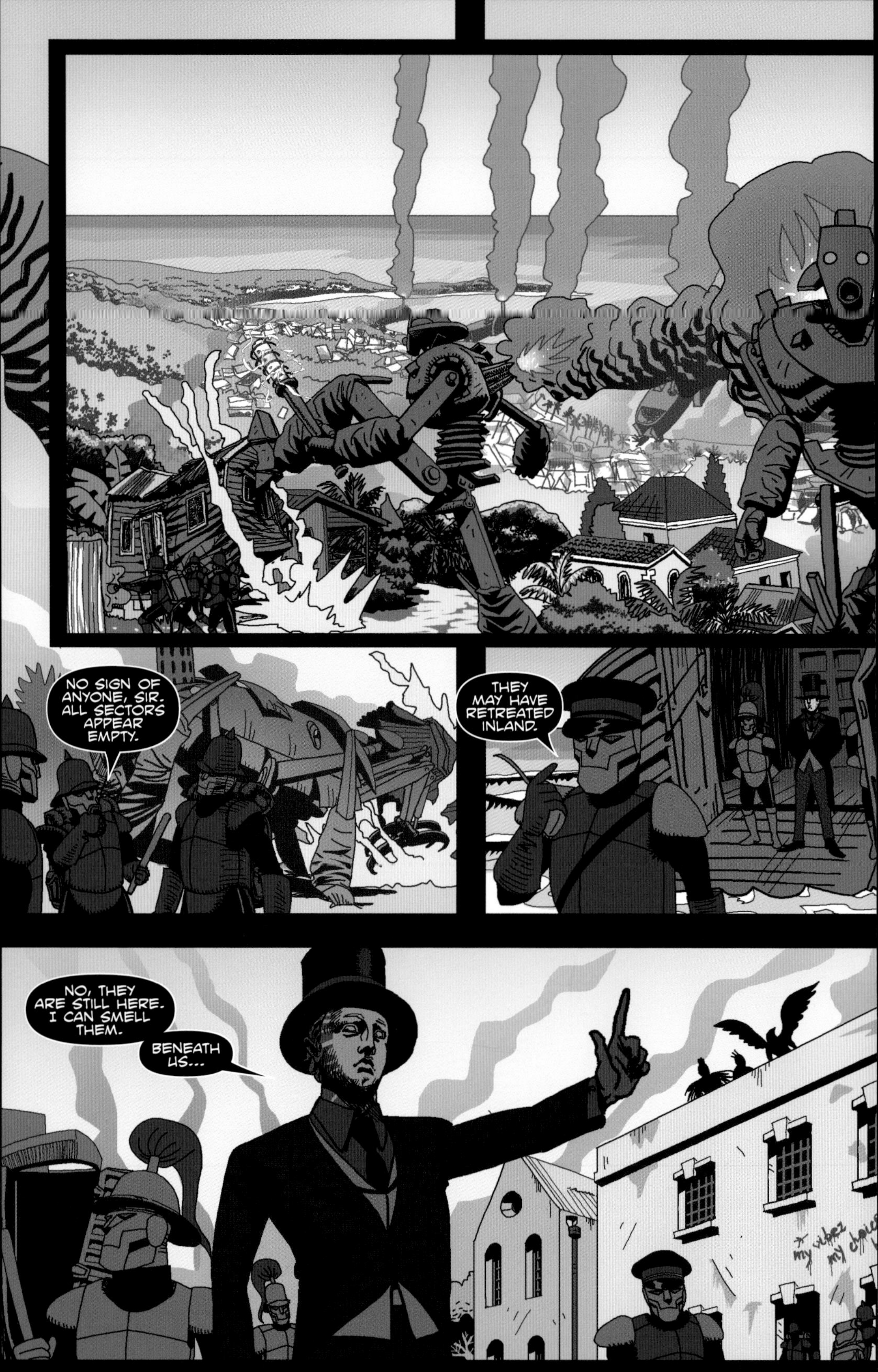
NO SIGN OF ANYONE, SIR. ALL SECTORS APPEAR EMPTY.
THEY MAY HAVE RETREATED INLAND.
NO, THEY ARE STILL HERE. I CAN SMELL THEM.
BENEATH US...

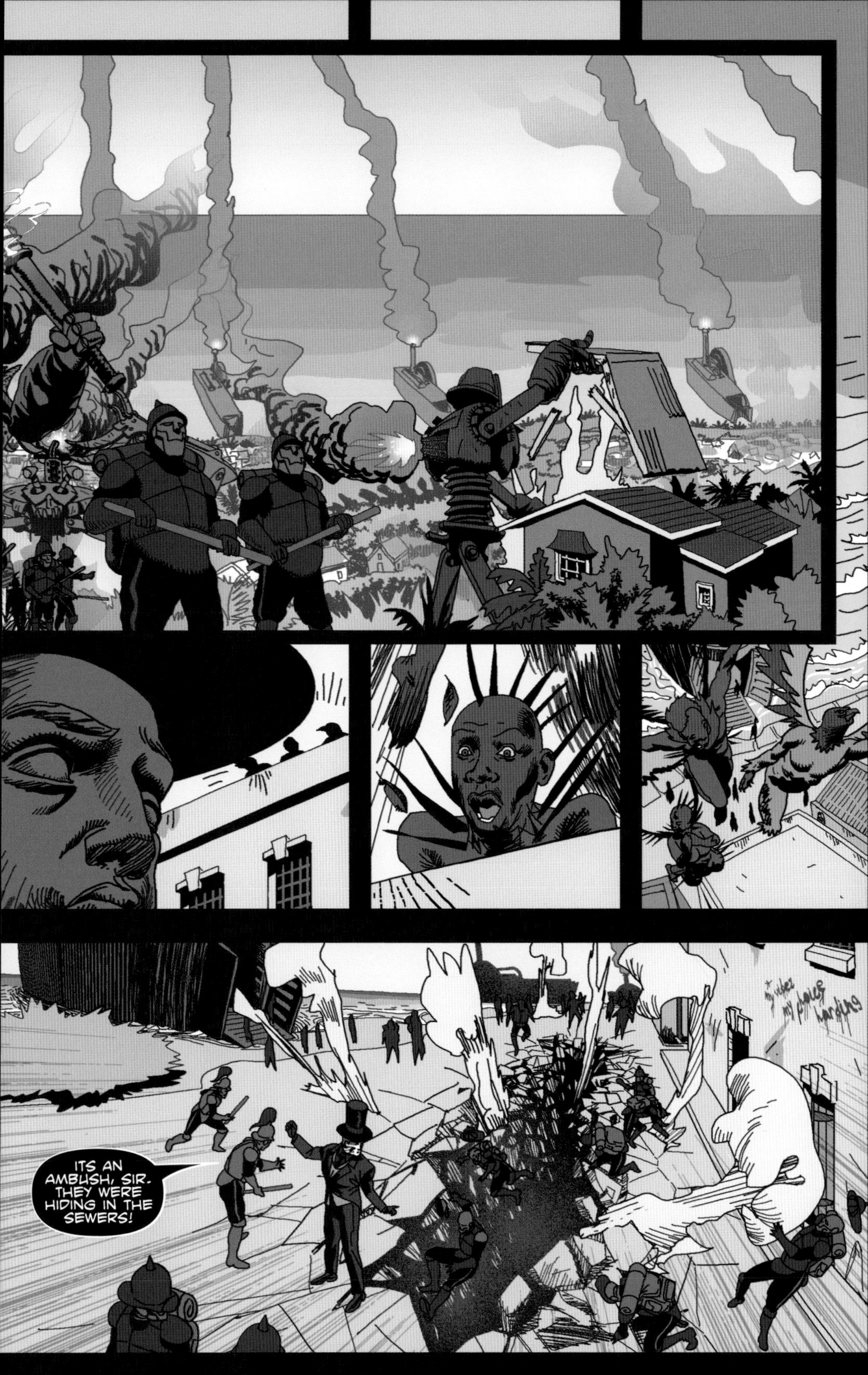
ITS AN AMBUSH, SIR. THEY WERE HIDING IN THE SEWERS!

COMMENCE PHASE THREE.

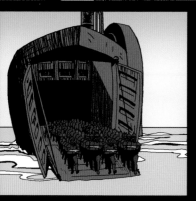

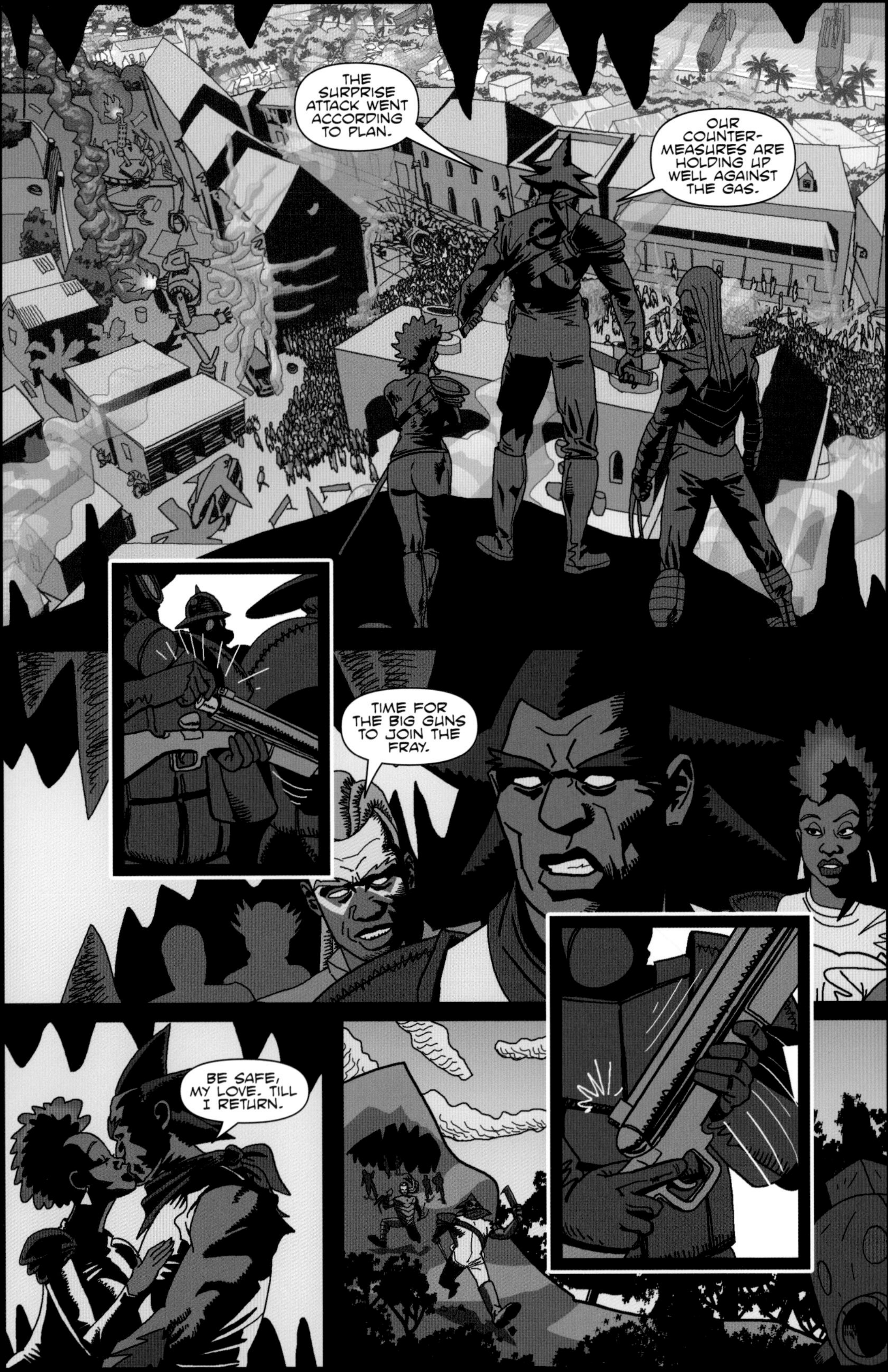
THE SURPRISE ATTACK WENT ACCORDING TO PLAN.
OUR COUNTER-MEASURES ARE HOLDING UP WELL AGAINST THE GAS.
TIME FOR THE BIG GUNS TO JOIN THE FRAY.
BE SAFE, MY LOVE. TILL I RETURN.

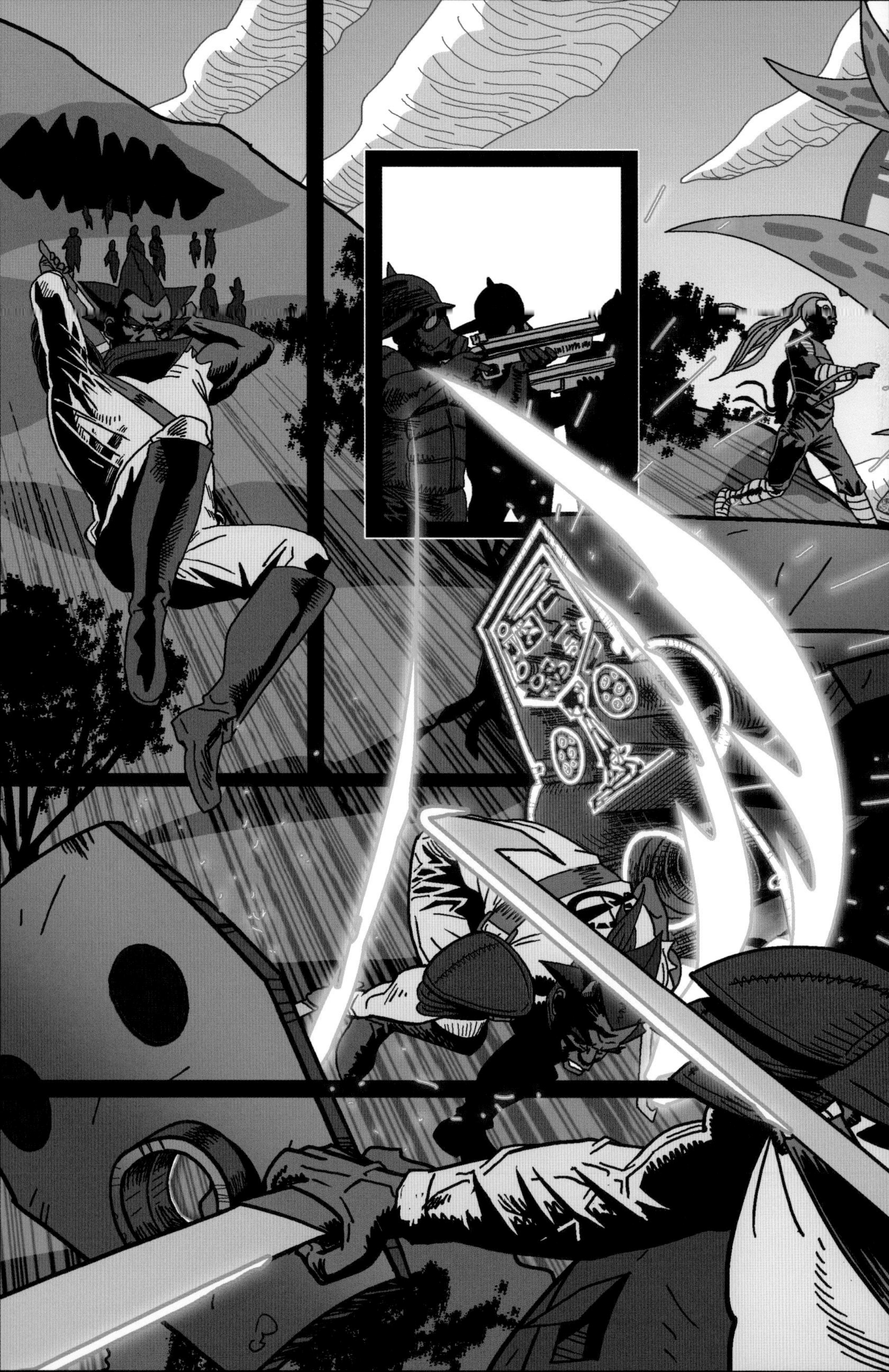

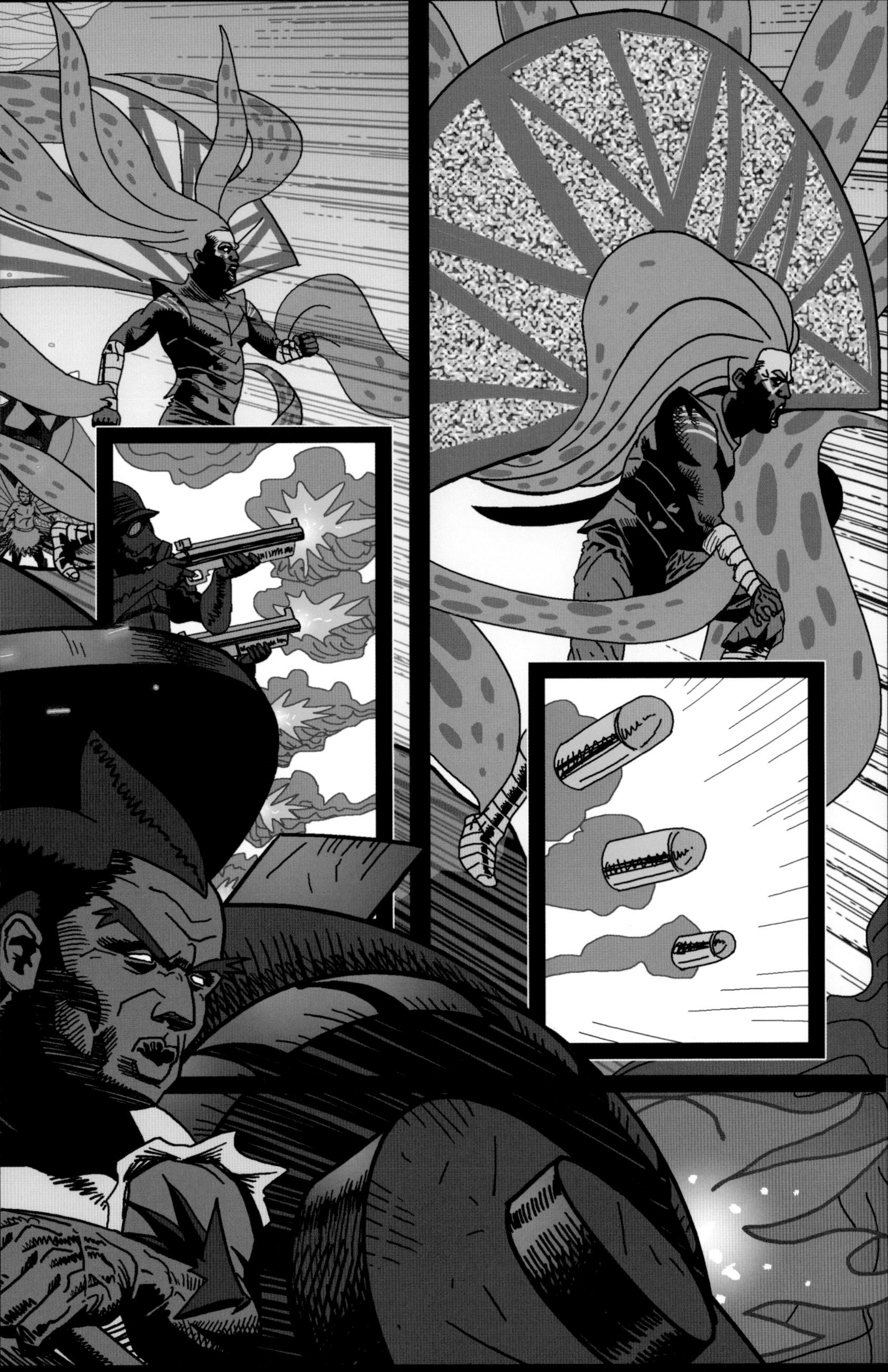

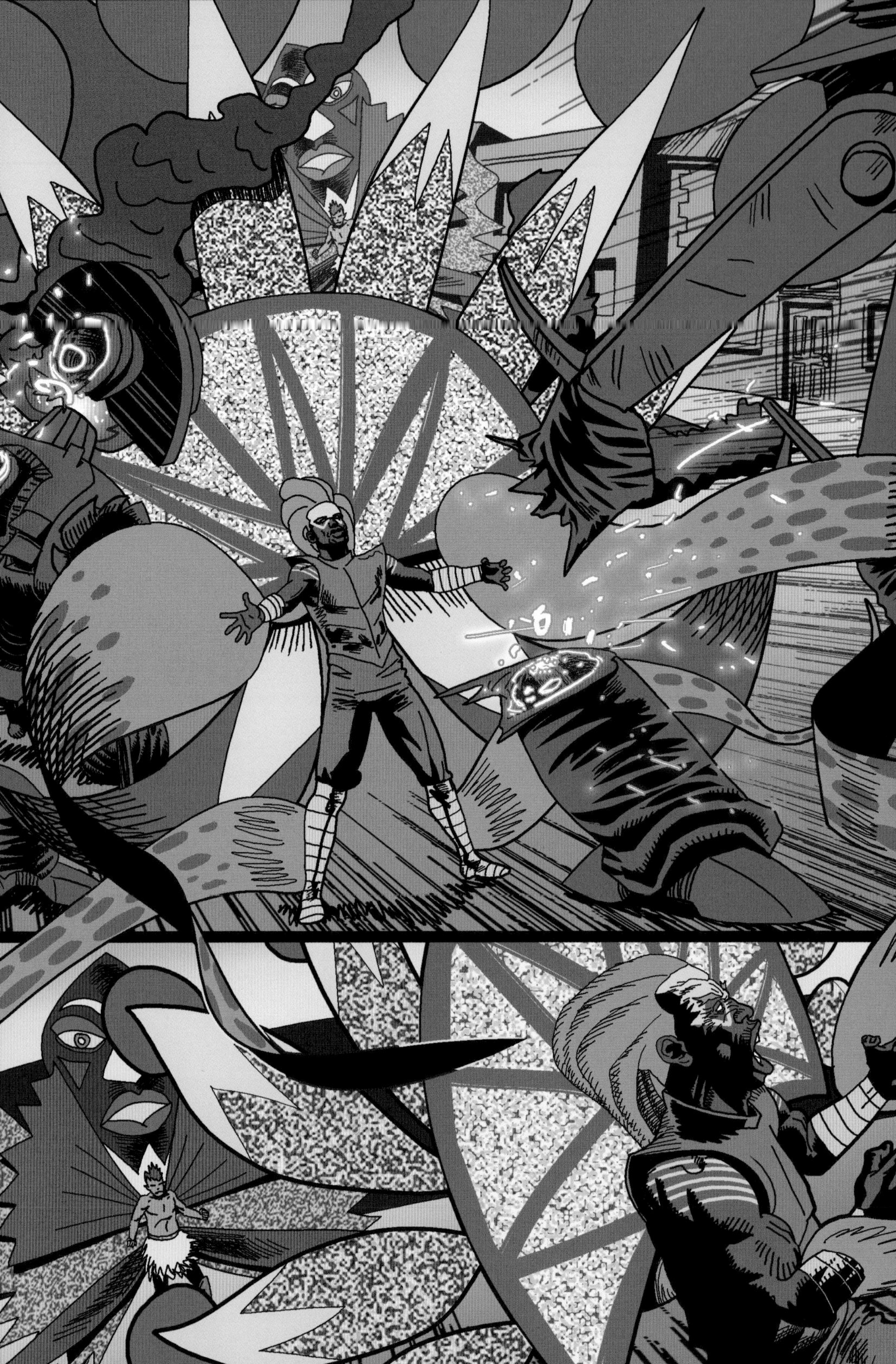

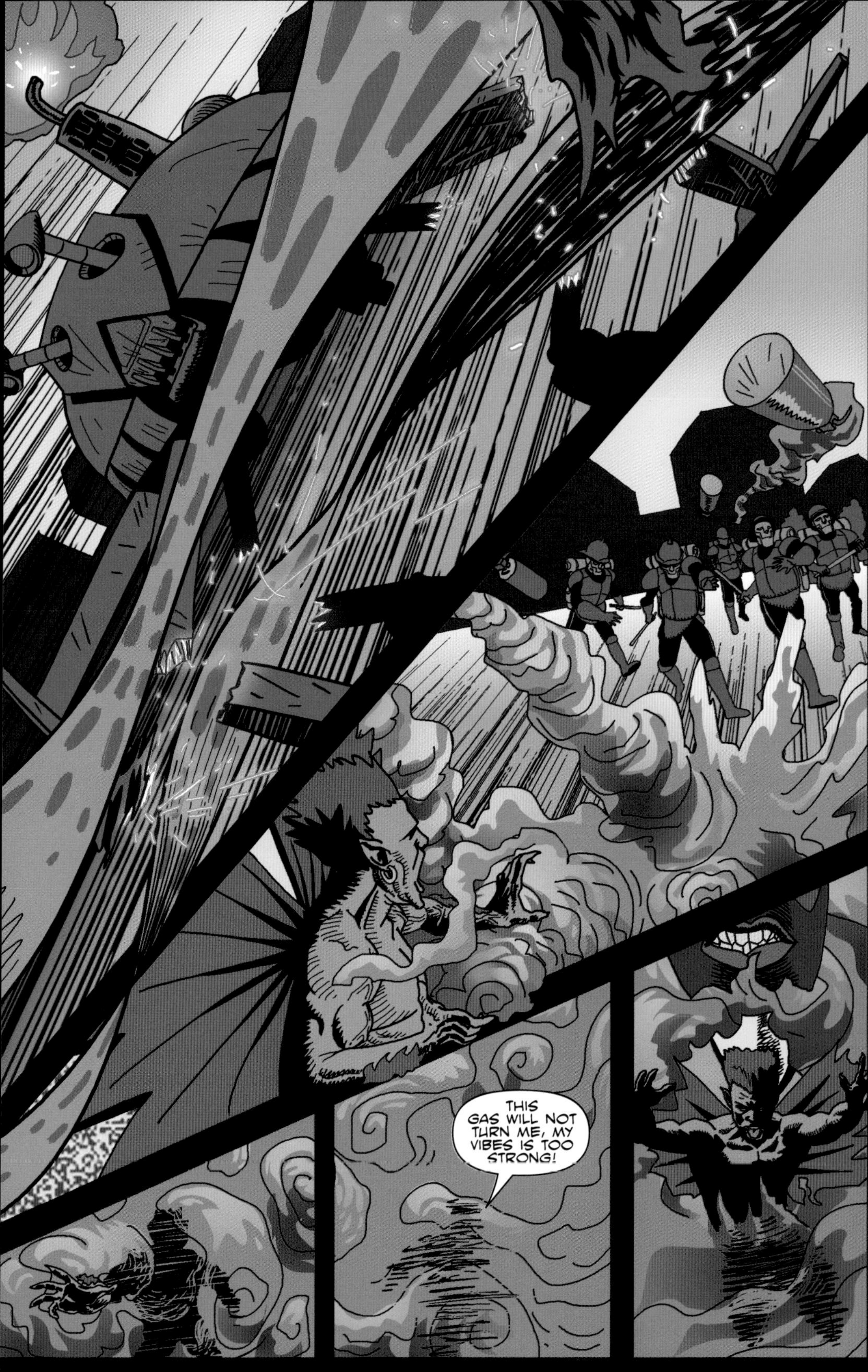
THIS GAS WILL NOT TURN ME, MY VIBES IS TOO STRONG!

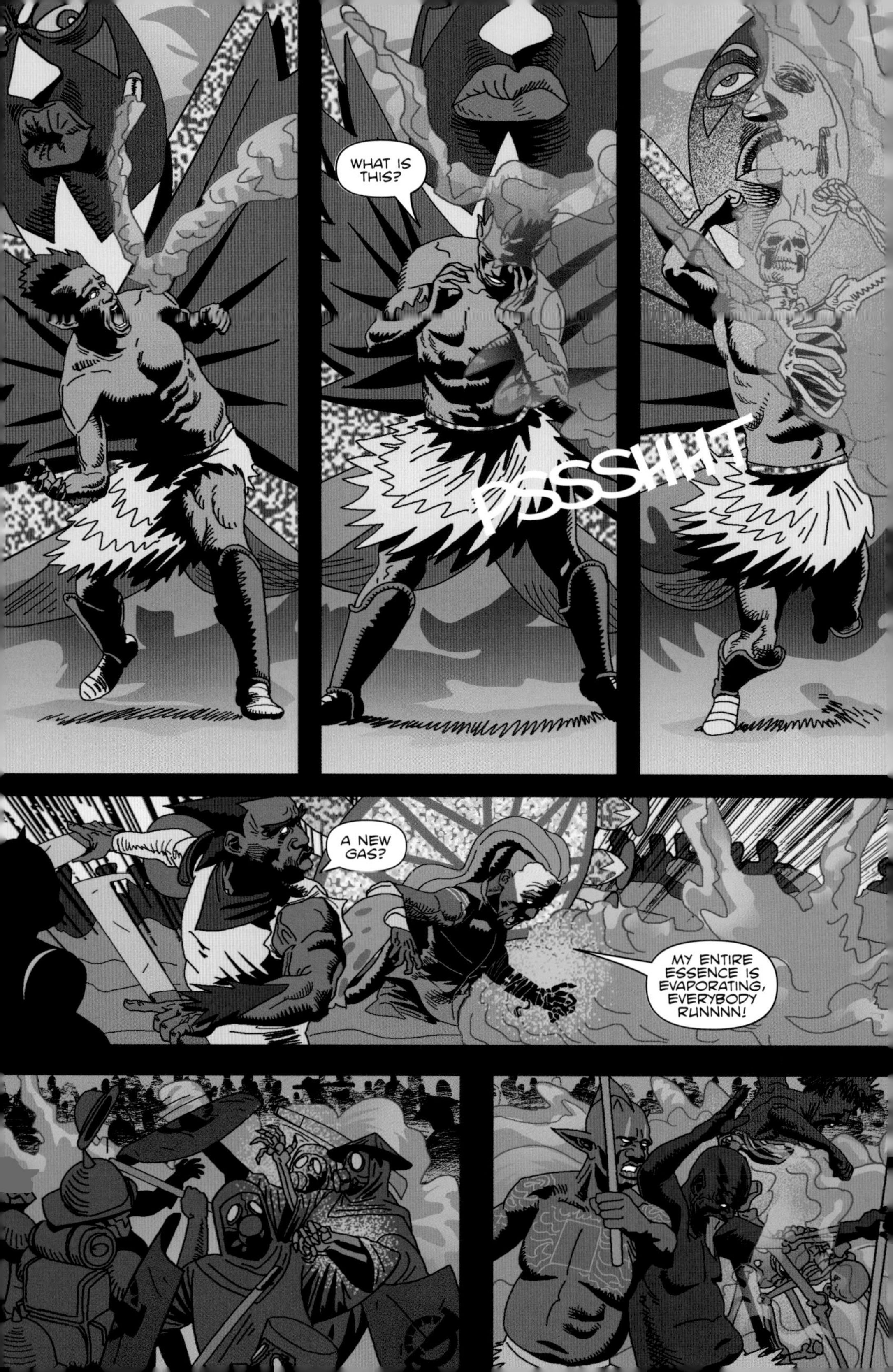
WHAT IS THIS?
PSSSHHHT
A NEW GAS?
MY ENTIRE ESSENCE IS EVAPORATING, EVERYBODY RUNNNN!

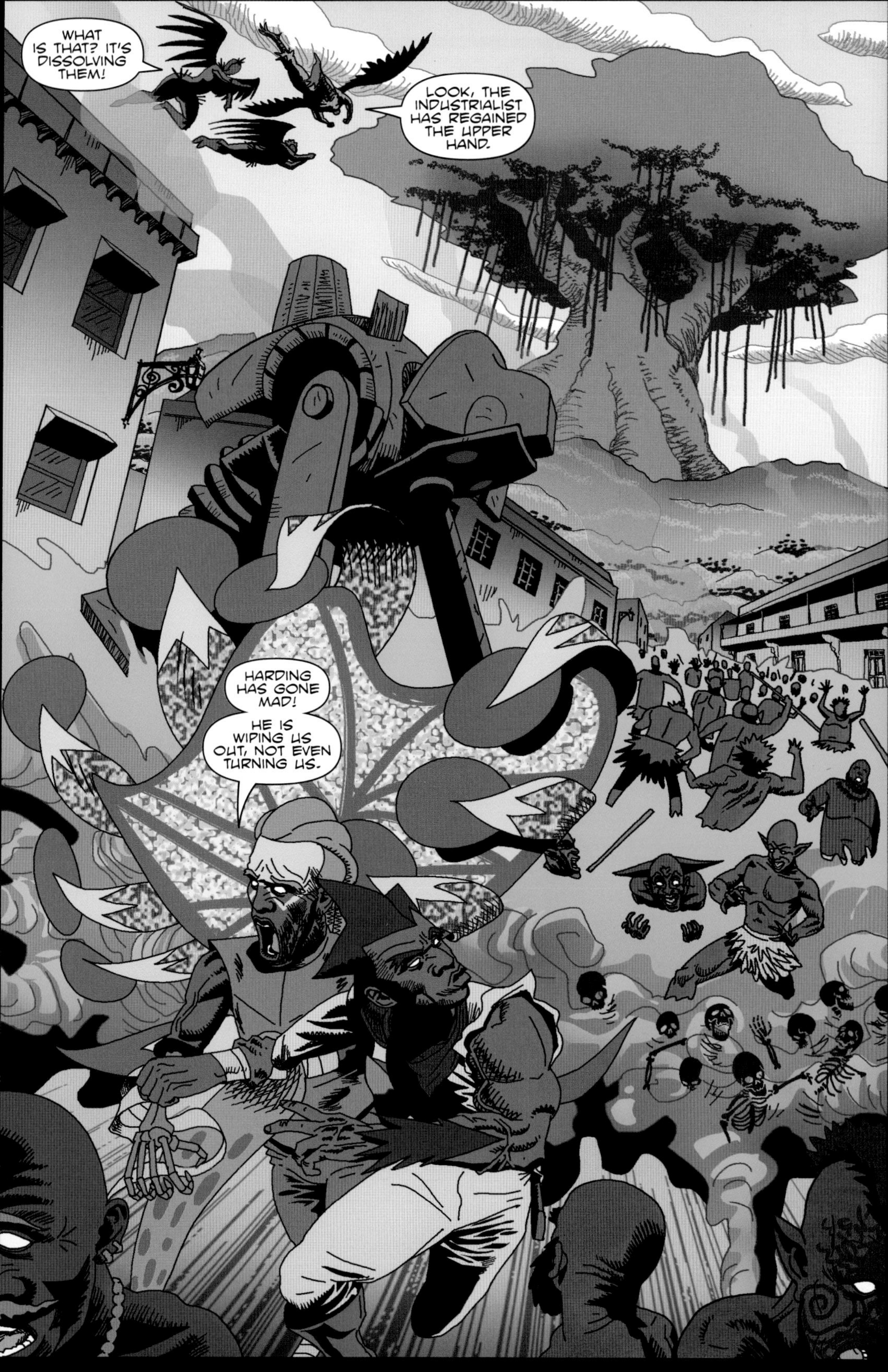
WHAT IS THAT? IT'S DISSOLVING THEM!
LOOK, THE INDUSTRIALIST HAS REGAINED THE UPPER HAND.
HARDING HAS GONE MAD!
HE IS WIPING US OUT, NOT EVEN TURNING US.

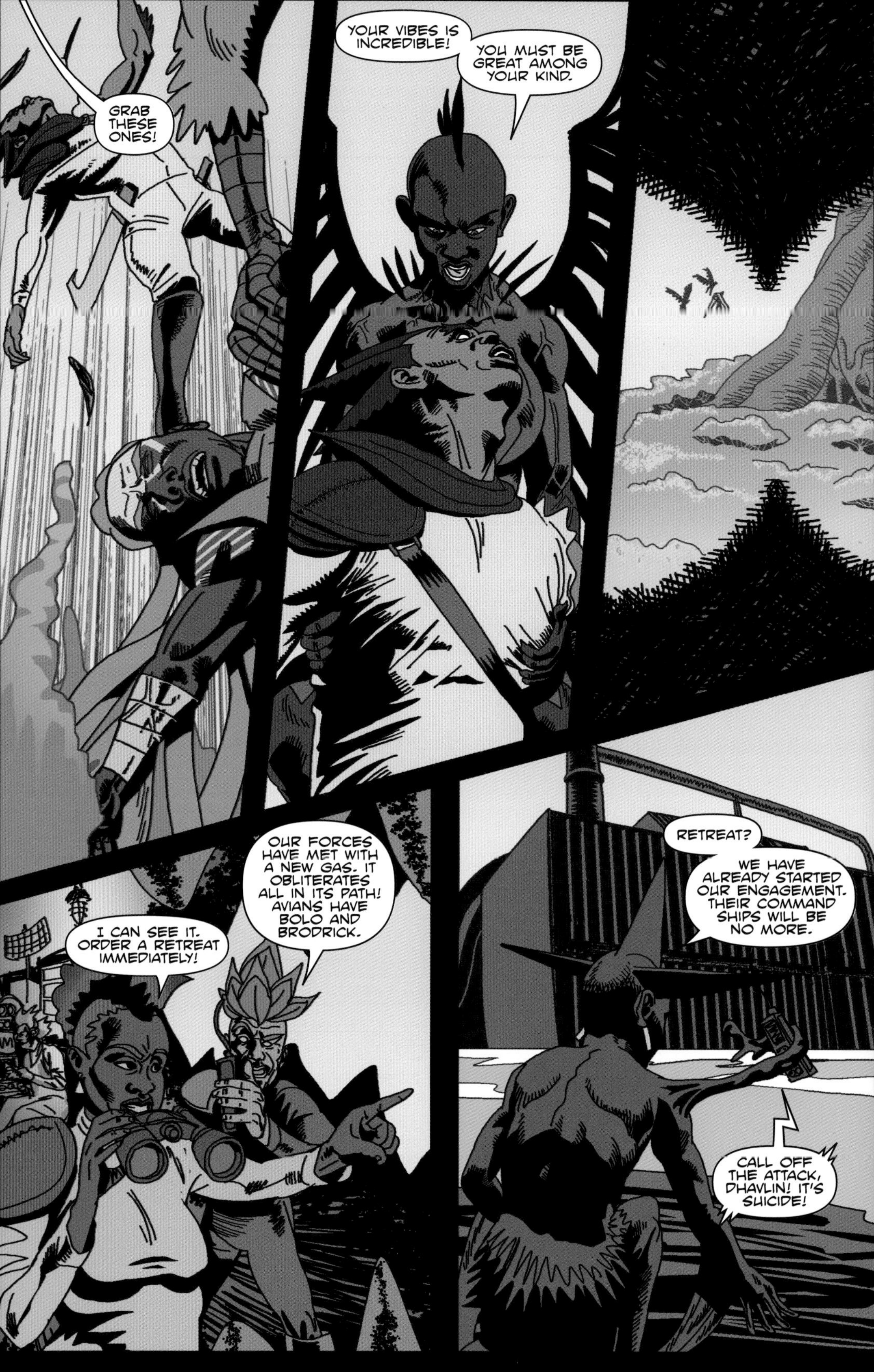
GRAB THESE ONES!
YOUR VIBES IS INCREDIBLE!
YOU MUST BE GREAT AMONG YOUR KIND.
OUR FORCES HAVE MET WITH A NEW GAS. IT OBLITERATES ALL IN ITS PATH! AVIANS HAVE BOLO AND BRODRICK.
I CAN SEE IT. ORDER A RETREAT IMMEDIATELY!
RETREAT?
WE HAVE ALREADY STARTED OUR ENGAGEMENT. THEIR COMMAND SHIPS WILL BE NO MORE.
CALL OFF THE ATTACK, DHAVLIN! IT'S SUICIDE!

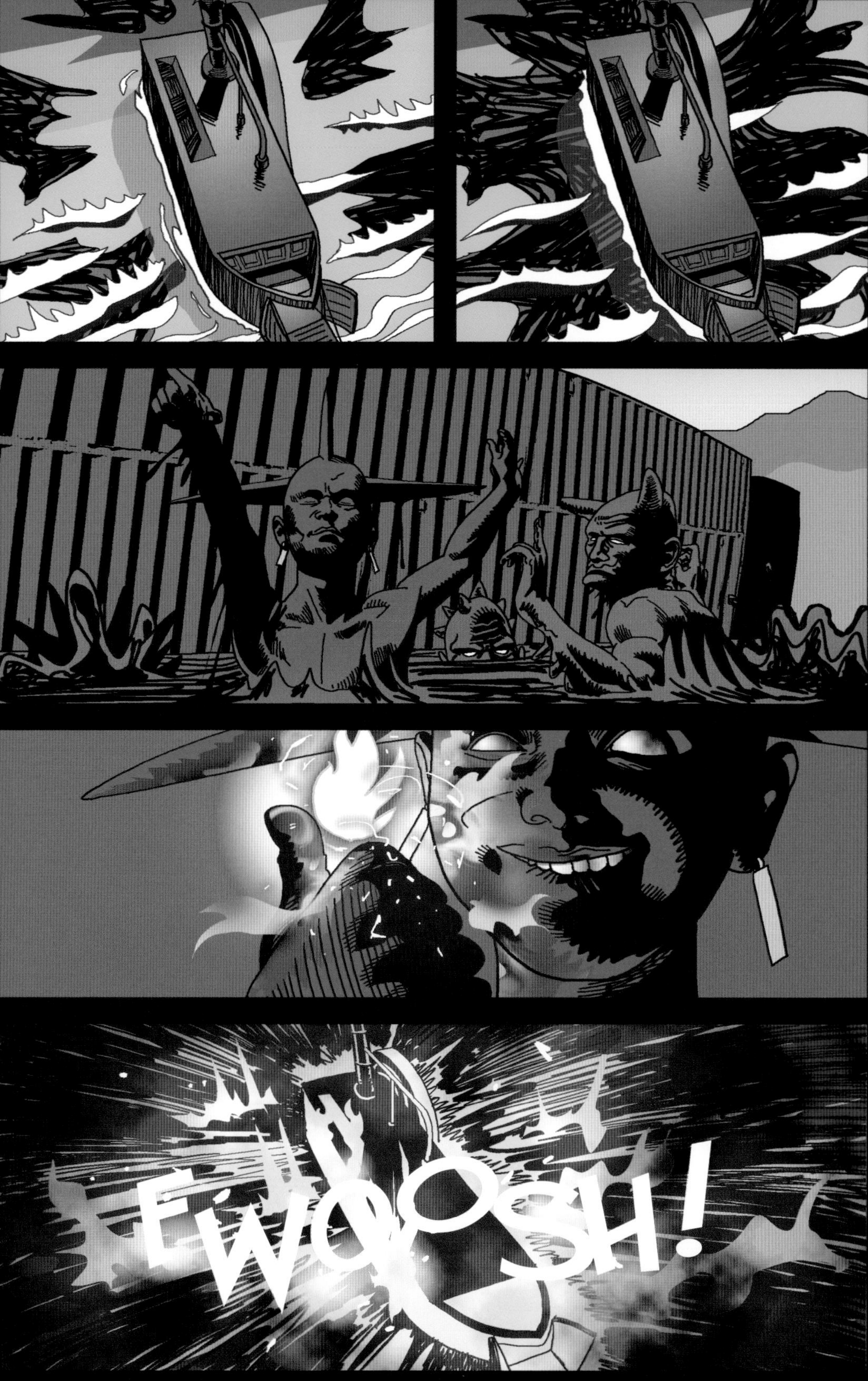
EWOOSH!

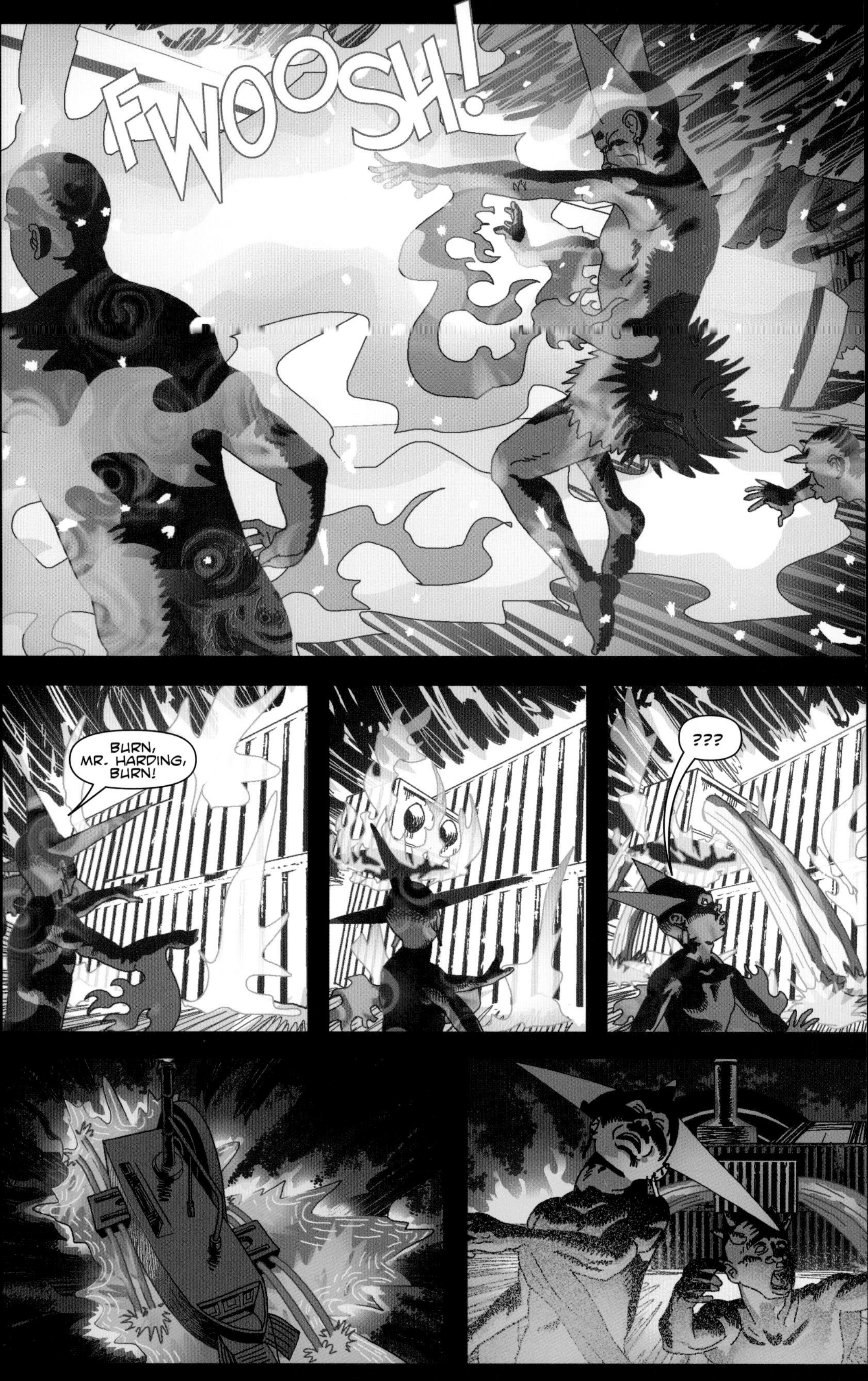
FWOOSH!
BURN, MR. HARDING, BURN!
???

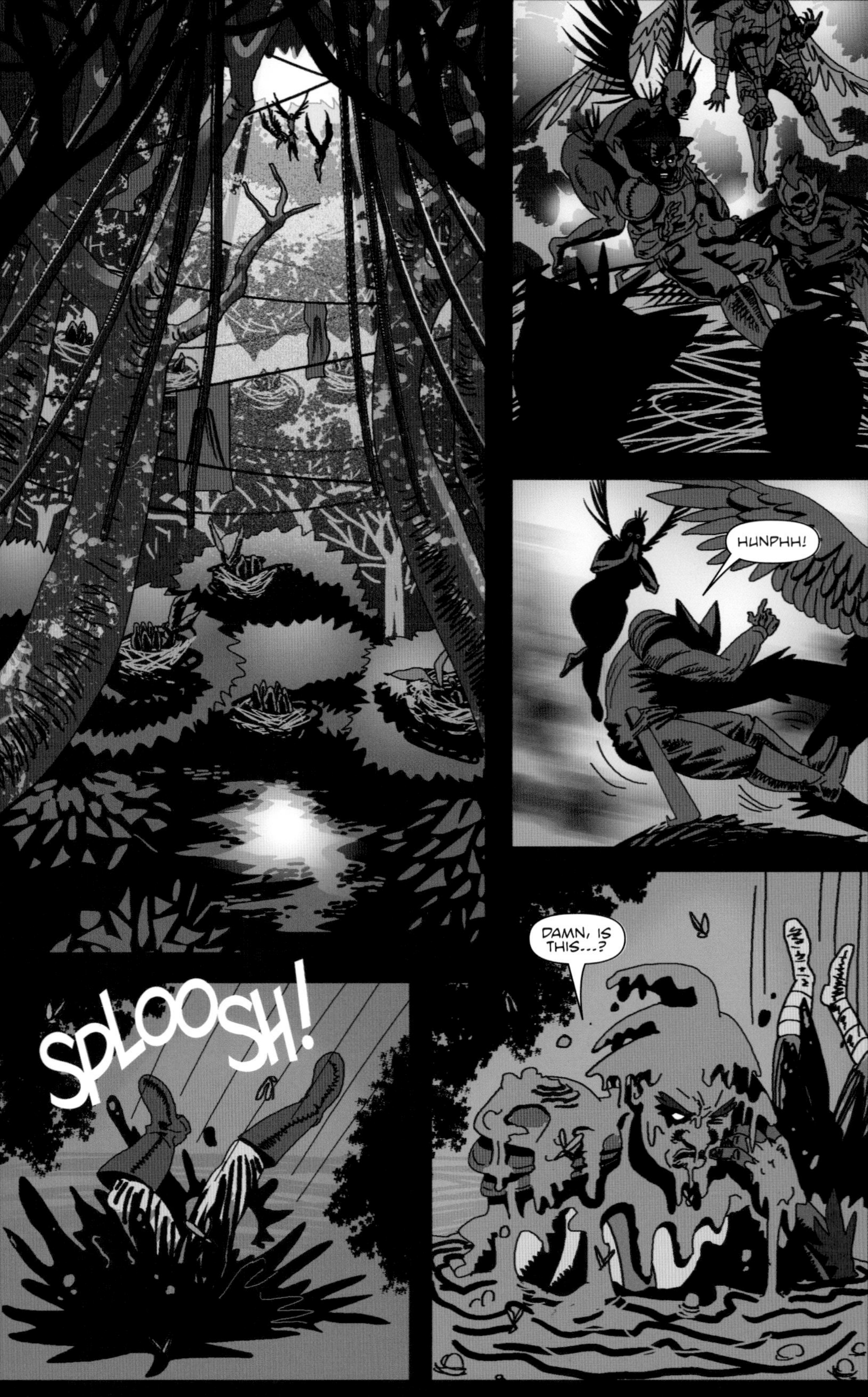
HUNPHH!
SPLOOSH!
DAMN, IS THIS...?

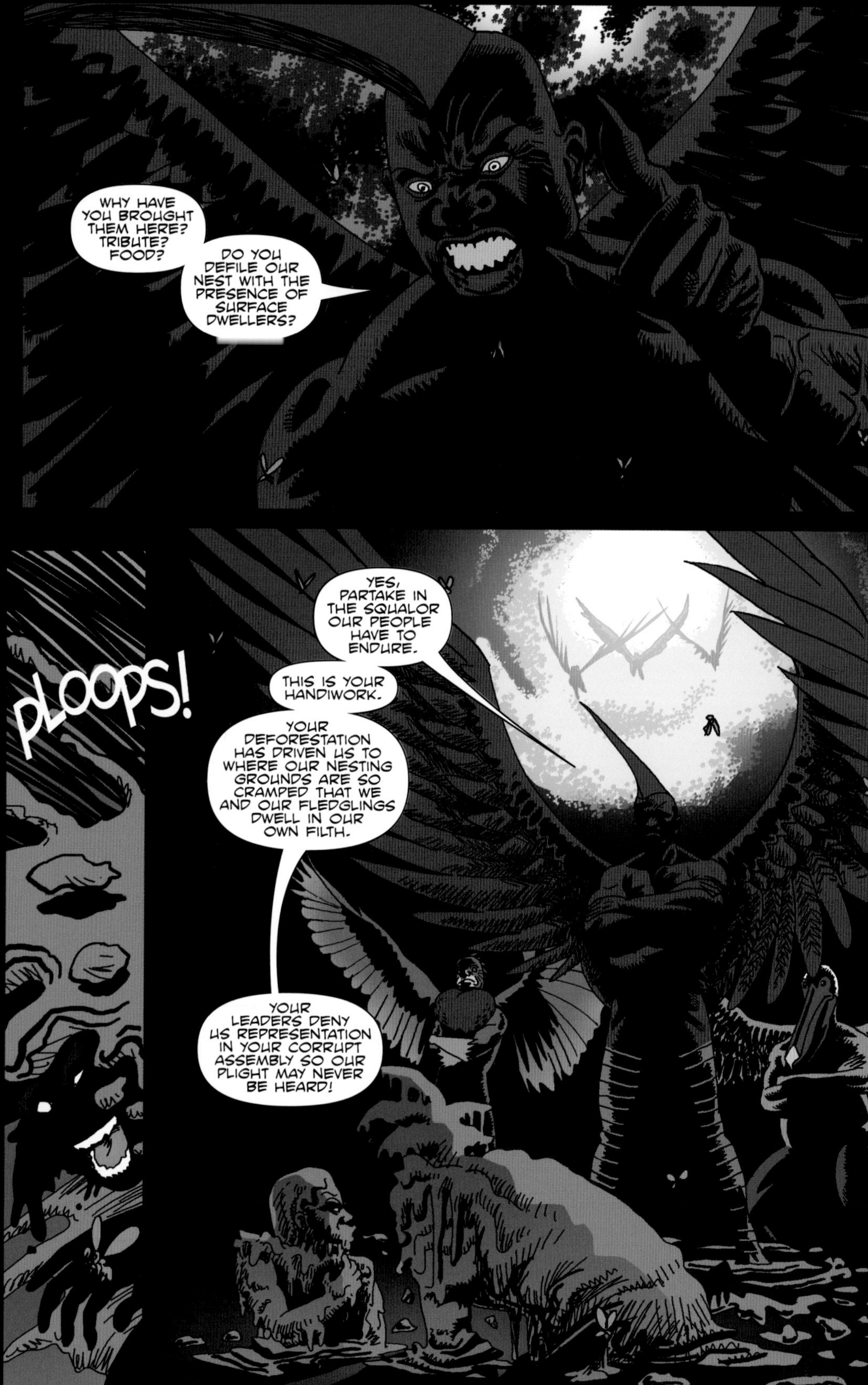
WHY HAVE YOU BROUGHT THEM HERE? TRIBUTE? FOOD?
DO YOU DEFILE OUR NEST WITH THE PRESENCE OF SURFACE DWELLERS?
PLOOPS!
YES, PARTAKE IN THE SQUALOR OUR PEOPLE HAVE TO ENDURE.
THIS IS YOUR HANDIWORK.
YOUR DEFORESTATION HAS DRIVEN US TO WHERE OUR NESTING GROUNDS ARE SO CRAMPED THAT WE AND OUR FLEDGLINGS DWELL IN OUR OWN FILTH.
YOUR LEADERS DENY US REPRESENTATION IN YOUR CORRUPT ASSEMBLY SO OUR PLIGHT MAY NEVER BE HEARD!

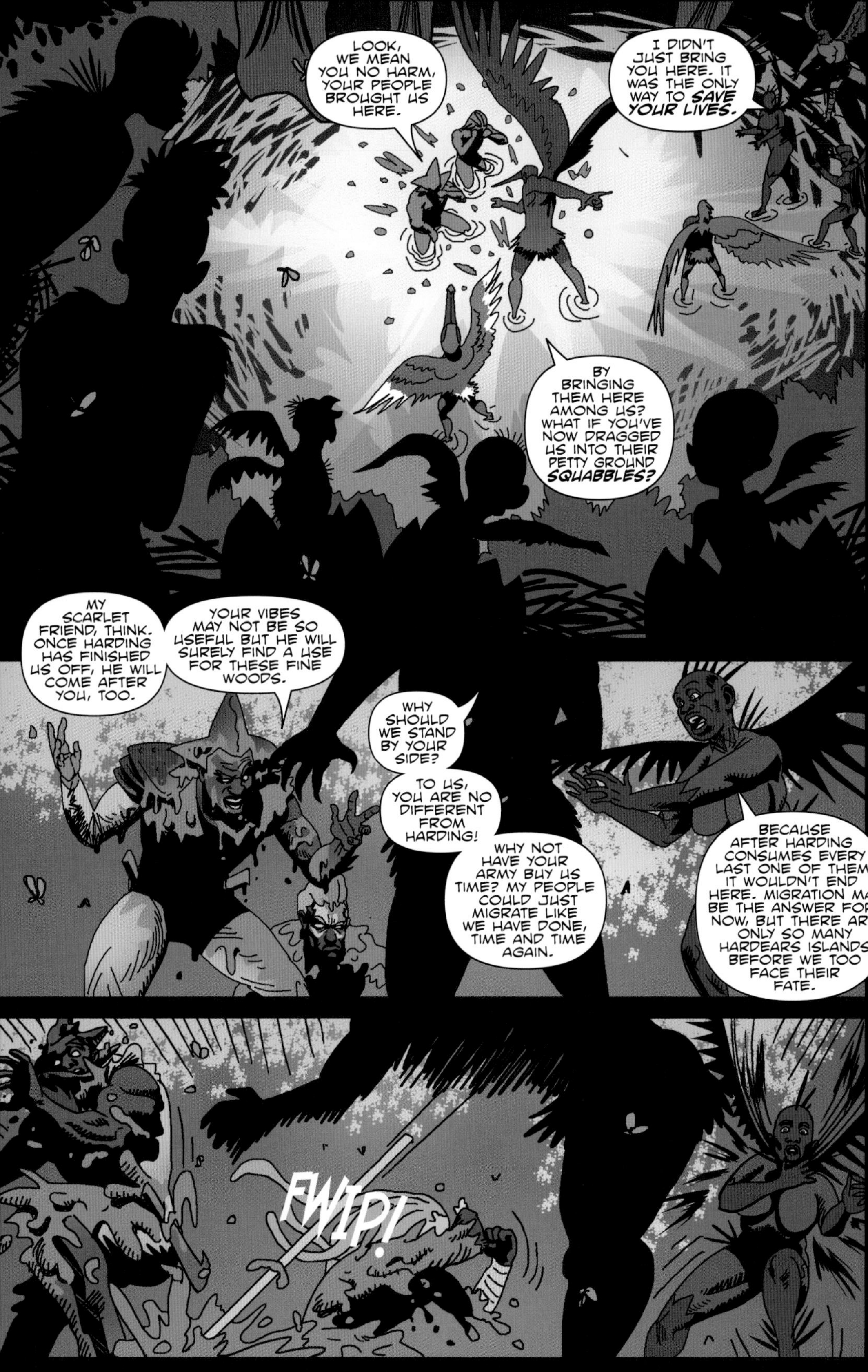
LOOK, WE MEAN YOU NO HARM, YOUR PEOPLE BROUGHT US HERE.
I DIDN'T JUST BRING YOU HERE. IT WAS THE ONLY WAY TO SAVE YOUR LIVES.
BY BRINGING THEM HERE AMONG US? WHAT IF YOU'VE NOW DRAGGED US INTO THEIR PETTY GROUND SQUABBLES?
MY SCARLET FRIEND, THINK. ONCE HARDING HAS FINISHED US OFF, HE WILL COME AFTER YOU, TOO.
YOUR VIBES MAY NOT BE SO USEFUL BUT HE WILL SURELY FIND A USE FOR THESE FINE WOODS.
WHY SHOULD WE STAND BY YOUR SIDE?
TO US, YOU ARE NO DIFFERENT FROM HARDING!
WHY NOT HAVE YOUR ARMY BUY US TIME? MY PEOPLE COULD JUST MIGRATE LIKE WE HAVE DONE, TIME AND TIME AGAIN.
BECAUSE AFTER HARDING CONSUMES EVERY LAST ONE OF THEM, IT WOULDN'T END HERE. MIGRATION MAY BE THE ANSWER FOR NOW, BUT THERE ARE ONLY SO MANY HARDEARS ISLANDS BEFORE WE TOO FACE THEIR FATE.
FWIP!

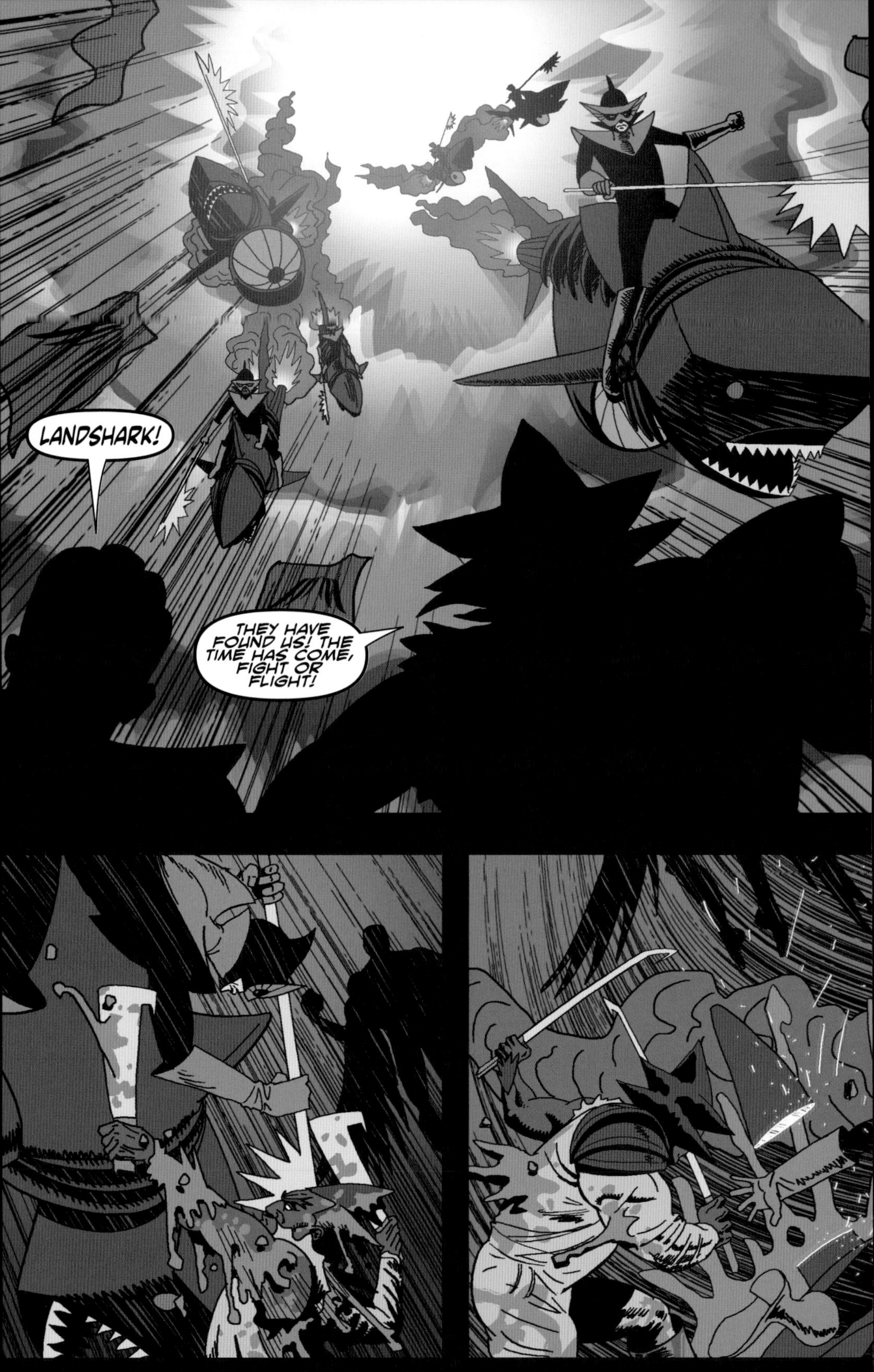
LANDSHARK!
THEY HAVE FOUND US! THE TIME HAS COME, FIGHT OR FLIGHT!

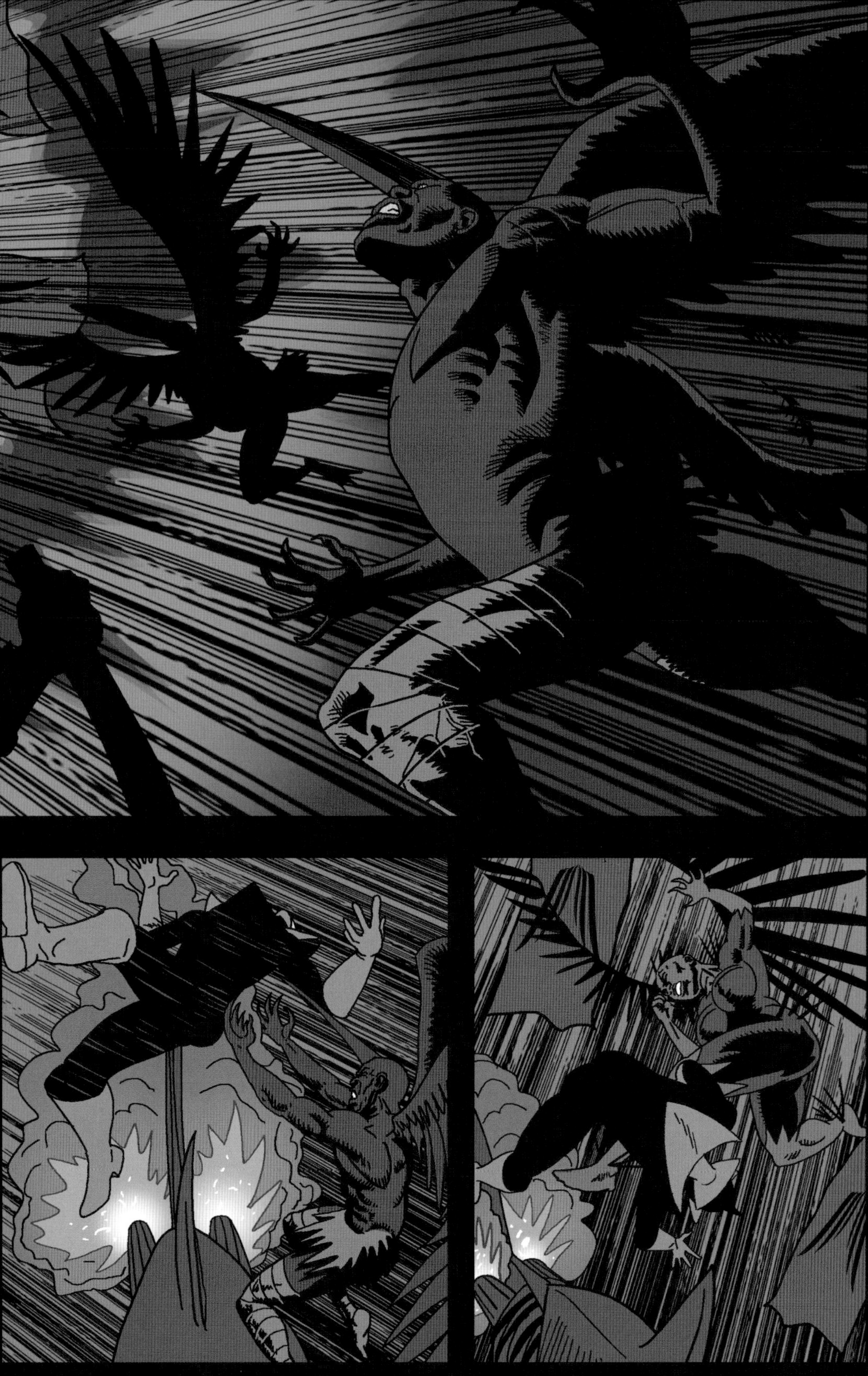

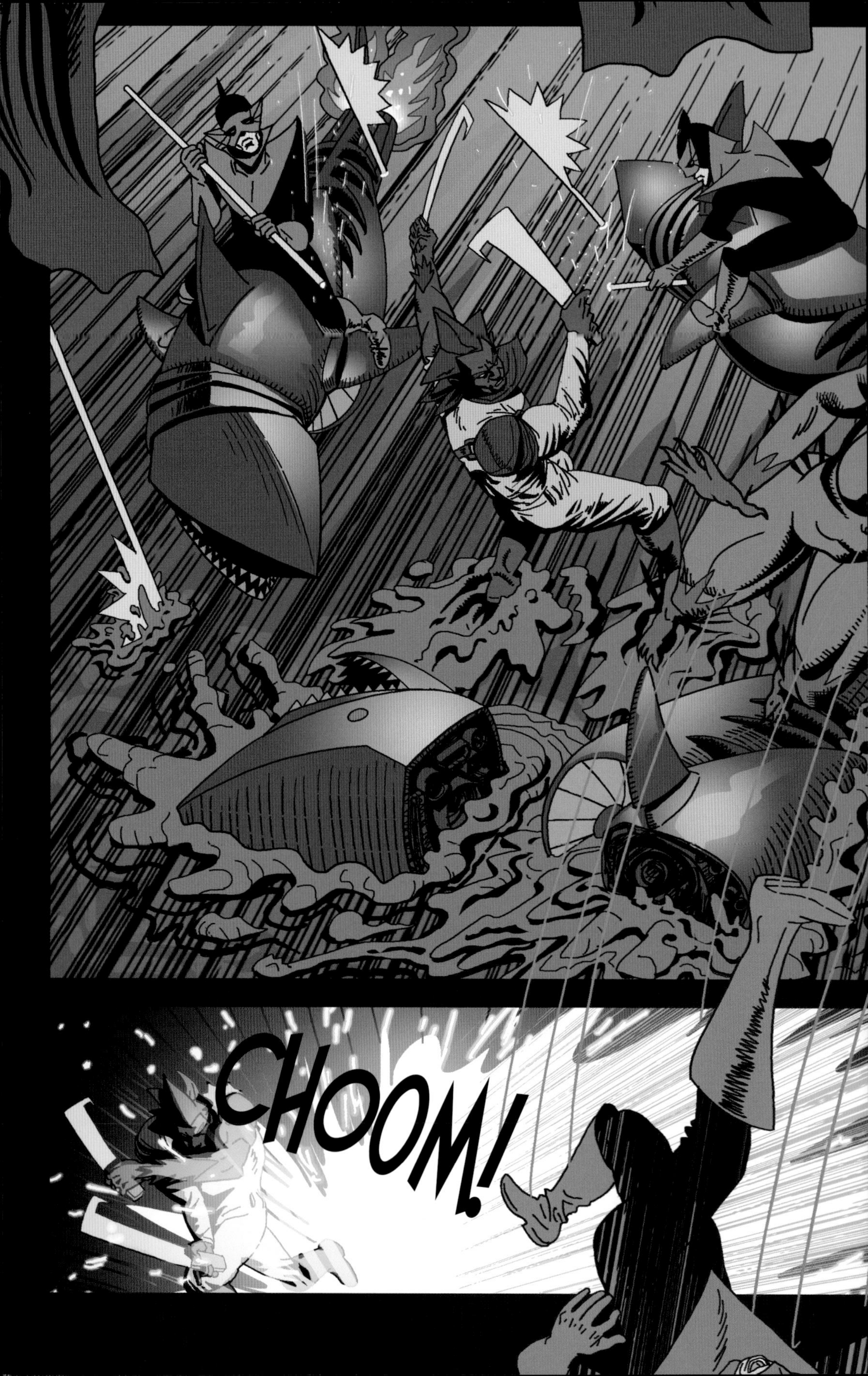
CHOOM!

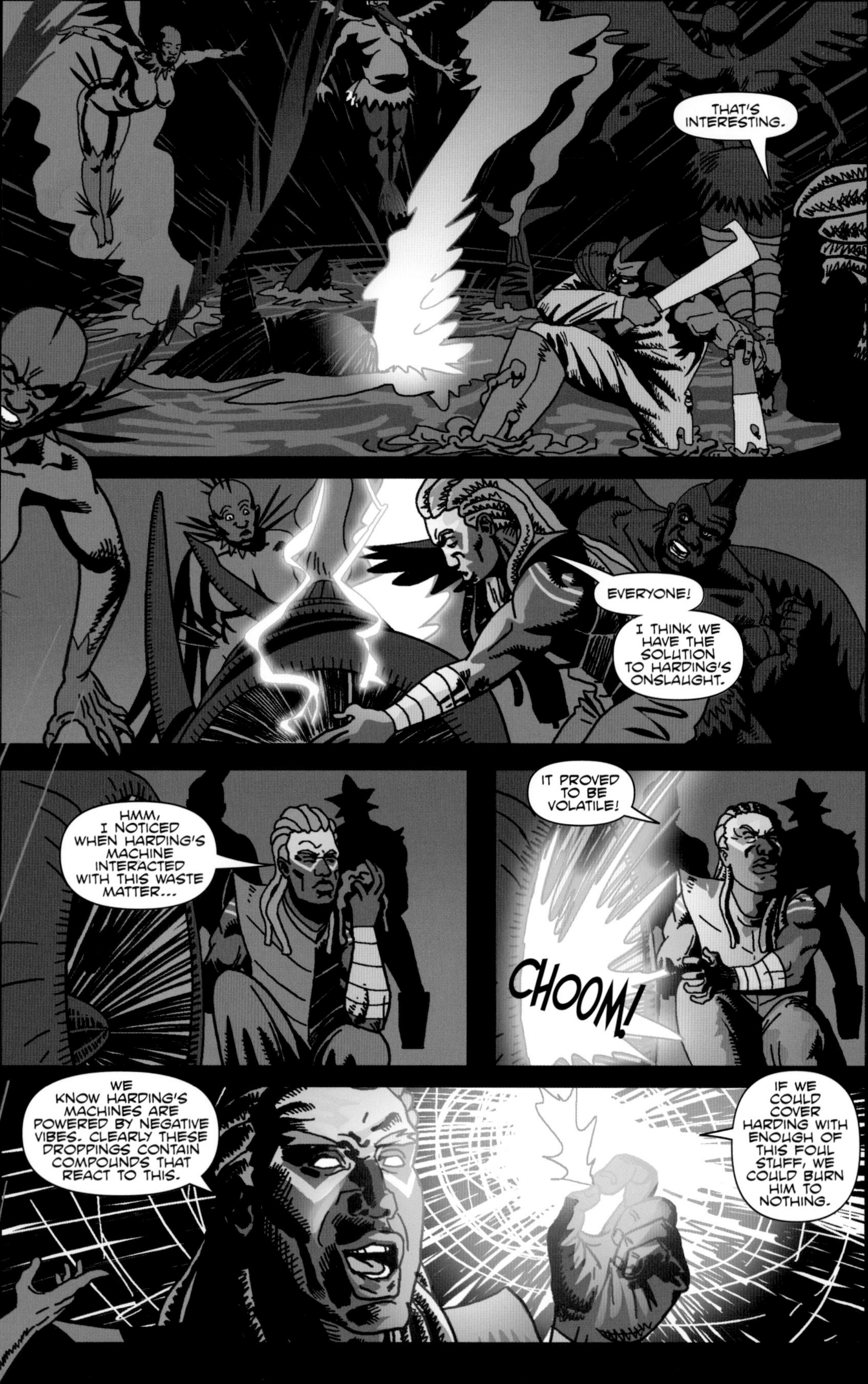
THAT'S INTERESTING.
EVERYONE!
I THINK WE HAVE THE SOLUTION TO HARDING'S ONSLAUGHT.
HMM, I NOTICED WHEN HARDING'S MACHINE INTERACTED WITH THIS WASTE MATTER...
IT PROVED TO BE VOLATILE!
CHOOM!
WE KNOW HARDING'S MACHINES ARE POWERED BY NEGATIVE VIBES. CLEARLY THESE DROPPINGS CONTAIN COMPOUNDS THAT REACT TO THIS.
IF WE COULD COVER HARDING WITH ENOUGH OF THIS FOUL STUFF, WE COULD BURN HIM TO NOTHING.

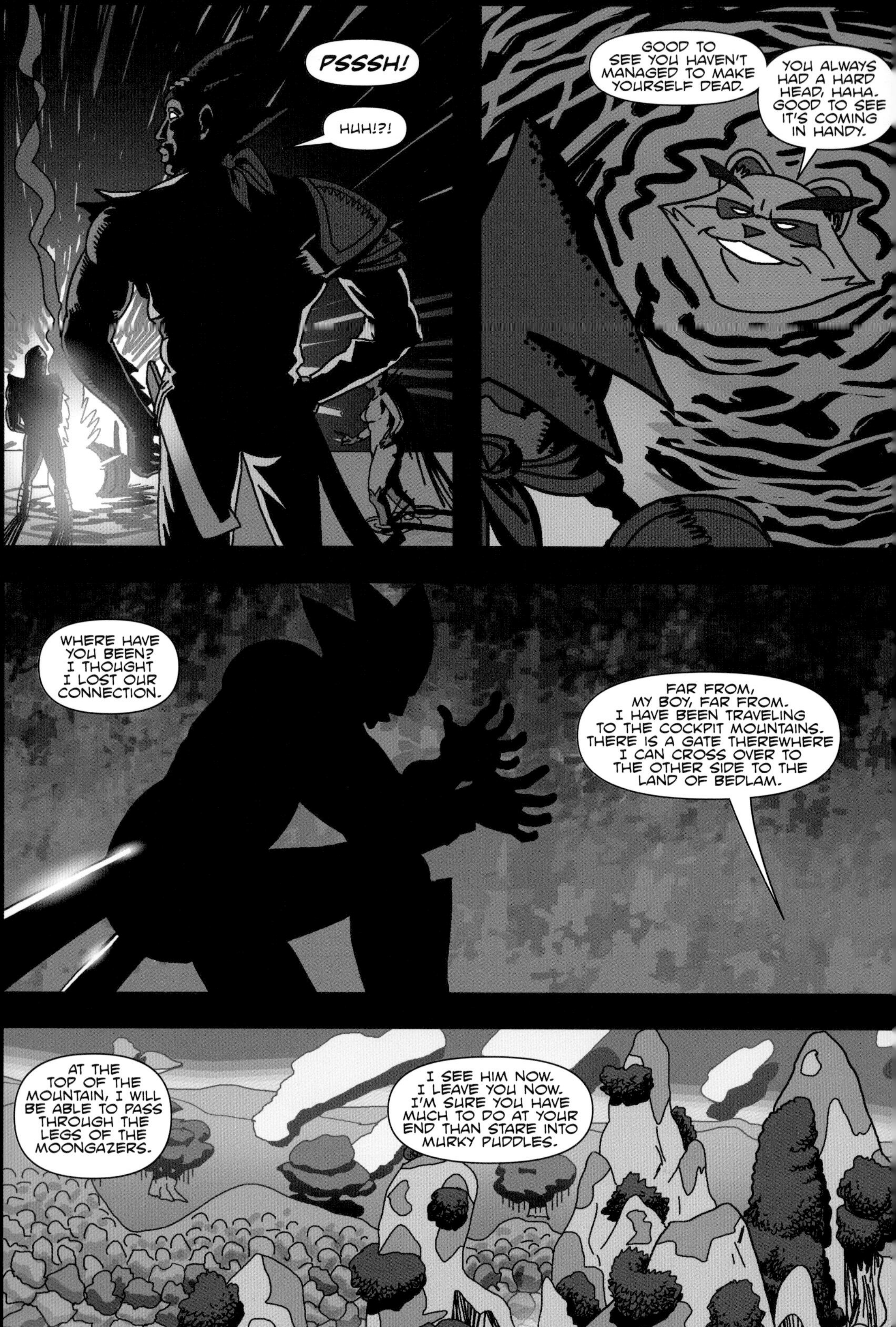
PSSSH!
HUH!?!
GOOD TO SEE YOU HAVEN'T MANAGED TO MAKE YOURSELF DEAD.
YOU ALWAYS HAD A HARD HEAD, HAHA. GOOD TO SEE IT'S COMING IN HANDY.
WHERE HAVE YOU BEEN? I THOUGHT I LOST OUR CONNECTION.
FAR FROM, MY BOY, FAR FROM. I HAVE BEEN TRAVELING TO THE COCKPIT MOUNTAINS. THERE IS A GATE THEREWHERE I CAN CROSS OVER TO THE OTHER SIDE TO THE LAND OF BEDLAM.
AT THE TOP OF THE MOUNTAIN, I WILL BE ABLE TO PASS THROUGH THE LEGS OF THE MOONGAZERS.
I SEE HIM NOW. I LEAVE YOU NOW. I'M SURE YOU HAVE MUCH TO DO AT YOUR END THAN STARE INTO MURKY PUDDLES.

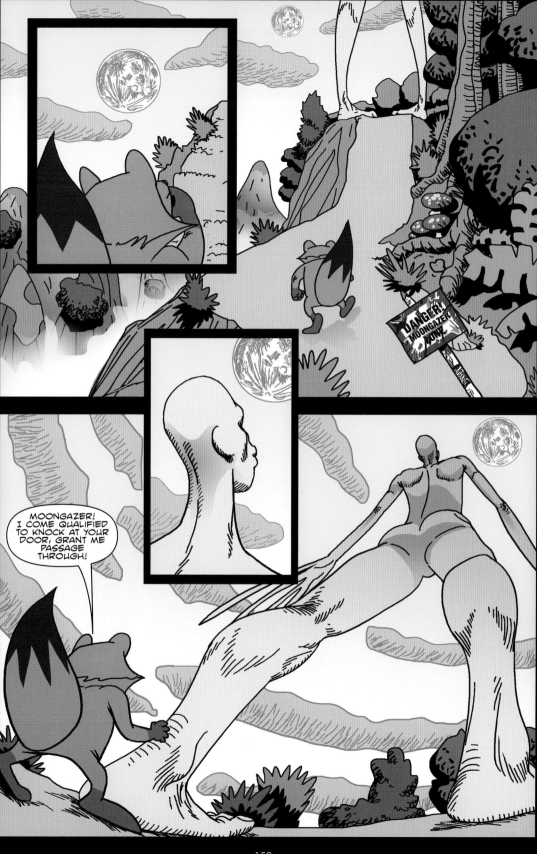

MOONGAZER!
I COME QUALIFIED
TO KNOCK AT YOUR
DOOR, GRANT ME
PASSAGE
THROUGH!

DANGER!
MOONGAZER
ZONE

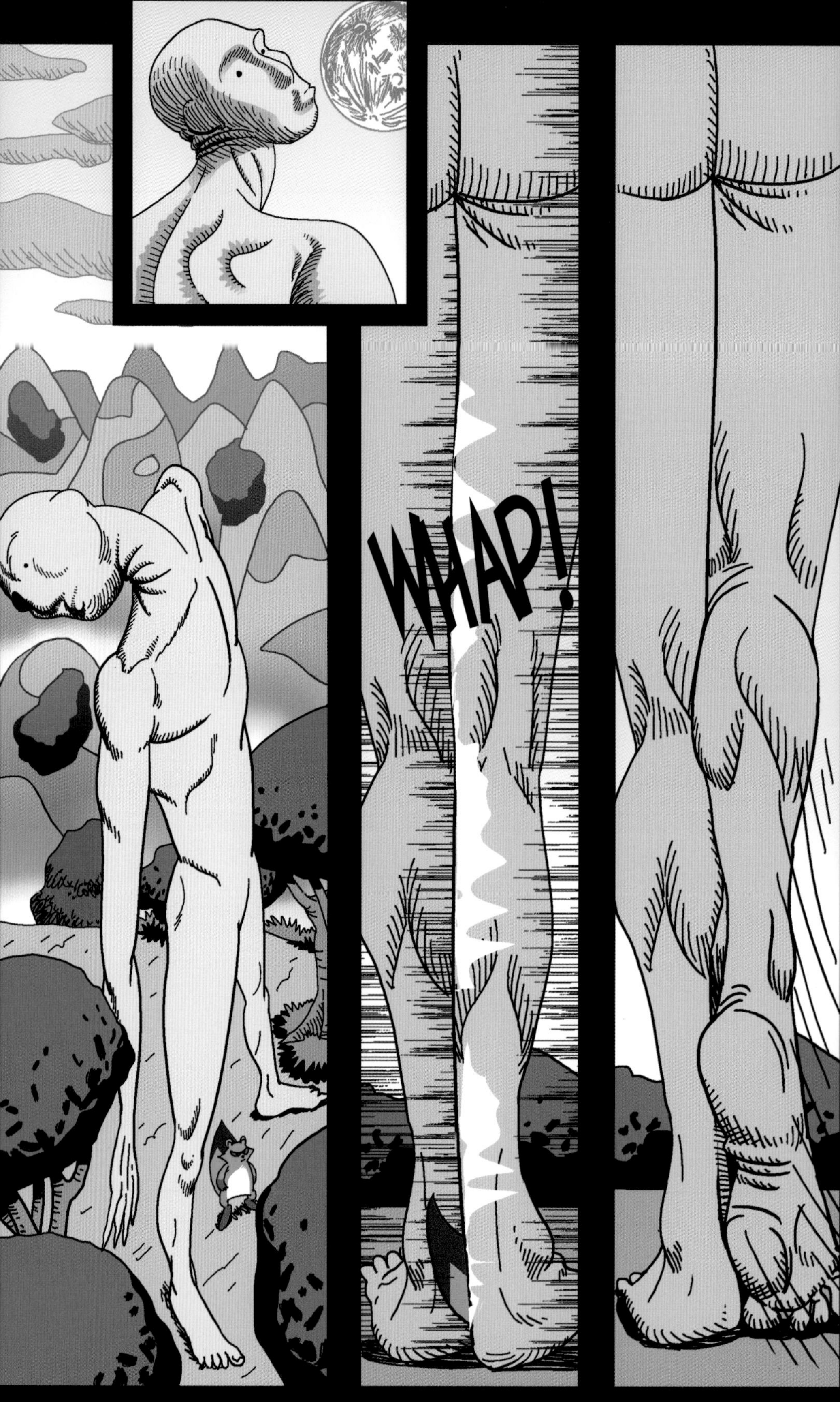

WHAP!

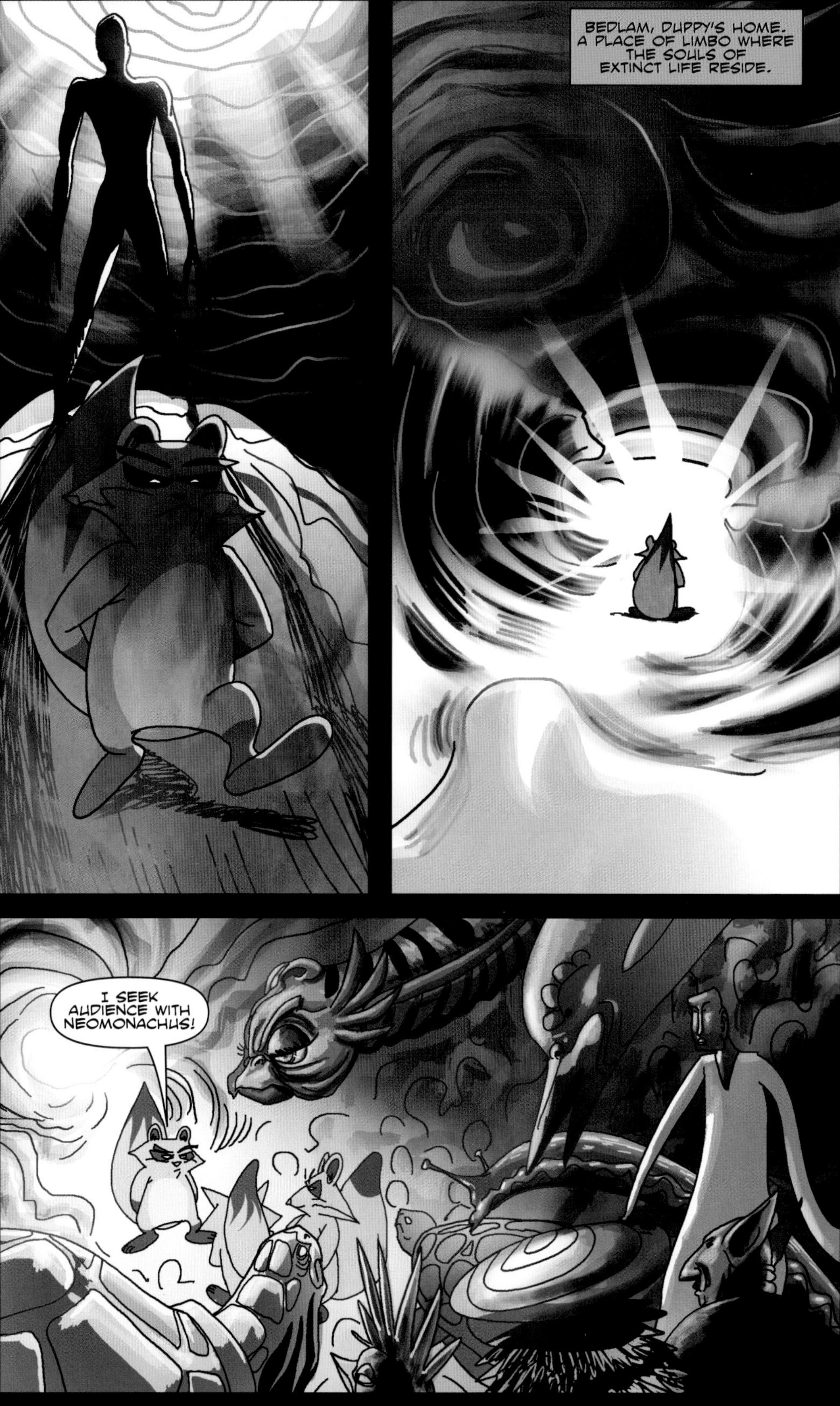
BEDLAM, DUPPY'S HOME. A PLACE OF LIMBO WHERE THE SOULS OF EXTINCT LIFE RESIDE.
I SEEK AUDIENCE WITH NEOMONACHUS!

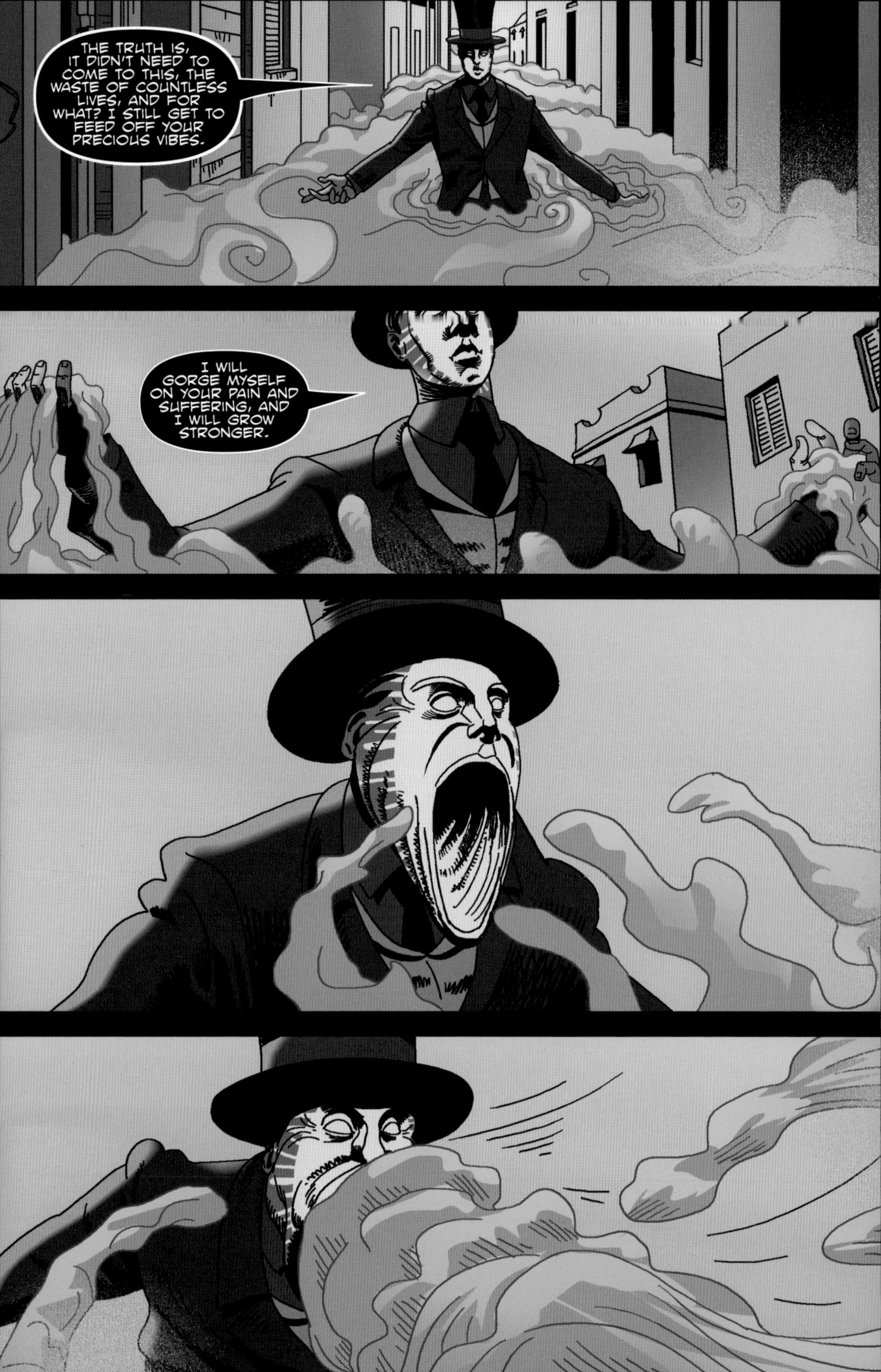
THE TRUTH IS, IT DIDN'T NEED TO COME TO THIS, THE WASTE OF COUNTLESS LIVES, AND FOR WHAT? I STILL GET TO FEED OFF YOUR PRECIOUS VIBES.
I WILL GORGE MYSELF ON YOUR PAIN AND SUFFERING, AND I WILL GROW STRONGER.

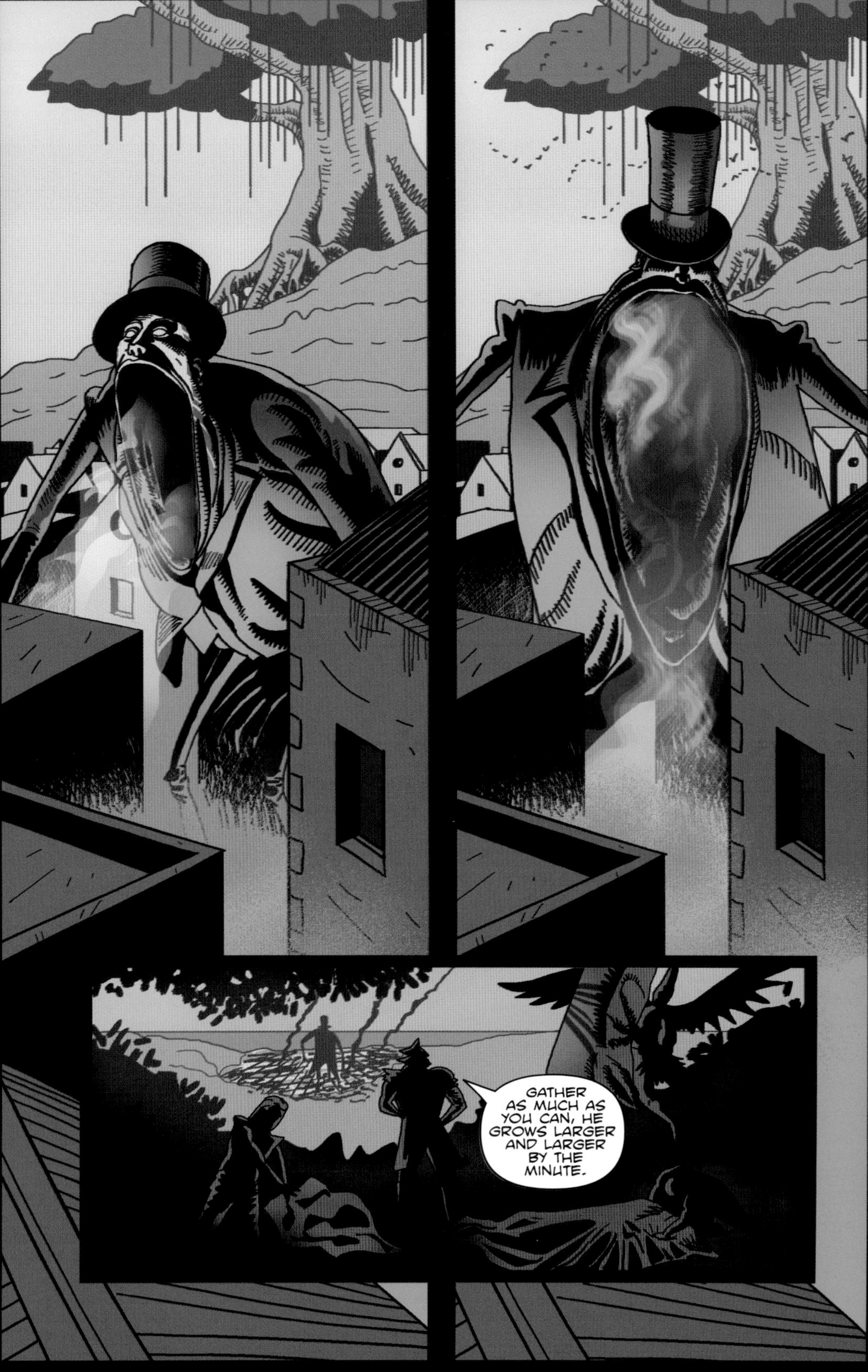
GATHER AS MUCH AS YOU CAN, HE GROWS LARGER AND LARGER BY THE MINUTE.

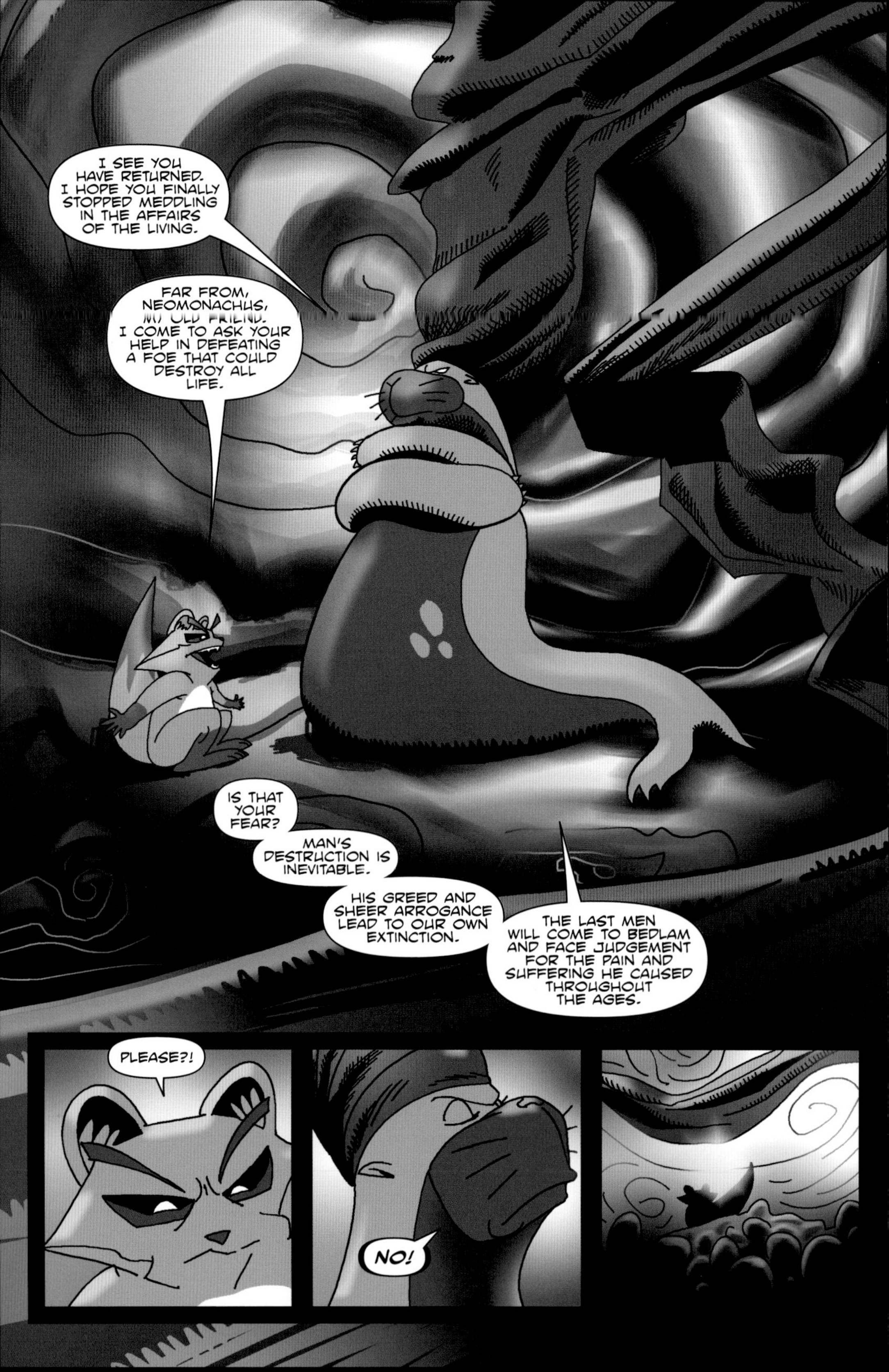
I SEE YOU HAVE RETURNED. I HOPE YOU FINALLY STOPPED MEDDLING IN THE AFFAIRS OF THE LIVING.
FAR FROM, NEOMONACHUS, MY OLD FRIEND. I COME TO ASK YOUR HELP IN DEFEATING A FOE THAT COULD DESTROY ALL LIFE.
IS THAT YOUR FEAR?
MAN'S DESTRUCTION IS INEVITABLE.
HIS GREED AND SHEER ARROGANCE LEAD TO OUR OWN EXTINCTION.
THE LAST MEN WILL COME TO BEDLAM AND FACE JUDGEMENT FOR THE PAIN AND SUFFERING HE CAUSED THROUGHOUT THE AGES.
PLEASE?!
NO!

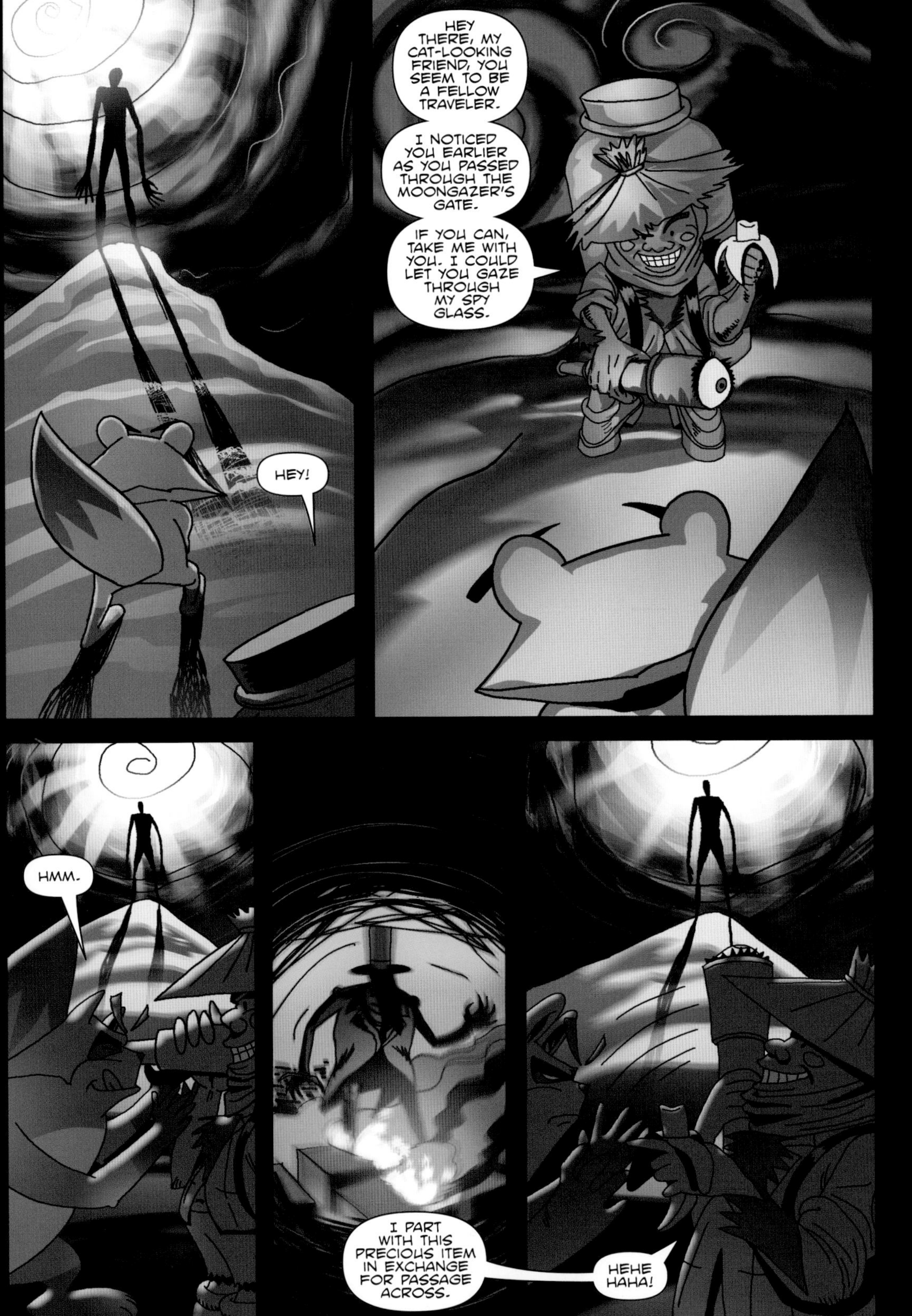
HEY!
HEY THERE, MY CAT-LOOKING FRIEND, YOU SEEM TO BE A FELLOW TRAVELER.
I NOTICED YOU EARLIER AS YOU PASSED THROUGH THE MOONGAZER'S GATE.
IF YOU CAN, TAKE ME WITH YOU. I COULD LET YOU GAZE THROUGH MY SPY GLASS.
HMM.
I PART WITH THIS PRECIOUS ITEM IN EXCHANGE FOR PASSAGE ACROSS.
HEHE HAHA!

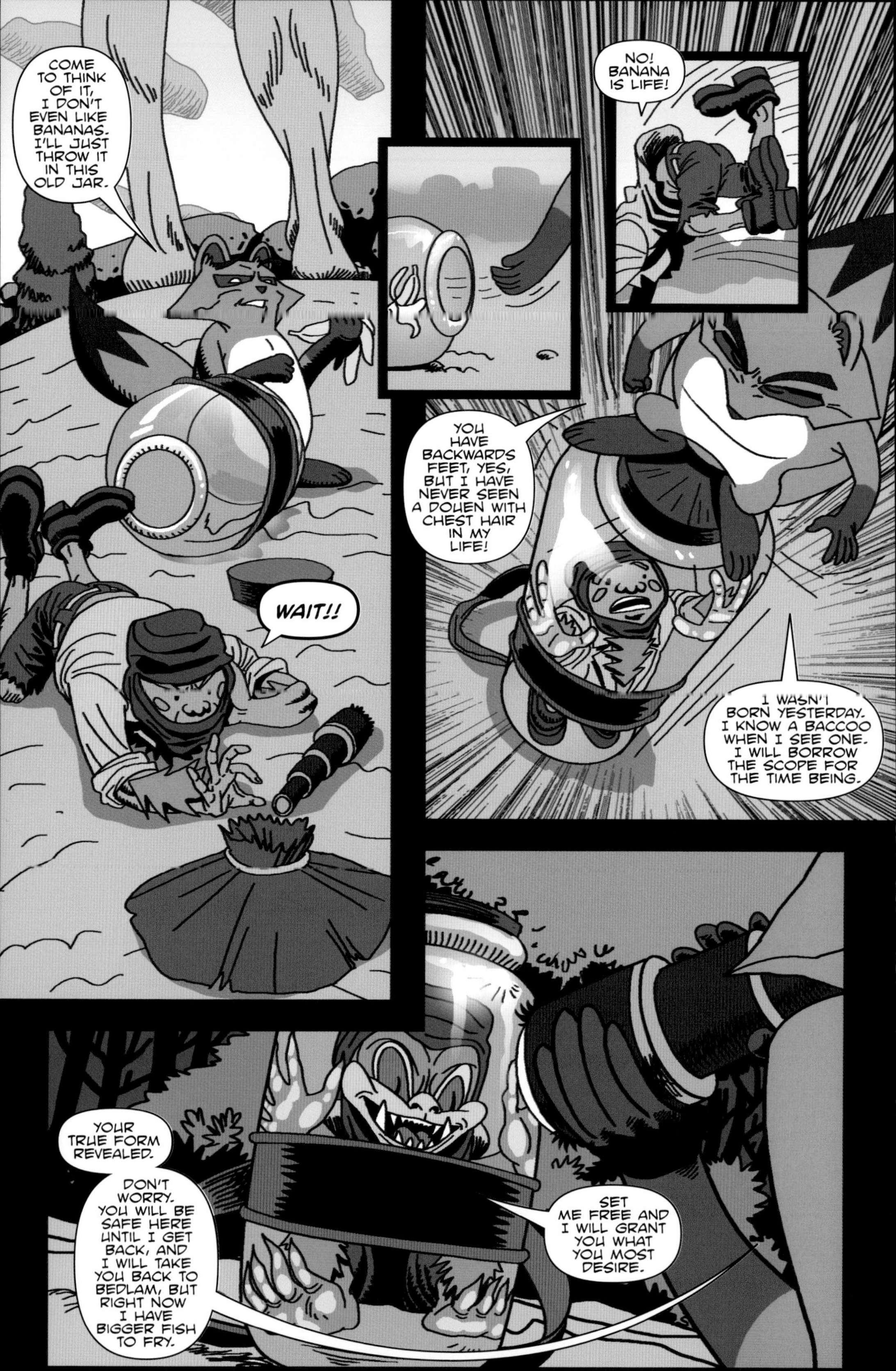
COME TO THINK OF IT, I DON'T EVEN LIKE BANANAS. I'LL JUST THROW IT IN THIS OLD JAR.
WAIT!!
NO! BANANA IS LIFE!
YOU HAVE BACKWARDS FEET, YES, BUT I HAVE NEVER SEEN A DOUEN WITH CHEST HAIR IN MY LIFE!
I WASN'T BORN YESTERDAY. I KNOW A BACCOO WHEN I SEE ONE. I WILL BORROW THE SCOPE FOR THE TIME BEING.
YOUR TRUE FORM REVEALED.
DON'T WORRY. YOU WILL BE SAFE HERE UNTIL I GET BACK, AND I WILL TAKE YOU BACK TO BEDLAM, BUT RIGHT NOW I HAVE BIGGER FISH TO FRY.
SET ME FREE AND I WILL GRANT YOU WHAT YOU MOST DESIRE.

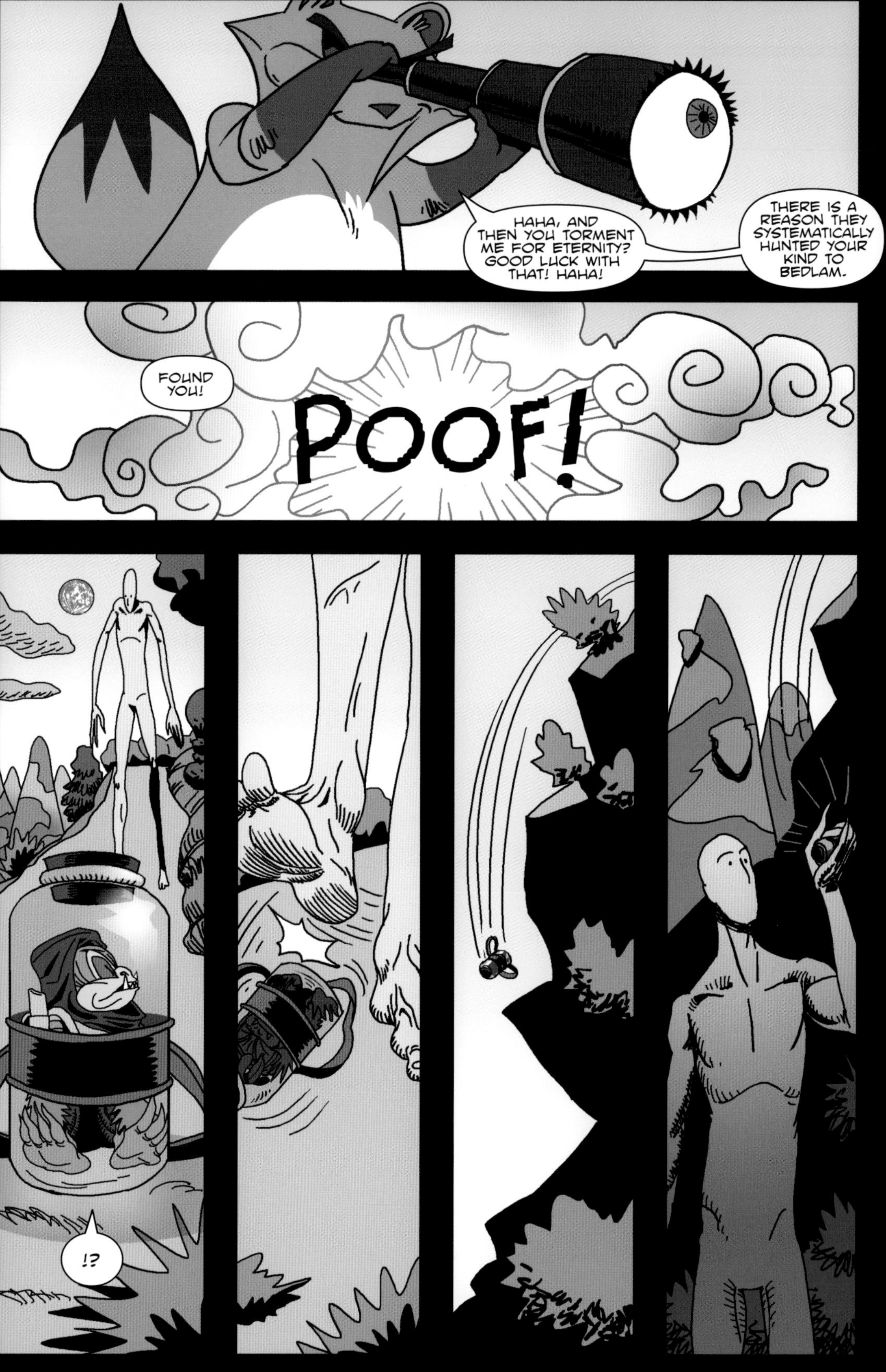
HAHA, AND THEN YOU TORMENT ME FOR ETERNITY? GOOD LUCK WITH THAT! HAHA!
THERE IS A REASON THEY SYSTEMATICALLY HUNTED YOUR KIND TO BEDLAM.
FOUND YOU!
POOF!
!?

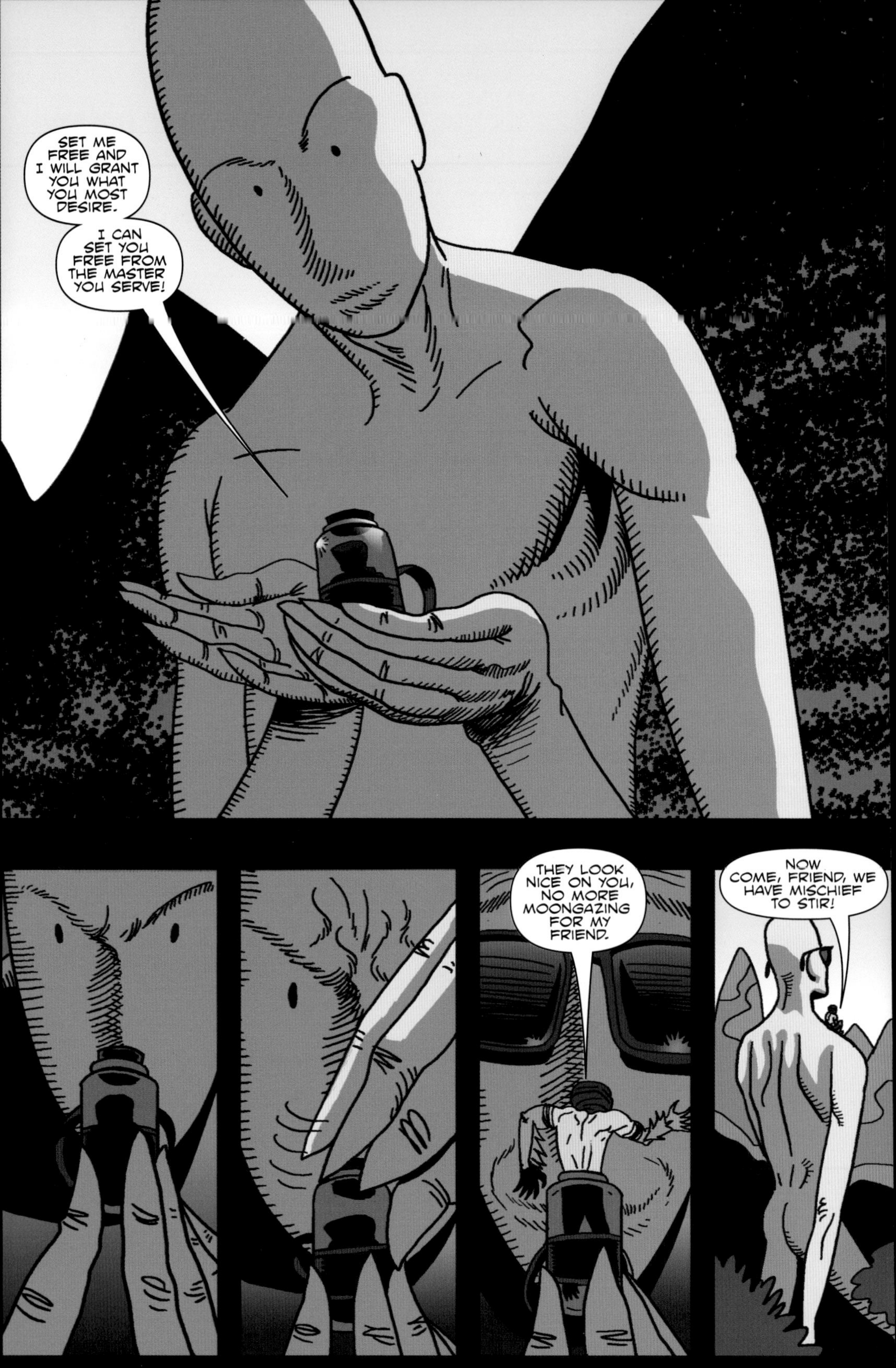
SET ME FREE AND I WILL GRANT YOU WHAT YOU MOST DESIRE.
I CAN SET YOU FREE FROM THE MASTER YOU SERVE!
THEY LOOK NICE ON YOU, NO MORE MOONGAZING FOR MY FRIEND.
NOW COME, FRIEND, WE HAVE MISCHIEF TO STIR!

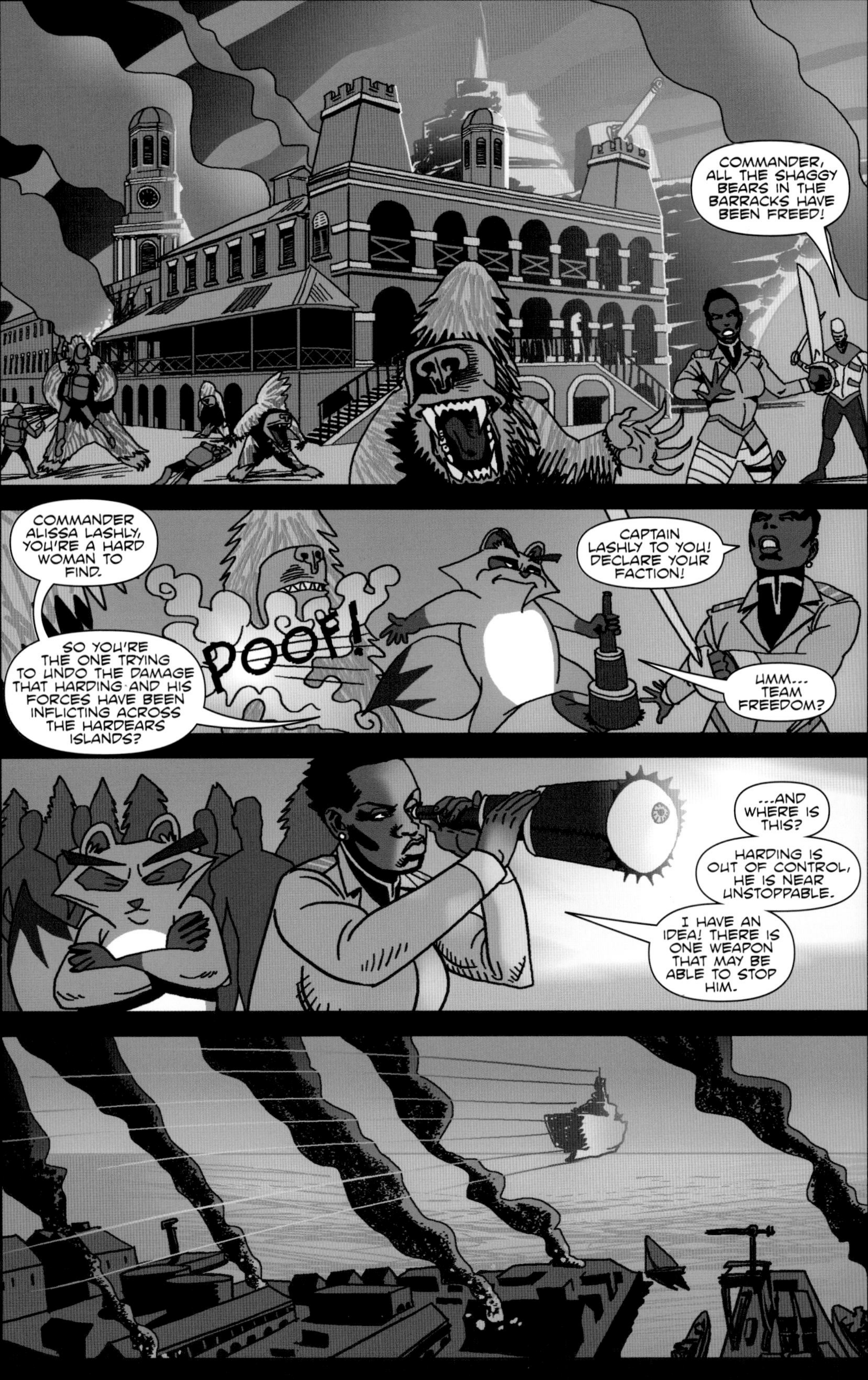
COMMANDER, ALL THE SHAGGY BEARS IN THE BARRACKS HAVE BEEN FREED!
COMMANDER ALISSA LASHLY, YOU'RE A HARD WOMAN TO FIND.
CAPTAIN LASHLY TO YOU! DECLARE YOUR FACTION!
POOF!
SO YOU'RE THE ONE TRYING TO UNDO THE DAMAGE THAT HARDING AND HIS FORCES HAVE BEEN INFLICTING ACROSS THE HARDEARS ISLANDS?
UMM... TEAM FREEDOM?
...AND WHERE IS THIS?
HARDING IS OUT OF CONTROL, HE IS NEAR UNSTOPPABLE.
I HAVE AN IDEA! THERE IS ONE WEAPON THAT MAY BE ABLE TO STOP HIM.

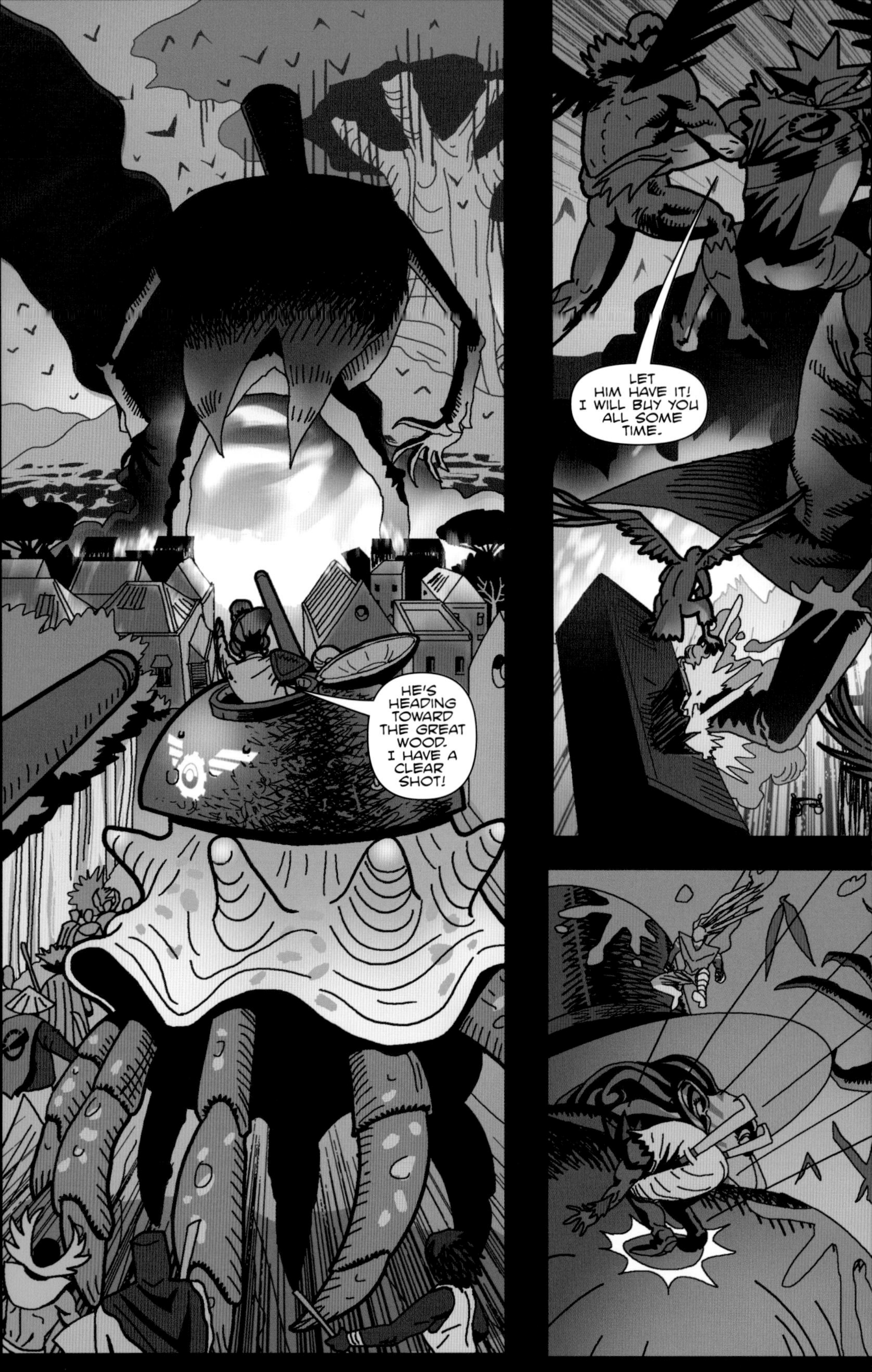
HE'S HEADING TOWARD THE GREAT WOOD. I HAVE A CLEAR SHOT!
LET HIM HAVE IT! I WILL BUY YOU ALL SOME TIME.

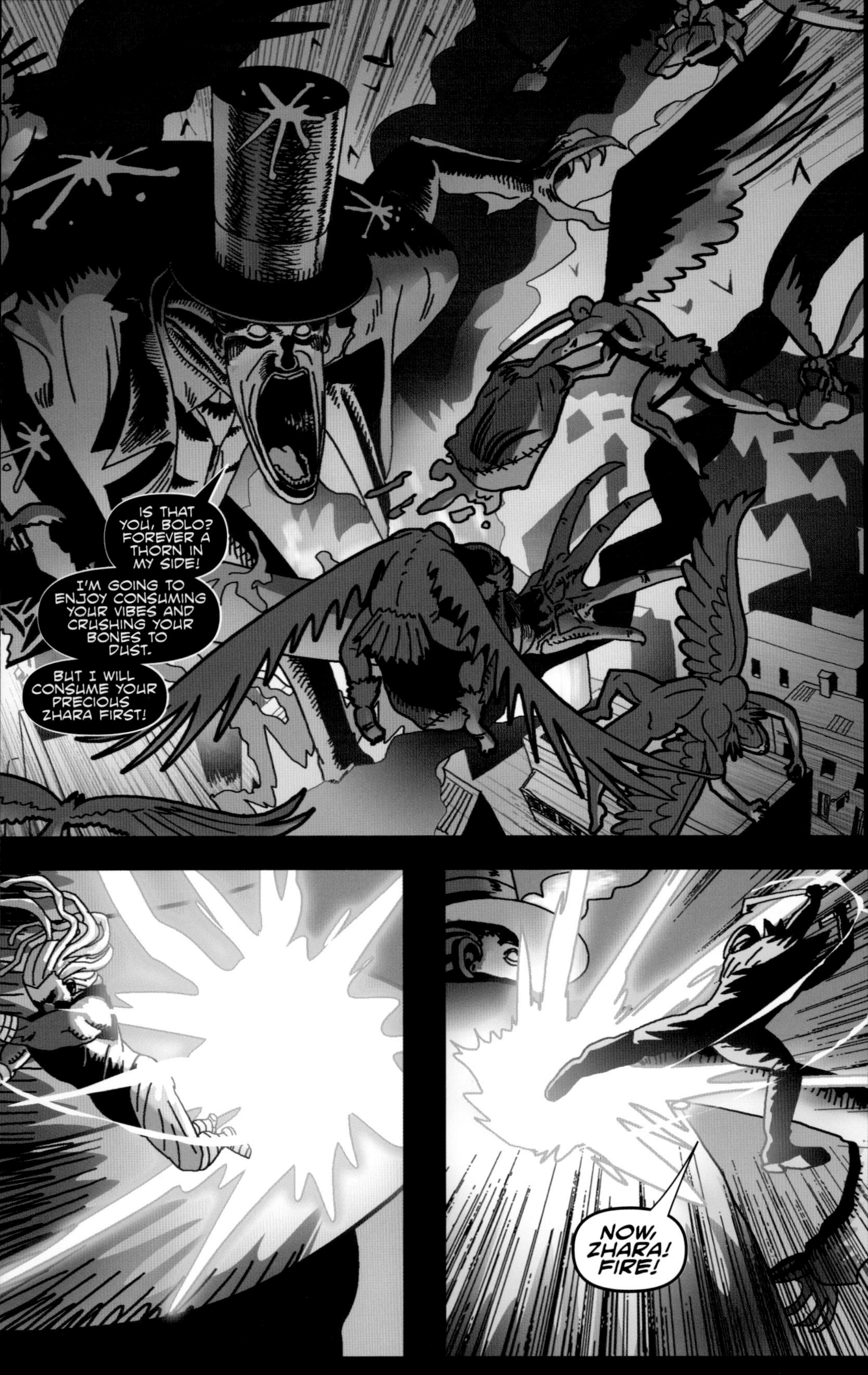
IS THAT YOU, BOLO? FOREVER A THORN IN MY SIDE!
I'M GOING TO ENJOY CONSUMING YOUR VIBES AND CRUSHING YOUR BONES TO DUST.
BUT I WILL CONSUME YOUR PRECIOUS ZHARA FIRST!
NOW, ZHARA! FIRE!

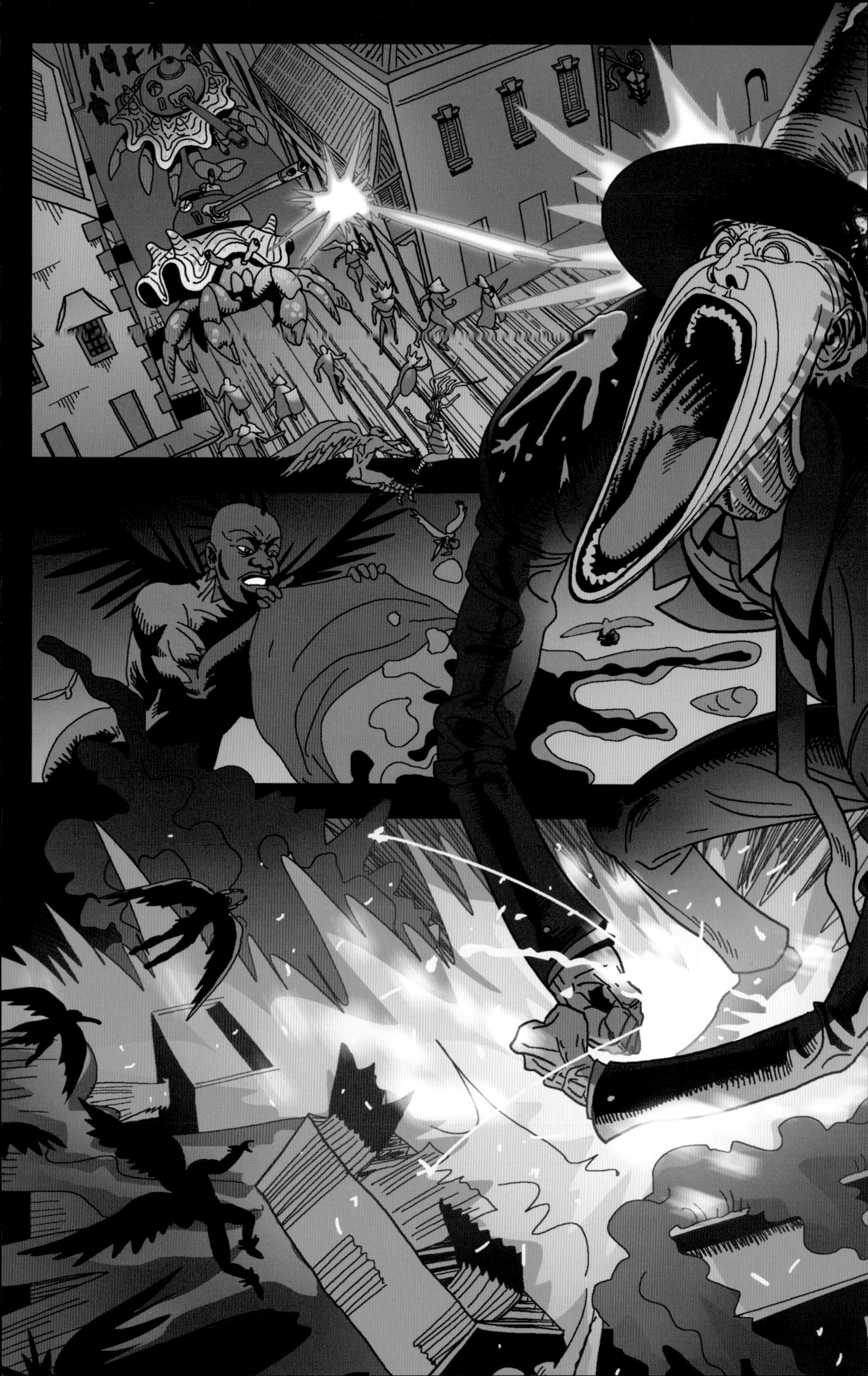

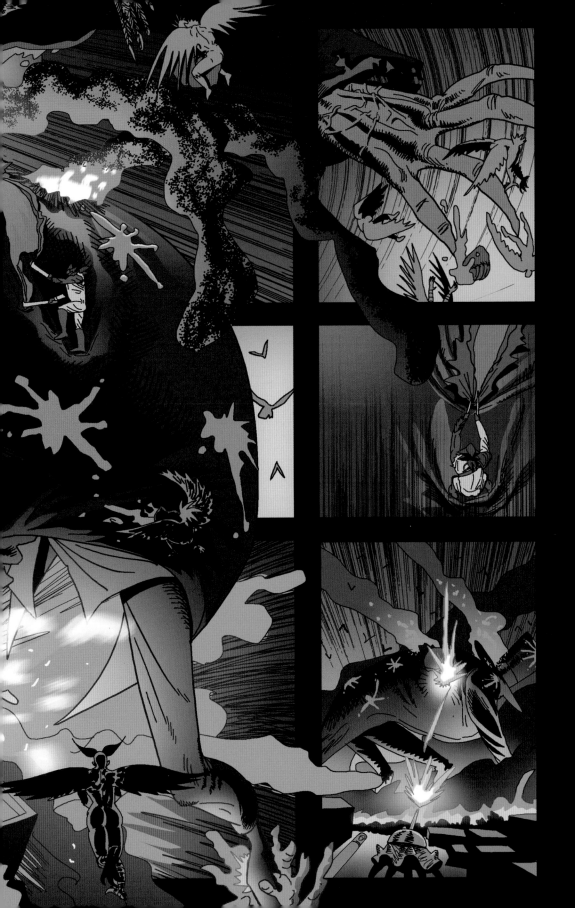

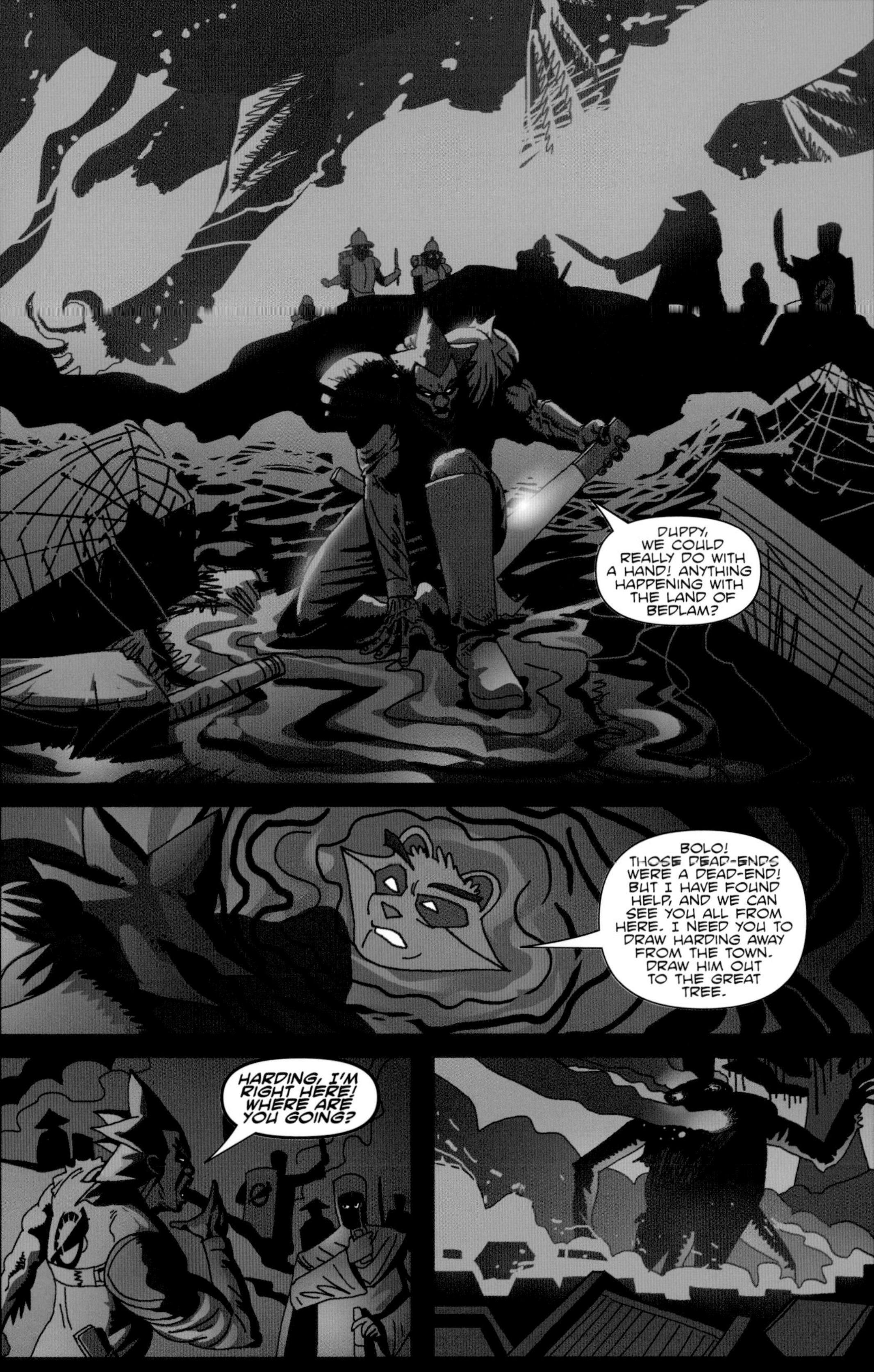
DUPPY, WE COULD REALLY DO WITH A HAND! ANYTHING HAPPENING WITH THE LAND OF BEDLAM?
BOLO! THOSE DEAD-ENDS WERE A DEAD-END! BUT I HAVE FOUND HELP, AND WE CAN SEE YOU ALL FROM HERE. I NEED YOU TO DRAW HARDING AWAY FROM THE TOWN. DRAW HIM OUT TO THE GREAT TREE.
HARDING, I'M RIGHT HERE! WHERE ARE YOU GOING?

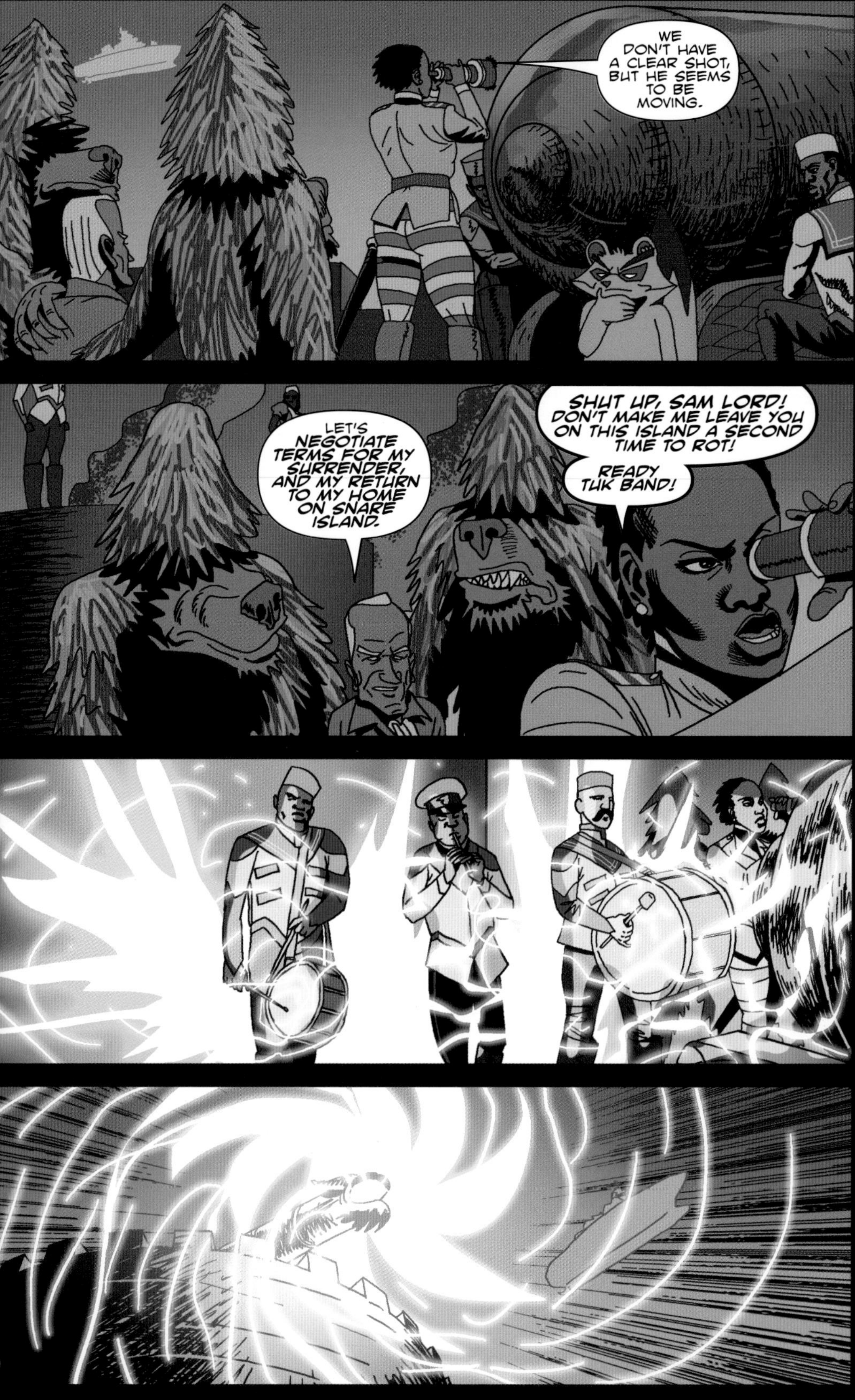
WE DON'T HAVE A CLEAR SHOT, BUT HE SEEMS TO BE MOVING.
LET'S NEGOTIATE TERMS FOR MY SURRENDER, AND MY RETURN TO MY HOME ON SNARE ISLAND.
SHUT UP, SAM LORD! DON'T MAKE ME LEAVE YOU ON THIS ISLAND A SECOND TIME TO ROT!
READY TUK BAND!

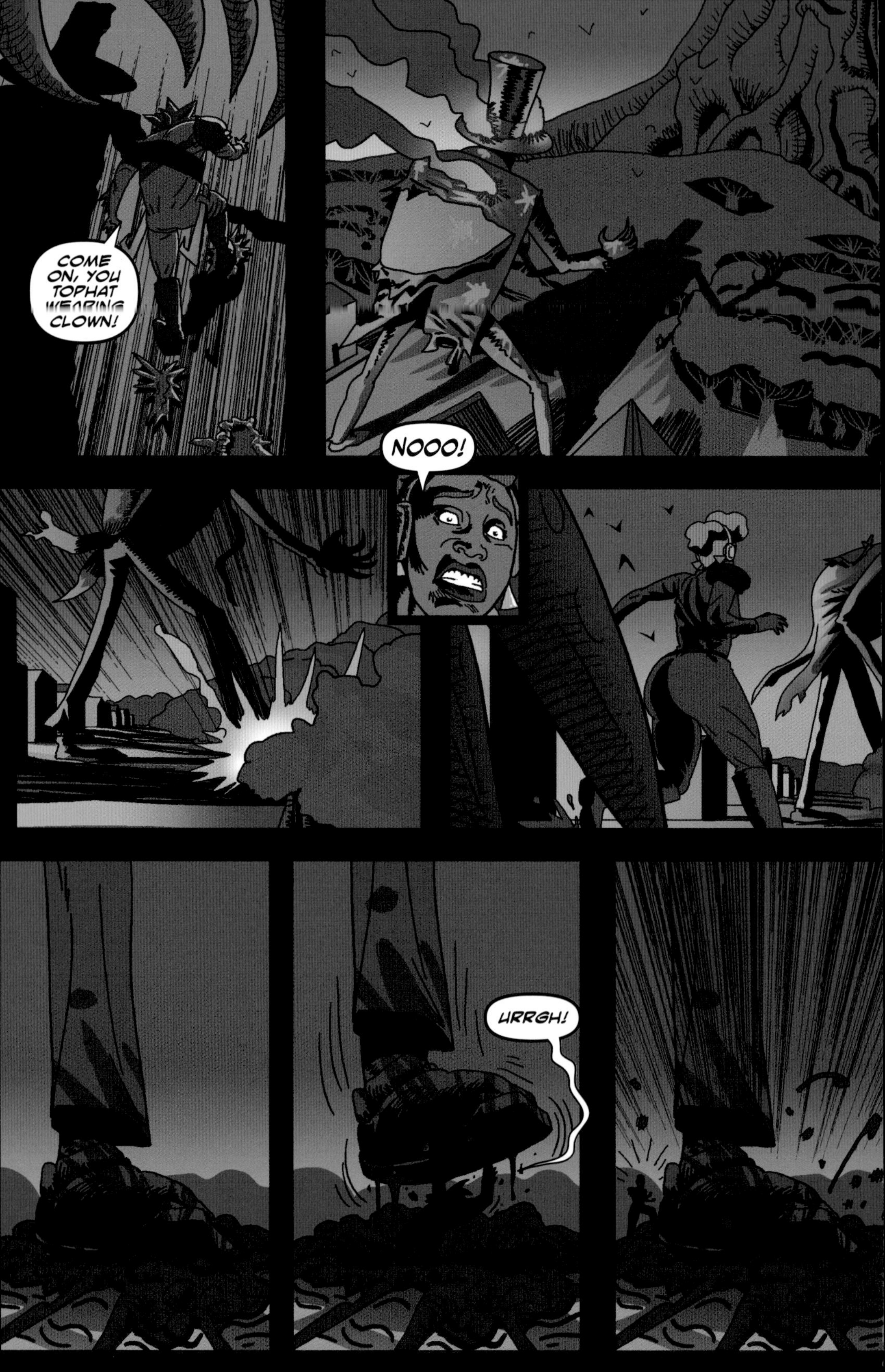
COME ON, YOU TOPHAT WEARING CLOWN!
NOOO!
URRGH!

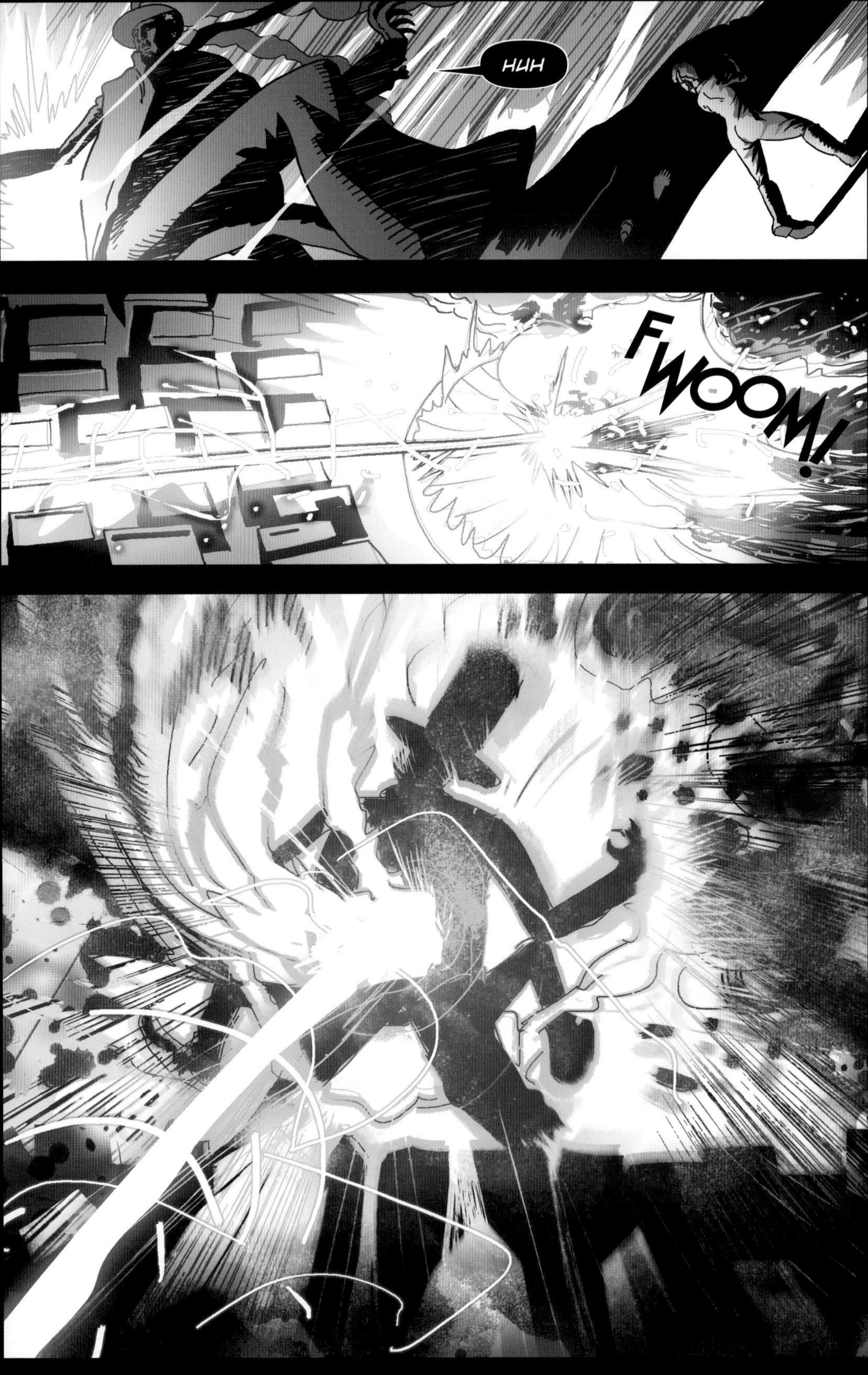
HUH
FWOOM!

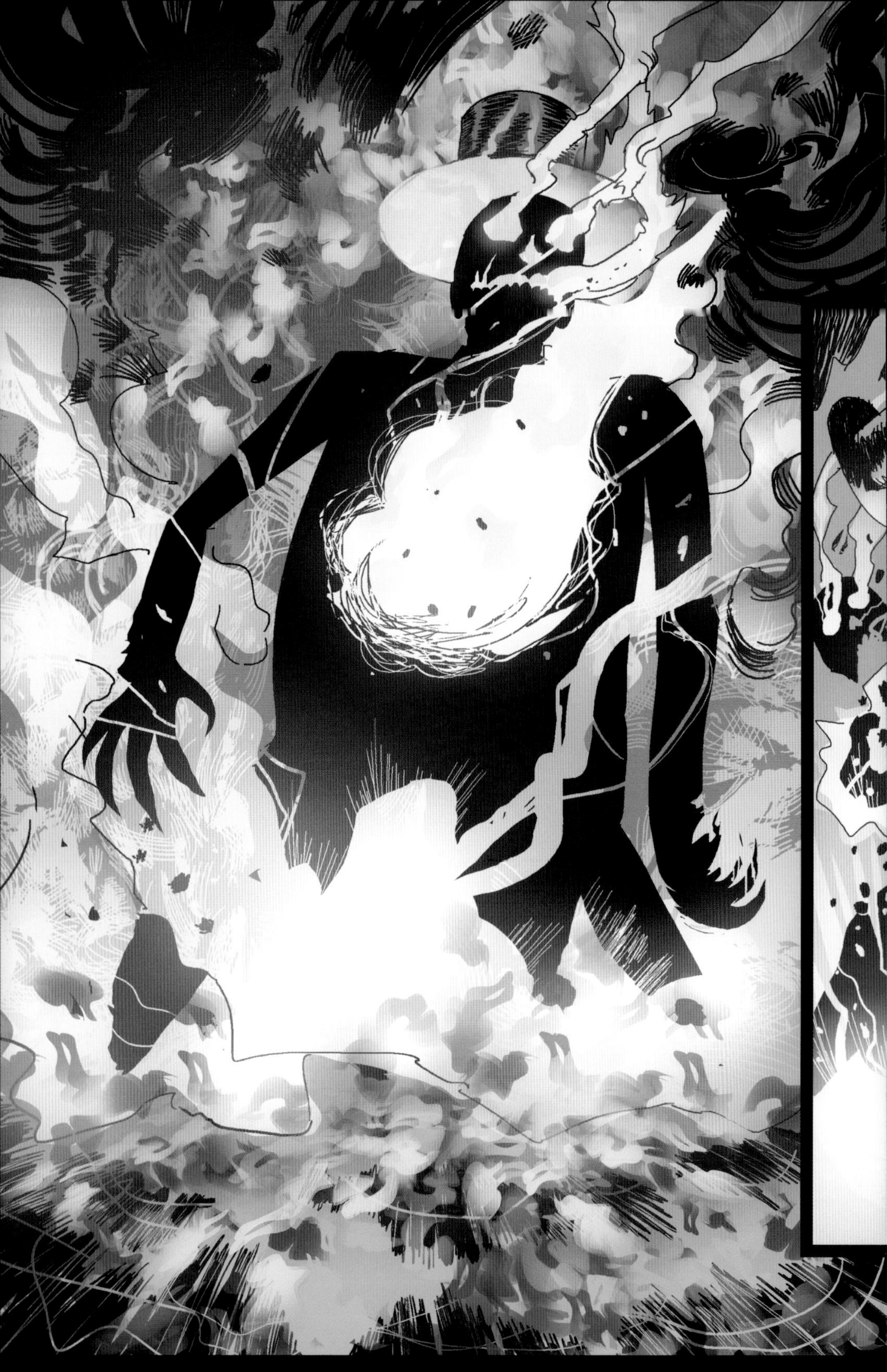

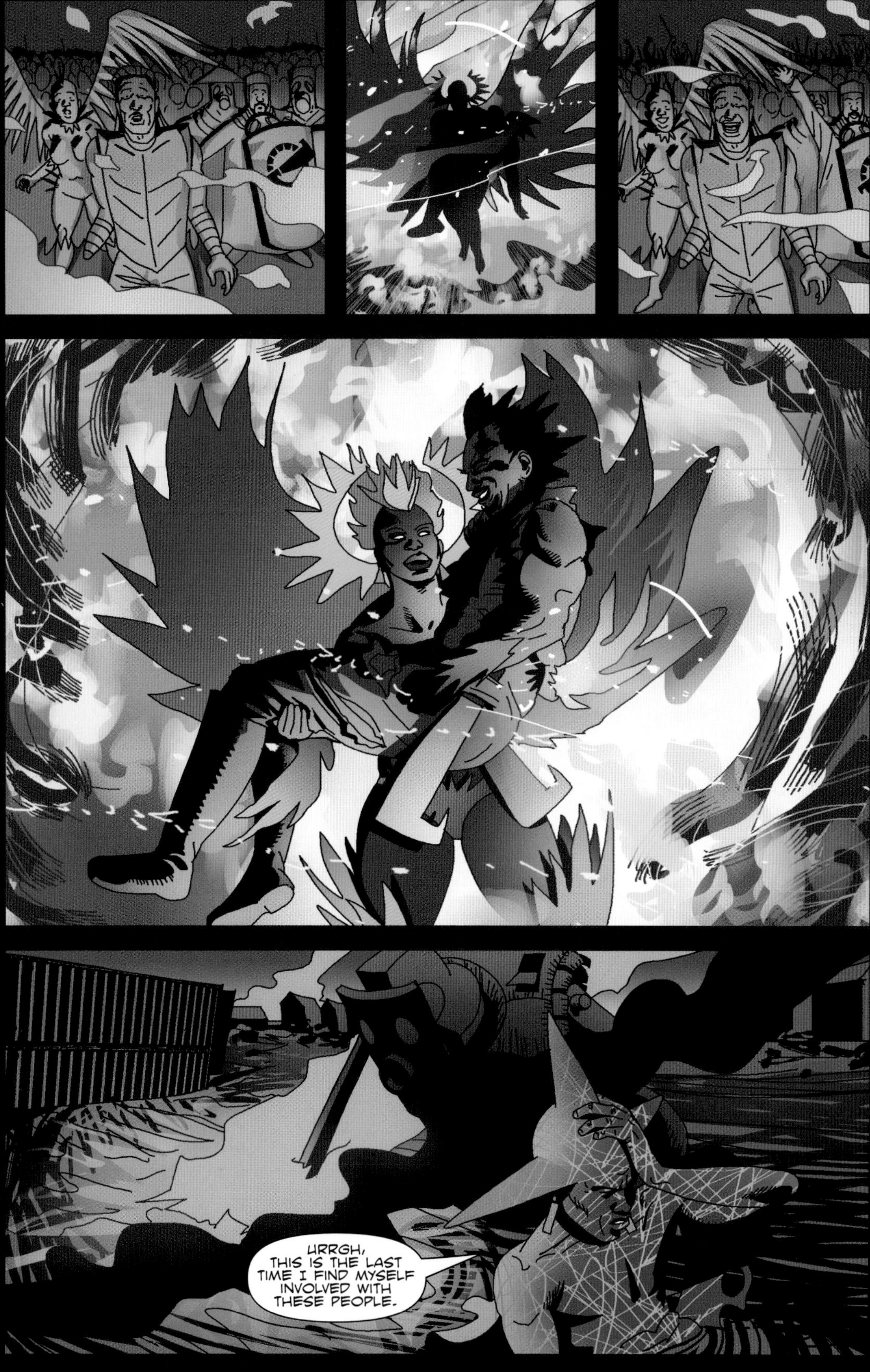
URRGH, THIS IS THE LAST TIME I FIND MYSELF INVOLVED WITH THESE PEOPLE.

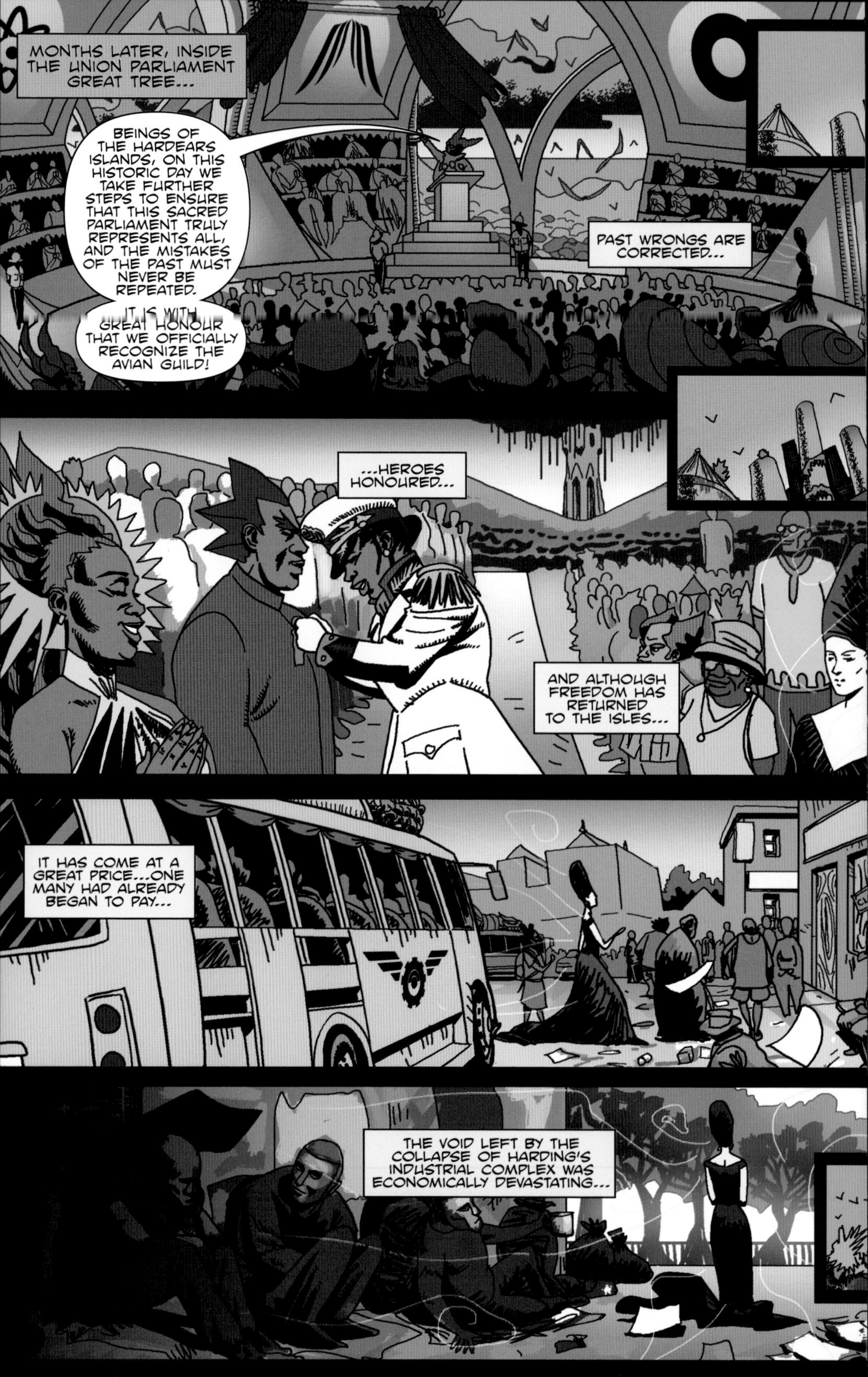
MONTHS LATER, INSIDE THE UNION PARLIAMENT GREAT TREE...
BEINGS OF THE HARDEARS ISLANDS, ON THIS HISTORIC DAY WE TAKE FURTHER STEPS TO ENSURE THAT THIS SACRED PARLIAMENT TRULY REPRESENTS ALL, AND THE MISTAKES OF THE PAST MUST NEVER BE REPEATED.
IT IS WITH GREAT HONOUR THAT WE OFFICIALLY RECOGNIZE THE AVIAN GUILD!
PAST WRONGS ARE CORRECTED...
...HEROES HONOURED...
AND ALTHOUGH FREEDOM HAS RETURNED TO THE ISLES...
IT HAS COME AT A GREAT PRICE...ONE MANY HAD ALREADY BEGAN TO PAY...
THE VOID LEFT BY THE COLLAPSE OF HARDING'S INDUSTRIAL COMPLEX WAS ECONOMICALLY DEVASTATING...

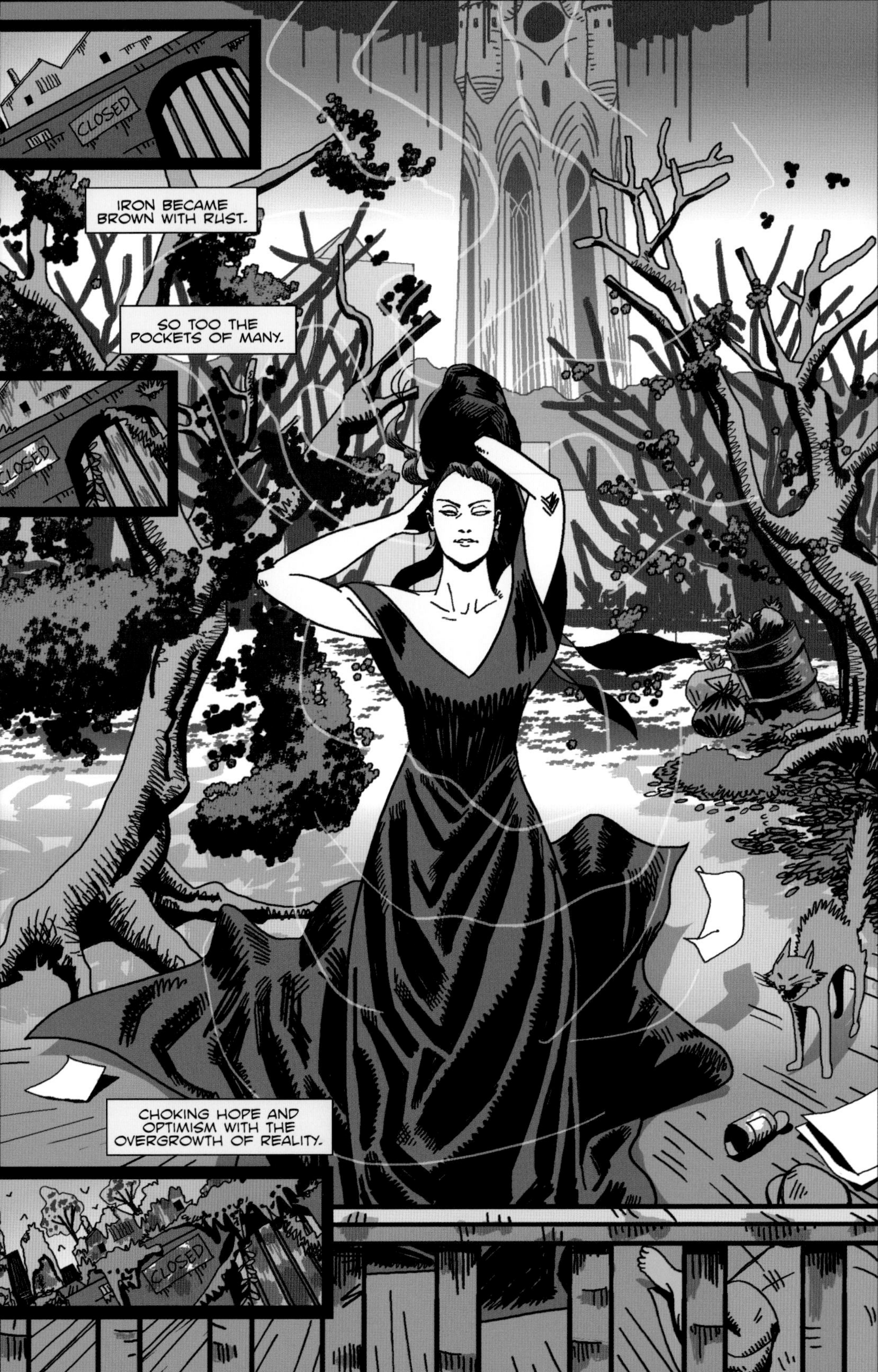
CLOSED
IRON BECAME BROWN WITH RUST.
SO TOO THE POCKETS OF MANY.
CLOSED
CHOKING HOPE AND OPTIMISM WITH THE OVERGROWTH OF REALITY.
CLOSED

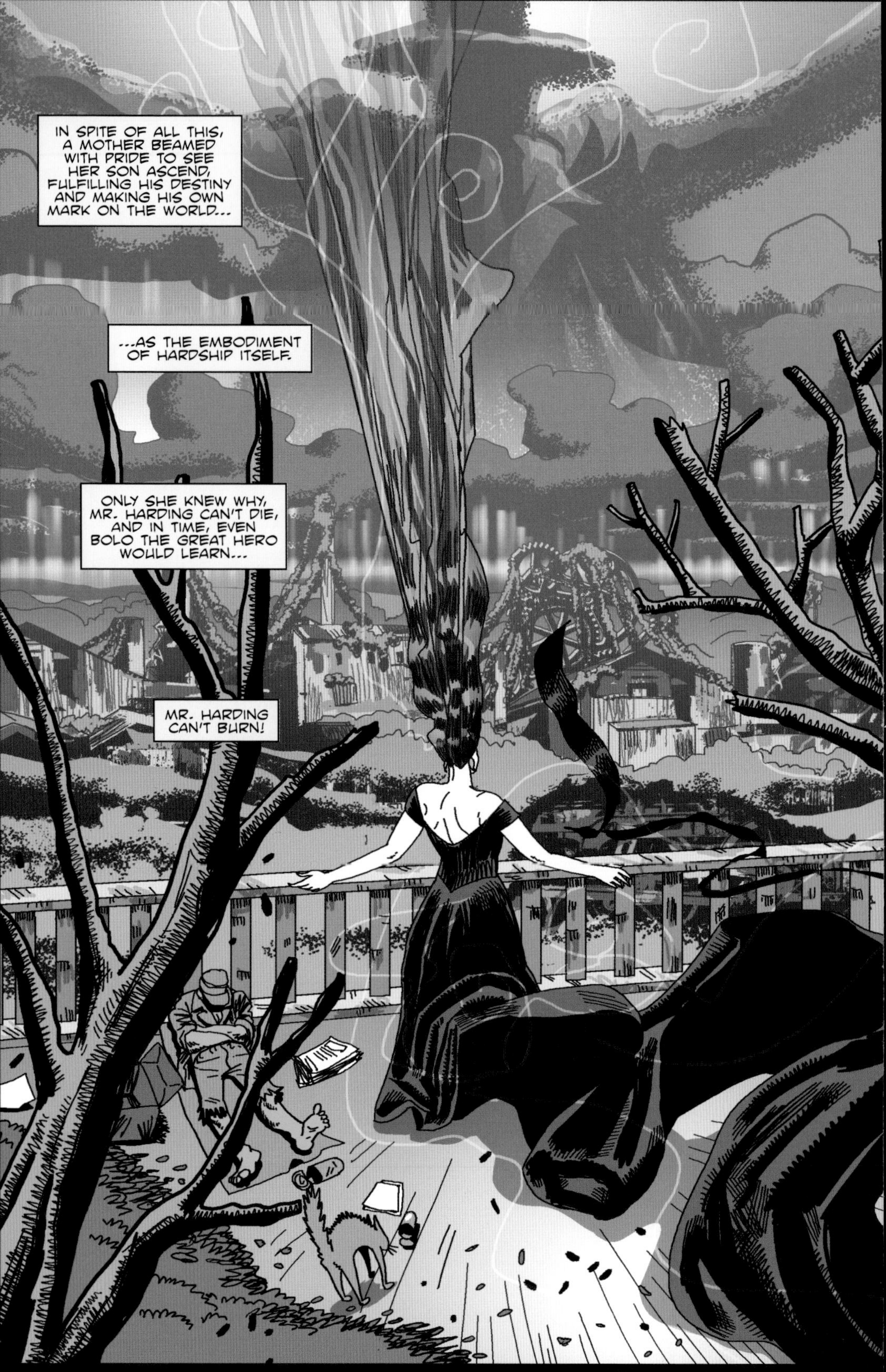
IN SPITE OF ALL THIS, A MOTHER BEAMED WITH PRIDE TO SEE HER SON ASCEND, FULFILLING HIS DESTINY AND MAKING HIS OWN MARK ON THE WORLD...
...AS THE EMBODIMENT OF HARDSHIP ITSELF.
ONLY SHE KNEW WHY, MR. HARDING CAN'T DIE, AND IN TIME, EVEN BOLO THE GREAT HERO WOULD LEARN...
MR. HARDING CAN'T BURN!

AFTERWORD

CARIBBEAN COMICS:
OUT OF PLACE, OUT OF TIME, OUT OF SIGHT

Chances are you can name at least five nations in the Caribbean. You may have traveled to a few Saint Somewheres with their cerulean waters and gold dust sands nesting between your toes. You may have learned about one being a tax haven for politicians, crooked industrialists, and Bond villains. You may have even heard of Crop Over in Barbados because you followed Rihanna down an Instagram rabbit hole where she is colored fête supreme in green, blue, and pink feathers holding a Julie mango like Alice's magical Eat Me cake. You may have happened upon *Hardears* because of pop cultural exposure to and awareness of repeated Caribbean icons and iconography, like Bob Marley. His patois lilt, sun-bleached locs, and signature Lion of Judah ring have become a global stand-in for Caribbean-ness.

But look closer.

This bejeweled lion, known as the Lion of Judah, wears a crown, holds a scepter, and walks on what could be grassland, fire, or water. Maybe all three elements. The imagery belies the complexity of the Caribbean cosmology that connects human and animal spirit to multiple political and spiritual identities, places, and times. Consider this:

Lion of Judah, or Conquering Lion of the Tribe of Judah, a symbol in Abyssinia.

the ring that was given to Bob Marley in 1977 by Ethiopian Emperor Haile Selassie I's son shows that same lion. Haile Selassie I was given divine status within the Rastafarian movement, the movement which in turn addressed the dislocation and oppression of Black people. The ring, or a fragment of it, is said to have belonged to King Solomon, who had given it to Queen Sheba for their son, a direct ancestor of Selassie. In a 1988 biography by Stephen Davis, Marley says he had a dream ten years earlier in which a man placed a ring on his finger saying, "This is all I give you." Though this ring has become mass-produced and is, perhaps, worn without thought, it connects Western beliefs to African diasporic insurgent practices to Caribbean dream spaces of freedom and futurity. Therefore, to imagine the Caribbean with its adornments, oceans, feathers, mangoes, music, hairdos, history, syncretic beliefs, and people, is to imagine *Hardears* and understand its vibes.

Hardears unfolds in an ethnosurreal Caribbean nation called Jouvert (jōō'vā) Island. In the story, Jouvert is part of an archipelago of other self-governing island nations that participate in the Hardears Islands Union and Federation of Guilds. Creators Matthew Clarke and Nigel Lynch's creation is simultaneously surreal and futurist. It is surreal because it mixes the work-a-day life for Zhara and Bolo with the fantasy of them commuting in a signature Bajan striped Maxibus but instead of a diesel engine, it is powered by a giant flying fish. It is also futurist because it predicts a world where Caribbean-style bureaucracy flourishes by way of its diverse citizenry, yet it still can be foiled by certain avaricious elected officials who are tempted by counterintuitive forces, like Mr. Harding. More specifically, and based on scholar Alondra Nelson's work, *Hardears* is an Afrofuturist comic because it has culturally distinct ways of approaching Caribbean Afro-diasporic culture that informs how techno-cultural practices, like Man Crab bulldozers and even hurricanes, show up.

Themes in *Hardears* follow a larger tradition within science fiction and fantasy comics about Black life. Mixing nature and technology can be seen in the Black Panther's Techno-Organic Jungle (*Fantastic Four* no. 52, 1966) and even earlier in Orrin C. Evans's Lion Man comic (*All-Negro Comics*, 1947). Cultural conservation, intellectual prowess, and the use of sonic energy can be seen in Marvel's Black Panther universe and DC's Tyroc character (*Superboy* no. 216, 1976). Combining African diasporic folk ways to create new heroes, villains, and foils can be seen in *Niobe* (Stranger Comics) and *House of Whispers* (DC Vertigo). And the crisis and radical refusal of oppression can be seen in *Bitch Planet* (Image Comics) and *Concrete Park* (Dark Horse).

Although the nature and techno-culture of *Hardears* strives to be in harmony, Clarke and Lynch are clever to not idealize congruity. The "real" in the ethnosurreal traces through the actual history of the Caribbean with chattel slave labor, species, and societal

LION MAN EXAMINES HIS RADAR ~~~ NO DAMAGE DONE ~~~ BUBBA SLINKS OUT.
LION MAN BEAMS HIS RADAR ALL AROUND~~TWO PERSONS NEAR THE MOUNTAIN!!

Lion Man uses nature and technology to protect his country from intruders. *All-Negro Comics*, 1947.

indictment on modernization but instead uses Mr. Harding to show how exploitation carries through the colonial plantation into the modern-day factory. One might say Mr. Harding, with his immortality and goals of corrupting the Hardears government and consuming the living vibes of Hardears, is a metaphor for hardship. Cultural critic Mark Dery famously coined the term "Afrofuturism" in 1994, asking, "Can a community whose past has been deliberately rubbed out, and whose energies have subsequently been consumed by the search for legible traces of its history, imagine possible futures?" In the Caribbean, of course it can.

With its many languages, people, spirits, and unpredictable weather, the Caribbean region is in constant flux. The characters, settings, and crises in *Hardears,* and even the title itself, ooze Caribbean culture and ecology. Both are created by a constant exchange of indigenous, African, Asian, and European influences plus their modern diasporic communities. Boundaries are porous. Thus, Caribbean surrealism and futurism, with its development that entangles many countries and with its cosmology that encompasses a larger imaginative geography, gives rise to what I call a "Caribatopia." Territorial borders may be set on a map, but not everything on a map can be defined or developed as a dwelling place. And while "atopia" means an inhospitable place, add the word "carib" and a Caribatopia becomes an illegible space. "Illegible" as in beyond any given rule. These Caribatopias are the spaces that, in Dery's words, "search for legible traces of its history" and "imagine possible futures." Consider the importance of *Hardears*'s Sea Guild and the Middle Passage. Along with *Hardears*, we can see examples of this confluence between being contained/being unruly and being tangible/being intangible in *Midnight Robber* (Nalo Hopkinson, 2000), *Madam Fate* (Marcia Douglas, 1999), and *X/Self* poems (Kamau Brathwaite, 1987); in the paintings of indigenous Guyanese artist and archaeologist George Simon; and even by participating in Caribbean carnival celebrations asynchronously around the world.

Now, the *Hardears* character Duppy is no Lion of Judah. But in the context of a Caribatopia, Duppy provides us an example of a living portal between worlds. Duppy is more than Bolo's imaginary friend. Duppies are spirits of people and animals that show up in many Anglophone Caribbean folk tales. Duppy could very well be appearing simultaneously for others elsewhere in Hardears. Another Caribbean word giving life to this graphic novel is the titular "Hard ears" which means stubborn, unwilling to listen, unable to take criticism, and doing it one's own way. One could say Bolo's refusal to believe a machine can beat (wo)mankind's drive means "heahaadyerri," or, he has hard ears. A Caribatopia has hard ears, too. As Bolo double-fists cutlasses in a John Henry–esque showdown against the mechanization of harvesting, this bring us to the word "jouvert."

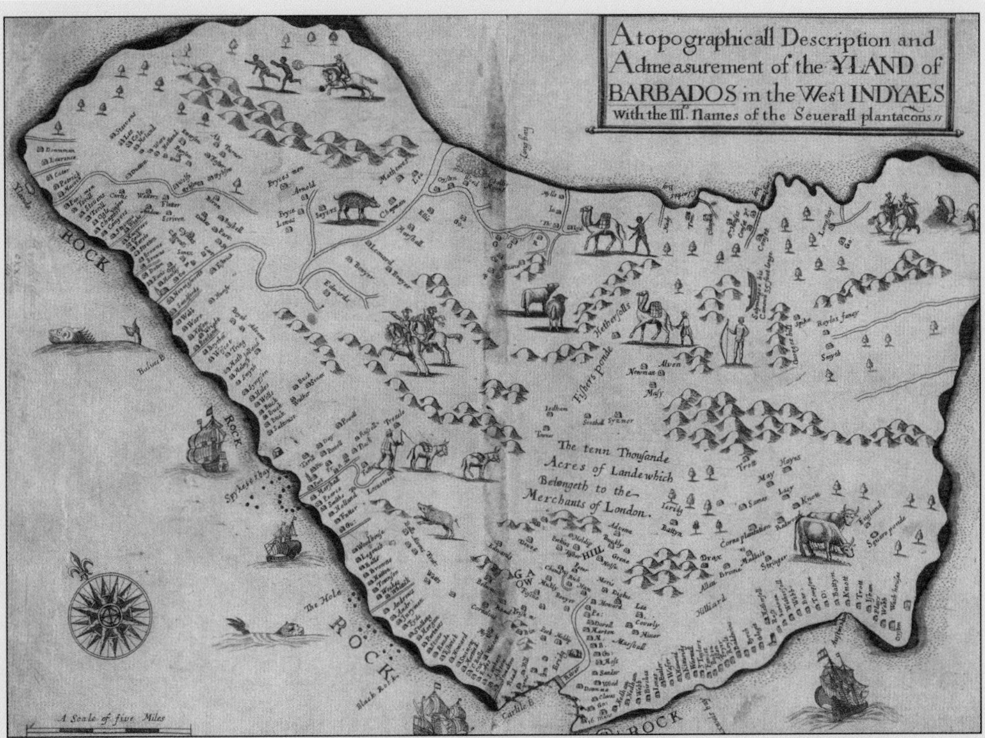
A topographicall Description and
Admeasurement of the YLAND of
BARBADOS in the West INDYAES
With the Ml. names of the Seuerall plantacons
ROCK
ROCK
ROCK
The tenn Thousande Acres of Lande which Belongeth to the Merchants of London.
A Scale of five Miles

"A topographicall Description and Admesurement of the YLAND of BARBADOS in the West INDYAES: With the Mrs. Names of the Severall plantacons," engraving by Richard Ligon, 1657.

In our world, "jouvert" (or J'ouvert) comes from the French-creole word meaning "dawn" and it is also the name for the annual street festival that happens the day before Carnival masquerade ("mas"). Some carnivals coincide with Lent and some coincide with the harvest season. Europeans introduced Carnival masquerade balls ("pretty mas") to the Caribbean in the eighteenth century but restricted enslaved people or free people of color from participating. Jouvert traditions include African ritual, folklore, and mocking the planter class. Jouvert is the transgressive "dutty mas," when oil- and mud-smeared jab devils like Dohylin roam the streets, as they've been doing from 1840s Trinidad into the current day Brooklyn West Indian Parades and beyond as inhabitants of Pitch Island in *Hardears*. The *Hardears* world is especially rooted in the Crop Over carnival originating in Barbados, the home of *Hardears* creators, Clarke and Lynch. *Hardears* uses many Crop Over elements to enrich its pages down to its amazing coloring. However, its use of the Landship and the burning of the white-faced effigy, Mr. Harding, deserve a closer look.

The Landship shows up in a 1931 article in *The Advocate News* being referred to as "Little England's navy en fete" comprised of "a band of their officers and sailors and red cross nurses . . ." Some critique the Landship movement as a farcical colonial artifact, but others have revealed their dance movements aren't just well-choreographed antics mimicking British naval routines but, rather, they are dance movements tied to an Afro-Caribbean legacy. The Barbados Landship existed as early as the 1860s as an organization collecting membership dues from which sickness and death benefits could be paid, as there was no such financial system in place for Black plantation laborers. So, it is out of the conditions of the Middle Passage, the plantation, colonial systems, and Carnival that the symbiotic choreography of Admiral Swift's Landship exists as the national defense system kept vibing by the Tuk band. The Landship is conjured up, out of time and space, to fulfill the needs of the people.

The Mr. Harding effigy burns on the last day of Crop Over. If the Landship is the body of the people, then Mr. Harding is the body of the hardship they experience as laborers. Mr. Harding is a necessary evil in his own right, being needed for economic growth and loathed for bringing misery. He must be fed *and* he must be stopped. In *Hardears*, Mr. Harding with his colonial, industrial, and magical roots, becomes that same Crop Over villain. Bolo's crowning as the King of the Crop in the beginning foreshadows his final showdown with Mr. Harding. It is no surprise that smearing Mr. Harding in the mix of mud and bird dung—nature's salvage, if you will—is what destroys him. But can he ever die? What new configuration will hardship take on and off a map?

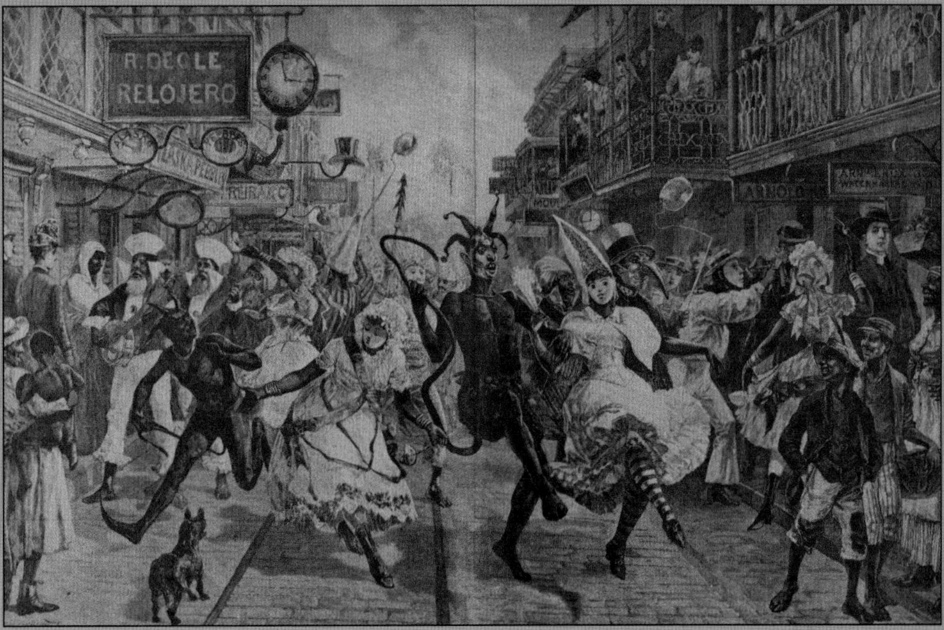
R. DEC LE
RELOJERO
"Carnival in Port of Spain, Trinidad," etching by Melton Prior, 1888.

For the sake of a sequel, or better still for the serialization of *Hardears*, let's hope Mr. Harding's next incarnation showcases Zhara's badass skills (a.k.a her jamette vibes). Because comic book world-building, like Carnival, illustrates how entwined myth and history are, I see similarities between Carnival masquerade and comic book cosplay. If Mr. Harding returns, he'll not only return to the pages of a book at your local comic book shop, but I wouldn't be surprised to see him make a white-face-in-top-hat appearance at a Comic Con near you. Cosplayers rolling up in convention halls in *mas band* squads dressed as members of a Hardears Guild like folk do for the Umbrella Corp. or dressed as a Moongazer like folk do for Sailor Moon is my imagined possible future. I'm already dreaming up my costume!

Cathy Thomas
April 2021
Riverside, California

CATHY THOMAS works on African American and Caribbean literature and is a comic arts scholar. Currently a postdoctoral fellow at University of California at Riverside, Thomas has also studied and taught at the University of California at Santa Cruz and the University of Colorado, Boulder.

BIBLIOGRAPHY

Barbados, Glory Tours. "A Bajan Tour Girl Exploring Barbados: Barbados Crop Over: Burning Mr Harding." *A Bajan Tour Girl Exploring Barbados* (blog). June 26, 2010, http://abajantourgirlexploring barbados.blogspot.com/2010/06/barbados-crop -over-burning-mr-harding.html.

Bates, Cary and Mike Grell. *Superboy Legion of Superheroes* no. 216. DC Comics, 1976.

Brathwaite, Edward Kamau. *X/Self*. 1st ed. Oxford: Oxford University Press, 1987.

Benitez-Rojo, Antonio. *The Repeating Island: The Caribbean and the Postmodern Perspective*. Translated by James E. Maraniss. Durham, NC: Duke University Press, 1997.

Burrowes, Marcia P. A. "History and Cultural Identity: Barbadian Space and the Legacy of Empire." PhD diss., University of Warwick, 2000.

Burrowes, Marcia. "Landship Ahoy." *Caribbean Beat Magazine*, September 2013, https://www.caribbean -beat.com/issue-123/landship-ahoy.

Davis, Stephen. *Bob Marley*. Garden City, NY: Doubleday & Company, Inc., 1985.

DeConnick, Kelly Sue, and Valentine De Landro. *Bitch Planet, Vol. 1: Extraordinary Machine*. Illustrated ed. Portland, OR: Image Comics, 2015.

Dery, Mark. "Black to the Future: Interviews with Samuel R. Delany, Greg Tate, and Tricia Rose." In *Flame Wars: The Discourse of Cyberculture*. Illustrated ed. Durham, NC: Duke University Press Books, 1994.

Douglas, Marcia. *Madam Fate*. London: The Women's Press, 1999.

Evans, George J., Jr and John Terrell. *All-Negro Comics*. All-Negro Comics, Inc., 1947.

Fenty, Robyn Rihanna (@badgalriri). 2017. "the @aura_experience caught by @dennisleupold no. BARBADOS no. cropover2017 no. culture." Instagram photo, August 7, 2017. https://www. instagram.com/pBXgaVpsDzfL/?utm_source =ig_embed.

Hopkinson, Nalo. *Midnight Robber*. New York: Grand Central Publishing, 2000.

Hopkinson, Nalo, Neil Gaiman, and Dominke Stanton. *The House of Whispers (2018-) Vol. 1: Power Divided*. New York: Vertigo, 2019.

Jones, Sebastian A., and Amandla Stenberg. *Niobe: She Is Life no. 1*. Edited by Joshua Cozine. Stranger Comics, 2015.

Klerk, Amy de. "A Comprehensive History of Rihanna's Carnival Ensembles." *ELLE*, August 9, 2017, https://www.elle.com/fashion/celebrity-style /news/g30225/rihanna-barbados-carnival -outfits/.

Lee, Stan, and Jack Kirby. *Fantastic Four* no. 52. Marvel Comics, 1966.

Mbembe, Achille. *Necropolitics*. Durham, NC: Duke University Press Books, 2019.

Menard, Russell R. *Sweet Negotiations: Sugar, Slavery, and Plantation Agriculture in Early Barbados*. Charlottesville, VA: University of Virginia Press, 2006.

Mignolo, Walter D. "Epistemic Disobedience, Independent Thought and De-Colonial Freedom." *Theory, Culture, and Society* 26, no. 7-8 (2009).

Nelson, Alondra. *Afrofuturism: A Special Issue of Social Text*. Illustrated ed. Durham, NC: Duke University Press Books, 2002.

Nunley, John and Judith Bettleheim. *Caribbean Festival Arts: Each and Every Bit of Difference*. 1st ed. Seattle, WA: University of Washington Press, 1988.

Puryear, Tony. *Concrete Park Volume 1: You Send Me*. Milwaukie, OR: Dark Horse Books, 2014.

Scher, Philip W. "'Landship', Citizenship, Entrepreneurship and the Ship of State in Barbados: Developing a Heritage Consciousness in a Postcolonial State." *Western Folklore* 75, no. 3/4 (2016): 313–51. https://www.jstor.org/stable/44791372.

Thomas, Cathy. "Dub, Saltfish, and Majah Hype: Caribbean Diaspora as a Praxis with Theory." In *Teaching, Reading, and Theorizing Caribbean Texts*. Edited by Emily O'Dell and Jeanne Jégousso. New York: Lexington Books, 2020.

Wieser, Chad. "Rihanna Is Pretty In Pink During Crop Over Carnival in Barbados." *The Blast*, August 5, 2019, https://theblast.com/c/rihanna-crop -over-festival-barbados.

PHOTO CREDITS

Page 178: Courtesy of Wikimedia Commons/תילגנא-יקיו; page 180: *All-Negro Comics* (Orrin C. Evans, 1947). Photo by Cathy Thomas; page 181: British Library, https://www.bl.uk/picturing-places/articles/mapping-the-british -caribbean-in-the-early-modern-atlantic-world; page 183: *Illustrated London News*. Port of Spain, Trinidad. 1888. A hand-colored original antique wood engraving. 20″ x 14″. https://drbrowne.me/prior1888/

ACKNOWLEDGMENTS

FROM MATTHEW CLARKE:

I would like to thank my mother, Ann; Alan and Leslie Lynch; Delvin Howell; Tristan Roach; Alexandre Haynes; Aguinaldo Bellegrave; John Jennings and the Abrams team; Shawn Alleyne; Mellisa Young; Omar Kennedy; Khalil Goodman; all the people who supported Alan and myself over the years creating comic books; and saving the best for last, our readers past, present, and future.

FROM NIGEL LYNCH:

First and foremost, I would like to thank my friend and co-creator Matthew Clarke for inviting me on this creative journey into the world of *Hardears* and giving me the opportunity to bring this amazing world to life. Without his amazing insight and creativity, this project would not have been possible.

To my wife, Leslie Lynch, thank you for the support and encouragement for the past fifteen years. From the first time I picked up the pen to when I published my first comic book, you have been by my side. Whether it was typing my almost illegible notes or listening to creative rants, you have always been someone I could rely on and a source of strength in my darkest moments. I value our love and friendship. Life's journey would be impossible without you.

To Richard Lynch, my brother and fellow writer, thanks for being the first ear to my storytelling, way before I ever honed a writing skill. Your drive and tenacity continue to motivate me to thrive.

To my legacy and greatest accomplishment, my son, Alan Lynch, may this inspire you on your path to success, and serve as a reminder that anything is possible if you dare to try.

To Kamaria Connell, an extraordinary friend and project assistant—without you, a lot of this would not be possible.

I would be remiss if I did not mention my parents, Frederick and Angela Lynch—thank you for never giving up on me.

To the Beyond Crew: Aguinaldo Belgrave, Tristan Roach, Delvin Howell, Alexandre Haynes, Julian Moseley, and all past members—we started together as a team and we all share in the success of this project.

SPECIAL THANKS TO:

James Rodriguez, for giving me my first big break as an aspiring comic book writer, and Amanda Martinez

Omar Kennedy, Gail Niles, and Erica Hinkson for establishing the platform for Caribbean comic book writers to be seen and heard.

Ayesha Gibson Gill for your continued support and confidence in us.

To John Jennings and the publishing team at Abrams: thank you for giving us this opportunity.

To my super fans: Alvin Sandiford, Tracy-Ann Gibbs, Fabian McCollin, Halim Moses, Frank O'Neil, Datus Corbin, Justin Thompson, Fabian Wood, Lamel Bishop, and Mark Gibson—thank you for reading and supporting me throughout the years.

And to all my friends and family, I thank you.

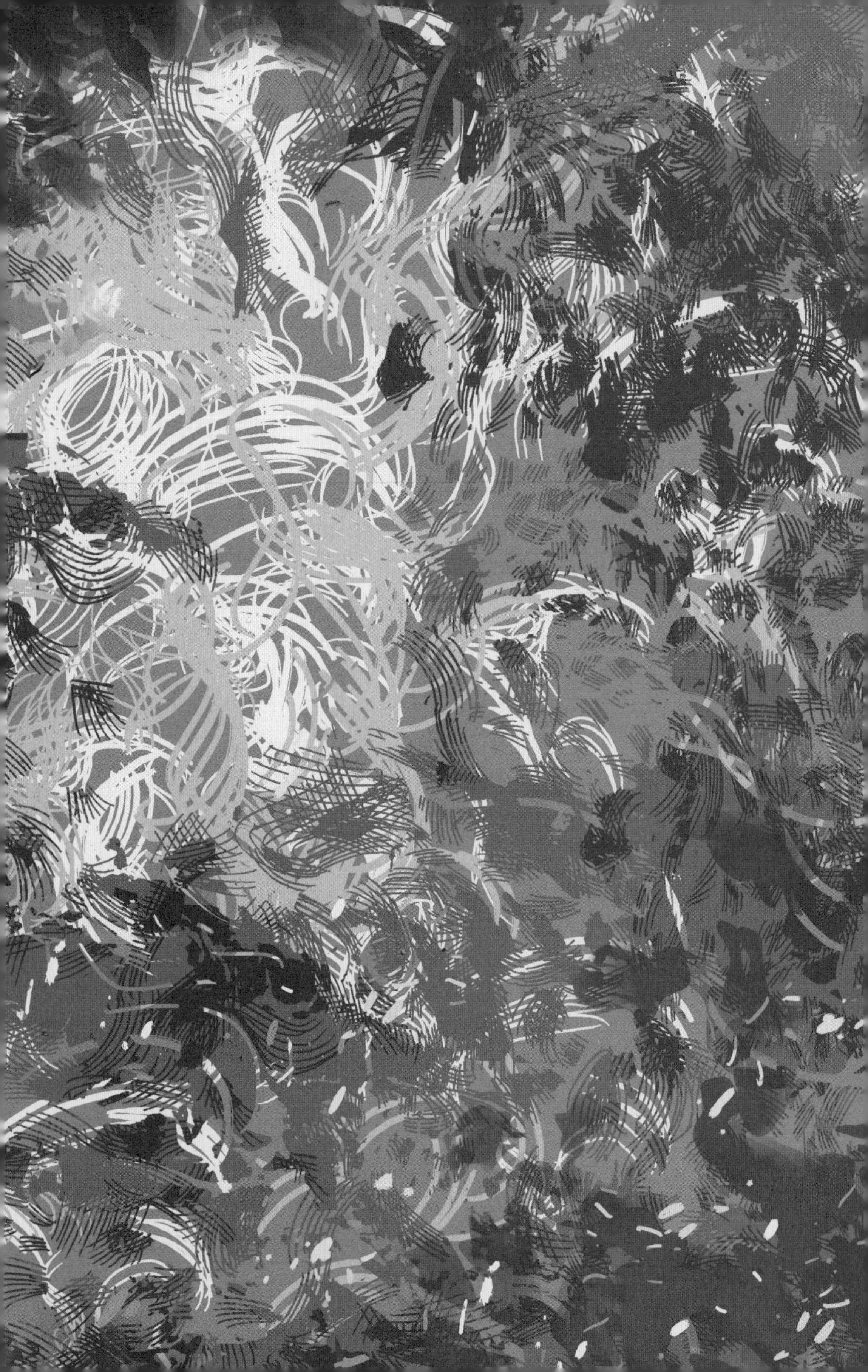

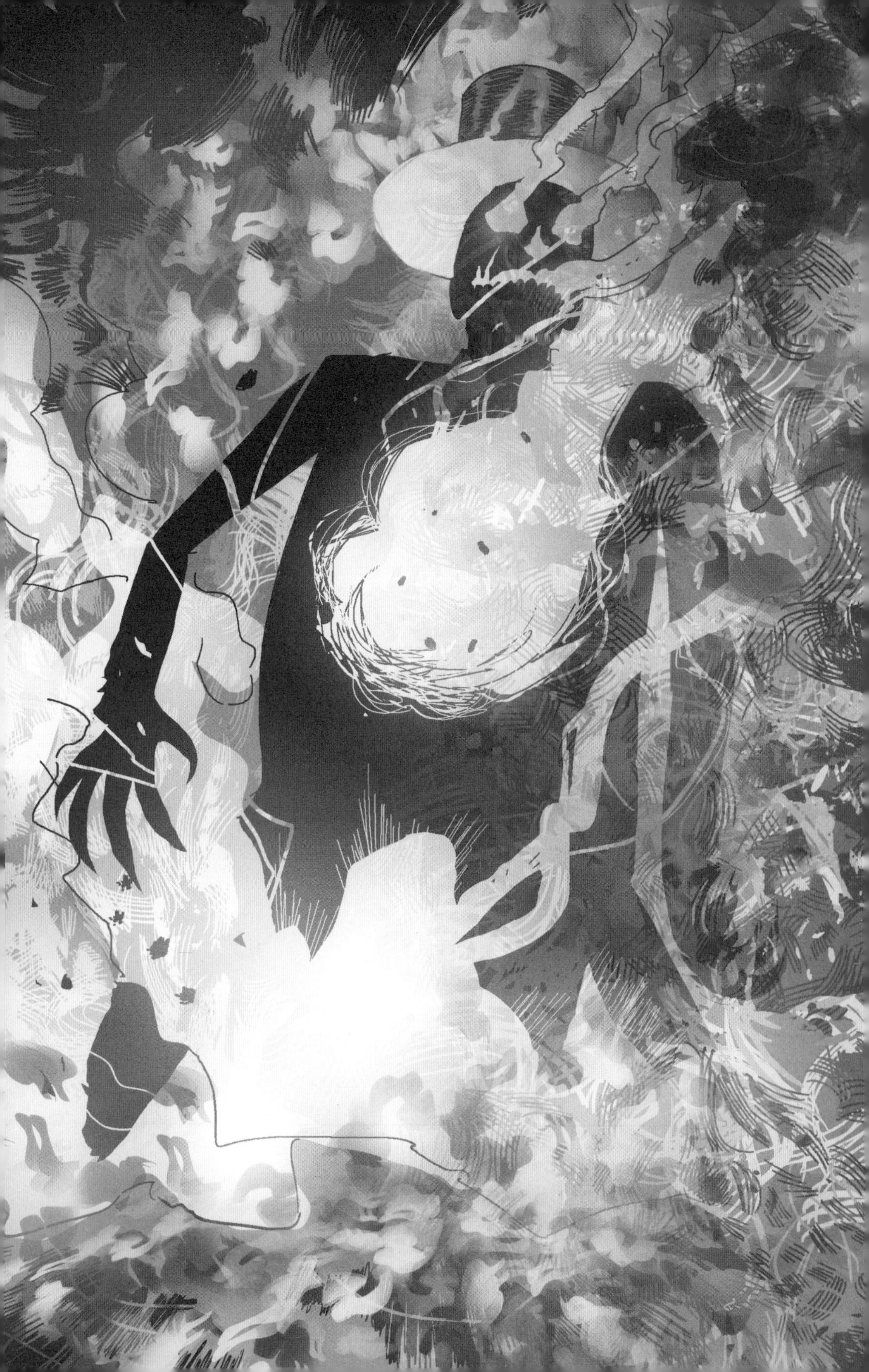